G000096682

PICTORIAL ATLAS
OF NORTH AMERICAN WINES

1st Edition

Author-Thomas K. Hardy   Photography-Milan Roden

"Andre Tchelistcheff At Buena Vista"

Published by Grape Vision Pty. Ltd
33-35 Raglan Street, Port Melbourne, Vic., Australia, 3207
155 Connecticut Street, San Francisco, CA., U.S.A., 94107

ISBN: 0-932664-63-6

Directed and Written by: Thomas K. Hardy
Visual Concept, Art Direction & Photography by: Milan Roden
Print Consultant & Art Direction (Artwork) by: Joe Murray
Co-ordination & General Assistance by: Rose Roden
General Assistance — U.S.A. by: Susan Dwyer
Editing by: Michael Muschamp
Design & Finished Art by: Anthony Shaw & Sue Wood
U.S.A. Consultant: The Wine Appreciation Guild Ltd. San Francisco
Printed at: Bell Group Press Pty. Ltd. (Western Australia)
Colour Reproduction by: Scantec Pty. Ltd. (South Australia)
Typesetting by: Southern Cross Typesetting (Victoria, Australia)

Foreword

No wine producing continent in the world is more diverse in terms of climate and topography than North America. It has been my honour and privilege to traverse this vine-land, as it was so aptly named by the Norse explorer Leif Ericson around 1000 A.D. some 500 years before wine was first produced in the sixteenth century.

This experience has been especially enriched by the company of my friend and brilliant photographer, Milan Roden, who has such deep insight and feeling for the natural beauty and wonderful people of the wine regions of this continent. For almost 2 years we have travelled constantly driving almost 50,000 miles and flying over 100,000 in this labour of love.

The reflection of the beauty of the industry and its people captured by Milan and his camera is enhanced by the magnificent maps created from satellite photographs providing the wine adventure with a much needed guide previously unavailable.

The Wines of North America have greater variety than any other continent on earth. The traditional European vinifera vines now grow successfully in almost every corner of the country but there are also the native American vines making their own distinctive wine styles along with the French and American hybrids bred to combat the phylloxera and other vine diseases and to survive the harsh winters in much of eastern and midwestern America and of course, Canada. This viticultural and climatic base means an incredible array of wine styles the overall standard of which is extremely high by world standards. I have had the pleasure of tasting many thousands of these and have been constantly amazed at the exciting and often wonderful wines that come from the most unlikely places. Although science plays an increasing part in winemaking it is still very much a human skill and an artform and the only true test is how you enjoy what is in the bottle.

The creation of this Pictorial Atlas would not have been possible without the support of some great North American corporations such as Kodak, Holiday Inns Inc., Continental Airlines we owe them a great deal. The assistance of the North American Wine industry and particularly those wineries featured in detail has been fantastic. We trust we have done justice to all and that you will derive some of the pleasure and knowledge from the following pages that we experienced in creating it.

Introduction — Raymond H. De Moulin

At first glance, the participation of Kodak's Professional Photography Division in the "Pictorial Atlas of Nth American Wines" seems an unusual collaboration. Yet, we are proud to help sponsor this volume, for its exceptional photographs and rich descriptions focus upon themes common to both the wine industry and photography; namely, those of heritage and tradition.

We at Kodak share much with the wine industry. Many wineries and vintners are, in fact, our neighbours. Kodak is a company with global activities, but our international headquarters in Rochester, New York, is just a few miles from the Finger Lakes wine country. In these rich hills and valleys, Konstantin Frank helped revolutionise the region's long heritage of grape growing and wineries; many of those wineries today are 100 years old or more. The area's wines and champagnes have earned national recognition and are widely enjoyed.

When wine experts compare fine wines, they often speak of vintages. At Kodak, many of our endeavours focus upon capturing the essence of a time and place in photographs;

Raymond H. DeMoulin, General Manager, Professional Photography Division, Vice-President, Eastman Kodak Company.

"vintage photography", so to speak, where excellence in creating classic imagery is the goal.

The nearly 600 images of rolling valleys, lush vineyards and rustic wineries in this volume are among the best examples of professional photography's ability to add a dimension of timelessness to these locales. Fresh perceptions of landscapes and wine cellars emerge in each new image. Professional photographers strive to immortalize textures, richness and details of their subjects, whether their objective is artistic or commercial. Often, the results expand photography's role as a communications medium; it truly becomes an artistic craft.

In this volume, Milan Roden's photographic craftsmanship and Thomas K. Hardy's prose combine to capture the very essence of vintners and winemaking in North America. Through Kodak professional photographic products, we are pleased to help bring their rich images together here for your enjoyment.

Introduction — Robert Mondavi

For many years I have advocated the philosophy that truly fine wines can be produced throughout the world where one could bring together all the necessary elements — climate, soil, grape varieties and wine growing. This ideal combination exists every bit as well in North America as it does in Europe.

In the last 22 years, a wine revolution has taken place in North America. Today, we are producing wine belonging in the company of the world's best, proven through innumerable tastings since Steven Spurrier's first Paris tasting in 1976. Some of the finest white Burgundies and red Bordeaux were tasted with California Chardonnays and Cabernets.

Thomas Hardy and Milan Roden have approached an almost insurmountable task presenting the wines of North America in a positive, exciting, professional and pictorial review.

The beautiful photographs by Milan evoke the variety and the spirit of the land of the grape. Tom's text reveals detailed knowledge and is a valuable addition to our

wine library.

Their second book, as did their first book on Australian wines, brings to the attention of wine lovers everywhere a new, enormous and important selection of fine wines from North America. We are grateful to Tom and Milan for this fascinating and fact-filled book.

I would like to close my comments by saying wine is the temperate, civilized, sacred, romantic, mealtime beverage recommended in the Bible, the liquid food praised 8,000 years ago, since civilization began, by rulers, poets, philosophers and physicians for life, happiness and longevity.

Wine is the only natural beverage that feeds not only the body, but the soul and spirit of man; stimulates the mind and creates a more gracious and happy way of life.

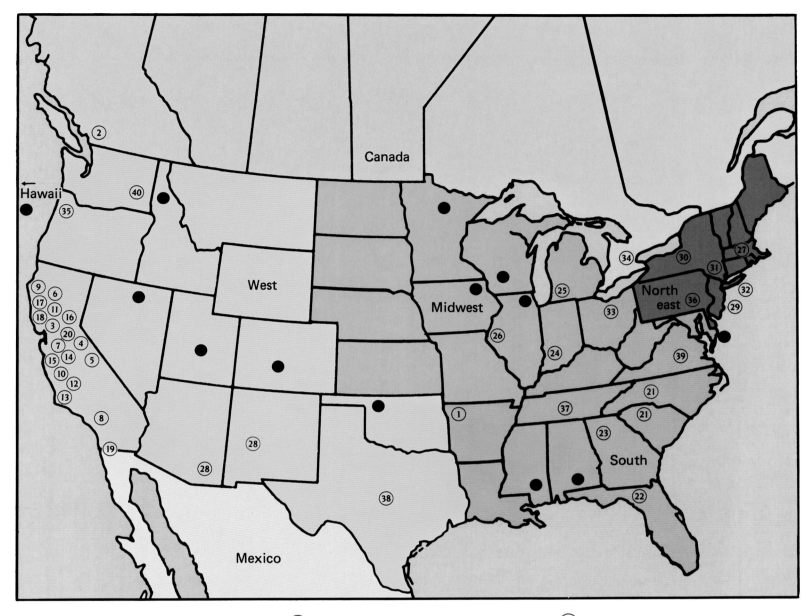

WINE REGIONS LISTED AND NUMBERED.

1. Arkansas
2. British Columbia, Canada
3. Carneros
4. Central Valley North, Ca.
5. Central Valley South, Ca.
6. Clear Lake, Ca.
7. Livermore & Santa Clara Valleys, Ca.
8. Los Angeles & Cucamonga, Ca.
9. Mendocino, Ca.
10. Monterey & Salinas, Ca.
11. Napa Valley, Ca.
12. Paso Robles & San Luis Obispo, Ca.
13. Santa Barbara & Santa Maria, Ca.
14. Santa Clara Valley, Ca.
15. Santa Cruz Mountains, Ca.
16. Sierra Foothills, Ca.
17. Sonoma Valley North, Ca.
18. Sonoma Valley South, Ca.
19. Temecula; San Diego; Mexico-Baja, Ca.
20. Yolo-Solano, Ca.
21. North & South Carolina
22. Florida
23. Georgia
24. Indiana
25. Michigan
26. Missouri
27. New England
28. New Mexico-Arizona
29. New Jersey
30. Finger Lakes, N.Y.
31. Hudson Valley, N.Y.
32. Long Island, N.Y.
33. Ohio
34. Ontario, Canada
35. Oregon
36. Pennsylvania
37. Tennessee
38. Texas
39. Virginia
40. Washington State
● Other Wine Producing Regions

Contents

History of Wine in North America

When one considers that the North American Wine industry has been stopped dead in its tracks twice within the last century it is remarkable that it is now certainly leading the new world of wine. It seriously challenges the great wines of the old world, even eclipsing them on a regular basis in international tastings.

Establishing today's strong, dynamic industry through these two major setbacks and many others unique to the North American continent has involved many generations of people, not only determined and persistent but also blessed with ingenuity and foresight.

Having travelled the length and breadth of the country a number of times, we have had the pleasure of meeting and learning from today's generation, whose dedication goes far beyond the search for meagre profits the cultivation of vines and the making of wine usually rewards them.

Wine is a long term business. There is no "quick buck" to be made. Constant risks are involved, not only through the vagaries of nature, but changes in taste whose pace often outstrips the slow growth of the vine and necessary time it takes to make good wine. It takes normally between 5-8 years to have a commerical quantity of wine on the market. Those involved must have a love for their enterprise and plenty of patience.

Today's wineries vary enormously from the benevolent giant Gallo company, the world's largest winemakers, to myriads of small "boutique" wineries that often strive to make a small quantity of just one wine that is unique and of absolutely top quality. The development of this structure and strength has happened largely over the last 20 years which has been marked by greater progress than the previous four centuries of winemaking in North America.

To trace the history of wine in North America we must go back almost a thousand years to the Norse explorer Leif Ericson, who landed near Newfoundland and discovered what were probably native American vines growing. He named this newly found land Vineland, a somewhat prophetic choice when today the vine thrives from the extremely high latitude parallels in British Columbia-Canada, to the sub equatorial areas of Southern Mexico In fact, it was in Mexico that the cultivation of the vine and the making of wines first took place some five centuries after Leif Ericson's pronouncement of Vineland and at the opposite extreme of the continent. The Spanish conqueror Cortez imported vines from his homeland and in

1524 issued a proclamation that every Spaniard with a land grant plant 1000 vines per year for each Indian worker he employed. This scheme went on for 5 years establishing the basis for a strong wine industry. So strong that the King of Spain, Philip II acted to stop planting later that century, as Spanish wine shipments to their colony fell so dramatically.

About 1564, the first American wine was produced in Florida by the French Huguenots

from the native muscadine grapes, probably the scuppernong variety from the "Vitis Rotundifolia" family.

The seventeenth century saw two major developments, both with results that have taken until recently to be fully realised. One was the planting of vines by the Franciscan fathers from Mexico in New Mexico as a fore-runner to their founding of the California wine industry. The other was the vain attempts by prominent east coast Americans to cultivate the classic European "Vitis Vinifera" varieties in eastern America. Chief among these was Thomas Jefferson, later to become president, who went to some extra-ordinary lengths including importing vines from the famous Chateau D'Yquem in France and even French soil. The soil however, was not the problem, not even the harsh Virginia winters as today's successful new vinifera based Virginia wine industry demonstrates, but rather insects, pests and vine diseases encouraged by the humid summers, not then able to be controlled by modern viticultural practices, chemicals, pest management and disease-resistant vines.

During the 1600's several native American "Vitis Labrusca" varieties were isolated that made wine which was not too harsh and overpoweringly "foxey" in taste. First amongst these was the "Alexander" named for its founder James Alexander, gardener to the son of William Penn, Thomas Penn. This was followed by others in the early 1800's such as Catawba, Isabella and Concord, the latter still being the basis of the grape juice and grape jelly industry. These varieties were disease-resistant and winter hardy offering the ability to grow and make wine in almost any North American Region. Their significance in saving the world's wine industry some 100 years later will be covered shortly.

In 1769, Californian wine was born when Father Junipero Serra brought the Mission (Criolla) vine from Mexico and planted it at Mission San Diego, the first of 21 Alta California Missions spreading north as far as Sonoma, taking viticulture and winemaking with them.

The first commercial winery however, started when the Pennsylvania Wine Company was formed and made wine from Alexander grapes in underground cellars at Spring Mill on the banks of the Susquehanna River near Philadelphia.

As early as 1811 the commercial wine industry of Canada started when Johann Schiller, a retired German soldier who had made wine on the Rhine in his homeland, founded a small winemaking operation at

Cooksville, Ontario (now Mississunga).

It was not until the 1850's that California, now producing over 90% of American wines, seriously challenged for its pre-eminent position.

In 1861 Agoston Haraszthy, known as the Hungarian "Count" and often seen as the father of the Californian wine industry, brought 100,000 vine cuttings from Europe, covering over 300 varieties to plant in California. He also founded the famous Buena Vista Winery in Sonoma, where he made his home. A year later French viticultural experts visited America to study the potential of the Vine and reported Californian wines as having the potential to compete with those of Europe.

During the 1870's, whilst just out of its infancy and having established itself as the premier wine state, California was decimated by the vine louse Phylloxera (which attacks the roots of the vine, eventually killing it). This dreaded vine disease struck Europe about the same time and, miraculously, the cure was an American one. The native American vine species such as "Vitis Raparia" "Vitis Labrusca" and "Vitis Rotundifolia" are resistant to the disease. The French actually came up with the solution by grafting their classic varieties onto the roots of American vines. They also created Hybrid vines (widely planted in eastern America and Canada) by crossing the French and American varieties. Specially bred American rootstocks then came back from Europe to provide the cure in California. The whole process took many years, however, and it was not until into the 1890's that California fully recovered.

In 1900 American wines won 40 awards at the Paris exhibition. During the next two decades wine flourished with the great strength being table wines. Then, in 1920, National Prohibition struck down the budding industry, until its repeal in 1933. Grape growers survived and in some instances prospered by supplying grapes to the home winemaker. This traffic mainly from California to the east was assisted by the introduction of refrigerated rail cars. Some innovative moves were made including a couple of ingenious products "vine-glo" a brilliant idea of Captain Paul Garrett the creator of America's most successful pre-prohibition wine "Virginia Dare". Vine-glo consisted of a concentrated grape juice in a can with all winemaking instructions and a clever marketing plan to home deliver.

However, the prohibitionists put the lid on it very smartly. The other ''invention'' was the ''Grape Brick'' dehydrated processed grapes — just add water, it even came with a yeast pill and a ''tongue in cheek'' warning not to use it as wine would result, which would be illegal! Over 100 wineries stayed open during prohibition with permits to produce sacramental and medicinal wines.

Following the end of Prohibition, a flood of hastily made bad wines created a bad image for wine, most good grape varieties having given way to coarse varieties to supply the home winemaker. Quality regions such as the Napa and Sonoma Valleys had run right down. It wasn't until the 1950's, when the renaissance started by post-war European immigration and European travel by North Americans started to change the

lifestyles of much of the country that ''wine with meals was in''.

Consumption per head of table wine started to rise and by 1968 surpassed the high alcohol ''fortified'' wines which had been the norm since Prohibition. Small boutique wineries sprang up all over the continent, run by devoted amateurs and disillusioned professional and business people looking for an alternative life. Large wineries began research and enforced strict quality standards. America developed some of the world's leading wine educational facilities notably at the Davis campus of the University of California.

Since 1968 table wine consumption has increased four fold and is now approaching two and half gallons per head per annum, far short of the over 20 gallon annual levels of

France and Italy, but placing North America amongst the leading wine producing countries being currently the sixth largest with over 500 million gallons produced annually. Premium bottled wines have seen the greatest increase over the last few years, showing wine has really arrived in this continent.

The pop wines of the 1970's have given way to the remarkable wine cooler beverage boom of the 1980's which at least is wooing people from hard liquor, which wine exceeded in consumption only as recently as 1980.

Before the turn of the century North America will more than likely produce over a billion gallons of wine with an increasing percentage being premium bottled table wine, a reflection of wines true place in life as an accompaniment to food and civilized living.

An Introduction to Arkansas

Arkansas is certainly not a state that comes to mind with the mention of wine. It does however, have a long history of wine growing going back over a century. The early settlers cultivated the native muscadine varieties that are native to this part of the south. Prohibition put an end to winemaking but not grape growing and large acreages of concords were planted for grape juice and grape jelly production. After Prohibition many wineries opened with some government protection to use the surplus grapes caused by the Depression. Most wines were "fortified" dessert wines but gradually changing attitudes and tastes forced most to close.

Swiss and German settlers continued on making table wines mainly around the town of Altus in the Arkansas River Valley nestling under Mt. Magazine in the Auchita Mountain Range, the largest range in mid-western America and the only one to run in an east-west direction. This range creates a unique micro-climate by forcing up the freezing Arctic air coming southward from Canada and lifting the mild air from the river valley up over the vineyards on the slopes of Mt. Mary on the opposite side of the river to the higher Mt. Magazine.

Two wineries stand out, Wiederkehr Wine Cellars at over 1.5 million gallon capacity is the largest most modern and impressive winery between the east and west coasts. The Weiderkehrs, along with their cousins the Post's who run the other significant wine operation, Post Familie Vineyards & Winery, have done much in terms of large plantings of French Hybrid grapes and Vitis Vinifera varieties. Many of the wines, I have tried recently, particularly some Chardonnays from Post's and Johannisberg Rieslings from Wiederkehr are world class examples of their styles.

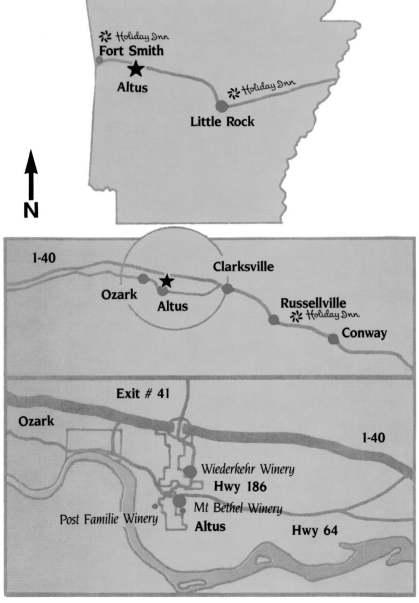

Post Familie Vineyards & Winery

Founded in 1880 by Jacob Post from Bavaria, Post's Winery is very much a family business. Mathew J. Post is a fourth generation son and has 10 of his 12 children working in the business. They make no less than 28 different wines and are also heavily involved in table grapes.

Whilst on a recent visit I tasted their 1987 Chardonnay from only the second crop off their vines. The wine was superb with full rich apricot-nectarine flavours with just a touch of wood influence from barrel ageing Mathew has also found time to do a stint as the Mayor of Altus, his son Andrew is winemaker, Thomas runs the vineyard and Paul looks after packaging and marketing his daughter is a very talented photographer and her works adorn the walls of the winery,

Wiederkehr Wine Cellars

Al Wiederkehr, recently awarded the Golden Vine Award by the Knights of the Vine in California for his work with Vinifera, is one of the genuine characters of the American wine industry. He exudes enthusiasm and an intensity of purpose that has built up a business his father nearly closed, into the largest and most prominent between the east and west coasts of the continent.

The Wiederkehr wine village, because it is much more than just a winery, perches atop St. Mary's Mountain at the summit amid the vines. Al has built a tower from which one gets a spectacular view of the Arkansas River Valley with the Auchita Range in the background, together these topographical features create the mild microclimate that enables virtually all species of vines to thrive. Herman Wiederkehr, an immigrant from Weinfeld in Switzerland, arrived in Altus around 1880 and started making table wine from the native grapes, much as his father Johann Andreas had done in his Swiss homeland.

Today, visiting Wiederkehr's is almost like discovering a little piece of Switzerland in rugged middle America. The Swiss Chalet-like buildings are beautifully presented with flower boxes full all year round. The original log cabin, home of Herman Wiederkehr, has been faithfully restored and rebuilt above a delightful cellar restaurant, Swiss and German cuisine predominates, using fresh local produce.

Each September since 1966 has seen the Wiederkehr wine festival with activities for young and old alike.

Al's children his son Johann Andreas (John) named after his Great Grandfather and daughter now studying in Lausanne Switzerland have both shown an interest in the business. Wiederkehr's have created a unique and wonderful environment in the most unlikely place — long may they prosper.

The wine industry of British Columbia which exists today has only developed during the last 25 years, although winemaking in this beautiful province of Canada goes back to the 1860's, when Father Charles Pandosy planted vines at the Oblate Mission seven miles south of Kelowna, near the shores of Lake Okanagan.

This deep and narrow glacial lake stretches for 80 miles in a north south direction. Today's British Columbian wine industry is largely based around its shores, where the harsh climate is moderated by the large body of water. The latitude of the Okanagan region is actually about the same as the Rhine Valley in Germany, and the Champagne region of France. It has virtually a desert climate with only about 6 inches of rain per year in the south and not much more in the north. Irrigation is essential, but there is plenty of sunshine with its northerly latitude and clear skies, the heat in mid summer days can be intense up to and over 100° farenheit. Ripening is no problem; acids also stay high as the nights, even in the hottest months are cool to cold. Slopes around the lake are generally steep, offering as in Ger

aspects and micro climates, many of which are yet to be discovered.

It was not however, until over 60 years after the Oblate Fathers had planted their vines that a commercial vineyard of any size was planted in the region. This occurred in 1926, when local farmer Jesse Hughes planted a 45 acre vineyard near the Oblate Mission in Kelowna.

Hughes' vineyard was successful and the only wine producer of any note at that stage, the Growers Co-operative Winery, were making wine on Vancouver Island from loganberries growing on the Saanich peninsular, in the south near Victoria. With the encouragement of Hungarian wine expert, Dr. Eugene Rittich, Hughes bought 20 acres on Black Mountain and planted them with vines. He had plans to expand to 300 acres, but the vines were wiped out by Winter Kill (most European vines freeze and die when the temperature goes below about − 23°F).

Rittich still believed some varieties could survive on Black Mountain and he introduced a Hybrid that became known as Okanagan Riesling, although it makes wine which is not

fruity character that is appealing and has adapted well to the region.

The major development of the wine industry started through apples, not grapes. During the depression Giuseppe Ghezzi, an Italian immigrant and winemaker floated an idea to use apples to make apple-based wines, cider and all manner of fruit based products.

He talked two prominent local citizens, Bill Bennett and Cap (Pasquale) Capozzi in joining him in the venture they named Domestic Wines and By-products. The apple wines were a dismal failure but by 1936, they were making wines from grapes and had re-named the company Calona Wines after the native Indian name for their location.

Bill Bennett went on to serve in the provincial government in 1940 and became premier in 1952, he introduced reforms and incentives for the local wine industry and gradually the planting of vines increased.

In the 1960's, the real developments started with many of the larger operations of today, being founded to take advantage of the provincial preference for local wine.

In 1961 Andres set up a substantial winery on the outskirts of Vancouver in Port Moody: Mission Hills' beautiful winery was built in 1966, Casabello Wines were founded in 1966 as Southern Okanaga Wines Ltd.

The next development was that of the Estate wineries, the first being Claremont in 1979 followed quickly by Sumac Ridge, Uniake Cellars (now Cedar Creek), Gray Monk and more latterly by Le Comte, Divino and the exciting Gehringer Brothers in 1985.

Brights Wines, Canada's largest winemaker also joined in the industry in 1981, when they completed their striking $5.5 million winery on the Osoyoos Indian Reserve, near Oliver, south of Lake Okanagan.

The other main winery of the province is the Ste Michelle Cellars in Surrey on the southern outskirts of Vancouver. This facility originated through the transfer to the mainland of the merged Growers Co-operative and Victoria Wineries, who had both outgrown their premises. The Winery was completed in 1978 and is now owned by Brights, but still run as Ste Michelle Cellars.

The Germanic vinifera varieties, like Riesling and Gewurztraminer seem most

successful in British Columbia along with some of the new German crosses such as Scheurebe, Ehrenfelser and Optima, although the Burgundian varieties of Chardonnay and Pinot Noir show promise.

The free trade agreement with the United States will put increasing pressure on the

costly wine production of British Columbia, but in certain styles they shine and this is where the future will be.

Possibly the most suitable region for viticulture in the province: the Lee Shore of Vancouver Island has no vines, but this may change.

British Columbia

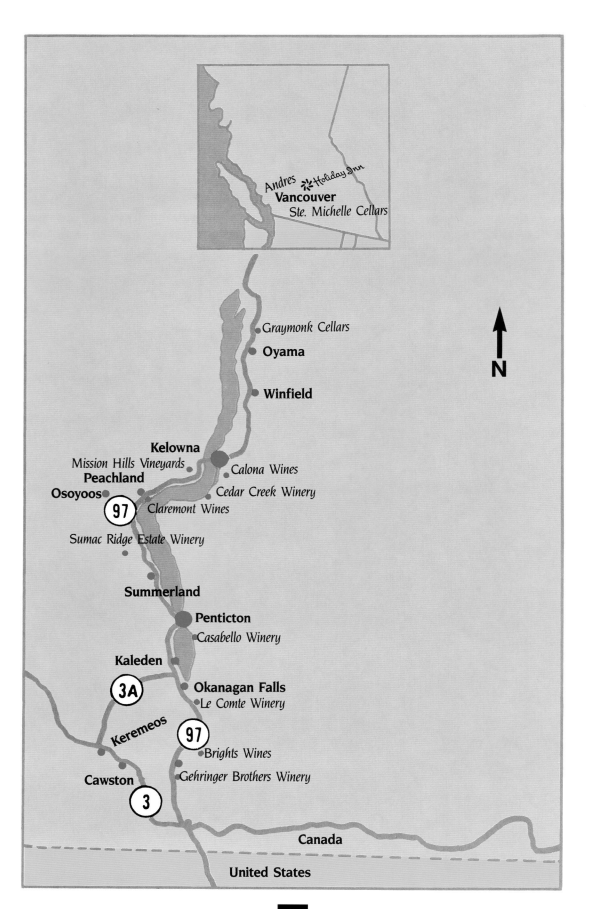

Andres Wines

The story of Andrew Peller, founder of this significant wine enterprise, is a fascinating one with a recurring theme of persistence and hard work towards worthy goals, often in adverse situations. Now in his 85th year he still takes an active role in the business.

Andre is Andrew's given name. Born in Hungary of German parents, after a childhood of considerable hardship he migrated to Canada in 1927, leaving his pregnant wife and surviving son Joe to follow him. Tragically his newly born son Andrew died in infancy, before he could see him, this the second time this terrible fate had befallen him and his wife Lena.

By the time Lena and young Joe arrived in Canada, Andrew was in the brewing business. His background in engineering took him through a number of jobs during the Depression but he eventually came back to brewing and gained his Brewmasters certificate in 1933. On the outbreak of war in 1939, his German background lost him his job. Not to be deterred he started "Peller Machine Industries" making supplies for the war effort.

Following the war, he opened his own Brewery in Hamilton, Ontario. "The Peller Brewing Company", the first new Canadian Brewery since Prohibition. In 1953, he sold the brewery to the legendary E.P. Taylor from Canadian Breweries, at a considerable profit. His next venture was publishing a newspaper the "Hamilton News", he bought and ran for two difficult years, next came a General Motors car dealership. Over the previous five years or so Andrew had nursed an urge to start a winery following his family's viticultural heritage.

The Liquor Control Board of Ontario made a full winery licence almost impossible to get, so Andrew went to British Columbia. In 1958, he bought a vineyard in the Okanagan and after a number of set backs obtained a licence, then built a modern efficient winery at Port Moody, suitably enough on Vintner Street. The new winery was outfitted with equipment purchased in California. His first winemaker, who capably got the winery together was Wallace Pohle from Lodi, California.

In 1964, Andres built a large winery in Calgary, Alberta, followed closely by Truro, Nova Scotia. The following year his son Joe left medicine to become president of the growing enterprise.

In 1967, Andres purchased a large modern winery in Winona, Ontario which has since become the head office. Since 1970 wineries in Quebec and Manitoba have been built giving Andres a truly national presence and the biggest wine business in Canada until the recent Brights/Jordan Ste. Michelle merger in 1987.

In 1971, Andres created a sparkling wine, "Baby Duck", which quickly became Canada's largest selling wine, a position it held until recently, appealing to the country's growing taste for lighter wines.

Andres produce a number of varietal wines from the Indian Reservation vineyards they helped create near Oliver in the Okanagan. They also make two very good proprietary wines, Domaine d'or Blanc Superieur and Domaine d'or Rouge Superieur as well as their German style Hochtaler.

Extremely competent winemaster, Ron Taylor has 18 years with the company, Ann Sperling is winemaker, a young third generation member of a pioneer grape growing family from Kelowna, keen and innovative, she has cherished a life-long wish to be winemaker.

Andres care for their staff and it shows in the wines

Brights House of Wine

When T.G. Bright, Canada's largest winemaker, decided to attack the British Columbia wine market they did so in a most unique fashion.

"Indian Head", a massive rugged precipice, whose profile resembles an Indian face, frowns sternly down on the winery. Legend has it that the local tribes used to drive their prey over the edge and come down to collect the meat. It is somewhat appropriate that in fact the winery was built on the Indian "Osoyoos" reservation by the Indian band and with the co-operation of the Provincial Government, at a cost of $2 million. It has been leased by Brights, who have put in $3.5 million of equipment. The first vintage was in 1981, although the winery was not officially opened until 1982.

The Indians have also planted 250 acres of vines, stretching south of the winery, which is near Oliver, towards Osoyoos. There are a further 6,000 acres suitable for planting. The climate is warmer than further north and quite rich flavours develop in the wines. The vineyards are 80% Hybrid varieties with 20% vinifera; 45 types were planted in trials going back to 1976, but gradually they have been weeded out. A number of German Riesling crosses have been planted, partly due to the influence of Dr. Helmut Becker from the Geisenheim Wine Institute, who consulted to the industry during the mid —

late 1970's.

Some of these varieties are Optima a Riesling/Sylvaner cross, (which I found particularly good), Oraniensteiner, Bacchus, Ehrenfelser and a few Russian white varieties Rkatsiteli and Matsvani. The overall standard of the wines is very high and the warm 1987 vintage has produced some outstanding wines; many feel it is the best vintage ever in the region.

Winemaker at Brights is Lynn Stark who has been with the winery since its inception. She previously worked at Andres before establishing an 86 acre vineyard with her husband; she has a well earned respect for the grape grower. Lynn continually updates her knowledge with study at such places as U.C Davis in California and European wine schools.

Brights have been a welcome addition to the British Columbian wine scene and everyone has benefited from their presence. They are also carrying out some interesting experiments under the I.R.A.P Government research scheme; the day we were there they were fermenting a batch of "Sereksya Chonaya" a light red Russian variety.

British Columbia is at the crossroads with Free trade. Brights, I feel, are pointing the way to follow.

Calona Wines

Calona Wines started its life in 1932 through the adversity of the Okanagan applegrowers created by the Great Depression when entrepreneurial Italian immigrant, Giuseppe Ghezzi saw a way of utilizing the huge surplus apple crop which lay virtually rotting on the ground. The company was registered as ''Domestic Wines And By-products Ltd.'', but after several unsuccessful years making wine, cider and a multitude of other fruit products based on apples, they decided to move into the traditional wine field and started purchasing grapes mainly from California. In 1936 the name was changed to Calona Wines — a native Indian name associated with their site.

The other partners in Calona were Pasquale ''Cap'' Cappozzi and W.A.C. (Bill) Bennet, who sold his share in 1940, when he went into politics. Becoming premier in 1952, he implemented many policies that have had the direct result of strengthening the B.C. Wine Industry. ''Cap'' continued on, bringing his sons into the business, when he sold in 1971 to Standard Brands of Montreal he became a multimillionaire, certainly he worked for it.

Calona are the biggest wine producer in British Columbia and have introduced some innovative wines over the recent decades including Canada's largest selling bottled wine ''Schloss Laderheim'' a crisp, fruity white with some residual sugar in the German style.

The Calona stable also includes an excellent Gerwurztraminar and late harvest Johannisberg Riesling, along with their ''Spring Hill'' range of excellent table wines.

Le Comte Estate Winery

About half way between Penticton and Oliver, a few miles up Green Lake road is a very pretty, small winery — Le Comte. This Estate winery was only opened recently, the first crush was in 1983, although the winery did not obtain its ''Estate'' licence until 1986. The vineyard was established many years ago and commands a majestic view over the Southern Okanagan Valley. The wines are produced in the French tradition and their Chenin Blanc is a lovely, crisp, fruity style with a little herbaceousness.

If you are in the region it is well worth the scenic drive to visit this Estate winery, why not also drop in on the Okanagan Falls, which are only three miles north east of the winery.

Gehringer Brothers

At the annual Septober Festival in Penticton in 1987, a new star emerged. The Gehringer 1986 White wines scooped the pool and judging from their 1987 wines I tasted at the winery other B.C. wineries had better look to their laurels.

Walter Gehringer went to Germany, where he underwent a two year apprenticeship at a winery near Stuttgart, on Lake Constance. This experience Walter followed by three years at Geisenheim, from where he graduated, with an engineering in winemaking.

Walter's brother Gordon has followed Walter's footsteps to Germany, gaining his degree from Weinsberg. The two brothers now run the winery, whilst their father Helmut and Uncle Karl look after the vineyards.

The quality of their fruit and their skilled and careful handling of the wines has created some of the best Germanic wines I have tasted anywhere in the world.

Claremont Wines

Claremont was the first estate winery established in British Columbia. Bob Claremont virtually pushed the government into creating a special licence for local small wineries, giving them the ability to sell to the public from the winery and able to sell directly to hotels and restaurants The main stipulations were a maximum size crush each year of 30,000 gallons, all grapes to be B.C. grown and 50% from their own vineyard.

Bob Claremont studied enology in Ontario, working at Jordan Winery there before coming west to work for Mission Hill, followed by Calona until he started making his own wine in 1977 The first vintage at Claremont was in 1979. The winery and vineyard sits on top of a large hill near Westbank a few miles south of Kelowna.

The wines are full bodied and all see some wood particularly the reds, which spend at least two years in small oak, a Merlot and Pinot Noir have been released recently this not an easy winery to find, but worth the effort.

Cedar Creek Winery

This very attractive small winery situated on the eastern shore of Lake Okanagan has just gone through some extensive renovations including a thorough and very aesthetically pleasing landscaping of the whole Estate.

Accompanying this has been a change of name. It was formerly called Uniake Estate Wines — a name going back to 14th century Ireland and meaning ''unique'' or ''without-peer'', being founded by David Mitchell, his wife Sue and some other partners. The Mitchell's planted vines in 1974, but the winery's first crush was in 1980. Over 80% of the wine produced is white and very much in the Germanic style. Their Okanagan Riesling is acknowledged as probably the best in the region and usually has some Gewurztraminer blended with it and a touch of residual sugar. Apart from the Germanic styles, Cedar Creek produce a Chenin Blanc and a Pinot Blanc.

Ste. Michelle Cellars

This winery has only been built recently 1977 — but its history is a long and intricate one. The current winery is the second largest in B.C. and has been purchased, along with the Jordan Winery in Ontario, by Brights Wines in 1987, making them Canada's largest wine producer.

In 1923, retired jockey Steve Slinger, who had a good deal of business flair began a winery at Victoria, producing wines from loganberries grown on the Saanich peninsula. In 1936 he merged with the Growers Company who were making wine in Victoria from Okanagan grapes, they had shipped across to the Island. They also had a production facility in Vancouver. In 1955, a group of Vancouver businessmen took over the Company expanding it by purchasing a small winery near Langley east of Vancouver, where they produced sparkling wines.

Imperial Tobacco took over in 1965, buying the large Beau Sejour Vineyard in the Okanagan, from where they had been buying grapes for a number of years. In 1973, brewing giant Carling-O'Keefe took over, changing the name from Growers to Ste. Michelle Wines. They also owned the Jordan Winery in Ontario now known as Jordan & Ste. Michelle Cellars.

1977 saw the commencement of the new winery at Surrey on the southern outskirts of Vancouver, amalgamating the plants from Victoria and the mainland.

The new winery has a large ground level cellar with an impressive array of large German type oval casks as well as a large sherry Solera the winery also produces a massive amount of cider under the Growers Label. During the mid 60's, Ste. Michelle Cellars pioneered Vinifera.

Their Johannisberg Riesling is an excellent wine in the Germanic style with slight residual sugar, showing hints of passionfruit and pineapple in its lifted fruit aroma and flavour.

The winemaker is in fact German trained. Ivan Lessner's family had a winery on Lake Balaton in Hungary. He trained at Geisenheim in Germany and spent some time working in southern France making a wide array of wines. In 1981 he came to Ontario on a research project, staying with relatives, who had vineyards and caught up with friends he had studied with at Geisenheim. Enjoying the lifestyle very much he decided to emigrate and returned to Canada several months later. He worked at the Jordan Winery then for the Ste. Michelle group in Calgary before coming to British Columbia in 1985. Ivan has a very pleasant disposition and enjoys his work very much. He is ably assisted by long time employee Joseph Vollmer. Between them they are making very good wines. I was most impressed with a well-priced red wine simply called "Selection Red" which had a delightful vibrant ruby hue and lovely cherry, raspberry fruit flavours, a well rounded and generous wine. For those who like dry wine with a touch of sweetness and plenty of fruit, the "Vin Blanc Sec" is good value.

Ste. Michelle Cellars is a particularly attractive winery for a modern building and those who operate it seem extremely happy. It's a good place to visit if in Vancouver.

Mission Hills Vineyard

One of North America's most beautiful wineries sits majestically perched on top of a large hill above the town of Westbank, commanding a spectacular view of Lake Okanagan. On our visit during the Septober wine festival we had the rare privilege of watching the harvest moon rise above the lake. With a glass of their superb Gewurztraminer in our hands, what could be better!

This mission-style winery was built in 1966 by local orchardist R.P. (Tiny) Walrod and a group of his professional friends. Tiny, unfortunately, died before its completion. In 1969, Mission Hills was sold to Ben Ginter, a beer Baron, whose crass marketing ideas and ego crazed methods of operation saw the winery fall into hard times. At one stage he sold the winery but bought it back again.

In June 1981, the property was purchased by a dynamic duo trading under the name of The Mark Anthony Group. Anthony Von Mandl had built up a very successful Wine and Beverage Merchandising Company in Vancouver, with great style. In a very short time, he was joined in the venture by the equally dynamic Nick Clark, the one time Director of Purchasing for the B.C. Liquor Distribution Branch.

They immediately returned the winery to its original "Mission Hills" name from Ginter's last trading "Golden Valley Wines". The winery received a total clean up and has been redecorated with considerable flair. The tasting and sales area is one of the most pleasant you will find anywhere on the North American Continent.

Their first winemaker was Austrian Helmut Dotti now at Okanagan Vineyards. His assistant Joe Praffener is still with the company.

September 13th, 1982 was a very significant day for Mission Hills. Daniel Lagnaz joined as winemaker, he has proved a wonderful asset to the winery, not only making great wines, but handling a mind boggling array of beverage products from cider to coolers through to distilling Eau de Vie.

Daniel is Swiss born and trained as an industrial chemist. Though he served in the Swiss army, his first experience with wine came in Spain making bulk wine for the European market. After three and a half years as a wine lecturer he spent six months with his family's wine company in Chablais, Switzerland. Daniel then went to Australia on a five month contract with Lindemans, a large wine company there. He ended up with them for three years in various parts of the country. When he arrived in Seattle to visit his brother in 1982 with no job, he heard about a possible job at Mission Hills, so visited and talked with Tony and Nick, they hired him immediately and have not looked back. Daniel married his Australian girlfriend, Fran in 1983.

The Mission Hills range of wines includes Semillon, Johannisberg Riesling, Muller Thurgau, Gerwurztraminer and the Swiss variety Chasselas. All whites are made in a dry style, but packed with fruit flavour and all from B.C. grapes. A Chardonnay is made

Mission Hills Vineyard

from Yakima Valley. Washington grapes and a Sauvignon Blanc from Sonoma. California grapes.

The reds include an excellent Pinot Noir and a Cabernet Sauvignon made from grapes grown in the Oliver region.

Mission Hills have expanded quickly and in 1987 crushed 1500 tons of grapes, their previous biggest vintage being 998 tons in 1983. The wine quality and presentation is excellent. A visit to Mission Hills is a pleasure — the staff all enthusiastically embrace their work and the tour is a real eye-opener. The physical beauty of this winery and its location is truly inspirational and a visit if you are in the area is compulsory.

MISSION HILL VINEYARD
Address: Boucherie & Mission Hill Roads, Westbank (Okanagan Valley) British Columbia
Phone: 604/768 5125
Year of Establishment: 1981
Owner: The Mark Anthony Group Inc.
Winemaker: Daniel Lagnaz
Principal Varieties Grown: Okanagan Riesling. Marechal Foch, Johannisberg Riesling. Verdelet
Average Annual Crush: 2,000 tons
Principal Wines & Brands
Mission Ridge White/Red
Mission Hill Vintage Dry White/Red
California Cooler
Okanagan Premium Brand Cider
Trade Tours – Available
Retail Room Sales – Available
Hours open to Public: 7 days a week (Times vary throughout the year)
Retail Distribution: Government controlled outlets. privately owned wine stores operated by parent company, The Mark Anthony Group Inc.

Sumac Ridge Estate Winery

The title of North America's most unusual winery must surely go to Sumac Ridge. Harry McWatters and Lloyd Schmidt bought a private golf course, with its restaurant club house in 1979, shortened the course and planted 10 acres of vines mainly Johannisberg Riesling, Gewurztraminer and Chardonnay. They then built their winery under the Club House. It has since expanded into an area behind the restaurant also.

Lloyd's family ran the large Beau Sejour Vineyard in Kelowna supplying the Growers Winery from Victoria with grapes. They sold it to the Growers Company in 1965 but Lloyd stayed on until 1971 running it. After two years with the Agricultural Department, Lloyd went to Casabello, where he met Harry, then in charge of marketing. Harry had been brought up with wine in an Italian neighbourhood in Toronto and had in fact made his own wines as a teenager, including a "Potato" Champagne.

In 1986, "Bud" Richmond bought out Lloyd Schmidt's share of the business and he, Harry and their families run the vineyard, winery and restaurant together. They also operate another vineyard at Naramata across the lake growing Verdelet and Okanagan Riesling.

Harry is quite a character, a man of substantial proportions both physically and mentally. He has taken wine education and promotion in British Columbia and Canada onto a higher plane.

The Sumac Ridge Chardonnay of 1986 has just been released, from young vines. It has a fairly high acid but great varietal flavours and will age well. The 1987 I tried out of the barrel is richer again and benefited from the warmer vintage. It can certainly hold its own in any company. Harry's Chancellor red wine is an exceptional one and the 1985 was recently served to Queen Elizabeth, at the Commonwealth Heads Of Government Conference in Vancouver. Sumac Ridge have a number of other wines including the rare Pearl-of-Csaba, an exotic member of the muscat family. The winery is set up in a most professional way and is operated in a very innovative fashion.

For the lucky scorer of a hole in one on the golf course Harry and Bud are delighted to present a bottle of their fine wines. Sumac Ridge has added an enriching aspect to the developing B.C. wine industry.

An Introduction to California

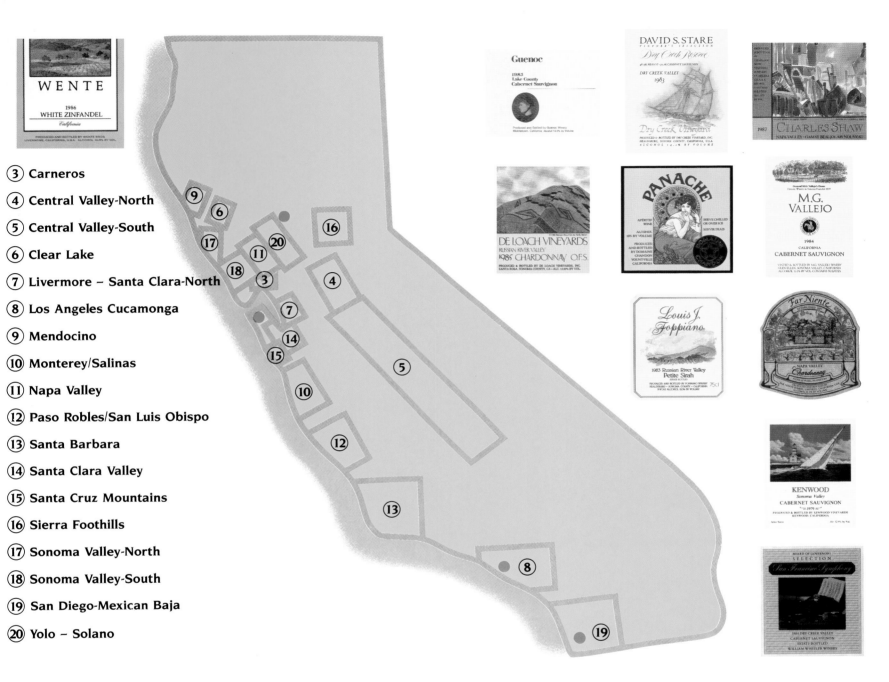

3 Carneros

4 Central Valley-North

5 Central Valley-South

6 Clear Lake

7 Livermore – Santa Clara-North

8 Los Angeles Cucamonga

9 Mendocino

10 Monterey/Salinas

11 Napa Valley

12 Paso Robles/San Luis Obispo

13 Santa Barbara

14 Santa Clara Valley

15 Santa Cruz Mountains

16 Sierra Foothills

17 Sonoma Valley-North

18 Sonoma Valley-South

19 San Diego-Mexican Baja

20 Yolo – Solano

California is blessed with one of the world's most hospitable climates for the culture of the vine. The traditional European vinifera vines thrive here and in many cases do better than in their original European locations. The summers are long and warm and in many regions tempered by the natural air-conditioning of the coastal morning summer fogs, stretching out the growing season, building and preserving the flavours in the grapes and certainly making some of the world's best wines. California also has mild winters with, in most cases,

sufficient rainfall and dry summers reducing the risk of a washed out vintage and vine diseases. Almost every year in California is a vintage one. Spring frost is the only real problem and many vineyards today have frost protection in the form of wind generators, smudge-pots releasing a covering warm smoke layer or sprinkler systems all to keep the vines above freezing point as the new season's buds are breaking through.

California has a multitude of climates with new vineyard locations being constantly developed in a progression towards the ultimate quality. Nowhere in the world is

there keener competition between wineries to produce ''the best'' which I feel is the main reason Californian wines are increasingly stealing the honours from the ''tradition-bound'' great wines of the Old World.

During the late 1930's, Professor Maynard Amerine, one of the world's great enologists and viticultural experts, together with a team from ''Davis'' the world's foremost wine school at the Davis campus of the University of California, came up with a new system of classifying vineyards climatically into regions I, II, III, IV and V. This system, using degree days (the number of degrees per day the

An Introduction to California

temperature exceeds 50°F) a yearly figure is calculated with region I being the coolest at less than 2500 degree days per year. This is really the lower limit of viticulture below which, as in some of the very foggy coastal and mountain regions of California, grapes will not ripen.

The vine is a peculiar plant, generally producing the best grapes with greatest intensity of flavour and character where conditions are toughest and yields small. The expense of viticulture in these areas is reflected in the price of many top wines. The sought after region I climates are being sought out in the most unlikely locations particularly in the higher elevations.

California produces some 85-90% of North American wine, much of which comes from the warm central valleys with their ideal even climates and irrigation. Grape yields are high and costs of production of the huge wineries such as the world's largest Gallo

(with two wineries both well exceeding 100 million gallons capacity, each capable of holding more than the total vintage of Australia or together with that of West Germany) are extremely low.

Quality coming from these regions is remarkably high. Californian techology in the vineyard and winery leads the world and lately viticultural research has yielded better grapes giving North America a standard wine rarely equalled anywhere in the world.

How did this all come about? California was in fact a late-comer as a commercial wine producing state with the oldest wineries only dating back to the 1850's.

Wine actually dates back to 1769 in the state when Father Junipero Serra planted the ''mission'' grape from Mexico at Mission San Diego, which began a progression of planting at most of the 21 missions spread through the state over the next 50 years.

Commercial winemaking actually started

in the Los Angeles area, which now has only one significant winery, the remarkable ''San Antonio Winery'', but no vineyards. In the 1830's a French immigrant, appropriately named Jean-Louis Vigne (Vine) started his El Aliso Vineyard made wine and introduced the first European vines into California.

The later days of the 1850's gold rush brought the first real boom of grape planting in the state starting an ominous ''boom then bust'' situation, repeating itself continuously into modern times. Now some stability finally seems to have crept in although only the future will tell us the true story. Phylloxera actually helped solve this problem by killing off some of the excess vineyards and heavy frosts affected the crops for some years.

Unfortunately, renewed prosperity of the early years of the new century forced another planting boom and by 1911 the whole market for grapes and wine collapsed yet again. Things were just returning to normal when

An Introduction to California

national prohibition struck in 1920. Vines were pulled out, then the boom in home winemaking mainly in the eastern states (as the only way alcohol could be legally produced for consumption) caused a massive explosion in planting. However the varieties needed were coarse and thick-skinned that would travel well. Even the classic European vines grown to make the leading table wines in quality areas such as Napa and Sonoma, were grafted to these coarse varieties.

Wineries anticipating the end of prohibition made large quantities of often very ordinary wine in the early 1930's. All in all, as prohibition ended, California held a legacy of entirely the wrong varieties and bad wines. It is no wonder that the high alcohol ''fortified'' dessert and aperitif wines the Port and Sherry styles captured an ever increasing share of the market. At least they were sound and palatable and usually somewhat sweet, appealing to palates and

purses of those unaccustomed to wine. In 1938 the surplus, mainly of the coarse varieties in the central valley became critical and the California state assembly passed a farm law — all growers having to convert 45% of all their grapes to brandy. This was a real shame for the growers in quality regions with classic varieties producing great table wines. However, this ''Grape Prorate'' often referred to as an ''artificial frost'', solved the surplus problem.

The war years brought wine shortages with imports stopped and many grapes being dried for food and used to make industrial alcohol. Following the war the old surplus problems returned resulting in another crash in 1947.

As the 50's and 60's unfolded table wines grew steadily as better educated and travelled American's started consuming wine with meals and in 1968 table wines finally overhauled ''fortified'' wines in consumption.

In the early 1960's the most significant American quality wine development started, ''the Boutique winery''. When Joe Heitz opened Heitz Cellars in 1961 there were only 18 wineries in Napa county; the number now is fast approaching 200 with almost 700 in total in the state.

These wineries usually started by hobby winemakers and disillusioned professionals, but more recently by high profile successful people from big businesses who often put enormous captial creating beautiful showplaces and often great wines.

The huge companies have been forced to increase quality dramatically by this development. The public now has, in California, superb wines, many at very competitive prices and magnificent wineries to visit. Wine is California's leading rural industry and a glowing example for the wine world to follow.

Introduction to Carneros

his unique viticultural area spans the southern portions of both the Sonoma and Napa Valleys. It is the word on the tip of everyone's tongue and its grapes, particularly Chardonnay and Pinot Noir, are highly sought after by leading wineries in both counties.

The attractive rolling hills of the region, flow down from the southern end of the Mayacamas mountains to the San Pablo bay, part of the San Francisco bay area. The name Carneros comes from one of the three land grants that go back to 1836, ''Rancho El Rincon De Los Carneros'', translated from Spanish this means Sheltered Narrow Valley of the Ram . The whole area was cleared of timber and mainly devoted to grazing sheep.

Vineyards gradually sprang up and in 1870 the region's first winery was built. By the 1880's grapes took over from wheat as the most important crop; William H. Winter from Indiana became Carneros' first Vintner in 1870, when he built his winery on the Huichica Creek, near the tower of Sonoma. Over the previous 15 years he had established one of the largest vineyards in the area.

The first vineyard was actually established in the 1830's, bought by the Kelsey brothers in 1846 and subsequently sold to Agoston Harasthy some 20 years later. It was from here he grew grapes for his Buena Vista Winery in Sonoma. Today history is repeating itself with Buena Vista's exciting Carneros developments that have shot it to the forefront of North American wine.

With Phylloxera, followed by prohibition, grape growing in Carneros all but disappeared and re-planting came much later than in most other regions. The development of the last 15 years has been staggering. From no producing wineries, there are now 16 either with wineries in the region or with their vineyards largely based in Carneros.

The Carneros has a unique climate and soil structure, which has proved particularly suitable for the Burgundian varieties, Chardonnay and Pinot Noir. The cooler climate and long growing season produces grapes of great character. More later of this and the exciting Carneros Quality Alliance, formed to promote this newly declared appellation.

Introduction to Carneros

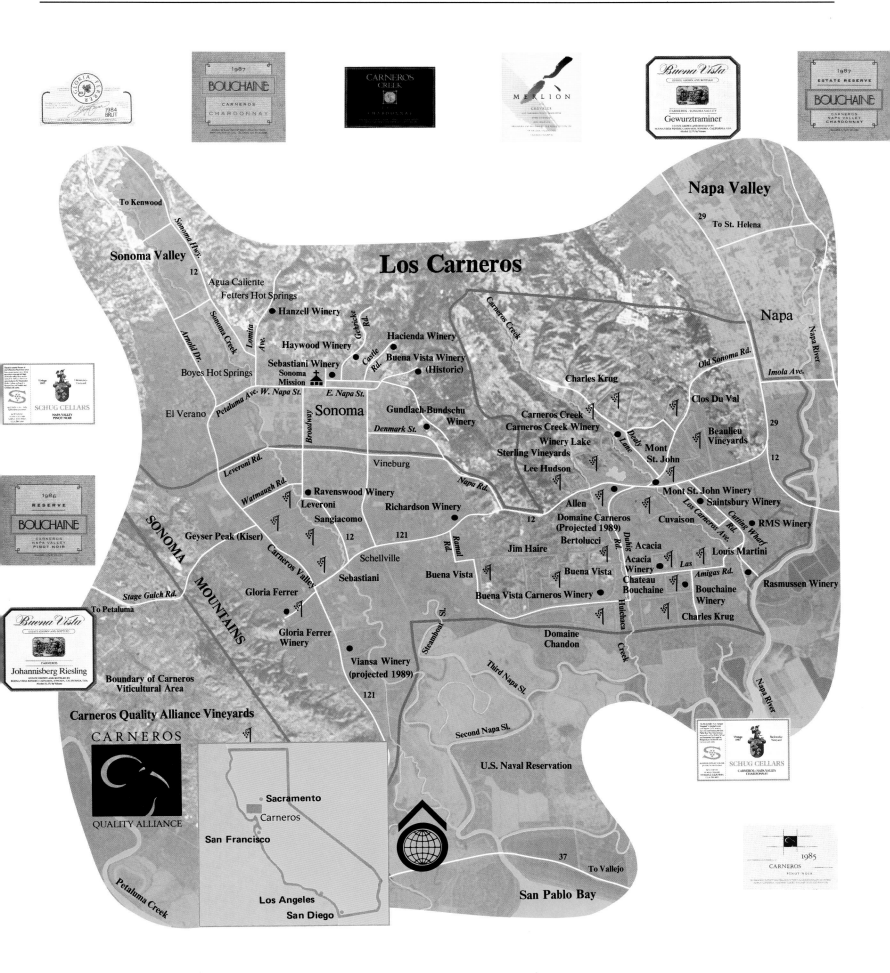

CARNEROS

QUALITY ALLIANCE

On September 19th, 1983 a most significant and unique event occurred, the declaration of Carneros as a viticultural appelation. This newly-defined region covers an area of two existing appelations, Sonoma and Napa. In total area it covers 36,900 acres. At present over 6,000 are under vine while the potential plantable area is about 16,000 acres. This is the first time in the United States an appelation has included two counties, let alone two famous wine growing regions.

What makes Carneros so special? Climate is probably the most important single determinant of grape quality. Generally the best quality grapes and wine come from the coolest climate, provided the grapes ripen fully. The climate of Carneros is classified as region I, or the coolest of all regions and common to the Rhine Valley in Germany, Champagne and Burgundy in France.

Three factors are at work moderating the Carneros climate: first the proximity of the region to the San Pablo Bay keeping it both warmer in spring and winter and cooler in summer. Second, the morning fog in summer, which helps cool both the Napa and Sonoma regions, has an even greater effect closest to the bay in Carneros. Third, in summer, a sea breeze invariably springs up around the middle of the day. Its first and greatest cooling benefits are felt in Carneros.

Soil is important in that too good a soil can be as bad as very poor soil. The best grapes come from vines that undergo some stress and therefore do not bear too heavy a crop; the berries are smaller, the colour and flavour are much more intense. The shallow, clay/loam soil of Carneros, often with heavier black underlying soils created by the area's long time under the sea, mean the vines must struggle to establish a root system, thus providing some stress, which keep yields in Carneros as low as 2.5 tons/acre.

Chardonnay and Pinot Noir grapes thrive in cool climates and account for 85% of the plantings in Carneros. Lesser plantings of Cabernet Sauvignon, Johannisberg Riesling, Merlot, Sauvignon Blanc and Gewurztraminer are also found throughout the region.

To achieve this aim they have devised a number of educational and informational programmes. Having witnessed their presentation at the 1987 Society of Wine Educators annual conference in Vancouver, Canada, I can attest to their effectiveness. Its members also sponsor much research on their region, its history, climate, soil and experiments in winemaking and grape growing. No stone is being left unturned in their search to explore fully the potential of this unique area.

The culmination of this joint effort and team work was the recent release of a Carneros Quality Alliance Pinot Noir, a wine blended from the best Pinots of 1985, chosen by the members from a masked lineup of all their wines.

The Carneros Quality Alliance, as it pushes the wheel of fate, has shown what can be achieved when everyone gets behind each other. This team work, combined with the natural assets of their region is showing the way to all other North American wine growing districts. Carneros is not only ``the region of tomorrow'', but ``the region of

Carneros Quality Alliance

today''.

In addition to the production of still wines, many of the Chardonnay and Pinot Noir grapes are used in sparkling wine. The prestige sparkling wine houses are zeroing in on Carneros as a desirable grape source; Freixenet of Spain recently built Gloria Ferrer Caves, while the French house Taittinger built Domaine Carneros. Both new facilities produce super-premium sparkling wine by Methode Champenoise. Domaine Mumm is drawing fruit through Winery Lake Vineyard, while Domaine Chandon owns over 800 acres in Carneros. Others such as Schramsberg buy in the region also.

Although grapes were first planted in Carneros in the mid-1850's, the combined threat of phylloxera and Prohibition slowed production in the early 1900's. Renewed interest began in the 1930's when Louis Martini planted two large vineyards. In 1938, Andre Tcheltistcheff started making Beaulieu Vineyard Pinot Noirs from the Stanly Ranch. A flurry of construction began in the 1970's when Acacia, Carneros Creek, Mont St. John and Ravenswood wineries were founded. Bouchaine, Ferret and Saintsbury wineries followed in the early 1980's.

Some of the larger growers in the region include Buena Vista and Sangiacomo Vineyards, with over 900 acres each. Buena Vista is also a pioneer in the production of Cabernet Sauvignon from the Carneros region, as well as being the largest producer of Carneros-designated wine.

In December 1985, the ''Carneros Quality Alliance'' was born. Its conception came from a realisation of the modern day pioneers of the region that they had something special. Today the Alliance has 13 winery members and 60 growers. These members all share a very strong commitment to Carneros and a desire to promote this to the wine drinkers of the world. Yes, their efforts are being felt world-wide. The primary objective of the Alliance is to promote the identity of Carneros and its growers and wineries, both nationally and internationally as one of the world's few classic premium wine regions.

Acacia Winery

Acacia started its life in 1979, when a group of 49 San Franciscans, many of them doctors, planted a 40 acre vineyard in the southern portion of the Napa side of Carneros. In 1982 a winery was built on a rise in the property and on a clear day the San Francisco skyline is visible across the San Pablo bay.

Chief movers amongst the partners were Los Angeles solicitor Jerry Goldstein, Texan Michael Richmond and winemaker Larry Brooks. The wines were made at other wineries for the first three vintages and were an instant success. Acacia specialises in Chardonnay and Pinot Noir, releasing a number of vineyard designated wines from each variety each year.

In 1986, Acacia was bought by Chalone Incorporated, a specialist wine producer publicly listed on the stock exchange. A measure of their strength, that although not large, is the fact they escaped unscathed from the October '87 stock market crash.

Chalone own two other vineyards, the original Chalone Vineyard established on the rugged slopes of the Pinnacles National monument in Monterey County and the Carmenet Vineyard in the Mayacamas Mountains in Sonoma County. They also have a share in the Edna Valley Vineyard and Winery in San Louis Obispo County.

Each winery is highly specialised and both have enviable reputations for their wines.

The Acacia Chardonnay's are a real mouthful of wine and age particularly well. The style has been lightened a touch over recent vintages, but the rich style with well balanced oak treatment is highly sought after. Several vineyard designations are produced along with a blended Napa Valley version.

All the Pinot Noirs come from Carneros. Five vineyard designations are usually released — Madonna, Lund, Lee, St. Clair and Winery Lake. Richer than most with a lovely cherry, strawberry flavour and earthy undertones, they often have a touch of mint/eucalyptus about them. Acacia almost more than any other winery have set the pace for American Pinot Noirs of recent years. Acacia have also brought out a well-priced Johannisberg Riesling and an unusual wine also well-priced, called "Vin de Lies" a Chardonnay produced from the fined and filtered lees of their barrel fermented Chardonnay. In 1984, they produced a Cabernet Sauvignon blended from five vineyards incorporating the Carneros and the Mayacamas Mountains, a Merlot was also made.

Acacia is well positioned to continue its success.

Bouchaine Vineyards

The Bouchaine Winery was built in 1980 around the shell of the Garratto Winery, a pre-Prohibition producer long since abandoned. The winery and vineyard are situated on the eastern side of the rolling hills and look over the Napa Valley.

The project was put together by David Pollak, a one-time DuPont executive, the name Bouchaine dating back to his ancestors. He was joined in the venture by a number of investors, chief amongst them being Barret Copeland, an heir to the DuPont fortune. Publisher Austin Kiplinger also has a share, along with renowned winemaker Jerry Luper, who made a big reputation for himself at Chateau Montalena, is in charge of the winery.

Bouchaine traded for a number of years under the Chateau Bouchaine banner. The winery itself is one of the largest in Carneros and makes wine under contract for a number of other wineries. This procedure, known as "custom-crushing", is essential to the viability of many new vineyard ventures.

Although Bouchaine concentrate on the Carneros strengths of Pinot Noir and Chardonnay, they also produce a Sauvignon Blanc and a Cabernet Sauvignon, both made from fruit grown further north in the warmer parts of the Napa Valley. The Cabernet is from the highly renowned Rutherford Bench area.

Bouchaine also have a second label, "Poplar", which is certainly sold at a popular price; the grapes for these wines come mainly from Sonoma County. In this range a Chardonnay and a Riesling are produced. Bouchaine has 30 acres of its own vines and selects fruit from other vineyards.

Bouchaine is a no-nonsense producer of quality wines and an active member of the Carneros Quality Alliance.

Buena Vista Winery

I find it somewhat fitting that the winery with probably America's richest wine history was risen again from obscurity to become arguably North America's most successful winery, producing award winning wines of all styles. Wine Country magazine awarded Buena Vista the platinum medal status as 1987 ''Winery of the Year''.

Buena Vista's belief in and persistence with the Carneros has cost them dearly in financial terms, but they are now reaping the rewards. A large part of their success is attributable to a young German couple Marcus Moller-Racke and his wife Anne, who came to California three years after Marcus' family company had bought Buena Vista from a Los Angeles liquor distributor.

A. Racke was founded at Bingen Am Rhein in 1855, two years before the redoubtable Hungarian ''Count'' Agoston Harazathay founded Buena Vista. Racke also own a champagne house, Bricout and Koch.

Marcus has had an interesting life for such a young man. He was appointed President of Buena Vista whilst still in his 20's, after graduating in Agronomics from the University of Keil and with a degree specialising in viticulture from the University of Bern. He travelled to Brazil to oversee the agricultural interests of the Volkswagen Corporation then returned to Germany to work for his family company. After a year in 1982 he came to California as Director of Vineyard Operations, and then became Vice-

President and Technical Director, then in 1983 President of Buena Vista. He has been instrumental in not only guiding Buena Vista to its now lofty position in the premium wine field, but also in being the driving force behind the Carneros Quality Alliance, which has made such an impact on the wine world since it was founded in December 1985.

Like Buena Vista's far-sighted founder Harazathy, Marcus is gifted with a visionary nature. On Buena Vista's 130th anniversary in August 1987, he arranged a symposium ''Vintage 2,000, a challenge to meet the Future'' bringing together four of the greatest living winemen along with a leading medical expert, a market researcher skilled in wine, two leading members of the wine media and

Buena Vista Winery

Californian Congressman Robert T. Matsui.

The relevance and importance of this move cannot be underestimated. Its contribution to the future of wine not only throughout North America, but reaching far beyond its shores will only be realised as time goes by.

All that has been achieved at Buena Vista over recent years could not be done without a real team effort, from the old guard to the young, everyone shares the same enthusiasm, a constant thread through time has been Andre Tchelistcheff, the pre-eminent winemaking genius, who has consulted with the winery for over 30 years. He in fact made his first Carneros wine a Pinot Noir for Beaulieu, from grapes grown in the Stanley

Vineyard, during his very first Californian vintage in 1938. Others such as Vice President Emeritus Rene Lucasia, who set up Carneros I for the first 700 vineyard in Carneros and Richard Nagroka Vineyard Consultant on Carneros II have laid an excellent foundation.

Buena Vista's young winemaker, Jill Davis, a 1978 Davis graduate, who worked for four years with the legendary Myron Nightingale at Beringer, is achieving great things.

A very big part of the success of Buena Vista also rests on the shoulders of Anne Moller-Racke, Marcus' beautiful and talented young wife. Anne's family have a history in viticulture dating back 200 years, owning one of the largest winemaking and vineyard operations on the Middle Rhine. Anne has studied in biology and chemistry in Germany. As Director of Vineyard Operations at Buena Vista she not only runs the vineyards, Carneros I and II now over 830 acres out of a possible 1,700, but oversees all new planting and conducts much research. Her contribution is invaluable. Today's wine is "made" in the vineyard. Grape quality and character are paramount.

On their 130th anniversary Buena Vista have released a special wine L'Annee, a Cabernet Merlot blend from the spectacular 1984 vintage. The wine has been bottled only in magnums with 8,000 produced, each one individually numbered. This rich full-bodied wine with its velvety texture is a fitting tribute to the remarkable renaissance of California's oldest premium winery.

Why not share in Carlifornia's wine history? Pay a visit the original Buena Vista Cellars (on the outskirts of Sonoma) and taste some of the exciting new Carneros wines of today's Buena Vista.

BUENA VISTA WINERY & VINEYARDS
Address: Ramal Road, PO Box 182, Sonoma, California, 95476
Phone: 707/938 1266 – tasting room
Year of Establishment: 1857
Owner: A. Racke/Marcus Moller-Racke
Winemaker: Jill Davis
Principal Varieties Grown: Chardonnay, Fume Blanc, Sauvignon Blanc, Johannisberg Riesling, Gewurztraminer
Acres Under Vine: 1,700
Average Annual Crush: 22,000 tons

Principal Wines &
Brands
Cabernet Sauvignon P.R.
Pinot Noir P.R.
Chardonnay P.R.
Trade Tours – Available by appointment only.
Retail Room Sales – Available.
Hours open to Public: 10am to 5pm 7 days a week, except Christmas, New Year's and Thanksgiving Tasting Room – 18000 Old Winery Rd, Sonoma.

Carneros Creek Winery

One of the early pioneers of the modern era of Carneros as a wine growing region was Francis Mahoney, who, with his partners, Anita and Balfour Gibson started Carneros Creek Vineyards in 1971. As the Gibsons run a San Francisco company called Connoisseur Imports, their interest in premium wines is understandable. The winery was built on the 30 acre vineyard in 1973 and is situated north of Highway 121, in the foothills of the Mayacamas Mountains, adjacent to Winery Lake Vineyard.

Francis is both energetic and enthusiastic with a quick mind. His Pinot Noirs set something of a standard, when they started being released in the mid 70's, justifying his faith in the region.

Carneros Creek was one of the first wineries to acknowledge the critical role of the grower by keeping the wines separate and giving vineyard designations on the label.

Carneros Creek also produce Fume Blancs and Sauvignon Blancs from various regions outside Carneros. The same applies to their Cabernet Sauvignons and Merlots, which often come from further up the Napa Valley.

Francis is also a fan of the red wines of Amador and Yolo counties. He trucks in grapes from selected vineyards in these regions, producing both Zinfandel and Cabernet Sauvignon. These wines, often intense in colour with rich berry and earthy flavours, repay long ageing. Carneros Creek is an important winery in this exciting viticultural area. Francis Mahoney, with his down-to-earth approach and inquisitive nature, is constantly, albeit subtly, developing his well established wine styles.

Cuvaison Vineyard

Cuvaison Winery is actually located some 25 miles north of Carneros at the opposite end of the Napa Valley, situated on the Silverado Trail, just south of Calistoga. One might well ask, "Why am I including this significant winery in this chapter on Carneros?" The reason is their main vineyards are situated in Carneros and the viticultural base of any winery is more important than its location.

Cuvaison is the French term for the fermentation and extended maceration of red wine on the skins of the grapes. The winery was founded by a group of scientists from the Silicon Valley, later selling it to "Commercial Clearing House", a publisher of technical books. The current owners are a Swiss firm, Isenhold Inc., who also own and operate a Swiss vineyard.

In 1980, they bought a 350 acre parcel of land in Carneros just south of Winery Lake Vineyard. There have, so far, been approximately 200 acres planted largely to Chardonnay and, sometime in the future, a new Cuvaison Winery may be built on the property. The skilled winemaker, Philip Tong, worked at Cuvaison for a number of years and oversaw the purchase and early planting of the Carneros Vineyards. He created a good reputation for the wines and was capably followed by his assistant John Thacher in 198.

The main wines produced by Cuvaison are a Chardonnay from Carneros fruit and a Napa Valley Cabernet Sauvignon. They also make a Zinfandel from Napa grapes.

Cuvaison also run a second label under the name "Calistoga Vineyards". These wine are from classic varieties such as Chardonnay and often from Napa grapes, but are very reasonably priced.

Cuvaison is another of the leading wineries of the Napa Valley to be taking a very strong interest in Carneros and the quality grapes it produces.

Gloria Ferrer

The world's largest Methode Champenoise producer, the Spanish Freixenet firm owned and operated for centuries by the Ferrer family, have left no stone unturned in their quest to create the world's best sparkling wine.

They have chosen as the site for this battle the rolling hills of Carneros, which they feel are ideally suited in terms of climate and soil, to provide them with the highest quality grapes.

Pedro Ferrer, son of the Freixenet President Jose, has overseen the building of one of the true show pieces of the American wine industry. This gracious Spanish style complex is a delight to the eye and a statement of good taste. It also provides subterranean cellars for the production and aging of the Pinot and Chardonnay-based sparkling wines. Only Carneros-grown grapes are used and the first gently pressed juices are utilised in creating the base wines for the Cuvees.

Initially, Pedro was assisted in setting up the operation by Eileen Crane and Robert Iantosca. Robert, whose background includes fine arts and a wide industry experience is now in charge of winemaking. The track record of his Cuvees in wine shows is enviable to the say the least, seriously challenging all comers world-wide.

The decor, furnishings and outlook of the Gloria Ferrer tasting area would do a five star restaurant proud. Spanish "Tapas" are served while you taste either the "Brut" or the "Royale Cuvee", created in honor of Spanish King Juan Carlos I and his Queen Sofia.

I know of no other winery which offers quite the same uplifting feeling of grandeur with the magnificence of its appointments and its product.

Mont St. John Cellars

Louis Bartolucci is a pioneer of the modern day Californian wine industry. His father Andrea came to San Francisco from Tuscany with his brother-in-law in 1913, to work on the Pan Pacific Pavilion. After completing his work on the project he moved to the Napa Valley to work in a magnesium mine.

In 1919, with his wife and young son Louis, Andrea became involved in the wine industry, shipping grapes east during Prohibition. In 1922, he moved to Oakville and shortly after bought a 24 acre vineyard and winery, with a permit to make sacramental and cooking wines. He also bought additional vineyards in the Napa Valley and at Lodi in the Central Valley. During the 1930's his son Louis joined him in business and between them they built a winery calling it the Madonna Winery — Mont St. John Cellars.

Louis ran the business up until it was sold to Oakville Vineyards who unfortunately went broke. The Bartolucci family re-purchased the vineyards and finally sold them to United Vintners in 1976.

Meanwhile, Louis' son Andrea Jnr. (known as Buck) had bought 160 acres in Carneros planting Pinot Noir, Chardonnay, Johannisberg Riesling, Gerwurztraminer, Sauvignon Blanc, Muscat Cannelli and Zinfandel.

Louis became restless in his early retirement, so he and Buck decided to build a new winery. Starting in 1979, they built much of it themselves. The attractive cellars are situated right on the Old Sonoma Road. Recently Cabernet Sauvignon and Petit Sirah have been added to the vineyard and all the wines are made from estate-grown fruit.

Buck has a degree in viticulture and enology from Fresno State and has undertaken further studies at U.C. Davis, his Pinot Noir making a name for the winery in its early days.

The rebirth of Mont St. John Cellars under Andrea with help from his father Louis has maintained a family tradition and added another high quality winery to the fast expanding Carneros region.

Schug Cellars

Walter Schug's rich and varied background shines through not only in his personality, but in his wines. His life has been totally devoted to wine. Born in Assmannshausen in the German Rheingau, his father was director of the State Domaine Winery in his home town, (the only producer of red wine in this famous region). Perhaps it is no coincidence Walter's mission has been to master the difficult Pinot Noir variety, the same one his father battled with in Germany.

Walter migrated to America in the late sixties complete with degrees in viticulture and winemaking from his homeland. He worked for a time with the giant Gallo Company, but his first break was when Joseph Phelps hired him to buy vineyard land and design a winery for him in 1973. After 10 distinguished years at Phelps, including a string of Pinots from the Heinemann Mountain Vineyard, he left in 1983. Phelps gave up the battle with Pinot, but Walter continues and now buys the fruit from Heinemann. Schug Cellar's first home was sharing a winery facility with Dr. Jerry Seps at Storybook Mountain Vineyards, north of Calistoga. This five year arrangement ended in 1985, when Walter bought a small speculative winery south of Yountville.

Walter has formed a strong bond with Carneros and only produces Chardonnay and Pinot Noir, the favoured varieties of this region. Two of his growers, Beckstoffer and Ahollinger, feature in vineyard designated labels. Walter plans to buy some vineyard land and build a new winery in Carneros in the future. A lot more will be heard from this modern day wine guru, whose wines speak for themselves.

Saintsbury Winery

It seems somehow suitable that a fast-rising area like Carneros should have its fast rising stars like Saintsbury. David Graves and Richard Ward met whilst studying enology and viticulture at Davis University. They then went their separate ways, working in different wineries for several years, before getting together and deciding to start their own winery. They named it Saintsbury, after an English literary figure because "it sounds good".

They both shared a love of Burgundy wines and set out looking for cool climate sources, of Chardonnay and Pinot Noir, to make the wines they were looking for. The first Saintsbury wines were made at the old Ehlers Lane Winery, north of St. Helena, where David and Richard rented space. Their search for Pinot Noir and Chardonnay suitable for their purposes led them to Carneros and it is here they built a small, but since expanded winery.

Saintsbury wines have captured the premium wine drinkers' imagination and won many awards and much critical acclaim. David Graves is also heavily involved with "Pinot Noir America", an organisation whose aim is to promote this classic variety and its

wines within the North American continent. Saintsbury wines surely exemplify the sort of wines this variety should be making.

"Saintsbury" is a name that will be increasingly seen, where good wines are enjoyed.

R.M.S. Vineyards

In 1983, a unique venture was launched in the Napa side of Carneros. The prestigious Cognac House of Remy Martin teamed with Schramsberg Vineyards, (one of the pioneers of premium Methode Champenoise in North America), to create a true Cognac-style brandy producer.

No expense was spared or detail overlooked in setting up the venture. They imported a number of the traditional Alembic stills, made in Cognac, copper stills which gently boil the wine and catch the vapours to produce brandy. In fact, the "heart" of the first distillation (the best and most favourful brandy comes from here, not at the start or at the end, but the very middle) is sent back to the still a second time and only the "heart" of this distillation makes R.M.S. Brandy.

This is a time-consuming and expensive process, but there is no short cut to great brandy, although cheaper brandy is made in huge quantities in continuous stills, as used in the central valley.

The grapes are chosen only from the cool coastal valleys of northern California and include French Colombard, Pinot Noir,

Chenin Blanc, Palamino and Muscat. Each is chosen because it adds different and desirable aromas and flavours to the finished brandy. Only Limousin oak casks, imported from Cognac, are used to age the brandy and an aged "Reserve" is planned for release shortly, in addition to the already Marketed "Alembic Brandy". The Heriard-Dubreuil

family of Remy Martin have continued in the venture, while the Davies of Schramsberg have decided to return to Methode Champenoise production, after their initial five years or so of involvement. California should be proud of this unique and splendid addition to its wine industry.

Domaine Carneros

D riving towards Sonoma from Napa on highway 12, a magnificent French Chateau sweeps into view. This newly constructed and superbly finished building is the headquarters for Domaine Carneros, inspired by the grand Chateau de la Marquetterie of the famous French house of Taittinger, one of the world's premier Champagne makers.

France's lastest foray into the North American wine scene is actually a joint venture between Taittinger and the owner of the 138 acres estate, Mr. Peter Ordway, a grandson of the founder of the 3M company, plus the Kobrand Corporation, distributors of Champagne Taittinger.

Heading this ambitious project is Eileen Crane, already experienced in Methode Champenoise management, having been assistant winemaker at Domaine Chandon and, more recently, establishing the impressive Gloria Ferrer Champagne Caves, also in the Carneros region.

Carneros is ideally suited for producing first class grapes for Methode Champenoise production; its cool temperate climate and difficult soils lead to small crop yields of high quality grapes with good acid balance, so necessary for top sparkling wines.

Chardonnay and Pinot Noir, the traditional Champagne varieties, flourish here. Taittinger have long been renowned for their elegant styles and were, in fact, the first French house to produce a Blanc de Blancs made entirely from Chardonnay grapes. Eileen is determined to capture their style, although, of course, with a Californian interpretation to suit the conditions. She will work closely with Claude Taittinger to achieve these aims.

Claude's father, Pierre, established the house of Taittinger in 1931, when he bought the venerable old house of Forest-Fourneaux, founded in 1734. He came into the Champagne business through a gastronomique passion and a desire to make more elegant and refined Campagnes to suit the emerging lighter and more natural cuisine. Over the next few decades he built the largest family-owned Champagne house.

Eileen Crane came into the Methode Champenoise industry in almost the same way, having firstly gained a master's degree in nutrition and trained at the prestigious Culinary Institute of America before teaching nutrition for two years. Her love for wine led her on to the U.C. Davis wine faculty from whence she went to Domaine Chandon on graduation. She is also president of the Carneros Quality Alliance which she helped found in 1985.

In another interwoven coincidence, the Domaine Carneros Vineyards were established by James and Steven Allen, owners of Sequoia Grove Winery, whose products are distributed by Kobrand.

Domaine Carneros is set to bring all these forces together to produce a strictly limited amount of fine Methode Champenoise which North America can be proud of.

Hyde Vineyards

Larry Hyde is a man with great intellectual capacity and a real feel for his environment. He is constantly fine-tuning his vineyard and experimenting with vine clones and viticultural techniques. His grapes are keenly sought after by wineries and various clones of varieties and locations within this 120 acres of vines are earmarked by leading wineries. Larry's 15 winery clients are extremely fortunate recipients of his long-term thinking and the fact he keeps his grape prices at very reasonable levels, preferring a lasting and mutually beneficial relationship with them.

Larry has a theory about the soil structure of Carneros. He believes the 120ft. elevation level was the old floor of the San Pablo bay and above this top soil is deeper and yields are greater, though it may not be quite as suitable for Pinot Noir. In the warmer northern portion of his vineyard he has planted some Cabernet and Merlot. He is also one of the few growers in the region with Sauvignon Blanc and Semillon, making a little Semillon wine, which I found exquisite, for his own use. Larry Hyde is a real asset to Carneros.

Beckstoffer Vineyard

Andrew Beckstoffer has more than a touch of the gentleman farmer about him; his astute mind and perseverance over the last two decades have built one of Napa's most dynamic and profitable vineyard operations.

Andrew was involved in construction engineering and finance in Virginia when Heublein lured him in 1969 to set up the "Vinifera Development Company" to ensure them a premium grape supply of grapes for their Beaulieu and Inglenook labels.

The Vineyard company sought investors to buy Napa land which could be developed as a joint venture. In 1973, Andrew bought out the company and now controls eight parcels in the Napa amounting to 1350 vineyard acres in all. Two of the vineyards, "Los Amigos" and "Carneros Creek" are in the Carneros region, where Andrew was one of the pioneers of the areas renaissance in the early 1970's.

In fact, he introduced two vineyard techniques to the region, drip irrigation and close vine spacing both now accepted as the norm, but at the time quite revolutionary. His work with Andre Tchelistcheff, then the winemaker at Beaulieu, he found most enlightening.

Today, Beckstoffer Vineyards supply many prestige vignerons including Stag's Leap Wine Cellars and Schug Cellars.

Andrew Beckstoffer's quiet, easy confidence and skill have created a string of top quality vineyards whose reputation is growing each day.

The Truchard family are very happy with their lifestyle as one of Carneros' premier grape growers. Anthony and Jo-Ann first planted in 1974, when they put in 20 acres comprising six varieties: Chardonnay, Pinot Noir, Cabernet Sauvignon, Cabernet Franc, Merlot and Riesling. The Riesling did not fare so well and was budded over to Pinot Noir in 1983.

In 1979, they planted a further 30 acres, mainly Chardonnay and in 1982 another 10 acres. 1985 and 1986 bought a change of direction, as, being one of the northern-most Carneros growers, on the Napa side they found that Bordeaux red varieties have done well and have planted 65 acres mainly of these varieties.

They sell to many prestige wineries including Saintsbury, Acacia, Carneros Creek, Newton, Sinskey and Conn Creek.

It is the Truchards' wish that their six children help carry on their grape-growing tradition into future generations.

Hudson Vineyard

Lee Hudson is irrepressible, enthusiasm bubbles from him constantly. His energy is fast making his dreams come true.

Lee followed a Horticultural degree from Arizona State with viticultural training in Burgundy. Perhaps it was this experience that drew him towards Carneros with its ideal conditions for Burgundy varieties.

He purchased 1200 acres in 1981 adjacent to the famed Winery Lake Vineyard. Much of his land is extremely hilly and rocky (the tail end of the Mayacamas Range) and only 100 acres are plantable.

Lee is creating a real Shangri-La. He has constructed a large lake beneath the hills and surrounded it with vineyards. Thirty-four large-mouthed bass released in the lake have now produced several hundred thousand. On the southern shores, he has built a delightful high roofed verandahed building, he calls his "Tibetan Train Station". Foundations have also been laid for an Italian villa, which will become home for Lee, his vibrant wife Becky and son Ed.

The ancient alluvial deposits on their volcanic ash base create ideal soils for viticulture. Lee's skill in the vineyard is obvious. He has nine very happy wineries to which he supplies grapes. In his spare time, he also has written a very useful book entitled "Carneros Quality Alliance Growers Profile" on the Carneros growers. He has also founded the C.Q.A. Grape Exchange, a

unique way of bringing potential winery grape purchasers in touch with the growers.

Lee exemplifies the dynamic nature of the new Carneros.

Sangiacomo

S angiacomo is a byword in Carneros for no less than thirty-five leading Napa and Sonoma Wineries are proud to acknowledge this families' vineyards as the source of some of their greatest wines. Many vineyard designate these wines as Sangiacomo.

The vineyard operation, comprising six sites around Carneros, is run by an extremely hardworking and modest family of three brothers and a sister led by Angelo Sangiacomo. His father, Vittorio, known as "Mike", founded the enterprise in 1927, when he bought fifty-six acres of orchard land. Angelo speaks with great respect of his father who worked right through until his death in November 1987, at ninety-one years of age.

Over the years, the Sangiacomos bought more land, much of it under fruit trees such as apples, pears and plums. Gradually these have been replaced by vines, the last eight acres being converted to the vine in 1988. The green fingers have been transplanted from the father to his offspring, who with their real feel for the land and their vines, consistently produce some of North America's finest grapes. Small wonder there is a constant queue of winemakers seeking their produce.

The Sangiacomos also have a joint venture with prominent Napa vigneron, Joe Phelps. Part of this area is planted to Merlot an unusual variety for Carneros, but resulting wines so far have been exciting.

Angelo, his brothers Victor (Buck), Robert and sister Lorraine richly deserve their success and the esteem they hold in Carneros. The next generation of the family is already set to become involved.

An Introduction To Central Valley North

This major region stretches some sixty miles from the Sacremento delta town of Lodi, southward to Modesto and encompasses the San Joaquin and Stanistaus Counties. This northern section is part of the massive central valley, where almost six hundred thousand acres of vines are grown. The valley is about fifty miles wide, three hundred and fifty miles long and lies between the Sierras and the Coastal Range. Soils are rich alluvial silt washed down from the mountains and well over half of California's table wine is produced here along with virtually all its Sherry, Port and Brandy.

The climate of the northern portion of the valley is milder, mainly due to its proximity to the Bay area and the waterways of the Sacremento delta. Around Lodi the Fume Tokay table grape thrives, only in this area does it obtain its' bright flame-like colour. Further south, in the hotter climate, it will ripen only with a dull brown hue. In the Lodi region premium varietal vineyards are expanding at a rapid pace and well versed vintners such as Robert Mondavi have always recognised its potential. At his Woodbridge winery Mondavi produces some excellent table wines now varietally labelled, under the R. M. insignia. The dynamic Franzia brothers of the Bronco Winery fame have just commenced planting one of America's largest Chardonnay vineyards at Forest Lake north of Lodi.

Other noteable winemakers in the region are the Indelicato Family with their Delicato Winery at Manteca, producing an increasing range of premium varietal table wines. The original Franzia Winery forges ahead under the "Wine Group" banner with marketing wiz Art Ciocca at the helm and highly respected Lou Quaccia in charge of winemaking.

The Northern Central Valley is also headquarters for the world's largest wine enterprise, E & J Gallo, at Modesto as well as probably the fastest-expanding large winery, the Bronco operation of the Franzia Brothers.

The Coastal counties have the glamour of wine tied up, but here its heartbeat and muscle are felt.

Cooks Champagne Cellars

The Guild Winery in Lodi, California is now home for Cooks Imperial Champagne, whose story is one of the most fascinating "webs of intrigue" surrounding a wine product in North America.

In a maze of stone arched cellars in the centre of St. Louis, Missouri, founded in 1832, the first Cooks Imperial Champagne was made in 1859 by Isaac Cook, a famed political figure and connoisseur of the day. After a number of years, the cellars closed, but were re-opened after Prohibition. The American Wine Company took over, headed by Champagne master, Adolf Heck from Alsace, who later went on to California and eventually took over Korbel. A Swiss firm helped him with finance in 1939, and only later was the secret owner traced to be Hitler's infamous foreign minister Ribbentrop. After government seizure and many ownership changes, The Guild Winery bought the brand and took its production to their Lodi Winery.

Cooks Imperial is one of the largest selling "American Champagnes" and

represents excellent value for money. It is certainly an institution and will no doubt be the centre of many celebrations in the future.

Central Valley North

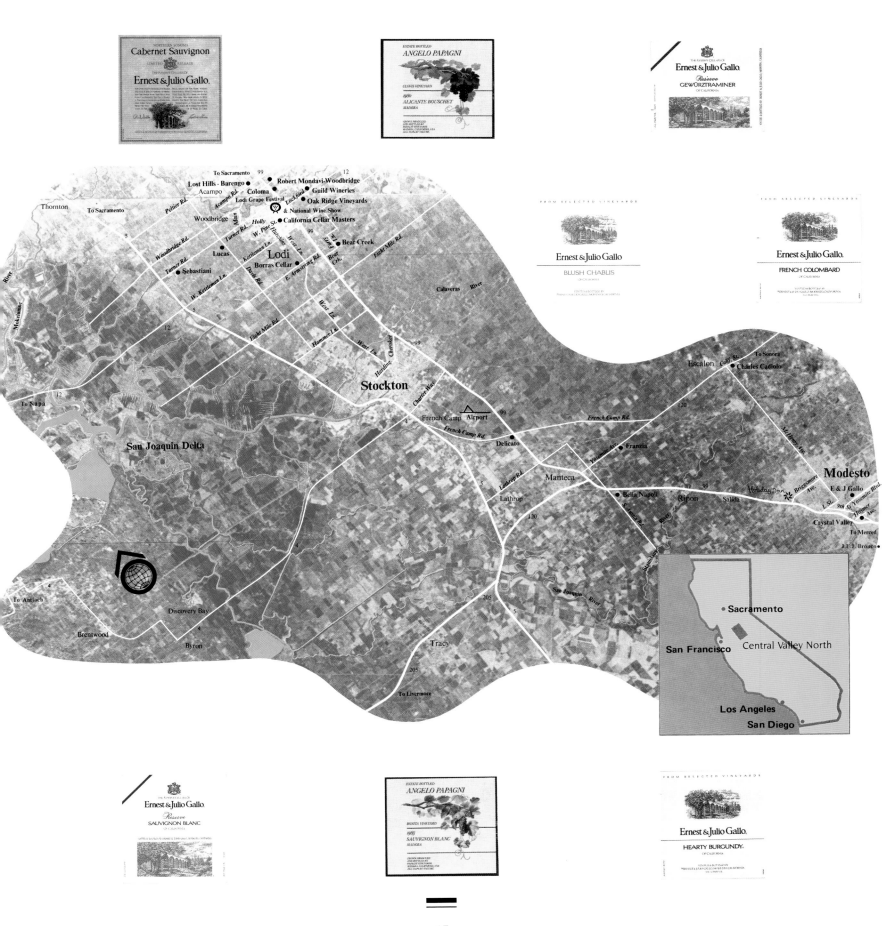

J. F. J. Bronco

At lightning pace, Joseph, Fred T. and John Franzia have built a wine enterprise that looks set to outstrip all but the mighty Gallo in size.

The Franzia brothers are the third generation of their family to be involved in wine. They have learnt their lessons well and have mastered the many aspects of the wine industry superbly. Just say to any one of them "It can't be done" and they'll prove you wrong.

One of the secrets of Bronco is that it has been built the opposite way to most wine companies; that is, distribution came first. A little history is needed at this point just to put you in the picture.

The brothers' grandfather, Giuseppe, came to California from Genoa, Italy in 1893. He worked in vegetable gardens around San Francisco until he raised enough capital to buy vineyards. In 1915, he started a winery only to be forced into closing it when national Prohibiton arrived. His five sons helped him re-establish after repeal and built a substantial business in both bulk and bottled wine. In 1971, the family had mixed feelings about the direction they should be pursuing and decided to sell.

Since the early 60's, the younger generation had called the tune and expanded the business base of Franzia considerably. So, it was no surprise when they launched "Bronco" in 1973 as three equal partners — the same way they operate today. Firstly, they set up distribution of leading wineries products in Southern California. Many leading vignerons including Robert Mondavi, gave them a chance and today they distribute in both Northern and Southern California for many of the state's leading producers. The likes of fast-growing companies such as Glen Ellen and Round Hill are with them.

The entry into distribution led naturally to setting up a winery, which they did at Ceres, just south of Modesto, the home of the mightly Gallo, (coincidently, their uncle is

J. F. J. Bronco

Ernest Gallo who married their aunt Emelia).

The Bronco name was chosen because it means, colloquially in Italian, "brothers or cousins" and in fact that's just how Bronco is made up. Of course Bronco also brings to mind a spirited bucking horse and to a degree that's just what Bronco Winery is about. The Ceres plant is constantly expanding and over 30 million gallons of wine were produced in 1988.

In the mid 70's, when the brothers first started putting in a battery of massive 700,000 gallon tanks (that is 6,000 bottles of wine per inch) they made a very generous gesture of dedicating each one to great industry people who had inspired and helped them. What other industry could boast such a magnanimous act? The names of Ernest and Julio Gallo appear, along with Robert Mondavi and Auguste and Sylvia Sebastiani. Wine runs in the veins of the Franzias, but their approach is extremely business-like. Quality is paramount and, although it is on a massive scale, the principles of good winemaking are applied in the same way as a boutique winery. Refrigeration, controlled fermentation, even separate 100,000 gallon parcels are made. John Franzia firmly believes there is no such thing as a perfect wine — there is always room for improvement.

The brothers have expanded into bottling and marketing their own wines, while the winery also makes and bottles for many leading wineries.

Even in the vineyard area they have not been idle and are currently planting a massive 1300 acre Chardonnay vineyard, in the moderate climate north of Lodi at Forest Lake. This will be one of the world's largest single Chardonnay vineyards and I am sure their product will take a lot of beating for quality and value-for-money.

Certainly at Bronco they call a spade a spade and not a shovel, but they certainly know what to do with it. Don't be surprised if in several decades, they challenge even the mightly Gallo. They are big thinkers and they follow their vision with action.

When the Franzia brothers launched their new Bronco wine venture in the early 1970's, they had visions of creating their own premium wines, but at much more affordable prices than the coastal wine regions can offer.

The "leading" varietal white wine is, of course, Chardonnay and, being one of the few truly classic white wine varieties, its popularity is set to continue for many years to come.

With these things in mind, the brothers

Joseph, Fred and John along with their cousin and vineyard manager Bill Rossini, purchased a parcel of land north of Lodi. They named it Forest Lake, for the Californian oaks that surround a lake in the centre of the property. The soils are basically red loam and very suitable for viticulture; the climate is much cooler than further south in the central valley, being tempered by the waters of the Sacramento delta and afternoon breezes from San Francisco Bay. The decision was taken to plant only

Forest Lake Vineyard

Chardonnay, somewhat of a risk knowing the changes of taste and fashion wine has been subjected to over the years. Still, the brothers are men of action and certainly not afraid of bold moves.

To establish this 1,300 acre vineyard, one of the world's largest Chardonnay plantings, as quickly as possible, they have used one year old rooted seedlings encased in tubes, which break up in the soil as the vine establishes itself. This could mean a small crop is possible after only two years.

When we visited the vineyard in Spring 1988, there were literally hundreds of workers involved in the planting process. The total area involving over one million vines should be finished this year.

The plan is to produce top class Chardonnay and to this end special 100,000 gallon controlled fermentors using all the technology applicable to the boutique winery operation have been built. These are on a grand scale some thought not possible, but one thing the Franzias are not short of is

ingenuity. The wines will be creatively and beautifully packaged and, knowing the "Bronco" connection and skill in distribution, sales will no doubt take off at a rapid pace. I am sure the pricing will be as attractive as the wine and package.

Forest Lake is set to become a well used name by wine lovers far and wide.

Delicato Vineyards

The Indelicatos, a family of gentlemen, make largely for other wineries, although they have worked very hard on their own premium bottled wine over recent years. Today, they produce a range of fine table wines under the Delicato brand name and could rightly be called the Boutique of the giant central valley makers.

The family's involvement with the vine started in 1925, when Gaspare (Jasper) Indelicato, who had migrated from Italy, set up a grape shipping business. This was during the depths of Prohibition, so he must have been a cheerful optimist, much like his descendants.

After Prohibition, he and his brother-in-law Sebastiano (Sam) Luppino, built a small winery naming it Sam-Jasper Winery, after their anglicised names. Grape growing still remained their chief livelihood, along with the sale of fresh grape juice to home winemakers.

In 1968, at the height of the wine boom, Jasper's three sons, Vincent, Frank and Anthony, decided to start a large winemaking operation under the Delicato banner, an obvious streamlining of the family name.

Today it has grown into a big business, crushing 125,000 tons of grapes in 1987. The third generation is now involved with Vincent's son Robert being particularly active. Some of their big investments in pursuit of premium table wines have been a very efficient gas-expansion heat exchanger to chill the juice immediately the grapes have been crushed and a barrage of 50,000 gallon controlled fermenters.

The proof of their endeavours lies in the bottled wines. I found their Chardonnay from Santa Barbara grapes and a special 50th anniversary "Napa" Chardonnay to be particularly impressive. Their Californian Cabernet Sauvignon was a very attractive wine and one of the best value buys I have seen. An unusual wine wine produced, to which I gave top marks was the "Green Hungarian", a white with crisp melon, pineapple and quince overtones, but beautifully dry and fresh.

Vincent's wife Dorothy oversees their very attractive tasting and sales area and even has a few of the family's secret recipes in her wine cook book. This is a delightful winery and family to visit if you are on the trail through the central valley; it is also quite convenient to the San Francisco Bay area.

F ranzia today is in the hands of the dynamic management of Art Ciocca and "The Wine Group" comprised of the Franzia management team that bought the winery along with Mogen David and Tribuno Vermouths in 1981. The group has recently expanded with the purchase of Corbett Canyon Vineyards and Shadow Creek Champagne Cellars in Paso Robles on the Central Californian coast.

The Franzia Winery has never suffered from a lack of action. Founded in 1915 by Italian immigrant and grapegrower, Giuseppe Franzia, but closed during Prohibition, it was opened again by his five sons in 1933. It was mainly involved in bulk wine production until the new generation of the Franzias became involved in the 1960's. They revamped the winery and started producing and marketing bottled premium wines. Sadly, the family could not agree on the direction they wished to follow and Franzia was sold to Coca-Cola in 1971, when the current owners were the Coca-Cola management team, headed by Art Ciocca, a former Gallo sales executive. Winemaking is still in the capable hands of Lou Quaccia, whose father Lawrence was the long time winemaster at Guild Winery; he has made the Franzia wines since the commencement of the modern era in 1966.

Franzia have over 4,000 acres of their own vineyards and use a great deal of grapes from the Sacramento Delta region. The winery has expanded from 3,000,000 gallons capacity in 1970 to over 30,000,000 gallons in 1988. Franzia purchased the "Summit" brand from Geyser Peak recently and produced a big selling "bag in the box" wine cask under this banner.

A range of premium varietal wines is produced which sells at the remarkable price range of two to four dollars. The red wines, particularly their Cabernet Sauvignon at under three dollars, I found very impressive. Several well-produced sparkling wines including one from Napa fruit and an almond flavoured Champagne are made.

The tasting room at Franzia is a true oasis surrounded by well-kept gardens and weeping willow trees, a pleasant spot to stop on a journey through the valley.

E. & J. Gallo Winery

Certainly North America's most important and significant premium wine producer is the E. & J. Gallo Winery; also by far one of the world's superior quality wine producers.

Ernest and Julio Gallo were brought up working in their father's vineyard. The boys worked from dawn to dusk seven days a week with mule teams to cultivate the vineyard.

On the repeal of prohibition in 1933, Ernest and Julio scraped together $5,900.23 in capital, rented a railroad shed in Modesto, bought a crusher, some redwood tanks on terms and started business. They obtained two pre-prohibition winemaking pamphlets, talked to professors at the University of California, and then began making wine.

Now you may make good wine, but you've still got to sell it. When the Gallos received a letter from a potential Chicago distributor, Ernest boarded a plane, travelled to Chicago, and made the deal. The first barrels of wine were sent East by rail.

Gallo wine in those days was sold in bulk to be bottled under many different labels. It was not until the early 1940's that the first Gallo label appeared.

The Gallos purchased the large 'American Vineyard' in Livingston and in 1946 began studying different grapes and the wine made from them. Working closely with the University of California, they eventually planted more than 400 different varieties, evaluating the vines and the wines; thereby helping to build the foundation for the growing of fine wine grapes in California.

Then, as now, two things dominated their operation – hard work and thorough research. The success this has brought has not only made them one of the world's finest winemakers, but they have enriched the North American and world wine scene enormously with the generous sharing of their extensive research and also by the training and experience they have endowed on many of today's industry leaders and winemakers (many of whom have worked at Gallo).

Since 1951, Gallo has released 57 separate research papers on grape growing and winemaking.

Gallo has become North America's leading quality winery in virtually every wine type from fine dessert wine to superior varietals and table wines. Julio insists on the best quality grapes from growers and uncompromising standards of wine quality control.

E. & J. Gallo Winery

E. & J. Gallo Winery

''Nobody can make good wine from bad grapes'', probably sums up Julio Gallo's philosophy and explains why Gallo has such a strong viticultural base. Based on decades of field trials and other research, in 1968, Julio made another pioneering move by offering California growers generous 10–15 year contracts if they would plant premium varieties and accept Gallo's viticultural standards. Gallo thereby became the first winery to encourage the planting of classic grape varieties to replace the coarser, high-yielding varieties planted and encouraged during prohibition. Today, Gallo harvests more varietal grapes from the North Coast (Napa, Sonoma, Mendocino) and the Central Coast than any other California winery.

The winemaking teams at Gallo enjoy almost ideal conditions directly attributable to Julio's research and technical orientation. They have one of the world's finest and most complete wine libraries, which obtains world-wide technical literature. This material is translated and circulated to the winemaking teams. The central 'University' style research and winemaking department can find answers for the toughest problems. Every Gallo wine has an individual winemaker and his team responsible for it; no wonder quality is so high and consistent.

Gallo winemakers have at their disposal the finest winemaking facilities available including an underground wood maturation cellar which contains 658 – 4,000 gallon oak casks. French oak casks are used to age white wines such as Chardonnay, and Yugo-slavian oak has been selected for Gallo reds such as Cabernet Sauvignon and Zinfandel. The cooperage was hand crafted by a father and son team of coopers over a three-year period.

Today, E. & J. Gallo Winery is still very much a family-run business. Ernest is Chair-man and still active at 79 years of age. He has almost single-handedly set the marketing and sales standards for American wines.

He brought wine from the back of the retail store to a product which is actively merchan-dised as a front-of-the-store item. He has ensured Gallo is always represented by knowledgeable, skilled wine sales people. His two sons are also very much involved; Joseph runs the Gallo sales network; David, the marketing and advertising. Julio, at 78 years of age, is President and runs the production side of the Winery. His son, Robert, is in charge of vineyard operations and also is involved in winemaking, while son-in-law, James Coleman, runs the production and bottling departments at Modesto.

What of the future? Plans are afoot to launch Estate bottled varietals from their Sonoma County vineyards. (See Gallo Sonoma page 225.)

Ernest and Julio have been honored as recipients of the American Society of Enology and Viticulture's prestigious Merit Award and ''Wines & Vines'' Magazine's 'Man of the Year' award. They have also

appeared on the cover of Time Magazine in 1972.

Throughout the years, in competition after competition, the wines of Ernest and Julio Gallo have been awarded top medals and honors.

North America's wine industry is much richer for the presence of Gallo, who has contributed to and shared so much with the whole wine industry, both large and small.

As the New York Times put it, ``Gallo is to wine what the Statue of Liberty is to New York.''

Robert Mondavi's Woodbridge Cellars

To tie in with his philosophy of bringing quality premium table wines to people from all walks of life, Robert Mondavi introduced a range of three bottled wines; a Red, a Rose and a White all under the R.M. insignia and affectionately known to many as "Bob White" and "Bob Red". All are sold at remarkably low prices and quality is excellent.

The wine was made under contract for Robert under his supervision in the Lodi region until 1979, when he bought the winemaking facility formerly owned by the Cherokee grapegrowers, but one which lately had made wine for a number of large wineries including the Mondavi family at "Charles Krug". Robert had dealt with them in this context.

With the sales of his "Bob" wines burgeoning, Robert entered negotiations and bought the winery in 1979, re-naming it "Robert Mondavi Woodbridge Cellars". The cellars have been totally updated and outfitted with the Mondavi-style, state-of-the-art equipment. The buildings have had a complete facelift and now sport a very attractive Spanish mission-style facade with landscaped gardens and pergola-covered walkways.

The "R.M." wines are some of the best in the value category and the red and white have just become varietals as they now contain over 75% of their chief varieties. The red table wine is now labelled "Cabernet Sauvignon" and the white "Sauvignon Blanc". They both have excellent varietal flavours on the palate.

Robert Mondavi is once again leading the world of wine in an inspired direction.

Oak Ridge Vineyards

Right in the heart of the town of Lodi are situated the Oak Ridge Vineyards Cellars. The front of the winery is easily distinguishable as a 50,000 gallon Redwood tank has been placed under the trees and converted to a pretty tasting cellar called "Das Weinhaus".

The winery was established in 1934 by frustrated German grape growers, who were being offered a mere pittance of a few dollars a ton by the wineries of the day. Today, there are one hundred and thirty grower members and a large range of wines is produced, many of them actively marketed, some of which use the recently established Lodi appelation. Three wines which appealed to me a great deal were their Gamay Beaujolais Blanc (their Lodi appelation White Zinfandel) and a 1985 Gran Shirah made from Shiraz grapes of the Hermitage area of the Rhone Valley of France. This wine has a spicy, peppery cassis fruit, yet was quite soft and drinkable.

Winemaker for over thirty years was the legendary Herman Ehlers, who won many awards for the winery.

Introduction to Central Valley-South

South of Modesto the central valley stretches for over 300 miles and is up to 50 miles wide in places. Much of this area is covered with vines; some, to be sure, are table grape varieties and while there are still large acreages of the ubiquitous multi-purpose grape, the Thompson Seedless, increasingly premium table wine varieties are the norm.

Once you travel southward from the area around Modesto and Ceres, the climate is classified as region V, the warmest of all with over 4,000 degree days per year. Despite this, with the advances of viticultural techniques and early picking, the quality and varietal character of the grapes are often excellent. The resulting wines are often of very high quality, although not as long-lived as those from cooler regions. Prices, of course, reflect this difference.

Wineries vary from the world's largest, the Gallo Livingston Winery, with over 130 million gallon capacity to the valley's first boutique winery, Ficklin, with its 40,000 gallon cellar, specialising in premium port and table wines. Andrew Quady has lately added a welcome addition, with his classic fortified Muscats and Zinfandels produced near Madera.

The winegrowing history of the central valley dates back to the 1870's and is largely tied in to the establishment of irrigation channels from the Sierras because, although the soil of the valley is rich, having been washed down from the volcanic mountains, rainfall is extremely low — only six to fourteen inches per annum.

The modern history of this region (it accounts for over half of all wine produced on the North American continent) has been turbulent. Since Prohibition, many of the large wineries have changed hands many times in the political and power struggles for control of the means of production. The large grape grower co-operatives such as Guild are still strong, but increasingly it is the entreprenurial companies such as The Beverage Source (incorporating I.S.C. and Sierra Wines), The Wine Group (including Franzia) and The Bronco Company, who are the power players. Large corporations such as Gallo and Heublein are, of course, still extremely powerful forces and will, no doubt, remain so.

From a wine consumer's point of view, the central valley is extremely important. It produces not only a large percentage of the continent's wine (of an ever increasing quality), but acts as a balance in the market forces to ensure good wine at value prices.

B. Cribari-Sons Cellar

The creeper-clad Cribari Cellars look somewhat out of place in the industrial area of Fresno-they would be much more at home in Italy's Piedmont. Surrounded by lush green lawns and large trees this is a real oasis in the desert.

The winery's history goes back to the turn of the century, when it was built by the Cella family and called Roma. It was subsequently bought by the Schenley Distilling Company, under Lewis Rosensteil.

The Guild Winery Group bought the Roma Winery from Schenley in 1971 and the then vice-president Albert Cribari took over, the winery being re-named B. Cribari and Sons. Albert's grandfather Benjamin had founded the House of Cribari in 1904, with large vineyards holdings in the Santa Clara Valley, operating wineries in Madrone and Fresno as well as New York City, before selling out to Guild.

The Cribari Winery has a large air-conditioned cellar. Many of the large maturation casks of days gone by are still in use, adding an attractive old world charm in tone with the gracious old buildings.

Cribari make a large range of wines of all styles, but have recently begun marketing premium varietal table wines.

The Cribari Cellars are well worth stopping at for a visit and tasting.

Villa Bianchi

On the banks of the San Joaquin River, on the border of Madera and Fresno counties lies the Villa Bianchi Winery. Its turretted Gothic tower and surrounding buildings have a distinct medieval feeling about them.

All this old world feeling belies what is inside Villa Bianchi, which has some of the most modern and efficient winemaking equipment available. In 1974, Joseph Bianchi, who had over forty years experience in chemistry, pulled out the entire winemaking plant and storage vessels, replacing them with the world's best from both Europe and America. Joseph has also experimented with viticultural and winemaking practices and produced some innovative products such as low alcohol wines and wine coolers in cans. The wines I tasted here were particularly impressive, showing strong varietal fruit flavours, proving Joseph's investment in new plant and techniques has been a wise one.

Papagni Vineyards

Right next to main Highway 99, a few miles south of Madera, is the modern winery of the Papagni Family.

In 1973, at the height of the wine boom, Angelo Papagni decided to build a "super-modern" winery and to become one of the first to produce premium table wines in the central valley. Angelo's father Demetrio, emigrated to California from Italy in 1912, and, seeing the boom in grape growing and grape juice supply to the eastern states with the onset of Prohibition, he planted vines in 1920.

Angelo operates the winery and vineyards with the help of his wife Blanche and daughters Kathy and Dana. The Papagnis are careful to not overcrop their vines and strive for quality grapes to make top class table and sparkling wines. The winery is well set up with all the modern equipment and technology necessary. The winemaker, John Daddino has long experience in several of the Valley's leading wineries.

Many Papagni wines have won awards at wine shows and these are proudly displayed in the company's attractive offices.

Clear Lake

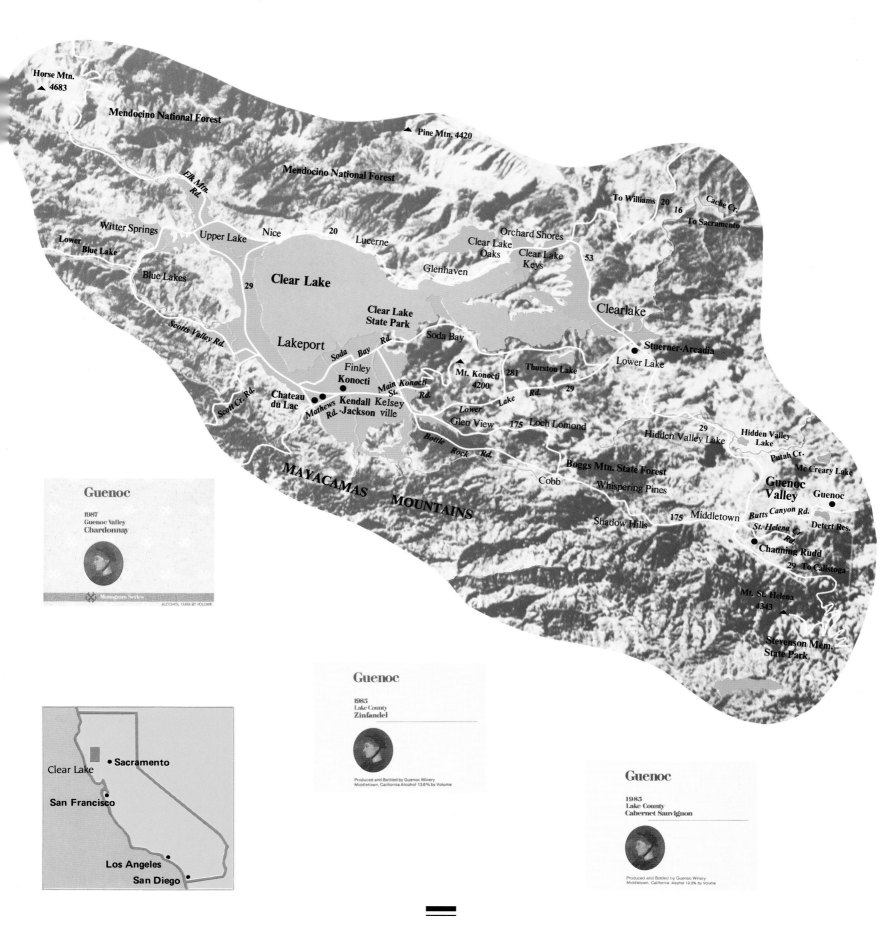

Horse Mtn.
▲ 4683

Mendocino National Forest

▲ Pine Mtn. 4420

Mendocino National Forest

Elk Mtn. Rd.

To Williams 20
16
Cache Cr.
To Sacramento

Witter Springs

Upper Lake Nice 20 Lucerne

Orchard Shores
Clear Lake Oaks
Clear Lake Keys

Lower Blue Lake

Blue Lakes

Clear Lake

Glenhaven

53

Clearlake

29

Scotts Valley Rd.

Clear Lake State Park

Lakeport

Soda Bay Rd. Soda Bay

Stuerner-Arcadia
Lower Lake

Scott Cr. Rd.

Finley Konocti

Main St. Konocti Rd.

▲ Mt. Konocti 4200 281 Thurston Lake

29

Chateau du Lac

Mathews Rd. Kendall Jackson Kelsey ville

Lake Rd.

Lower Glen View 175 Loch Lomond

29 Hidden Valley Lake

Hidden Valley Lake

Bottle Rock Rd.

Putah Cr.

Mc Creary Lake

MAYACAMAS

Boggs Mtn. State Forest
Cobb Whispering Pines

Guenoc Valley Guenoc

MOUNTAINS

175 Middletown

Butts Canyon Rd.

Detert Res.

Shadow Hills

St. Helena Cr. Rd.

Channing Rudd

29 To Calistoga

▲ Mt. St. Helena 4343

Stevenson Mem. State Park

Guenoc

1987
Guenoc Valley
Chardonnay

Monogram Series

ALCOHOL 13.8% BY VOLUME

Clear Lake • Sacramento

San Francisco •

Los Angeles •
San Diego •

Guenoc

1983
Lake County
Zinfandel

Produced and Bottled by Guenoc Winery
Middletown, California Alcohol 13.8% by Volume

Guenoc

1985
Lake County
Cabernet Sauvignon

Produced and Bottled by Guenoc Winery
Middletown, California Alcohol 13.0% by Volume

Introduction to Lake County

Lake County is fast developing into a major wine growing region. Once again, vineyard acreage is expanding toward 5,000 acres from a mere 300 acres in 1965. The adjoining county of Mendocino has more vineyards, but Lake County is catching up.

During the latter part of the last century the position was reversed, with around 1,000 acres of vines planted near the Lake and only 300 in Mendocino. Even until fairly modern times the lake district has been isolated from major transportation links, which certainly slowed its re-development, until recent times.

Prior to prohibiton there were some 33 wineries — the area seemed to have attracted some famous and colourful characters no doubt partly due to its stunning physical beauty and isolation. California's first Chief Justice Serranum Clinton Hastings was one,

with his Carsonia Vineyard and Champagne Cellars.

Colonel Charles Mifflin Hammond, was another whose wines won awards at the Paris Exposition in 1900, but English actress Lillie Langtry overshadows them all. Born Emily Charlotte Le Breton Langtry on the Isle of Jersey, she escaped the island by marrying a visiting yachtsman and became an actress, known for her charm and beauty, having a notorious affair with Albert Edward, the Prince of Wales and heir to the British throne. In 1888, desiring to escape the limelight, she purchased a large ranch in the Guenoc Valley and planted vineyards as a sideline to raising horses. She built a winery and even employed a French winemaker, Henri Deschelles. Her Guenoc Winery has recently been re-established.

The modern history of Lake County

only goes back about a decade. Although vineyards were planted in the early 70's, the first commercial crush was not until 1977. Today there are not many wineries but three in particular have made quite a name for themselves, the largest is "Kendall-Jackson" also known as "Chateau du Lac", who recently entered a partnership with Robert Mondavi to take over the Tepesquet Vineyards in Santa Barbara County. Kendall-Jackson wines have received much critical acclaim.

Konocti Winery, a partnership between the growers of the region and the Parducci brothers from Mendocino have made an impact and the Guenoc Winery has been revived by the Magoon family from Hawaii.

Lake County is firmly re-establishing itself as a super premium wine region and exciting developments are sure to follow.

Introduction to Lake County

Guenoc Winery

As far as romance is concerned Guenoc Winery is in a league of their own. Lillie Langtry, the famous British actress bought a 4,190 acre ranch in the Guenoc Valley (Guenoc is derived from an Indian name for the Valley) with the intention of raising horses and escaping from the public eye. Lillie was a woman of considerable life and vitality as well as beauty; she had been immortalised in verse and prose by literary giants of the day, her form was captured in canvas by many famous artists. It was she who so infatuated Albert Edward the Prince of Wales, that he entered into a brief liaison with her.

In creating her paradise by the lake, she planted vines to supply her needs with wine, even bringing in a French winemaker, Henri Deschelles, from Bordeaux. Such was her attraction to men a suitor Fred Gebhard, a wealthy horse fancier from Baltimore and smitten with Lillie, bought the 3,000 acre ranch next door. Lillie however, moved on when she married the English aristocrat Hugo Gerald de Bathe, later becoming Lady de Bathe when he inherited the family's baronetcy.

The wine history of Guenoc disappeared into obscurity until 1963, when the Magoon family moved into the Valley. They, too, have a story of romance and adventure. The original Magoon was a Scottish sea captain who married the daughter of a Hawaiian Chief. Together he and his princess developed a number of plantations. The family had held onto their land holdings and in the 1960's they still owned 34 acres in downtown Honolulu. Meanwhile, Genevieve and her two son, Orville and Eaton, moved to the Guenoc Valley in 1963. After negotiations the family exchanged their 34 acres in Honolulu with the University of Hawaii for 23,000 acres of land that had been bequeathed to the University in the Guenoc Valley.

Orville Magoon took a great interest in the ranch, although still practising as one of the world's leading Marine Engineers, involved in designing harbours and breakwaters. In the early 1970's a test plot of 25 acres was planted in conjunction with U.C. Davis, by 1979 this was expanded to 270 acres. In 1981 a winery was built, cleverly designed to blend in with the Langtry barn.

Orville has also restored the Langtry house to its former splendor, which although not open to the public is used to accommodate visiting dignitaries. Many of Lillie's original possessions have been found and bought by the Magoon family.

The Raymond family, descendants of the Beringers, have assisted in the establishment of the vineyard and making the wine. Bob Roman is the current winemaker.

Generally the Guenoc wines are very well priced and very high quality; their Chenin Blanc is one of the best of this variety. Their Cabernet Sauvignon is highly sought after and ages particularly well. Other varieties produced are Chardonnay, Sauvignon Blanc, Petit Sirah and Zinfandel, along with good value white table wine and

Guenoc Winery

red table wine blends.

The Magoon family are to be applauded for their enterprise, in not only recreating the magic of Lillie Langtry, but creating a great winery for which they have obtained their own goverment appellation, the first single winery and vineyard to do so.

Konocti Winery

Named after nearby inactive Volcano Mt. Konocti, this winery was constructed by a Lake County growers' co-operative in 1979. Feeling the need to expand and to bring in some more wine industry expertise, the growers embarked on a joint venture with Mendocino winemakers and growers, John and Geroge Parducci in 1983. The winery was expanded and has won many medals in the last few years.

Konocti typifies the re-emergence of Lake County as a real force again in California wine. (During the later part of the 19th century it was a much bigger wine producer than Mendocino and had 36 operating wineries). The slopes of the lakeshore form the vineyard land for most of the growers. The soils are rich, red, alluvial, volcanic deposits that produce grapes of strong varietal flavours. The large body of water (California's largest lake) moderates the climate considerably and also decreases the risk of frost in Spring.

Bill Pease, who had been making wine in Kentucky, came back to his home state to make the wines and very successfully so. He has moved to the new Clos Pegase but has been ably replaced by Jac Jacobs in 1986.

Konocti has received considerable acclaim for its Sauvignon Blanc. The 1986, in fact, won the Platinum award at the American Wine Competition in New York being named "the best Sauvignon Blanc in the world", marking the sixth year in succession it had won a major award.

Kendall-Jackson

Meteoric would be an understatement when describing Kendall-Jacksons rise to a position of pre-eminence in the North American wine industry. Only founded in 1982, as strictly a family owned business by San Francisco lawyer Jess Jackson and his then wife, Jane, it has scooped the pool in many wine competitions and now produces well over 200,000 cases of wine annually.

Jess Jackson is now devoting most of his time to the wine business but still maintains a law practice specialising in Constitutional cases. The Kendall name came in through Jane's family and although they are now divorced both she and Jess still work in the business. Daughters Jennifer and Laura also work for the winery, handling sales in most

states between them, as well as public relations.

The winemaker is Jed Steele, formerly with Edmeades Winery in Mendocino County. Ted actually studied psychology at Gonzaga University near Spokane, Washington, working in a wide variety of jobs including a stint with the railways and some time as a bar-tender. In the late 1960's, he worked two crush seasons at the legendary Stony Hill Winery in the Napa Valley, an experience which motivated him to enter the wine course at U.C. Davis. During his time at Davis he worked part time at the Edmeades Winery in Mendocino, which he joined full-time on graduation, becoming head winemaker and eventually a partner. After nine years with Edmeades, Jed branched out

into consulting. He was hired by Jackson during the 1982 harvest (their first) as they had problems with their Chardonnay. Steele not only corrected them but the wine went on to take the top position in the 1983 American wine competition.

Kendall-Jackson believe strongly in blending from the leading coastal county wine regions. Their two Chardonnays are glowing tributes to the success of this philosophy. Their very affordable Vintners Reserve and their Proprietor's Chardonnay have both won a large number of awards. Other varieties have also been very successful including Sauvignon Blanc, Cabernet Sauvignon and Johannisberg Riesling.

Another cornerstone of Kendall-Jackson

Kendall-Jackson

is their policy of making wines which appeal to a wide range of consumers, packing a lot of fruit in the wines, sometimes a faint touch of residual sugar even in the dry wines if it improves their balance.

In late 1987 Kendall-Jackson pulled off a real coup when they bought the large Chardonnay vineyards of Tepusquet in the Santa Maria region of the central coast (Robert Mondavi bought the Cabernet Sauvginon).

Already Kendall-Jackson are approaching 200,000 cases of premium wine and in only six years have developed an awesome reputation. They have examined every area of the industry with a critical eye and come up with a formula that is hard to beat.

The two closest wine regions to the fast expanding cities of the San Francisco Bay region are the northern portion of the Santa Clara Valley on the eastern outskirts of San Jose and the Livermore Valley, about 40 minutes drive east of Oakland.

Climate of both regions is warmer than that of Napa and Sonoma, but the evenings are cool and the sea breezes from the bay and the ocean have a further moderating effect.

Northern Santa Clara was the second main commercial wine producing region in California and boasts the substantial Mirassou Vineyards winemaking operation continuously operated by the family since 1854 making them North America's oldest wine growing family. Wine in the region actually dates back to 1777 when vineyards were established at the Mission Santa Clara de Asis. By midway through the 19th century a number of wineries had been established and by 1870 wine was the most important industry in the region.

Phylloxera struck in the 1880's, but by then grafting onto American root stocks, developed for the purpose in France had become the accepted prevention and the region survived the vine louse better than most. At the turn of the century the region was one of California's most prominent, boasting over one hundred wineries and large acreages under vine. The French immigrants had quite a strong influence in the establishment of the industry and the style of wines produced.

Prohibition did not take too heavy a toll, with grapes in demand for home winemaking and over sixty wineries survived when repeal finally came in 1933.

The urban sprawl of San Jose took over much of the original vineyards, but in the last few decades a number of small "boutique" wineries and vineyards have sprung up. Some large wineries such as Weibel and Mirassou now draw their grapes from other vineyard areas, where land is cheaper and large vineyards can be established using

modern viticultural techniques. Weibel vineyards have expanded north to Mendocino County and Mirrasou have substantial plantings in Monterey County to the south.

The Livermore Valley only some 15 miles to the north has a long history in wine growing and includes Wente Bros. and Conncannon Vineyards, two of California's most significant wineries with rich family sagas and both founded in the same year 1883. Wente's have further safeguarded and enriched the Valley by purchasing the historic ''Cresta Blanca'' Cellars and Vineyards, the first vineyard in the region established by Charles Wetmore in 1878 an outspoken newspaperman with a special interest in wines and in France.

In fact, he actually talked the Marquis de Lur-Saluces, the proprietor of the famous Chateau d'Yquem, into giving him cuttings of his Semillon, Sauvignon Blanc and Muscatelle vines to take back to California.

Wente's have spent a great deal of money and effort converting this beautifully located winery in its amphitheatre like valley into a Methode Champenoise winery with a magnificent 350 seat restaurant with its surrounding courtyard areas, where concerts and festivals are held regularly during the summer months. Wine history was created at Cresta Blanca in 1956 when Myron Nightingale infected Sauvignon Blanc and Semillon grapes with Botrytis Cinerea ''the noble rot''

by spraying them with spores of the mould. He subsequently made America's first classic Sauternes style wine, ironically coming from vines grown from the cuttings of Chateau d'Yquem, the world's greatest Sauternes maker.

With such historic and strong wineries together with the boutique newcomers, all now protected by a green belt status from urban taxes and development, wine will continue to flourish in these historic valleys between their beautiful rolling hills.

Livermore — Santa Clara

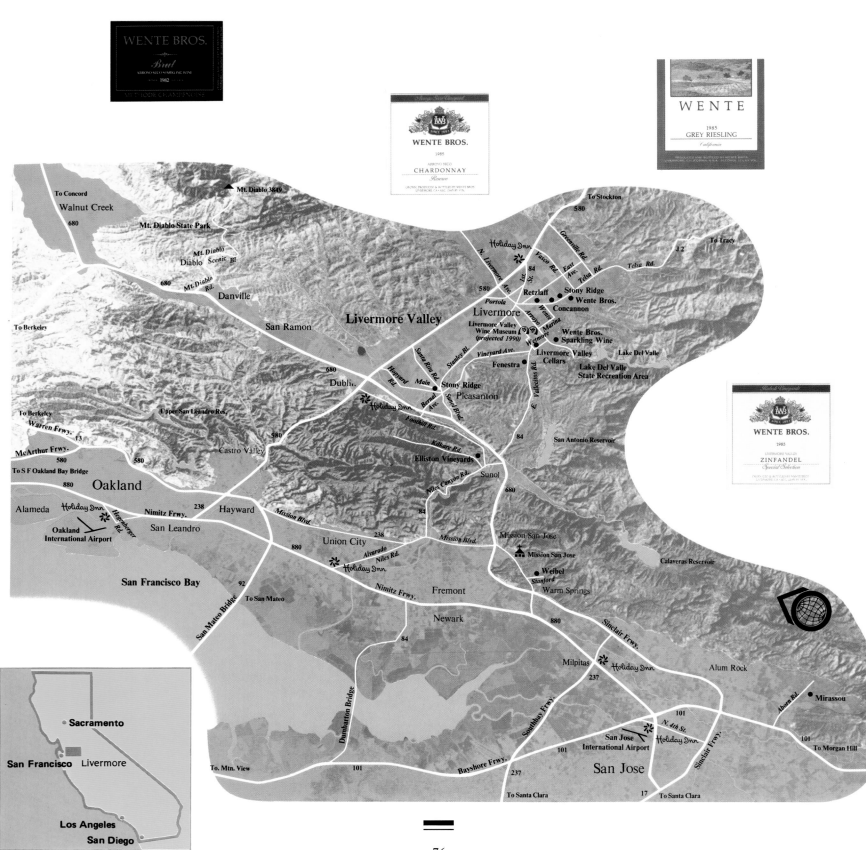

Concannon Vineyard

Steeped in one of California's richest vinous histories going back to 1883, Concannon has recently undergone a rennaissance, which, in a few short years, has taken it probably further forward than in its first century of operation.

Eighteen year old James Concannon arrived from Ireland in 1865. After establishing himself in the hotel trade, this young adventurer then took off west selling a new invention, "the rubber stamp". His travels took him to California and even down to Mexico City where he obtained Mexico's first street cleaning franchise from strong man dictator, Diaz. This connection was to have great significance later.

On travelling back to San Francisco, he obtained a license to produce altar wine for the Catholic church. This he did by purchasing a 250 acre property in Livermore and planting it with vines from France. Needing capital, he travelled back to Mexico in 1889, convincing Diaz that the Mexican wine industry needed new varieties and viticultural knowledge. He obtained the franchise to do this and, during the next 15 years, with the help of his brother Thomas, placed millions of cuttings from Livermore throughout Mexico. In 1904 he returned to Livermore to establish more firmly Concannon Vineyards.

Altar wines saw the company through Prohibition and the family, in terms of his son, Captain Joseph, and current President grandson James continued.

Like many medium-sized wine companies they struggled with a lack of capital and the difficulty of competing with the big wineries.

In 1981 a Swiss consortium under Augustin Huneeus, now president of Franciscan Vineyards bought the winery while James Concannon remained as president.

Many changes were wrought, the most significant being the employment of Sergio Traverso, a Chilean winemaker with a Ph d. from U.C. Davis, who had worked at Sterling Vineyards.

Sergio started at "grass roots", replanting the vineyards to those most suited to the Bordeaux-like soils of the Livermore Valley and rationalising the range down from 18 to 9 wines. The winery received much attention with new equipment and new small French cooperage.

The range now includes a Sauvignon Blanc with a touch of Semillon, a Petit Sirah, Cabernet Sauvignon and Chardonnay (from selected coastal grapes). These are the wines the modern day Concannon is making a big reputation with today. The D.C.L. Spirits corporation took over in 1983 and in 1988 the Deinhard German wine company bought the company. Their commitment to quality wine is sure to see Concannon on to an even more illustrious future.

Mirassou Vineyards

Being of the fifth generation of an Australian winemaking family founded in almost the same year as Mirassou. I felt very much at home talking with the Mirassou brothers America's oldest wine growing family to be continuously involved in the business. Their hospitality centre with its food and wine educational scene is a joy to visit.

Like much of Santa Clara, Mirassou owes its beginnings to the French connection. In 1853 Pierre Pellier, great great grandfather of today's fifth generation running the enterprise, arrived from La Rochelle France with cuttings (including America's first Pinot Noir and French Colombard) ordered by his brother Louis, who had founded the San Jose city's gardens a few years before. A resourceful fellow he was caught with a problem on the ship bringing out the cuttings. In those days it was a six month journey from Europe around Cape Horn and thence to California. With water running low he negotiated with the ship's captain and purchased the entire stock of potatoes on board, he then carefully split each one and placed the vine cuttings in them to prevent them drying out and dying.

In 1881 his eldest daughter Henrietta married Pierre Mirassou a French winemaker in the region. Although he died at a young age, his wife and their young sons kept the business going. Peter the eldest son also had two sons Norbert and Edmund. These fourth generation members of the family saw the company safely through Prohibition and the Depression.

Right up until the 1960's Mirassou wines were all sold in bulk to other wineries. The first development of this decade however, was in a different region. Land was becoming scarce and expensive in the Santa Clara region so Norbert and Edmund, along with Peter, Ed's eldest son, pioneered the Monterey area where they were joined shortly after by the Wente's. Monterey proved a bonanza with ideal viticultural conditions, with top quality wines resulting.

Mirassou have just celebrated the 25th anniversary of their Monterey vineyard. During this time they have pioneered a number of techniques of international significance. Firstly, the horizontal T-head trellising system, mainly used to combat the strong Monterey winds but with the benefits of a bigger canopy exposure for the vine, which ripens and adds flavour to quite large crops. Later when they developed a mechanical harvesting machine this trellising proved ideal. Since those days in the early 60's mechanical harvesting has revolutionised viticulture, although it is not suitable for all grape varieties in all regions. The Mirassou family have not left it at that and under the watchful eye of Peter they have developed a system of not only crushing in the vineyard as the grapes are being harvested, but also pressing the grapes. This and the fact it is all done in the cool of the night means all the wines have a great freshness and fruit quality.

In 1966, after more than a century of winemaking, the first Mirassou wines were bottled and sold under their own banner.

The hallmark of Mirassou is great value. They have presented excellent varietal table wines of all styles plus very good sparkling wines at exceptionally good value for money. Whilst Peter has been toiling in the vineyard and winery to produce these excellent wines, his two brothers Daniel, who is now President of the company and Jim, who assists in the marketing area have done an excellent job of packaging and promoting them.

In August 1987 the brothers signed an agreement with "Seagrams Classics Wine Company". This agreement, covering the national distribution of Mirassou Wines, is already proving a most beneficial one in gaining extra outlets of all types around the continent and bringing their worthy wines to more and more wine drinkers.

A sixth generation of Mirassou's has already joined the wine industry and Peter's daughter has travelled to Australia to study and gain wine experience there.

The harvest season at Mirassou is quite an international affair. The 1987 crush brought together a crew of 12 very keen young winemakers representing many different countries including Finland, France, Australia, New Zealand and Ireland.

The Mirassou's are devoted to continuing as America's oldest family owned and operated wine company for many generations to come. I for one and, I am certain, wine lovers the world over are right behind them in this wish.

1982
Monterey Champagne
BLANC DE NOIRS
Alcohol 11% by volume
MIRASSOU

Weibel Vineyards

F red Weibel Snr. is one of the few people who can claim to have ushered in the new era of wine to North America in 1945, as the Second World War ended.

Fred and his father, Rudolph, who migrated to America in the late 1930's, had made wine together in their family winery just outside Berne in Switzerland.

The Weibels bought 100 acres of land at Warm Springs, just east of San Jose. The property contained a run down vineyard and a disused winery, so they put their skills in sparkling wine production to work. Only a year later did they discover they had bought the former vineyards and winery established by Leland Stanford, the legendary California Governor and U.S. Senator, who had passed the property onto his brother Josiah. Had this not been the case perhaps Stanford University would be situated there and not at Palo Alto!

By the late 1940's, production was up to some 5,000 cases, a far cry from today's 1,000,000 case production (which includes Weibels Redwood Valley Winery founded in 1968).

Weibel is a truly family enterprise with Fred Weibel Snr. in his 70's still at the helm as president. His son, Fred Jnr., runs the marketing and finance side of the business, whilst daughters Linda Weibel Lannon, Public Relations Director and Diana, Special Accounts Director, are also involved. Son-in-law Terry Lannon, National Sales Manager and Rick Casqueiro, winemaker, make up the tightly knit executive team.

Rick took over the winemaking in 1980 from Oscar Habeutzel, Rudolf Weibel's brother-in-law and co-founder, who had made the wines since 1945. Weibel produce 13 kinds of sparkling wine. Their Mendocino Brut, Chardonnay Brut and Blanc de Noirs are made by the traditional Methode Champenoise (the Weibel Mendocino operation is covered in Chapter Nine). A number of other sparklers are made using the Charmat method and then there are their Stanford Champagne range and many under special labels for prestigious organisations throughout America. Weibel also make 15 varietal wines including an excellent dry Chenin Blanc and six dessert and aperitif wines.

This unique family winery makes great value wines and looks set for a prosperous

WEIBEL VINEYARDS

WINERY ESTABLISHED 1869

Wente Bros

The Wente family, now in their fourth generation, is going from strength to strength, ably represented by Eric Wente, President, assisted by his sister Carolyn, Vice-president in charge of marketing and their large restaurant operation at the sparkling wine cellars in the old Cresta Blanca grounds and younger brother Philip, Vice-president in charge of winemaking.

Wente's greatest strength, is in fact, the great value for money their wines represent. Always strong in the premium wine field and with good distribution in all 50 states, they have managed to increase the quality of their already excellent wines, constantly by expanding their own vineyards in the Livermore Valley and in the Arroyo-Seco region in the Salinas Valley, Monterey County, as well as investing heavily in modern winemaking technology under Philip's Davis

trained eye. This quality increase has been an added bonus, as they have kept prices on all their many wines well below most of their competition.

The Wente saga began around 1870 when Carl Heinrich Wente migrated to America from Germany. He was the second son of a north German farmer and, rather than play second fiddle, he sought his fortune in a new land. After travelling across the continent he went to work with Charles Krug, a fellow countryman and the first commercial vintner in the Napa Valley.

After some years and with a good knowledge of winemaking he headed south. Perhaps it was the gravelly soils much like his native land that attracted him to the Livermore Valley, where he bought 50 acres of land in 1883, planted vines and shortly thereafter built a winery. The main Wente

Bros. Winery is still on this site but has now expanded to encompass the whole 50 acres.

His eldest son, Carl F., opted for the banking world, starting as a messenger boy and ending up as President of the Bank of America, while the other two sons went into the business. Ernest concentrated on managing and expanding the vineyard, whereas Hermann developed into one of California's greatest-ever winemakers.

Ernest's son Karl, became involved in 1949 after graduating from Stanford University. Wente's to this stage had almost exclusively white wines, which brought much higher prices on the bulk market to other wineries which they solely supplied prior to Prohibition. The original cuttings for their vineyards had come from the Chateau d'Yquem stock brought in by Charles Wetmore.

During Prohibition they survived by

Wente Bros

making Altar wines and selling grapes fresh to the home winemakers. Seeing the need to market their own wines and determine their own destiny, Herman and Ernest started bottling and marketing immediately after Prohibition. They were among the first to implement varietal labelling, first under the brand name of ''Valle de Oro'' meaning Golden Valley, anyone who has visited Livermore in the summer will relate to this name.

Fortunately, the family had perservered with the classic varieties through Prohibition and immediately began establishing a reputation. Their Sauvignon Blanc won the grand prize at the Paris International Exhibition in 1936 and a similar award at the 1939 Golden Gate Exposition nearer home in San Francisco.

The legendary wine entrepreneur, Frank

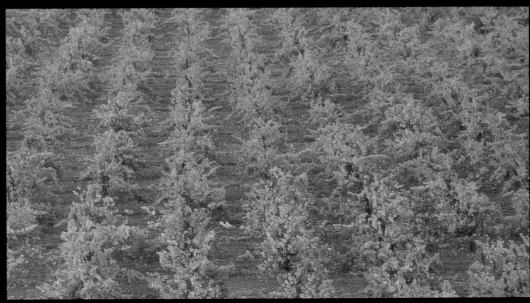

Wente Bros

Schoonmaker, started marketing a range of varietal wines nationally using the Wente name prior to the second World War. By this time the Wente's themselves had begun using their own name alongside "Valle de Oro". Apart from their Semillon and Sauvignon Blanc they were one of the few wineries to have Chardonnay planted, their 80 or so acres representing one third of the Californian total. It was in fact a glowing article in "Life Magazine" in 1959 on their Chardonnay that started the planting boom of the variety.

In 1960, Karl Wente purchased land in Monterey in what is now termed the "Arroyo-Seco" viticultural area in the Salinas Valley, 300 acres being planted to classic varietals. Today this has expanded to over 800 acres with Wente's owning well over 2,000 acres including those at Livermore. This makes them one of the few medium to large American wine companies who are self sufficient in grape supply and, more importantly, gives them a great control over quality.

The varying climates and soils of their two grape growing regions has enabled a large range of varieties both red and white to be successfully grown and presently 16 varieties are cultivated.

The first Californian wine I tasted some 18 years ago, was a Wente Grey Riesling, a little known variety, fruity but dry and somewhat spicy, one the family have carved a substantial niche in the market with, particularly in the Bay area.

Gradually their red wine range expanded with Pinot Noir, Gamay Beaujolais in the lighter styles and Petit Sirah and Zinfandel in the fuller bodied style — later Cabernet Sauvignon was added.

Early in the 1980's, Wente's purchased the historic Cresta Blanca Cellars at the southern end of the Valley. In this idyllic setting, nestled against the steep hillsides of the Canyon, they have faithfully restored the classic mission-style buildings and added a beautiful hospitality complex, including a 350 seat restaurant. The landscaped grounds are superb making the whole place one of America's most beautiful wineries. The facility is used for the production of Methode Champenoise sparkling wine — the first vintage and Wente's first ever sparkling wine being very suitably 1983 — their centenary year. Long arched drives (tunnels) have been dug into the hillsides for the tirage bottle ageing of these wines so necessary to producing a top quality product for this growing market segment.

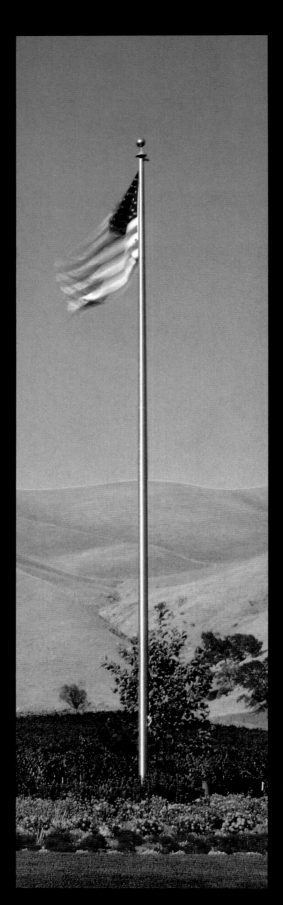

Karl's untimely death in 1977 had brought his three children into serious responsibilities in the business. At an early age they have certainly aquitted themselves admirably to the task and along with their mother Jean, who is still very involved, have added yet another successful chapter to this exemplary American wine company. I am sure their continuing efforts and those of future generations will add further lustre to this already shining jewel in the world of wine.

WENTE BROS/WENTE BROS SPARKLING WINE CELLARS
Address: 5565 Tesla Road/5050 Arroyo Road, Livermore, CA., 94550
Phone: 415/447 3603; 415/447 3023
Year of Establishment: 1883
Owner: Wente Family
Winemaker: Eric Wente
Principal Varieties Grown: Chardonnay, Sauvignon Blanc, Semillon, Pinot Noir, Cabernet Sauvingon
Acres Under Vine: 2,000
Average Annual Crush: 8,000 tons

Principal Wines & Brands	Cellar Potential (Years)
Chardonnay Reserve	5
Arroyo Seco Sparkling Wine	5
Sauvignon Blanc	5

Trade Tours – Available.
Retail Room Sales – Available.
Hours open to Public: Tesla Road tasting room: 9am to 5pm; tours hourly 10am to 3pm; Sparkling Wine Cellars Arroyo Road tasting room: 11am to 5pm; tours 12 noon to 5pm hourly.
Retail Distribution: U.S, Canada, Europe, U.K. and Japan

Introduction to Los Angeles & Cucamonga

Los Angeles, for a time, was the centre of the Californian wine industry when Jean Louis Vignes from Bordeaux became California's first commercial winegrower in 1833. When he established a vineyard and winery El Alsio on Aliso Street, his nephew made the first California Champagne in 1857.

Los Angeles first mayor, Benjamin Davis Wilson, won much acclaim for the wines of his Lake Vineyard near San Gabriel in the 1850's. This winery was taken over by his son-in-law, J. de Barth Shorb, who built it into what was then the biggest winery in the world in 1890 holding 15 million gallons. Others, such as one of the characters of the era, "Lucky" Baldwin, with his 1200 acre vineyard and winery at Arcadia, pushed Los Angeles to the premier position in North

American wines. His mansion is today an historical monument.

Anaheim, where Disneyland now stands, was established in 1857 by German immigrants as a wine growing community. The vine also spread eastward into the Cucamonga area of San Bernadino and Riverside counties. Thomas Vineyard, California's first winery, was founded in 1839 by Tibercio Tapia, who received the Cucamonga land grant, from the Mexican governor. This winery still stands today in what is now a residential district. Captain Paul Garrett of "Virginia Dare" fame, America's largest selling pre-Prohibition wine, sourced much of his grapes here from Tapia's 2,000 acres of vines.

The town of Guasti was named for

Secondo Guasti, who established a 4,000 acre vineyard which, just prior to Prohibition, was the world's largest.

The San Antonio Winery, right in the heart of downtown Los Angeles, no longer has its vineyards around it, but still produces a large volume of excellent bottled wines and has a rather unique restaurant/entertaining area and outdoor gardens, where one can sip the Riboli family's wines. They have no intention of doing anything else other than making and selling wine, on what must be one of the world's most valuable pieces of wine real estate.

A number of "boutique" wineries is springing up around L.A. and a wine renaissance appears in the air.

Los Angeles & Cucamonga

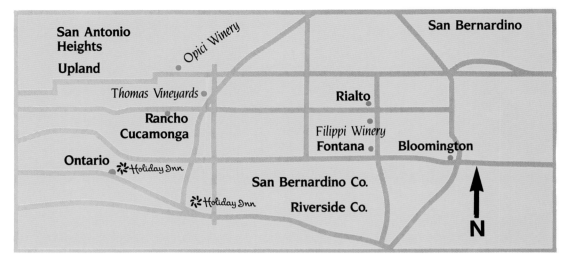

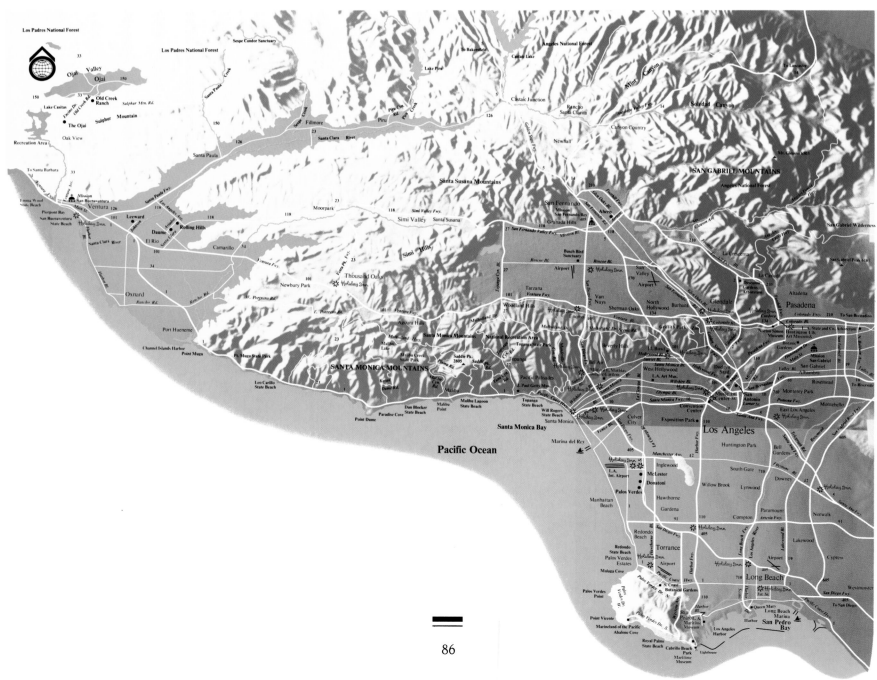

Thomas Vineyard

Tiburcio Tapia received the Cucamonga land grant, from the Mexican government in 1838. He planted vines and in 1839 built a winery and commenced making wine shortly thereafter. The original Thomas Vineyards winery now on corner of Highway 66 in a built up section of Cucamonga, is in remarkably unspoilt condition.

In 1967, it was bought by the Filippi family, who have a large winery in the region. Wines are no longer made at the Thomas Winery, but at Filippi. However, much of the old winemaking equipment is still on display at the winery and it is a good place to stop and drink in a little of the rich wine history of this region.

J. Filippi Vintage Company

Although the Cucamonga wine growing region, has contracted over recent decades, mainly due to the urban sprawl of Los Angeles and its resultant effect on the price of land, the Filippi family have expanded their enterprise, not only in their original cellars in Mira Loma (once known as Wineville), but by buying what is claimed to be California's oldest winery, The Thomas Vineyard in the heart of Cucamonga. Filippi have also built six tasting rooms and sales cellars, in Southern California under the Chateau Filippi banner.

The Filippi family started planting vineyards in the 1920's, perhaps foreseeing the end of Prohibition in 1934. Joseph and Mary began making wine in their basement, selling most of it to locals who bought their own containers to be filled. They expanded to their current location and began bottling. In 1967, they bought the historic Thomas Vineyards Cellars. They now make the wine for both brands at the Filippi Winery and look set for a successful future, with their three dozen or so different wines, covering most styles.

An introduction to Mendocino

Whilst Napa and, to a degree, Sonoma have been stealing all the limelight, there has been a quiet winegrowing revolution going on in Mendocino county. Like Northern Sonoma, but in a smaller way, Mendocino had been mostly involved in bulk wine production until the table wine boom of the 1960's.

Today there are over 12,000 acres of premium grape varieties planted through the beautiful, unspoilt river valleys of Mendocino. Much of the development has been by the larger vintners such as Fetzer, Parducci, The

Mendocino Vineyards of Guild wineries, plus Weibel. Many small wineries have also sprung up and at last count there were almost 30 wine producers in all.

The climate of Mendocino is generally cooler then the northern portions of Napa and Sonoma, ranging from Region I near the coast in the Anderson valley to Region II further inland. Mendocino borders Lake County on the east and the history of their wine developments have been reasonably parallel. Mendocino, however, was somewhat behind Lake in pre-Prohibition times, but has

had much greater vineyard development in modern times.

Mendocino pulled off an important coup in 1982, when the French Champagne house, Louis Roederer, bought 584 acres of land near Philo, in the Anderson valley to become only the third Champagne producer to invest in California. They have since planted vineyards and completed a winery in 1986.

Mendocino is quietly but quickly growing in size and stature as a leading North American wine producing region.

Mendocino

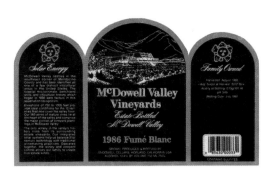

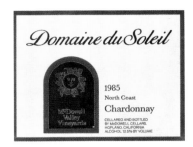

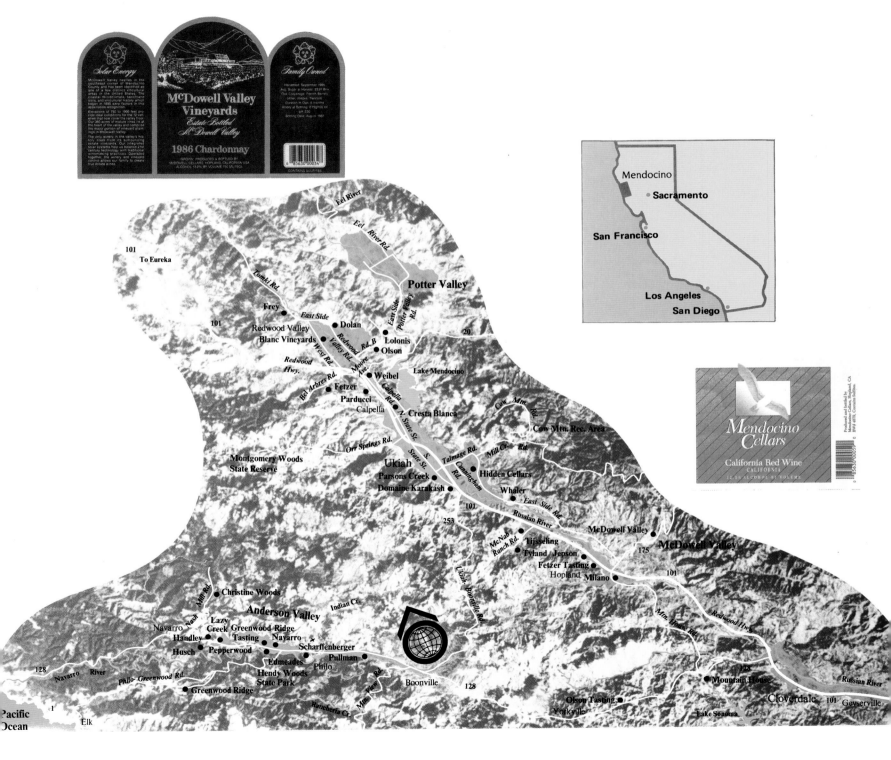

Fetzer Vineyards

If Barney Fetzer were alive today, he would be justly proud of his offspring. In seven years, they have increased the sales of Fetzer wines tenfold, that is a 100% increase for each of his ten children involved in the business. Barney had eleven children and the family participation may become unanimous if one of his daughters, with her Master's degrees in Tax Accounting joins the business. Her skills in this area would no doubt be welcomed!

The Fetzer operation of today is hardly recognisable from the small family winery created in 1968. Family businesses are not easy, but the Fetzers have a very strong sense of purpose; they are all aiming in the same direction and each one is happy to take the role that benefits the business, though many of them do not carry much glory.

The Fetzer family have not lost sight of what has brought them such success. Very good premium wines at exceptionally low prices: in fact they pioneered this concept right from their founding.

Whilst the family is involved in every area of the business from preparing the soil for planting, right through to designing the point of sale material, they have, however, not taken a stranglehold on every position, particularly when they acknowledge an expert is required. In 1977, winemaker Paul Dolan joined them. Paul is steeped in wine history, on one side of his family he is the great grandson of the famous Edmund Rossi one of the founders of ''Italian Swiss Colony'', on the other side he has the Concannon family from the Livermore Valley.

Although champions of consumer value in their wines, the Fetzers have evolved from a production-driven operation to a market-oriented one. Barney and his wife Kathleen

(who still adopts a strong role as matriarch of the family) bought their historic Redwood valley ranch, in 1958; of the 750 acres, sixty comprise an 80 year old vineyard. Desiring to help keep his large family together and involved, Barney and his eldest son John (now president of the firm) started building the winery in 1968. Barney's background was in the lumber industry, originally in Oregon but later in Mendocino county. He kept his executive position with a lumber firm and left the establishing and running of the winery to John, then only in his early twenties. The rest of the family, of course, were also involved.

Today, the Fetzer Vineyards holding have expanded to include not only 200 acres at their home Vineyard in the Redwood valley around the main winery, but 300 at their Sundial ranch with a planned 600 at their Valley Oaks vineyard both near Hopland. More planting is planned, but they also buy

Fetzer Vineyards

from many growers Lake, Mendocino and Sonoma counties.

The Fetzers have in fact built two separate wineries at Redwood valley, one solely for white the other for red, both with state of the art equipment and almost 15,000 small oak barrels. Their Sundial Chardonnay, a fresh style without oak and well priced has been a huge hit. The top of the range are their Barrel select wines from varieties such as Chardonnay and Cabernet Sauvignon.

During the last few years the family has brought together food, wine, hospitality and even music in a unique and beautiful way at their Valley Oaks property. This historic ranch has been restored and expanded to include a restaurant, function facilities and its own extensive gardens, where organic gardener of the year, Michael Maltas, grows magnificent produce for, Margaret Fox (who started Cafe Beaujolais) their renowned consulting chef.

Dan Fetzer manages the centre, the youngest son of the family. Diane Fetzer, fomerly assistant winemaker, is in charge of hospitality and guest facilities. This bold and courageous move by the family has come from a strong sense of responsibility and a recognition of wines role in life as a food itself and an adjunct to civilised living. Valley Oaks is truly beautiful.

Fetzers also have a new winery in Hopland under construction. They also have a large tasting facility on the main street, seen as you come northward on Highway 101.

The name Fetzer is synonymous with honest, value-for-money, premium wines and the family has no intention of changing that reputation. At the current break-neck rate of growth of their wine sales, it is hard to see any one of the ten of them idle.

McDowell Valley Vineyards

Set above the vineyards, a few miles west of Hopland, is a striking and unusual winery, McDowell Valley Vineyards named after Paxton McDowell, who pioneered the region in the 1850's, vines had been planted in the 1890's.

When built in 1979, it became the world's first solar heated and cooled winery. The vineyards, which cover some 360 acres are maintained with military precision, which is not surprising as they were established by Richard Keehn, an ex-military pilot. The winery also hosts concerts and art exhibitions, on a frequent basis. The wines have made an early impact. The first winemaker, George Bursick left to join Ferrari-Carano, in 1987 and has been replaced by John Buechsenstein.

The vineyards were actually established by the Keehns, shortly after they bought the property in 1970, working with mature and well cared for vines from the start, has obviously been an advantage.

Apart from some excellent Chardonnays

Fume Blancs and Cabernet Sauvignons. McDowell Valley have produced a Syrah — the main grape of the Rhone Valley region

This wine has been well received. Several other varieties including Zinfandel are grown and overall production is increasing quickly.

Roederer is one of France's most revered Champagne houses; their ''Cristal'' became legendary as the favourite of Alexander II, Czar of Russia.

Roederer is one of the few houses still under family control and the only one that still maintains ''estate'' status in France by growing all its own grapes.

Jean-Claude Rouzard, managing director of Champagne Louis Roederer and descendant of the founder, began a search of North America in the late 1970's to find a suitable viticultural region to make the finest Methode Champenoise Cuvee possible. His search led him to the Anderson Valley in Mendocino County, 90 miles north of San Francisco, where cool, foggy nights and mornings and warm sunny afternoons promote long, even ripening of the grapes and good acid retention, so important in Champenoise production. In all, he purchased 580 acres. A superb aesthetically pleasing winery and caves have been built partially into the hillside and surrounded by vines which are planted on unique floating wire trellises. Roederer also barrel-age their Cuvee material in new Limousin oak casks. Jean-Claude personally blends the Cuvee with Champagne master, Michel Salgues, a former professor at the Universite de Montpellier. The first release took place in October 1988.

Parducci Wine Cellars

Adolf Parducci was born in California but went back with his family to their Italian Tuscany homeland in 1907. Ten years later he returned to California and built his first winery in Sonoma County. After a fire destroyed the winery in the late 1920's he moved north to Mendocino, opening a new winery at its current location on the northern outskirts of Ukiah, in 1932. Upon the repeal of Prohibition, Adolf was ready and experienced. Business prospered mainly through passing trade and bulk wine sales to larger wineries in the Central Valley. His sons, John and George, joined him and still operate the winery today, although a majority interest in the winery was bought by the Teachers Management Institute in 1973. Fourth generation Parduccis are now coming into the business. In 1983, the Parduccis bought a half interest in the Grower established Konocti Winery in nearby Lake County.

Parducci make a wide range of wines which represent excellent value for money.

Weibel Mendocino

After more than two decades of winemaking at their Mission San Jose vineyard and winery, the Weibel family needed to expand. Many wineries in the Santa Clara Valley including their neighbours, the Mirrasou family, decided to go south to Monterey and other central coast counties. The Weibels looked carefully at the alternatives as the suburban sprawl, with its accompanying rising land prices and taxes, was forcing a decision. It was not to Monterey they went but Mendocino County, where they began buying vineyard land in 1968.

The Weibels believed the grapes from Mendocino were better suited to the production of sparkling wines than those of the central coast. Their business then was even more heavily based on sparkling wines than it is now. As the vineyards grew, they built a crushing and fermentation facility although the sparkling wines and champagnes, including the maturation and blending of the varietal wines, are made at their Mission San Jose Winery.

Chief winemaker, Rich Casqueiro, who joined the Weibels over ten years ago, is in charge of winemaking at Redwood valley. In front of the winery is a large tasting room, shaped like an upturned Champagne glass, just off highway 101 north of the town of Ukiah and quite easy to find.

The Weibel Chenin Blanc from Mendocino is one of the best dry Chenins in the country and has won a number of awards in recent years. It has just been very attractively repackaged.

Weibel have just released a new one litre range of varietals under the Redwood Valley Cellars label; these include a California Chardonnay, California Fume Blanc, California Cabernet Sauvignon and a California White Zinfandel.

As with their other sparkling and still wines the Weibel Redwood Valley wines are excellent value for money, wines that this long established family winery can be proud of.

Monterey — Salinas

Monterey Bay

Pacific Ocean

Big Sur Coast

1

G12

G11

G12

129

To San Jose

To Santa Cruz

Prunedale

101

156

Castroville

183

Marina

Salinas River

G17

Salinas

Mission San Juan Bautista

San Juan Bautista

Fremont Peak State Park
Fremont Peak
3171

G1

San Juan Cyn.

101

Main

John E. Branken

Abbott St.

Morgan

68

River Rd.

Chualar

101

Salinas River

Salinas Valley

To San Jose

101

San Juan

4th St.

Hillcrest

156

156

25

Fairview Rd.

Hollister
San Benito

Tres Pinos

Airline Hwy.

San Benito River

Cienega Rd.

San Andreas Rift Zone

Calera Wine Co.
Cygnet Cellars
Cienega

Limekiln Rd.

Cienega Rd.

Enz Vineyards
Limekiln Valley

Gabilan Range

Paicines

J1

25

Paicines

Airline Hwy.

San Benito River

Airline Hwy.

J1

Paul Masson Tasting & Wine Museum

Point Pinos
Lighthouse

Asilomar State Beach

Monterey Bay Aquarium
Bargetto Tasting

Cannery Row

Del Monte

Monterey State Beach

Fort Ord Military Res.

Monterey
218

68

68

Monterey-Salinas Hwy.

17 Mile Dr.

Cypress Point
Carmel Bay

Point Lobos State Reserve

Yankee Point

Garrapata State Beach

Carmel
Carmel Mission Chateau Julien
Carmel River State Beach

Carmel Valley Rd.

G16

Riverside Park

Garland Ranch Regional Park

Carmel Valley

Robert Talbott

Mt. Toro 3560

Sierra de Salinas

Carmel Valley Village

Durney Vineyards

Carmel River

Carmel Valley Rd.

Cachagua Rd.

Mason Rd.

Jamesburg

Tassajara Rd.

G16

Palo Colorado Rd.

Mt. Carmel 4417

Notleys Landing

Santa Lucia Range

Little Sur River

Ventana Cone 4720

Ventana Wilderness
(Hiking Trails & Campgrounds)

Point Sur
Lighthouse

1

Andrew Molera State Park

Big Sur

Big Sur River

Pfeiffer Point

Pfeiffer Big Sur State Park

Tassajara Hot Springs

Los Padres National Forest

Julia Pfeiffer Burns State Park

Junipero Serra Pk. 5862

Tassajara Rd.

Carmel Valley Rd.

G16

Arroyo Seco Rd.

Arroyo Secco

Arroyo Seco

Los Padres National Forest

1

John Little State Reserve
To San Luis Obispo

Taylor California Cellars
The Monterey Vineyard

Gonzales
River S. Alta

Gonzales

101

Mission Soledad

Smith & Hook

Fort Romie Rd.

River Rd.

Stonewall Cayn. Rd.

Pinnacles National Monument

Chalone Vineyard
Chalone

North Chalone Pk.

South Chalone Pk.

Soledad
Metz

146

146

25

San Benito

San Benito River

Airline Hwy.

Foothill Rd.

Ventana

G17

Los Coches

Thorne

Jekel

Walnut Ave.

Elm Ave.

Greenfield

Arroyo Seco

Metz Rd.

Salinas River

King City

San Lucas

To San Luis Obispo

Sacramento

San Francisco

Monterey

Los Angeles

San Diego

Monterey & Salinas Valley

A lthough small areas of vines had been planted in the large fertile Salinas Valley during the early part of the century, only 200 acres remained after Prohibition.

During the 1950's, the urban sprawl around San Jose was putting great pressure on the vineyards of Mirrasou, Paul Masson, Almanden and Weibel. Two of these companies decided that the soil of Monterey, assisted by supplementary irrigation, should be ideal for premium grape varieties and in 1957, Mirrasou and Paul Masson bought a large tract of land and in 1962 began planting. The vineyard explosion they started means that Monterey county now has more acreage under vine than Napa or Sonoma counties (over 40,000 acres in all). Other significant wineries to plant in the region have been Wentes and The Monterey Vineyard. Some extremely large new vineyard developments such as the 6,000 acre Southdown "Vina Monterey" Vineyard have also been established.

There are very few wineries in the region although some are very large — two of America's finest amongst them. In the Chalone Vineyard, established in 1960, on the rugged ledge beneath the awesome Pinnacles Mountains and the Jekel Vineyard, established in 1972, by movie-making twin brothers Bill and Gus Jekel.

As wineries learn to deal with the unique viticultural conditions and winemaking techniques that this region demands, some world class wines are resulting. The future of Monterey in terms of wine, looks very rosy indeed.

Chalone Vineyard

The most spectacular view from any vineyard in North America is the outlook from the top of the Chalone Vineyard. The eighty mile-long Salinas Valley spreads out before you, with its patchwork quilt of green vineyards and salad gardens amongst the grey-black tilled volcanic soils and sun-bleached grasses.

This would seem as unlikely a place as any to find any vineyard at all, let alone one of America's finest. Vines were first planted here in 1920 by William Silvear and their grapes eagerly purchased by Wente and Almaden who appreciated their high quality.

The vineyard is spread out on a number of rocky, limestone ledges covered with volcanic soil washed down from the spectacular Pinnacles of the Gavilan Mountains. Rainfall is sparse and crops extremely small. The intensity of flavour in the resulting wines, chiefly Pinot Noir and Chardonnay, is incredible.

Richard Graff bought the vineyard in 1965 from a group of hobby vignerons. He has now been joined by his brothers John and Peter, who, along with Philip Woodward, have formed a successful public company Chalone Vineyards Inc. they also own Carmeret Vineyards in Sonoma, Acacia Vineyards in Carneros and have a share in Edna Valley Vineyards in Paso Robles. Chalone is the jewel in the crown of these excellent enterprises.

Bill Jekel is a cultured gentleman and a model of quiet persistence. His ultimate statement is the wine he and his family produce from their vineyards, established in 1972. Bill's son Rick took over the winemaking in 1983, enabling Bill to travel extensively promoting not only his own wine, but also championing the cause of the Arroyo-Seco appelation and premium California wine, in almost every corner of the globe.

Bill's first career was as an artist for the Metro-Goldwyn-Mayer film company, after graduating with a fine arts degree from U.C.L.A. He also gained a law degree and practised for a time. Following this, he created his own film scenery company and then formed a film production company with his twin brother Gus. Bill remained President until 1984, when the winery required his full attention.

Bill and his wife Pat established the Jekel vineyard in 1972, and the winery followed in 1978. Their first Johannisberg Riesling from this vintage was sensational and caused a total re-think on this classic variety's place in California. The Jekels also produce a Cabernet Sauvignon the first vintage of which in 1978 won a taste-off against all comers at the Zinfandel club in London, including the French first growths. Other wines they produced are Chardonnay, Pinot Blanc and Pinot Noir; all have shown outstanding quality.

With such an auspicious start from their first vintage some thought it just a stroke of luck that would not last. The Jekels have certainly proved them wrong.

Jekel Vineyard

On evaluating their current releases on a recent visit, I tasted eleven wines. Six were certainly gold medal quality and the others very close behind.

Bill has been instrumental in the granting of a special appelation for the Arroyo-Seco region, first recognised for the grape growing potential of its climate, by Professors Amerine and Winkler, in their Californian climate analysis of the 1930's. The extremely long growing season of this Region 1 climate enables the creation and retention of rich and complex fruit flavours in the grapes.

The climate is also dry and reliable and although Jekel use some necessary supplementary irrigation, they employ a certain water stress to the vine to limit the crop and intensify the resulting flavours.

In several of the early 1980's vintages the ''El Nino'' conditions, of warm ocean currents off Monterey prevailed, causing some pre-vintage rains. This in fact caused Botrytis, the noble rot, to develop and helped create some interesting and outstanding wines. A 1985 Chardonnay I tried had the tell-tale apricot and honey

aromas and flavours created by this occurrence. This, combined with excellent Chardonnay varietal character and tasty vanilla wood aged overtones, has produced one of the best and most interesting Californian Chardonnays I have tasted.

Jekel are now one of North America's finest wine producers and knowing Bill's perfectionist nature, no stone will be left unturned in his quest for ever greater wines.

The Monterey Vineyards

The Monterey Vineyards Winery, one of the most attractive and yet functional in North America, was very much the creation of Dr. Richard Peterson, one of the industry's greatest winemakers.

In 1973, the McFarland land company, owner of thousands of acres of Monterey Vineyards, decided they wanted to become involved in wine production and marketing. They made a generous offer to Richard Peterson, then making wines at Beaulieu Vineyards, to let him set up the total winemaking operation and run it. The winery went through some turbulent times and, in 1977, it was purchased by Coca-Cola's wine spectrum. Subsequently in 1983, it was bought by its current owner, Seagrams Classics, who also acquired the large Taylors California Cellars next door.

Although Seagrams have sold Taylors, they have retained The Monterey Vineyards Winery and market a range of excellent varietal table wines at great value prices from this winery.

The Northern Salinas Valley, where The Monterey Vineyard is situated is one of the coolest wine growing regions.

Dr. Peterson became skilled in capturing the extra flavour and intensity that Monterey's climate offers. In 1974, he produced one of the first classic Botrytised Sauternes styles from Sauvignon Blanc and Semillon.

Since 1984 the winemaster has been Gary Cott (formerly with Corbett Canyon and Montevina wineries). Gary has been instrumental in upgrading the entire product line. Some of his shining stars are the Monterey Classic Red (predominantly Cabernet Sauvignon). Their Classic White an the Petite Fume a crisp and elegant Sauvignon Blanc. Monterey have also just marketed a Limited Release Cabernet Sauvignon.

Gary's good work at Monterey was aptl rewarded at the 1988 California State Fair, when his Limited Release Chardonnay from the 1986 vintage, carried all before it and became the champion Chardonnay.

The fact Domain San Martin is being featured in the Monterey chapter not in Santa Clara, where its winery is situated. is a comment on the dramatic change of direction this old winery has undergone in the last decade. The viticultural base for Domain San Martin has shifted to Monterey and San Louis Obispo counties, to provide the premium varietal fruit needed for their re-vamped wine styles.

San Martin was formed as a co-operative in 1906. In 1932, just prior to the repeal of Prohibition, it was bought by the Felise family and after repeal, they produced an enormous range of wines, including a number from other fruits marketed under the ''The California Fruit and Berry Wine Company'' label.

In 1973, the Southdown Company purchased the winery. Their winemaster, Edmund Friedrich, from Trier in Germany,

pioneered the production of low alcohol ''soft'' wines in America and was instrumental in having the minimum alcoholi content of Californian wines lowered from 10% to 7%.

In 1977, the Somerset Wine Company bought San Martin. 1981 heralded the arriva of Ron Nilno and dramatic changes. Ron completely updated the winery and, in his first year cut the number of wines produced by half. He also sold the fruit wine company

Domain San Martin wines are now largely premium varietals, made from centra coast grapes, beautifully packaged and sold at value prices. A range of magnum bottles of quality generic wines is also produced.

The winery featured on the label is an attractive brick structure reached through a beautiful avenue of fir trees. The tasting roor is well worth visiting, it is situated across the railway line from the winery

Taylors California Cellars

In 1977, after Coca-Cola's wine operations had bought Taylors and its associated company Great Western in New York State, they decided to expand to California. Their first move was purchasing Sterling Vineyards at Calistoga and the Monterey Vineyards Winery at Gonzales. Deciding they needed a broader market base, they introduced the Taylors California Cellars brand mainly for generic jug wines. These wines were blended from Monterey Vineyard wines and those from the central valley. So successful was the move that in 1981, a giant winery, Taylors California Cellars, was built right next door to The Monterey Vineyards facility. Two years later, Seagrams bought both properties from Coca-Cola and, although, Seagrams also owned Paul Masson, involved in the same market, the Taylors operation continued. The wines were masterminded by Dr. Richard Peterson, whose long experience as Gallo's research director and as enologist at Beaulieu fitted him well for the creation of excellent "value" wines.

In 1987, Vintners International was formed mainly by the executive staff at Seagrams. Under Michael Cliff's direction, they staged a leveraged buyout of some of Seagrams wine interests, including the Taylors New York winery, the Paul Masson operation and Taylors California Cellars. Seagrams maintained their ownership of The Monterey Vineyards and Sterling.

Taylors California Cellars has continued to expand and makes a range of bottled varietal wines as well as their "jug" packages. Quality is excellent and prices extremely reasonable.

An Introduction to Napa Valley

I n the world of wine the name "Napa" is magic, so great is the effect this simple four letter word has on a wine label that prices for what little land there is to further plant with vines in this county have become astronomical $35,000 — $40,000 per acre is not unusual. No other wine region in the world has developed such a high profile and become such a tourist Mecca as Napa. With over 5 million people annually visiting the valley it is second only to Disneyland as a Californian tourist attraction.

The number of wineries in the Napa County is fast approaching 200 and there are over 30,000 acres under vine. The wineries vary enormously in size and style from tiny private wineries producing only a few hundred cases and carefully secluded from the avalanche of tourists to the grand stately "Wine Mansions" such as Christian Brothers, Beringer, Charles Krug, Chateau Montelena, Beaulieu and Inglenook magnificently

preserved and presented as reminders of a bygone era of grandeur.

The Robert Mondavi Winery with its simple but stylish adobe Mission architecture, state of the art winemaking set up and strong emphasis on culture with art exhibitions, music festivals and all manner of culinary events has led the world into the modern era of wine since it opened in 1966. More of the visionary Robert Mondavi later. Needless to say his winery started a boom in state of the art wineries usually founded and funded by wealthy achievers from all walks of life intent on creating classy wines and wineries that are their ultimate statement. Styles and themes vary from the Old World charm style of the Wedding-Cake-like Far Niente through the space age Sterling, the oriental Xanadu like Newton Vineyards to the post-modern palace of the recently completed Clos Pegase.

Perhaps I am letting my imagination run a little far but I find a fascinating relationship

between the proprietors and the wineries they create and the wines they make. To me a definite personality emerges in the wines distinct to each winery and very much reflecting that of their mentor.

Hollywood has certainly touched the Napa. The somewhat reclusive Francis Ford Coppola, a lover of Bordeaux and Burgundies bought the old Neebaum Estate in Rutherford in 1978. Though nothing quite matches Michael Robbins Coup in securing the "Falcon Crest" series at his classic Victorian style winery "Spring Mountain".

The latest development in the valley is the "Napa Wine Train". The old Southern Pacific track unused for many years has been bought by an entrepreneurial group and soon Napa's version of the Orient Express will be running tourists. The "Carneros Quality Alliance" founded to promote the region and made up of most growers and wineries of the region is extremely committed to its task

An Introduction to Napa Valley

in doing an outstanding job. The climate of Carneros a classified cool region I continues up through the Napa through Yountville and north up the valley as far as Oakville. From here through Rutherford to St. Helena the climate is classified as the still cool region II as one approaches Calistoga the climate warms still further to region III.

The "Napa" were actually the tribe of Indians that inhabited this rich river valley before the white settlement started in the 1830's. Their 5,000 strong population was decimated by disease and bloody conflicts with the white settlers by the late 1800's very few remained.

The explorer George C. Yount settled in 1836 and built a log fortress just north of what is today Yountville. In 1838 he planted vines several others also planted vines over the next two decades, but it wasn't until German immigrant Charles (Karl) Krug established his winery in 1861 that commercial winemaking was commenced. Jacob Schram of Schramsberg fame started a year later in 1862. Prior to the phylloxera disaster nearly 5,000 acres of vines and almost 150 wineries in Napa County, although the vine louse destroyed most vineyards many were replanted.

The Valley itself runs right to the San Pablo bay in the south, this southern area is known as the attractive rolling hills of Carneros, this region has its own special micro climate influenced by the morning fog that rolls in off the bay and its cooling afternoon sea breezes and in 1985 was awarded its own appellation although the region covers two different counties both Napa and Sonoma, this the first time this has occurred in America.

Vineyard acreages have expanded dramatically and by 1920 10,000 acres were under vine. Prohibition did not destroy the vineyards, but most were grafted over the thick skinned coarse flavoured varieties for shipping east to the home winemakers, when the vine boom commenced in the mid 60's, there was little over 10,000 acres of vine. Today, there is over 30,000 acres.

Napa has the name and such strength that its premium position will remain for the foreseeable future but a number of other Californian regions and a few in other states are closing the gap certainly in terms of overall wine quality but also in terms of reputation and recognition. I am sure all involved in Napa's wine industry will strive even harder to produce the ultimate wine it is this search and painstaking effort that has made American wine great — long may it be so.

Napa Valley Wineries

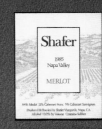

Beaulieu — beautiful place — was the name chosen by Georges de-Latour's wife, Ferdinande, for the property just north of Inglenook at Rutherford they bought in 899. Just over 40 years later when de Latour died they had created the most beautiful estate with its many wings, formal gardens and artifacts from all over the globe. ronically, it was the year after his death that what has become the most famous American wine was released. The "Georges de Latour" Private Reserve Cabernet Sauvignon, was the brainchild of Andre Tchelistcheff, certainly America's greatest-ever winemaker and still enormously active well into his 80's — consulting to many wineries including Beaulieu Vineyards.

Tchelistcheff was "discovered" by

Georges de Latour, when he went to France in 1938. De Latour was travelling with his son-in-law, the Marquis de Pins and visited Paul Marsais, then in charge of the "Institute National Agronomique" in Paris. He had no hesitation in recommending Tchelistcheff — his Research Enologist for the position. Little did any of them realise the significance this would have for the whole American wine industry.

Tchelistcheff was born in Moscow in 1901, but was educated in Czechoslovakia, the cultural centre of Europe in those times. He served in the Czarist and White Russian armies before travelling to France and joining the wine industry. On studying Californian wines, he decided Cabernet Sauvignon had the potential in the Napa to become world

class. He talked de Latour into building a maturation cellar with small oak barrels, solely for the purpose of creating wine in the Bordeaux style. His first, the Georges de Latour Private Reserve Cabernet Sauvignon of the 1936 vintage was released in 1941, the year after Georges' death. Like many innovative developments, it took time to create a reputation which has been only enhanced by the years. The Tchelistcheff tradition was passed on when Andre's son, Dimitri joined Beaulieu in 1970. Dimitri was a pioneer, in his own right having helped develop quality table wines for the Mexican wine industry, where he spent a number of years in the 1960's at the "Bodegas de Santo Tomas" on the Baja California Peninsula. Dimitri also helped Hawaiian wine pioneer

Beaulieu Vineyard

Emil Tedeschi, establish the first and only winery in the Island state.

Today Beaulieu is ably run by President, Tom Selfridge, a star graduate of Davis in the early 1970's and President, Legh Knowles, whose voice I heard many times on the airwaves promoting Beaulieu wines, as I was driving around California.

Beaulieu still produces a wide range of table wines covering many different varieties style and price ranges. Several dessert wines are also produced from Central Valley wines aged at Rutherford. Beaulieu has one of the best tasting and sales complex incorporating a theatre, where a most informative film on winegrowing is shown.

Beringer Vineyards

The classic Rhine House at Beringer Vineyards on the main road through St. Helena, is not only Napa's most beautiful and historic building, but the focal point of the Valley's oldest operating winery, where wine has been made continuously since 1876.

Fredrich Beringer, a maltster from the brewing industry in Mainz, Germany arrived in New York in 1865. In 1870, his brother Jacob joined him after working in his homeland as a winemaker and cellar-master.

Jacob set out across America in search of the ideal place to plant European vines and make wine. His search ended in the Napa Valley, where he found both the soil and climate perfect for his purposes.

He started work as a cooper (barrel maker) and then as cellar-master for Charles Krug, a fellow German immigrant. Jacob talked his brother into joining him. They bought the Hudson property in St. Helena in 1876 and commenced building a winery, chiefly constructed by carving tunnels hundreds of feet into the hillsides composed of "volcanic tufa". This task was carried out by the Chinese "coolies" (labourers), who had just returned from constructing work on the transcontinental railway. The cool cellars created are still in use today for wood ageing of the Beringer private reserve wines. Hidden amongst the barrels is a private museum containing some of the classic older vintages, including a 1937 Cabernet Sauvignon and a 1943 Pinot Noir.

The original winery operated on a gravity flow basis with crushing and pressing on the hillside and finished wine finally going into barrels in the tunnels.

Whilst Jacob lived in the Hudson house built in 1854 and currently being renovated as a culinary centre, his brother Frederick commenced building "The Rhine House". This classic German "castle-like" building, was modelled on the original family home on the Rhine River in Germany. Commenced in 1883, the 17 room mansion was built from Napa Valley stone, Pennsylvania slate, Californian Redwood and Honduras mahogany. When the gardens were re-landscaped in 1987, stone from the same Napa quarry was used. At the same time, Frederick's bedroom upstairs was painstakingly re-modelled and finished in Honduras mahogany. Called "The Founders Room", it has been set up as a special tasting area, where the public can pay to taste the rare and private reserve wines of Beringer and talk with the actual winemakers. This innovative approach is a wonderful way to meet a growing need amongst wine lovers.

The Rhine House was last lived in by the family in 1946, although for a period it was out of the family's hands, until bought back by Otto Beringer earlier this century.

In 1970, Beringer was bought by the Swiss based Nestle Company, which immediately started buying land and planting vineyards. Around 80% of Beringer wines are made from their own grapes, which is most unusual for such a large company — it gives Beringer great control over quality and the ability to bring out many Estate bottled individual vineyard wines. Practically the only grapes they buy are those for the White Zinfandel.

Beringer own almost 1,000 acres in the Napa, broken up between the following vineyards: Hudson Ranch, mainly Chardonnay and at the cool end of the Valley between Yountville and Napa, Gamble Ranch, at Oakville and mainly Chardonnay. State Lane near Yountville predominantly Cabernet Sauvignon. The Lemmon Chabot Vineyard, on the slopes of Glass Mountain, on the eastern side of the Valley again Cabernet Sauvignon is the main variety. The Home Vineyard, terraced into the hillsides of Spring Mountain, was the first established by Jacob

Beringer, its steep slopes, no doubt reminding him of the Rhine Valley of his homeland.

Beringer have also established a new and unique vineyard at Knights Valley, nestled under the watchful eye of Mt. St. Helena, some 17 miles north of the winery. This area is producing brilliant Cabernet Sauvignons and Sauvignon Blancs particularly and was recently awarded its own appellation.

Continuing in the quest for quality through vineyard ownership and control and to help supply top wine for their second label "Napa Ridge", Beringer have just completed the purchase in March 1988 of the Estrella River Vineyards and Winery in San Louis Obispo County.

Nestle are also adding to the new winery they built in the 1970's across the road from the original cellars. Nestle have a long term commitment to their wine division and plan to invest some $10 million per year for the next decade to add even further strength and lustre to the Beringer name.

Nestle have kept a very stable team together and their current winemaker, Ed Sbragia, a third generation winemaker from Healdsburg, who also holds a Masters Degree in Enology from Fresno State, joined them in 1976. Ed had also worked as a research enologist at Gallo. He spent a further eight years under the legendary Beringer wine-master, Myron Nightingale and took over from him on his retirement in 1984.

Beringer Executive, Michael Florian took me through an extensive tasting of current releases in early 1988. The wines were extremely impressive and Beringer's pricing is certainly competitve. I was particularly taken with the private reserve Chardonnay (mainly barrel fermented). The Lemmon-Chabot Vineyard Cabernet Sauvignon a big earthy/classic style wine with minty overtones and a very late harvest Johannisberg Riesling in the Trochenberenauslese style — luscious and complex. The Beringer Chenin Blanc is a very popular wine and rightfully so, slightly sweet, but clean and crisp with delightful fruit flavours. A visit to Berigner is a must, the Rhine House, gardens and wine tunnels are beautiful.

Relax and enjoy a glass of wine under the huge 350 old valley oak with its tortured branches, which as legend has it, used to be straight until the roots found a wine barrel in the cellar!!

Buehler Vineyards

The eastern hills surrounding the Napa Valley have been slow to develop although viticulture was well established here in the last century. Recently the Howell Mountain region obtained its own district appellation from the federal government.

During the 1970's, John Page Buehler Snr., a former engineer and executive with the Bechtel Corporation, bought a beautiful 75 acre estate on Greenfield Road a few miles east of the Silverado Trail, off Conn Street, which in turn runs off Lower Howell Mountain Road. John actually planned to just build a retirement home for he and his wife but he planted 60 acres and sold grapes to Napa Valley wineries.

His son John Jnr. decided to build a small winery and also moved to live on the property. The handsome winery was opened in time for the 1978 vintage. Only grapes from their own vineyard, named "Vista del Lago" after the stunning view it has of Lake Hennessey, are used and all wines are estate bottled.
The Buehler's have employed Heidi Petersen (now married to James "Bo" Barnett from Chateau Montelena) as winemaker.

Chappellet Winery

Donn Chappellet goes a long way towards proving the theory that wines reflect the character and personality of those that create them. Donn is a giant of a man who has tackled and tamed some of the toughest hill country east of the Napa. He has established his 100 acre vineyard and majestic pyramid shaped winery 700ft. above the Valley on Pritchard Hill, which overlooks Lake Hennessy.

Donn left a successful food vending business in Los Angeles at the young age of 34. He and his wife Molly started clearing and planting in 1965 and established the winery two years later. Certainly energetic, the Chappellets have found time to not only create some of the greatest Cabernet Sauvignons produced in California, but also raise their six children on the property. Chappellet also produce a Chardonnay and Chenin Blanc.

The winery has grown steadily in size and reputation. Donn is one of the quiet achievers and stays clear of much of the limelight enjoyed by many of the Napa wineries. This winery and its wines are well worth seeking out.

Cakebread Cellars

Jack and Dolores Cakebread were childhood sweethearts. Jack's parents had a ranch, but his father suffered badly from hay fever, so Jack got the job of driving the tractor when he was only eight years old. After they met at high school, Jack let Dolores drive the tractor, a gesture that marked the commencement of a close, warm partnership that lasts until this day — some 40 years later. Although they still live in Oakland, where both have elderly parents and Jack ran a successful garage, they have created a marvellous environment on their Napa Estate, which is just north of Robert Mondavi on the opposite side of the road.

The loving care and attention both bestow upon their projects and their enterprise is obvious. Jack is a complete perfectionist. On a recent visit, he enthusiastically showed me a new vineyard he was planting, having just bought an extra 25 acres of land adjacent to his property and right on the banks of the Napa River. Along with all his other vineyards, he has laid tile drainage 18 ft. below the surface, which collects all excess water from the vine roots and returns it to a central dam where it can be reused for irrigation. This very natural water control, amongst other things, has enabled Cakebread to produce outstanding fruit, which is very evident in the wines. All have very crisp, lively fruit flavours.

Their initial purchase of 22 acres of land in 1973 has been steadily expanded by their purchases of adjacent properties — 11 acres in 1982 and a further 25 acres in 1987. Most is planted with Cabernet Sauvignon with 10% being planted with Cabernet Franc — this has proved a most successful blend in the finished wines.

Their two sons, in their early thirties, are also involved. The eldest, Dennis, is involved in administration, sales and marketing, while the youngest, Bruce, studied pomology at Cal-Polytechnic as well as winemaking at U.C. Davis and is now the winemaker.

The Cakebreads have restored and added to an old house adjacent to the winery and created a wonderful "Winery Hospitality House" incorporating a commercial kitchen, entertaining areas and a superb garden complete with a fountain. This private entertaining facility is beautiful and Jack's other love — photography, is displayed on the walls.

Dolores grows all her own vegetables, herbs and flowers adding further to the total ambience.

The design award winning winery is both aesthetically appealing and efficient. Their Chardonnay made from fruit from a long time supplier in the Oak Knoll area is crisp with delightful melon and grapefruit flavours. The Cabernet made from their own vines, a special clone isolated by Cakebread and combined with 10% Cabernet Franc, has overtones of raspberries and cherries — a rich, yet superbly balanced wine.

The Cakebreads travel the world promoting their wines. Dolores also ran the highly successful California Grill at Vin Expo in Bordeaux in 1987 and is doing a similar job in Germany soon for a Californian wine promotion. I am sure though they would find it difficult to beat their own environment.

Caymus Vineyards

Charlie Wagner was a long time architect and grape grower in the Napa Valley when, in 1971, he decided to join the fast developing, but (compared with today), quite small winemaking fraternity. Charlie is known far and wide as one of the characters of the Valley, far different from many of the smooth-talking professional and business profile people, who have turned to the wine industry. Those visiting the cosy personal tasting room at Caymus will often find him dispensing his dry humour along with his full of character wines.

Caymus has built quite a reputation for their Cabernets, Sauvignons. One of their secrets is the blending of various districts, where they grow the grapes. Some are in the hills around the Valley, whilst others are on the Valley floor itself. Wines from the higher vineyards tend to have more acidity along with fresh herbaceous fruit, whereas the Valley wines have more strength colour and body.

Caymus is one of the few companies that seems to have found the right balance with the use of small oak. This fact shows through in their various Cabernet's from the mid 70's.

A number of Caymus wines appear under the "Liberty School" label, which appears with a painting of the one room school near to the winery and where Charlie attended in his youth.

Caymus was actually named after the original "Caymus land grant" of the last century. A number of other wines are produced mainly from Charlie's own vineyards. These include their Chardonnay, which is developing an increasing respect, Johannisberg Riesling, Sauvignon Blanc and Fume Blanc, in the whites. Whilst they also make a Pinot Noir in both Blanc de Noir style as well as a full blown red plus a Zinfandel and a Petit Sirah.

Caymus have earned a good reputation overseas as well as in America and are moving into the export market. They were part of the 1987 Vin Expo Californian promotion in Bordeaux and their wines were exceptionally well received.

Charlie's son, Chuck, is also involved adding further depth to one of Napa's best and most personal family wineries.

Clos du Val

Bernard Portet is one of the Napa Valley's most respected wine personalities and one of its strongest advocates. It was he who so eloquently presented Californian wines at Vin Expo in Bordeaux this last year as figurehead for the very professional Californian Contingents Exhibit. It seems almost ironic that not only he, but his younger brother Dominque, who has set up Taltarni Wines in Australia, should be promoting the wines of the new world so close to where their father Andre worked for many years as the Technical Director of Chateau Lafite.

Clos du Val's beginnings go back to 1971, when John Goelet, who spreads his time between America and France, set out in search of the ideal locations to make wines to rival the greatest of France. It was a stroke of genius surely that he persuaded the Portet brothers to assist him. Bernard a graduate of the French Montpellier Wine Course had worked in the South African wine industry as well as his native France.

Although not large, the winery has a certain Gallic grandeur. It is surrounded by vineyards that rise into the hills eastward from the Silverado Trail, not far from Stag's Leap. These vineyards are mainly devoted to Cabernet Sauvignon although some Merlot is grown. Clos du Val have also joined in the renaissance of the Carneros district and have a large vineyard there, chiefly planted with Chardonnay.

Clos du Val wines are individual and full of character and, like their creator, Bernard Portet, a welcome addition to America's developing wine industry.

CLOS DU VAL
Address: 5330 Silverado Trail, Napa, CA., 94558
Phone: 707/252 6711
Year of Establishment: 1972
Owner: John Goelet
Winemaker: Bernard M. Portet
Principal Varieties Grown: Cabernet Sauvignon, Merlot, Zinfandel, Pinot Noir, Chardonnay
Acres Under Vine: 250
Average Annual Crush: 950 tons

Principal Wines & Brands	Cellar Potential (Years)
Cabernet Sauvignon	10-15
Merlot	10-15
Reserve	10-15

Trade Tours – Available by appointment only
Retail Room Sales – Available
Hours open to Public – Daily 10am to 4pm
Retail Distribution – National

Chateau Montelena

One could be forgiven for thinking one had stumbled upon a Mediaeval French castle, when you reach the top of the winding drive to Chateau Montelena with its beautifully secluded location built into the pine covered hillside and overlooking a delightful lake complete with bird-life.

The winery goes back to the early days of California's commercial wine history. Alfred Tubbs was a very prominent San Francisco citizen and Californian State Senator. His background included setting up his own whaling fleet and building the first "rope making business" on the west coast, supplying the China Clippers.

Tubbs was somewhat infatuated with France to the extent of having his winery designed in the French Bordeaux tradition by a French architect. He himself sailed to France to choose the stone for the facade as well as bringing back the initial vine cuttings. To top it off, he employed a Frenchman, Jerome Bardot, as his first winemaker.

Chateau Montelena developed a big reputation in the early part of the century, but closed with Prohibition. After repeal in 1933, the winery was opened again by Alfred's son Chapin, but it closed again in 1940 and lay in disuse until 1958, when it was bought by a Chinese couple the Yort-Franks, who added Chinese gardens and a "Jade" lake with several islands, connected by traditional arched bridges and with red laquered partitions. A genuine Chinese launch was also added — this still floats serenely on the lake. This delightful scene features in some of the wineries packaging.

In 1972, the winery received a new lease of life when it was bought by a syndicate headed by James L. Barrett. The winery was immediately revived with new equipment and winemaking team, including the famous "Mike" Grgich. It didn't take long before exciting things started happening culminating in the victory at a Paris tasting in 1976, where Chateau Montelena's 1973 Chardonnay defeated all French white Burgundies causing a sensation and even reaching the pages of Time Magazine. The new partnership also revived the vineyard on its original sight, the rich volcanic plane at the foot of Mt. St. Helena. This 100 acre site has been planted predominately with Cabernet Sauvignon, as well as a little Zinfandel — over 95 acres in all. The Chardonnay is purchased from the Yountville area and also in the Alexander Valley, the Johannisberg Riesling comes mainly from the hillside vineyards and makes an excellent wine only available at the winery.

Current winemaker is James P. (Bo) Barrett, son of the managing partner, "Bo" has a long history with the winery. Although still a young man he first worked under Mike Grgich from 1973-1976 then Jerry Luper from 1977-1981. He then travelled to Europe to further his knowledge and experience to add to his winemaking degree from Fresno University. On his return he assisted in establishing a large vineyard and winery on the central coast, but was back at Chateau Montelena by the end of 1982. "Bo" sets his standards high and is constantly innovating whilst keeping the cellar style. Chateau Montelena's commitment to quality is most succinctly put by its huge 2,000 barrel

Chateau Montelena

maturation cellar — all French oak. Every wine is held in bottle until mature enough for sale and good drinking. Chateau Montelena can be summed up with one word — ''outstanding''.

The Christian Brothers

Probably the best known North American winery worldwide "Christian Brothers", is also Napa's largest producing winery. Over the last few years, the whole organisation has gone through a renaissance. From being slightly out of date and tradition bound in its making, packaging and marketing, Christian Brothers have invested some $25 million and employed some of the biggest guns in the industry. They now have a "state-of-the-art" winemaking facility, just south of St. Helena, which has plenty of room for future expansion. The packaging and marketing revolution has been even greater a new range of "super-premium", (they have already won a bundle of medals). Estate bottled varietal wines has been released along with many other new lines all magnificently packaged.

The two things that most changed the course of this grand old winemaking brotherhood, were the appointments of Brother David Brennan as Chief Executive Officer and his subsequent hiring of hot-shot industry guru Dick Maher as President. Brother David had achieved much as he also found winemaker Tom Eddy, who has proved such an asset in establishing the new St. Helena Winery and improved the quality of the wines out of sight.

Dick Maher is a tough no nonsense operator, whose background includes the United States Marine Corps and an M.B.A. from Stanford University. He learned his brand marketing skills with Proctor and Gamble, but first came into the wine industry in 1965, when he joined the giant E & J Gallo company, assisting building the Gallo brands through a period of dramatic growth. Next he ran the Nestle operation as President of Beringer for 9 years, following which he went to Seagrams to run the wine classics operation. It was about this time that Brother David first made overtures to him to come over to Christian Brothers. After he left Seagrams, this is exactly what he did. The number of cases moving out of the warehouses has increased dramatically up some 20% in 1986, 35% in 1987 and already up 60% in the early part of 1988. Dick has brought together a team with a similar commitment to his own.

Much of the success goes right back to the vineyard. With over 1,300 acres, Chrisitian Brothers are the biggest vineyard owner in the Valley and they have their vineyards in many different locations with varying soils and micro-climates. Over recent years much re-planting has gone on, firstly to rationalise the varieties down to Cabernet Sauvignon, Chardonnay, Merlot, Sauvignon Blanc, Johannisberg Riesling and Zinfandel, other varieties traditionally grown by the Brothers, but now unfashionable such as Pinot St. George and Pineau de la Loire have either been grubbed out or T-bud, grafted

over to other more fashionable types. Secondly, varieties have been matched to the micro-climate and soils giving a great base for the winemaker and the new "super-premium" range.

The Christian Brothers are a teaching arm of the Jesuit movement and any profits they make go to assisting the Brotherhood's work. Their wine history in California goes back to 1882 at Martinez where they produced only altar wines. In 1930, they bought the Mont La Salle property, in the hills west of Napa, already complete with a vineyard and stone cellars built in 1903. The name Mont La Salle is still used as the holding company that owns and operates all their vineyards and as the brand name they still use their altar wines.

1937 saw the Christian Brothers name first appear on labels. The previous year, the legendary Brother Timothy, born Anthony D.

Angeles, became winemaker. He is still a consultant and active in many Napa events — his contribution to wines has been immense.

Over the years the Brothers developed a wide range of table and higher strength wines, plus a brandy that is produced at their winemaking facility near Fresno. Until 1977 no Christian Brothers wine carried a vintage, but rather the wines boasted a consistent style and quality blended to suit the label. Around 1970, a labelling system using bin numbers made it possible to determine the vintage of the wine, but their 1976 Gewurztraminer was the first to sport an actual date.

In 1945, the Brothers started leasing space in the huge historic Greystone Cellars just north of St. Helena, which is quite coincidental as the building has a religious feel and look about. Erected in 1889, it was the largest stone winery in the world.

and had a number of owners until the Brothers bought it in 1950. The winery complete with ageing tunnels into the hills, was used for bulk champagne making for a number of years, as well as maturation and storage for table wines. The building was closed in 1984 for seismic renovation to prevent earthquake damage, but re-opened to the public in 1987. It is once again the biggest single tourist attraction in the Valley. As well as their traditional brandy Christian Brothers produce a range of fruit flavoured brandys in attractive packages that are selling well. They also make excellent premium ports. Their Napa Zinfandel Port fortified with 8 year old pots still brandy is particularly good.

Christian Brothers export to 45 countries. Their good name has only been enhanced both in America and overseas by the exciting developments of recent years.

Conn Creek Winery

Conn Creek early developed a big reputation for its Cabernet Sauvignon and Zinfandel, but over the last few years its Chardonnay and Sauvignon Blanc have helped the winery join the illustrious few at the top with both red and white.

The two main reasons for this meteoric rise to fame are the dedication and skill of their winemaker, Darryl Eklund and the resourses and understanding of the industry by the new owners "Stimson Lane", also proprietors of Chateau Ste. Michelle in Washington State. Nothing has been spared in the quest for great wines. Darryl has been given virtually a free hand and he has very much justified this faith laid in him.

Conn Creek draws its grapes from a number of sources, using regions within Napa suited to each variety. They have invested heavily in new French oak, but Darryl is very restrained in its use, believing that oak is a seasoning to create complexity, not dominate the wine. All the wines, both red and white receive at least a full 12 months in the bottle before release, giving them a chance to settle down and the flavours to marry together. Often the red wines have almost two years in bottle,

allowing an even greater opportunity for the integration of flavours and softening of tannins.

Conn Creek Cabernets from the Collins Vineyard often bring the highest price at the Napa Valley Barrel auction and rightly so. If Conn Creek wines of the past have been impressive, be sure they are working on those of the future being even better.

CONN CREEK
Address: 8711 Silverado Trail, St. Helena, CA., 94574
Phone: 707/963 5133
Year of Establishment: 1974
Owner: Stimson Lane Wine & Spirits
Winemaker: Daryl Eklund
Principal Varieties Grown: Cabernet Sauvignon
Acres Under Vine: 2
Average Annual Crush: 900 tons

**Principal Wines &
Brands**
Cabernet Sauvignon
Zinfandel
Chardonnay
Merlot
Sauvignon Blanc
Trade Tours – Available by appointment only
Retail Room Sales – Available
Hours open to Public –
7 days a week from 10am to 4.30pm

Domaine de Napa

Michel and Claudine Perret's Domaine de Napa exudes the simple Gallic charm of Provence, with its wisteria-entwined verandah and whitewashed walls. Michel is readily recognised — always attired in the French tradition, complete with braces.

This is one of the few wineries where the owners personally run the tasting and sales area. A visit with them is one of the real joys of the wine road. Michel has a sparkling eye and a wry sense of humour. He also knows the valley better than most of the locals and, having managed many of the leading vineyards, he has his ear to the ground on everything. Claudine is both gracious and charming.

Michel is still busy with his vineyard consulting business and has a New Zealand winemaker Grant Fowler. Between them they make the wines, a Sauvignon Blanc, Chardonnay and a Cabernet Sauvignon. It's hard to put your finger on it precisely, but they are different in style to most Napa wines. Although the winery was only completed in 1986 and is thus one of the newest in the Valley. Michel and Claudine have made wine under the Domaine de Napa label since the 1983 vintage, using other winery facilities.

The Perrets migrated to the States in July 1977, leased and ran a farm in the San Joaquin Valley. It wasn't long however, before the lure of wine brought them back to the industry they grew up with in France. Michel's 10 years experience running vineyards in all parts of the Napa Valley and in the Mayacamas Mountains has given him a great feel for the best areas for certain varieties. He uses this and his many contacts to source grapes for his own wines.

The Domaine de Napa wines are more subtle and complex than many others. Michel tends to pick a little earlier than most, giving his wines a well defined, crisp fruit character. He uses small oak for all his wines, but doesn't believe in too much new-wood character. I found his wines particularly well balanced with a good lingering flavour in the mouth.

Domaine de Napa is certainly a different and welcome experience amongst the hype of Napa. Long may Michel and Claudine preside over this charming winery among the vines.

DOMAINE DE NAPA WINERY
Address: 1155 Mee Lane, St. Helena, CA., 94574
Phone: 707/963 1666
Year of Establishment: 1985
Owner: Michel and Claudine Perret
Winemaker: Grant Taylor
Principal Varieties Grown: Cabernet Sauvignon, Chardonnay, Sauvignon Blanc
Acres Under Vine: 11
Average Annual Crush: 300 tons

Principal Wines & Brands	Cellar Potential
Cabernet Sauvignon	1700 cases
Chardonnay; Chardonnay barrel fermented	2500; 500 cases
Sauvignon Blanc	2500 cases

Trade Tours – Available
Retail Room Sales – Available
Hours open to Public –
7 days a week from 10am to 5pm

Domaine Chandon

Meeting John Wright and Edmund Maudiere together, one immediately gets the impression that Domaine Chandon is in good hands for not only are they delightful people but extremely talented and hardworking in their professions.

They alone could not of course, have created France's most successful wine venture, but they have built a thoroughly professional and devoted team around them, a team which can do everything from planting vines to serving a superb haute cuisine meal.

Domaine Chandon was born on March 26th, 1973. John Wright, a long time lover of wine had become involved, first, in his role of management consultant. The lure of the project was too much for him, particularly when he was given a virtual carte blanche to do the job.

Today Domaine Chandon produces over half a million cases of excellent "methode champenoise" wines, but the beginnings were very different. The first cuvee s were made from purchased grapes grown in the cooler parts of the Valley and pressed at the Trefethen Winery, whose vineyards still supply considerable fruit to Domaine Chandon.

Moët-Hennessy, the French multinational company, which is involved in luxury products as well as the hospitality industry, appointed their Conseillier Technique (Technical Director), Edmund Maudiere, to oversee the winemaking style and production. Edmund is a man of immense energy and zest for living, as much at home piloting a group of guests over Domaine Chandon in a light aircraft (as he often does) or evaluating hundreds of wines to determine the blend that will make the best cuvee and ultimately the perfectly balanced "Methode Champenoise" sparkling wine. On quizzing Edmund regarding his thoughts and philosophies on how to make the best champenoise style in California, his first reaction is "Fruit". He believes with California's ideal climate with grapes that are fuller in flavour and softer in acid than in his own Champagne district, one should let the fruit show through. The resulting product is fruitier and softer than the French equivalent and does not rely as heavily on malolactic fermentation and long ageing on the yeast for its body and character.

The first wines of Domaine Chandon were, in fact, still table wines. A Chardonnay from press wine called "Fred's Friends" was put out as a slightly tongue-in-cheek tribute to the then Moët chief, Count Frederic Chandon de Briailles. Later a Pinot Noir Blanc, also called Fred's Friends was needed, both proved so popular they are still sold only from the winery. Edmund still travels over from France four or five times a year, although winemaking is now in the hands of Dawnine Sample Dyer. Edmund of course, also makes the Moët Champagnes, including the most famous of all — Dom Perignon. His life and vitality is very evident in all the wines he oversees.

In 1977, Domaine Chandon completed their winery and methode champenoise caves on the site of what was once the adjacent Veteran's Home rubbish dump. The complex is superb — not ostentatious, but sculptured into the landscape and surrounded by beautiful gardens. The haute cuisine restaurant seating 90 inside and 40 outside, serves 70,000 meals a year of a quality I have rarely seen equalled. The presentation of the dishes particularly is sensational.

The three main products produced are the Chandon Brut, the Blanc de Noirs and the Reserve. All have in common good, rich fruit flavours yet are elegant, with great texture and excellent balance. The French have invested some $42 million into the project so far, including some 850 acres of vineyards, which only supply about one-third of their needs. So highly do Moët regard their Californian operation, that they have put them directly in charge of their largest project just outside Melbourne in Australia.

Domaine Chandon has given the North American sparkling wine industry an entirely new image and all other makers are benefitting from these efforts. They have created a whole new market that is still soaring ahead.

DOMAINE CHANDON
Address: I California Drive, PO Box 2470, Yountville, CA., 94599
Phone: 707/944 2280
Year of Establishment: 1973
Owner: Moet-Hennessy, Louis Vuitton
Winemaker: Dawnine Dyer
Principal Varieties Grown: Pinot Noir, Pinot Blanc, Pinot Meunier, Chardonnay
Acres Under Vine: 850
Average Annual Crush: 7,400 tons

Principal Wines & Brands	Cellar Potential (Years)
Chandon Reserve	
Chandon Brut	
Chandon Blanc de Noirs	
Panache	

Trade Tours – Available
Retail Room Sales – Available
Hours open to Public – I1am to 5.30pm daily May – Oct; Wed – Sun November – April
Retail Distribution: Schieffelin & Somerset Co.

Domaine Chandon

Flora Springs Wine Company

Right at the end of West Zinfandel Lane at the base of the Mayacamas Mountains, stands a substantial stone winery built in the 1880's by the Rennie Brothers from Scotland. Right from the start James and William were dogged by bad luck. First the roof burnt off the winery then phylloxera struck the vineyards. Finally, they abandoned the winery.

In the 1940's the property was bought by Louis Martini, who built a home there in 1946 and lived there the rest of his life, the winery being used to store some of the Martini sherries and red wines. After Martini's death the property was bought by Jerome Komes, the retired president of the Bechtel Corporation.

The 328 acre property had 110 acres under vine; now more has been planted while the Komes family have other vineyard holdings in various parts of the valley. These large vineyard holdings give Flora Springs a big advantage over many wineries — they can select only the best of their grapes for their own wines as three quarters of the harvest is sold to other wineries.

Jerry's daughter, Julie, and son-in-law Pat Garvey, have managed the vineyards since the property was purchased, but it was son John who had the idea to start a winery in 1978. He is an extremely energetic building contractor and has in fact, built many of the new wineries and additions around the Valley during the last decade.

Flora Springs winemaker, since 1980, has been Ken Deis, who previously worked with Joseph Phelps and Joe Heitz. Traditionally Flora Springs have only made a Cabernet Sauvignon a Chardonnay and a Sauvignon Blanc, although they are just releasing a new wine "Trilogy" a red Bordeaux blend, barrel selected from their very best wines and given extra bottle age — this wine is not cheap, but is one of the very best North American red wines.

Donald Patz is the very pleasant marketing chief of Flora Springs and has been successful in gaining wide distribution for the wines, which now also appear in Switzerland, Canada, Japan and the U.K.

With their commitment and skilled team, Flora Springs really have their act together.

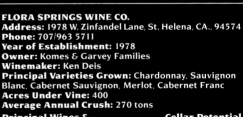

FLORA SPRINGS WINE CO.
Address: 1978 W. Zinfandel Lane, St. Helena, CA., 94574
Phone: 707/963 5711
Year of Establishment: 1978
Owner: Komes & Garvey Families
Winemaker: Ken Deis
Principal Varieties Grown: Chardonnay, Sauvignon Blanc, Cabernet Sauvignon, Merlot, Cabernet Franc
Acres Under Vine: 400
Average Annual Crush: 270 tons

Principal Wines & Brands	Cellar Potential (Years)
Flora Springs Barrel Fermented Chardonnay	5
Flora Springs Estate Chardonnay	3-5
Flora Springs Trilogy	10-15
Flora Springs Sauvignon	10-15
Flora Springs Merlot	10-15
Flora Springs Sauvignon Blanc	3

Trade Tours – Available by appointment only
Retail Room Sales – Available

Far Niente Winery

I t is hard to imagine a more beautiful winery than Far Niente, often referred to as the Wedding Cake of the Napa, as it sits perched on a knoll amongst its beautifully landscaped gardens and lake, overlooking its own vineyard.

Gil Nickel's background, running one of the biggest nursery businesses in America in his home state of Oklahoma must have attracted him to the aesthetic sleeping beauty and the potential of this turreted stone winery, which had been abandoned for half a century when he bought it in 1979.

The winery had originally been built by a Captain John Benson, who marketed wines under a charming label, featuring the legend "without a care", which relates well to the name "Far Niente", chosen by Gil Nickel when he discovered an Italian fable carved in stone above the uppermost window of the old building — translated it means "do nothing".

Certainly the environment Gil has created may make one feel there is nothing more to be done, but all around one notices the painstaking attention to detail that is also very obvious in the wines of Far Niente, probably the most attractively packaged of all American wines.

Until recently, Far Niente only made a Chardonnay, the first two vintages — 1980 and 1981 — were made in a makeshift winery in Sausalito, whilst the old winery was being restored. The hundred acre vineyard, which surrounds the winery was actually part of the famous To-Kalon Vineyards in the last century.

Far Niente now makes two wines, the other being an estate bottled Cabernet Sauvignon. The Chardonnay is a rich style with good wood treatment, fruit flavours of grapefruit and melon are complemented by a nutty vanilla overtone with a rich, creamy texture. The Cabernet Sauvignon is a Bordeaux-like style with some minty and herbaceous character and a pleasant, but restrained use of oak — both are extremely well made wines. One of the beauties of having only two wines is that the winemaker can devote all his efforts to making them good.

Gil is also a classic car enthusiast and has just completed a barn at the rear of the winery to house his fleet. All in all, Far Niente is paradise amongst the wines and a tribute to good taste.

FAR NIENTE WINERY
Address: #1 Acacia Drive
(PO Box 327, Oakville, CA., 94562
Phone: 707/944 2861
Year of Establishment: 1885
Owner: Mr. Gil Nickel
Winemaker: Mr. Dirk Hampson
Principal Varieties Grown: Chardonnay,
Cabernet Sauvignon, some Merlot and Cabernet Franc
for blending purposes
Acres Under Vine: 100
Average Annual Crush: 500 tons

Principal Wines & Brands	Cellar Potential (Years)
Napa Valley Chardonnay	8-10
Estate Bottled Cabernet Sauvignon	5-20

Trade Tours – Available by appointment only
Retail Room Sales – Not Available
Hours open to Public – Not open to public
Retail Distribution – All 50 states

Fairmont Vineyards

The Napa Valley is like a magnet that draws to it all people with their hearts in wine. George Kolarovich is one of those people. His family have cultivated vines in Yugoslavia since 1796 and George still has an interest in these vineyards. During the late 50's, he migrated to Australia to work for the Barossa Valley Growers Co-operative, later to become Kaiser Stuhl. George managed to introduce many new wine products and concepts to Australia, including the first bulk fermented sparkling wines, which really started the wine revolution in that country as well as Australia's first successful Rose. To a degree George was a man before his time.

Although not a young man, he still had new frontiers to conquer, so he and his vivacious wife Yelena, who had been raised in America, migrated to California and George secured a job with the Californian Wine Association based in Napa. The desire to make wine again was irresistible, so George started making his own wine at a friend's winery. In 1982, he and Yelena launched "Fairmont Vineyards".

Although still making wine at other wineries, Fairmont has grown into a substantial operation and plans are afoot to establish their own winery and tasting room in the Valley.

All Fairmont wines are 100% Napa Valley. George's skill, along with careful grape selection has produced outstanding wines with plenty of flavour and very good balance.

George and Yelena love what they do and their Fairmont wines are worth seeking out.

Fairmont Vineyards

Freemark Abbey Winery

Bill Jaeger and Charles Carpy are two of nature's gentlemen and growers in the Napa Valley for many years. In 1967, they drew together a syndicate and bought the old stone winery on Highway 29, north of St. Helena. They have not only gone on to produce exceptional wines, but developed Freemark into a beautiful complex, including gourmet shops and the "Abbey" restaurant upstairs.

The growers involved in the winery have vineyard holdings of some 600 acres around the Valley, giving Freemark access to very good fruit. Some of the wines are released with vineyard designations. Although Cabernet Sauvignon and Chardonnay are the main offerings, the Johannisberg Rieslings of Freemark are some of the best in the Valley, particularly the late picked wines made from botrytised grapes (noble rot).

The first of these luscious dessert wines was a 1973, released under the name Edelwein. The 1976 and 1982 vintages were particularly concentrated with around 20% residual sugar, equivalent to top French Sauternes or German Trockenbeerenauslese wines and were released under the name Edelwein Gold. Freemark have also produced some well balanced Petite Sirah reds from this hard-to-handle variety.

Charles Carpy, one of the managing partners, comes from a long line of winemaker ancestors. His grandfather came to California from Bordeaux and set up Uncle Sam Cellars in Napa in the 1880's and was the largest shareholder in the California Wine Association, when it was set up in 1894. At one stage he owned the historic Greystone (now Christian Brothers), then the largest stone winery in the world.

Both Charles and Bill are also partners in the Rutherford Hill Winery (see p. 152) they bought in 1976 as a second label to Freemark Abbey. It has actually outstripped their earlier winery in size and developed a very good reputation, particularly for its red wines. Freemark has stayed fairly small and concentrates on quality and dispensing hospitality.

Mike (Miljenko) Grgich has developed a most illustrious reputation as a winemaker. Born in Croatia, he worked in his father's winery and studied winegrowing at the Zagreb University. On arriving in California, he worked at a number of wineries including Robert Mondavi. In 1972 he went to the newly established Chateau Montelena where he became famous virtually overnight, when his 1973 Chardonnay took all before it at a 1976 Paris tasting.

In 1977, Austin Hills, of San Francisco coffee merchant, Hills Brothers offered him a partnership and Grigich Hills was born. Much of the fruit comes from Hill's own vineyards. Although not cheap his Chardonnay is very good and highly regarded, with its rich buttery style. Grgich also produces Fume Blanc and Johannisberg Riesling as well as a Cabernet Sauvignon and an excellent Zinfandel from Alexander Valley fruit in the red department.

Grgich Hills produces consistently good wines that justify the big reputation they have garnered. The winery has a pleasant low-profile tasting room, which is conveniently located at the front of the winery on Highway 29.

Girard Winery

Just off the Silverado Trail in the Oakville area is the spilt stone winery of the Girard's. The winery was built in 1980, but Stephen Girard had established his 40 acre vineyard in 1974, after retiring as Chairman of the board of Kaiser Steel.

Girard's son, also Stephen, who had been working in San Diego, took a great interest in the vineyard and eventually talked his father into building a winery. He is now President of the company. In 1982, the Girards started planting a new vineyard on a hillside near Domaine Chandon. Their objective is to eventually grow all the grapes required by their winery.

Girard runs a second label, "Stephens", under which all wines produced from bought-in grapes are labelled. One of the outstanding wines produced from their own vineyards is their Chenin Blanc, which unlike most wines of this variety, is made in a dry style. Also produced are Chardonnay, Cabernet Sauvignon and Sauvignon Blanc. Occasionally a classic dessert Semillon is produced from botrytis-affected grapes and

William Hill is an agricultural economist, which makes it all the harder to understand his penchant for establishing Mountain Vineyards, with their extremely high initial costs and low yields. It can only be explained by his desire to make the best possible wine from the high quality grapes they produce.

Bill's first contact with wine came when, as an Oklahoma agricultural consultant, he travelled to Napa on an investment project or clients looking at agricultural pursuits. In 1974, he began buying and developing vineyard land and, two years later, bought an old fruit juice plant in the town of Napa and commenced making wine for his vineyards on Mt. Veeder, in the Mayacamas Range to the west, and Atlas Peak to the east, where he has plans to eventually build a winery. His vineyard holdings have now expanded to an impressive 1,200 acres of Chardonnay and Cabernet. All wines are estate grown and bottled and represent another dimension of Napa wines with their mountain region origins.

Goosecross Cellars

Goosecross is one of Napa's newest wineries (construction of the winery only commenced in 1987, although the first vintage was made in 1982 by winemaker, Patty Sarant).

The owners, Patt and Rey Gorsuch, have been growers in the valley for a number of years and had supplied nearly all their Chardonnay to Far Niente in 1982, 1983 and 1984. Their son, Geoff, has been in charge of construction of the winery and will also oversee its operation.

The vineyard is located in the Turin Rivers appelation of the lower Napa and produces renowned Chardonnay grapes.

An interesting twist is the name Gorsuch meaning "where the goose crossed the stream". For the last eight years, a lone Canadian goose family has stopped in springtime on its northerly migration.

The Gorsuchs have a lovely English Tudor-style home and the winery has been erected adjacent to it with only one wine to concentrate on. The results so far have been outstanding. The name "Goosecross" when associated with leading Chardonnay, is set to become well known indeed.

Joe Heitz is a modern day wine pioneer. When he established Heitz Cellars in the Valley in 1961, less than 20 wineries were operating; today that total is fast approaching 100. His vision and enterprise sparked the remarkable transformation of the last quarter of a century.

Joe's first contact with wine came during World War II when, as a member of the U.S. Airforce, he was stationed in the Central Valley and assisted unloading boxes of grapes into the crusher at the local winery.

After the war he obtained his degree in oenology from U.C. Davis, and in 1949 he joined Gallo for a short time then spent nearly eight years at Beaulieu, which he left to set up the Enology course at Fresno State.

By 1958, he was keen to get back into the mainstream of wine and the Napa Valley, but there were no jobs. His old friend Hanns Kornell helped him arrange $5,000 finance and Joe purchased just over eight acres of grignolino vines on Highway 29, where he still has a tasting room. At the site of his original winery his vineyard holdings have now expanded to 16 acres. In 1964, Joe and his wife Alice, bought 160 acres including a disused winery and an old house in need of restoration, at the end of Taplin Road, off the Silverado Trail. The winery was restored and has been expanded several times. Joe has also bought 90 acres near the Conn Creek winery. Heitz Cellars produce 80% red wines and are nearing their overall target, set by him many years ago, of 40,000 cases annually.

Two of Joe's red wines, "Martha's Vineyard" and "Bella Oaks", both Cabernet Sauvignons, have become classics. Martha's

comes from the Oakville vineyard of Tom and Martha May, 1965 being the first vintage. The Bella Oaks, from the vineyard of the same name, commenced with the 1976 and has appeared every year since, except 1979 when it was not considered up to standard and blended into the Napa Valley Cabernet.

Joe's daughter Kathleen, assists in the marketing, whilst son David is now making the wines along with his father. The "Martha's" and "Bella Oaks" both spend a year in upright American oak vats before spending a further two years in small French oak barriques that have been first "seasoned" by being used for ageing Zinfandel and Pinot Noir. This long wood maturation in the partly

seasoned wood gives them complexity and a balance of flavours that is outstanding.

The Martha's Vineyard of 1984, due for release in early 1989, is absolutely outstanding with its deep ruby/mauve colour, the nose exhibiting cassis-like fruit with some floral violet and rose characters. On the palate, it has a wonderful texture with some mint, spice and a sandalwood/cedar background with soft, but firm tannins — my tasting notes marked it at 19.2 out of a possible 20, one of the highest marks I have awarded out of thousands of wines tasted.

The Heitz family are to be lauded for their contribution to American wine.

Inglenook Vineyards

Inglenook, meaning "a cosy nook by the fireside" hardly seems a likely place for a ship's captain who had made his fortune from the fur trade in Alaska. Gustave Niebaum, was only 37 years old and would have preferred to build a ship rather than a winery. His wife did not agree, so instead they purchased a vineyard already named Inglenook on the main road in Rutherford.

A man of vision and style, he imported vines from Europe and by 1887 had completed a magnificent Gothic style winery, which still impresses today. Niebaum left no stone unturned in his quest for the very best wines. His rewards came with a number of awards from the Paris International Exposition in 1900. Niebaum died in 1908 and the winery closed when Prohibition started in 1920.

Following Prohibition the new era started when Suzanne, Niebaum's widow, arranged for the winery to be reopened in 1933. Carl Bundschu, who had run the famous Gundlach-Bundschu Winery in Sonoma before Prohibition, got things going. Quality wines was the only objective. John Daniel, Niebaum's great nephew, took over the running of the company in 1939.

Inglenook built an enviable reputation for its wines and they were the first to prove the longevity of Napa wines, when old vintages, some from the 19th century, were provided for a commemorative dinner of the San Francisco Wine and Food Society in 1939.

Daniel started varietal labelling in 1940, when it was still very much a novelty. The "Navelle" name, after a creek on the Estate, was introduced by Daniel in 1935 as a brand name for a Rose, certainly a wine style not common in its day.

Although Daniel was involved in the operation of the winery until his death in 1970, Inglenook was sold to the Heublien Group in 1964, who showed considerable foresight in completing one of the first buy outs of leading wineries at the beginning of the wine boom. As the winery expanded a new crushing and fermenting facility was built at Oakville. The original winery became a maturation cellar and a new bottling facility was built.

Through an arrangement with Allied Grape Growers, access to 1,500 acres of Napa grapes was achieved. The range of Inglenook wines also grew to include other coastal counties, although the Napa wines have all remained under the Estate bottled label. One wine which, more than any other, has built Inglenook's reputation and that of the famed "Rutherford Bench" area is

Cabernet Sauvignon and the famous Inglenook "Cask Selection" is still a most sought after wine. Inglenook premium win cover a large range of price and style and their quality and value has grown over rec years. The gracious old winery is magnificer presented with many items of interest for visitor — a compulsory call on the main Na wine route.

Robert Keenan Winery

High up Spring Mountain Road is another of the successful hillside vineyards established in recent years. Robert Keenan had his own insurance company in San Francisco and, in 1977, purchased a 45 acre, overgrown vineyard and deserted stone winery, built in 1904, but not operated since 1937.

Using what was left of the original structure, he re-built and re-modelled it, putting in modern winemaking equipment. Robert re-planted the vineyard and winemaking re-commenced under Joe Cafaro, who had made wine for Donn Chappellet at his mountain vineyard, on the opposite side of the Valley. (He left Keenan in 1984).

The wines, particularly the Cabernet Sauvignon and Merlot, already highly regarded, have gone from strength to strength and are definitely propositions for long bottle ageing. A Chardonnay is produced, which is in the crisp, more elegant style, somewhat reminiscent of a French Chablis.

The Spring Mountain area overlooking St. Helena is particularly attractive. It is worth calling ahead and arranging a visit to this vineyard.

La Jota Vineyard Company

Bill and Joan Smith were looking for a retreat and somewhere to grow a few acres of vines. Near the state forest in the Howell Mountain area, east of the Napa Valley, they found a pre-Prohibition stone winery. They bought the property and after several years, had planted 30 acres of vines deciding they would like to make wine, which Bill had done as a hobby in the past as a break from his oil and gas business. The old winery was restored.

Today it is a real showpiece, outfitted with the beautiful 100 year old oval casks from the original Cresta Blanca Cellars, in Livermore. This historic connection is rather apt, as the winery previously produced wines that won awards at the Paris Exhibition in 1900. Although their wines only came onto the market in 1986, they have been well received and Joan in particular, has been travelling far and wide finding ready markets for them.

The Hess Collection

In the rugged mountain terrain of Mt. Veeder, Swiss businessman Donald Hess has spent more than a decade quietly carving out a world class vineyard and winery. Intent upon taming the powerful mountain grapes produced along the westerly rim of the Napa Valley, he has made a long-term commitment to achieving elegance, refinement and drinkability in The Hess Collection's Cabernet Sauvignon and Chardonnay wines, while maintaining the best of the concentrated aromas and flavours that characterise these hillside grapes.

He has approached this challenge with the same enthusiasm and business acumen that earlier led to successful diversification of his family's Swiss brewing interest into mineral water, agriculture, restaurant, international real estate and wine negotiant businesses, which are headquartered in Bern, Switzerland.

While on a California business trip in the late 1970's, Mr. Hess discovered first-hand the Napa Valley's growing stature as a wine region. With family ties in America (his mother was American and his wife is from Boston) he was immediately drawn to the prospect of participating in Napa Valley's emergence as a producer of world class wines. Studying the components of wine quality, he concluded that a key element was a reliable, uninterrupted source of premium grapes. He began assembling a group of vineyards on Mt. Veeder which have the ideal micro-climate and the rocky, well-drained soils to produce wines of great structure and flavour. Today, 900 acres of prime Mt. Veeder vineyard land make up The Hess Vineyards, with 280 acres of mature vines and another 160 acres to be planted, predominantly in Cabernet Sauvignon and Chardonnay varietals.

The Hess Collection's viticulture and enology team, all experienced with mountain grapes, has devoted ten years to studying the performance of these vineyards and developing a consistent winemaking style, blending small lots of wine from various parts of the vineyards. Robert Craig, who managed the vineyards with an earlier partnership, is the General Manager. A graduate of the University of Chicago with a masters degree in business, he combines management skills with an abiding affection for the mountain vineyards. Winemaker Randle Johnson is the resident expert working with Mt. Veeder grapes. In addition to an M.S. in viticulture from the University of California at Davis, he gained first-hand knowledge of mountain-grown grapes at Mayacamas, Stag's Leap Winery and the original Souverain Winery.

In 1986, a 50-year lease was signed with the Christian Brothers for the Mont La Salle

The Hess Collection

Winery facility near The Hess Vineyards. This historic winery is being restored and outfitted to be open to visitors in early 1989. Traditional wine making techniques are emphasized, such as open top, punch-down fermentation tanks, aging in French oak and extended bottle maturation. Mr. Hess will also house a major portion of his extensive contemporary art collection within the vine-covered walls of the original stone winery building, which was constructed in 1903. The aim is to have the wine and art operations complement each other, while having their own independent identity.

The Hess Collection's first Cabernet Sauvignon releases have been acclaimed as wines of extraordinary depth and character. They are drinkable while young, without sacrificing ageability. The Chardonnay is crisp in style, with pronounced varietal character and interesting complexity. Although made to

enjoy immediately, both the red and white wine have the firm structure necessary for aging potential.

The patience, commitment and long-term perspective which Donald Hess has brought to this unique winery bodes well for

the future of The Hess Collection and the reputation of the mountain vineyards that are the backbone of these world-class wines.

THE HESS COLLECTION WINERY
Address: 4411 Redwood Road, Napa, CA., 94558
Phone: 707/255 1144
Owner: Donald M. Hess
Winemaker: Randle Johnson
Principal Varieties Grown: Cabernet Sauvignon, Merlot, Cabernet Franc, Chardonnay
Acres Under Vine: 280 and planting 480
Average Annual Crush: 500 tons

Principal Wines & Brands	Cellar Potential (Years)
1983 Cabernet Sauvignon	3-6
1983/84 Cabernet Sauvignon Reserve	4-10/5-10
1986 Chardonnay	2-5
1985 Cabernet Sauvignon	4-10

Trade Tours – Available
Retail Room Sales – Available
Hours open to Public – Phone for hours
Retail Distribution – California and 6 other states

Hanns Kornell Champagne Cellar

It is a miracle that Hanns Kornell ever managed to make champagne in America at all. With the help of an American friend he had met whilst hitch-hiking through Italy three years before, he managed to arrange a release from the infamous Dachau prison camp, where, as a German Jew, he had been interned for a year. That was in 1939, when Hanns fled with less than $2.00 in his pocket, first to England, but soon after to America, where he arrived in New York in 1940.

He hitch-hiked across the continent to California and got labouring jobs. Hann's father had been a champagne master and Hanns himself was a graduate of the Geisenheim Enolgical Institute. He desperately wanted to get back into champagne making, in which he had worked in France and Italy. His chance came when the new owner of the historic Fountain Grove Winery in Santa Rosa started producing champagne. From here he travelled east making champagne for the Gibson Winery in Kentucky and at the famous Cooks Imperial Champagne Cellars in St. Louis.

By 1952, Hanns was ready to strike out on his own, he did this by leasing the old Tribuno Winery in Sonoma for $100 per month with a $3,000 loan from a friend to buy equipment. He produced by night and sold by day, until he had accumulated enough capital by 1958 to purchase the Larkmead winery in St. Helena, an attractive stone winery built around 1870. He also married Marie-Louise Rossini, whose grandfather started the Souverain Vineyard. She immediately involved herself in the business and remains his right hand helper to this day. Their children Paula, Peter-Hanns, in their twenties are now involved also.

Hanns Kornell is one of the very few American winemakers still making champagne by the full traditional Methode Champenoise technique — that is every bottle is individually fermented, shaken down on racks, checked with a candle flame and finally disgorged of its yeast plug, which is frozen in the neck of the bottle by inverting it in a chilled solution. This process means handling the bottle some 200 times — it is expensive, but Hanns says: "When your name is on the label, you have to put something of yourself in the bottle".

Hanns makes champagne from many different cuvee's (base wines), all of which he blends himself, after carefully choosing the wines and purchasing them from other wineries.

Hanns': premier Cuvee is the "Signature" made from Johannisberg Riesling, using a 25 year old cognac-based dosage. Older vintages have been known to fetch astronomic prices at auctions.

Truly a pioneer in the premium champagne field in America, Hanns along with his family, richly deserve their success.

Lakespring Winery

I t is unusual for three brothers to get on well enough to start a new business together. Frank, Ralph and Harry Battat were already partners in a successful food processing and exporting company, Liberty Golf Fruit company, wine was a natural diversification for them.

Although Frank was a successful home winemaker, the brothers decided they needed an expert. In 1980 they hired Randy Mason, a U.C. Davis graduate and let him design the winery. Randy was given a free hand to put in the best equipment possible.

Five varietal wines are produced, Chardonnay, Chenin Blanc, Sauvignon Blanc, Merlot and Cabernet Sauvignon. The accent is on quality with a limited production. Suitably enough their second label is called "Trois Freres".

Lakespring is situated just south of Yountville, west of Highway 29.

Silverado Hill Cellars

At present there are over 30 acres of vines — only Chardonnay Pinot Noir and Sauvignon Blanc are grown.

The total production of the winery is supplied to the Hotel and Restaurant trade. The wines have been showing a constant improvement and the future looks bright for this exclusive small winery.

SILVERADO HILL CELLARS
Address: 3105 Silverado Trail, Napa, CA., 94558
Phone: 707/253 9306
Year of Establishment: 1979
Owner: Stockholder of the Corporation
Winemaker: Dr. John D. Nemeth
Principal Varieties Grown: Chardonnay, Sauvignon Blanc
Acres Under Vine: 30
Average Annual Crush: 300 tons

Principal Wines & Brands	Cellar Potential (Years)
Napa Valley Chardonnay, Estate	10
Art in Wine – Wine in Art	10
Napa Valley Pinot Noir	8

Trade Tours – Available by appointment only
Hours open to Public – 9am to 4pm weekdays; special arrangements for weekends
Retail Distribution – Los Angeles & 9 other states and Japan

I n 1986, Minami Kyushi, the bottlers of Coca-Cola in California bought this winery, resurrected in 1982 by Louis Mihaly, a Hungarian born international businessman who with John Nemeth, also Hungarian, with a winemaking degree from the University of Budapest, had started the "Pannonia Winery" with other partners in 1979.

The winery in the south part of the Valley facing the Silverado Trail had fallen on hard financial times. Mihaly came to the rescue and the name was changed to his own. Although Louis is retired from his other business he became very involved with the winery. Under the new owners the plan is to only make and bottle wines from the estate.

Charles Krug Winery

Charles Krug was the first commercial winery in the Napa Valley, founded by a Prussian immigrant, Charles Krug who first came to America in 1847. A teacher, he returned to Germany, but finding the political scene not to his liking returned to America becoming the editor of a German newspaper published in Oakland.

He became interested in wine and followed Haraszthy to Sonoma, where he worked for him at Buena Vista for two years, he also befriended General Vallejo and married his grandniece, the dowry from her father Dr. Edward T. Bale, was a 7,000 acre property at St. Helena. In 1861 Krug started planting and the following year built the winery.

His wines proved very successful and he became a leading industry figure but had problems to contend with. The winery burnt down in 1875 and again in 1880. Phylloxera followed and, by 1892 when he died, the estate was in debt. The winery continued under his nephew with new owners but closed at Prohibition. After repeal it opened and after a shaky start was purchased in 1943 by the Mondavi family. This marked the start of a remarkable contribution to American wines by this highly respected family.

Cesare Mondavi arrived in America in 1906, after working in the iron mines in Northern Minnesota he commenced a grocery business there. In 1922, he moved to Lodi in California and became involved in the grape business. He did very well during Prohibition shipping grapes east and survived the Depression. Both Cesare's sons Peter and Robert attended Stanford University and on graduating expressed a wish to become involved in the wine industry. Cesare by this time was making some wine at the Acampo winery at Lodi. He believed, however, that the future was in quality table wine, the Napa Valley in particular.

So, in 1937 he bought the Sunny St. Helena Winery. By this time his sons had studied winemaking, under professors from the University of California and immediately started innovating. Peter was the first to utilise cold fermentation for white wines in 1937 and the first to use inert gas cover of wines along with sterile filtration. In 1943 the family bought Charles Krug and it wasn't long before the wines started winning awards.

In 1957, Peter Mondavi introduced the first glass lined tank to the wine industry,

Charles Krug Winery

Charles Krug now has 3,500,000 gallons of these vessels with individual tanks up to 35,000 gallons capacity. They are all temperature controlled and the wines are stored around 38°F, a real advantage with white wines as it keeps the flavours young and fresh.

The introduction of these tanks came about when blends at Krug became large and had to bottle several times a year.

In 1965, Robert left to start his own winery and shortly after this Peter was joined by his two sons Marc, who studied at Davis and Pete Jnr., who graduated in engineering from Stanford. Between them they have created an amazing winery with the most modern equipment and computer technology it is both efficient and offers excellent quality control.

The Krug grounds are superb, Charles also ran a big horse ranch and the Carriage house now makes a wonderful wine cellar,

between 58°F — 62°F.

The Mondavis were the first to introduce a winery newsletter and their quarterly "Bottles and Bins" has been published for over 40 years. The August concert series held on the lawns amongst the gardens on summer evenings were the first such events held in the Valley they and other events are held regularly.

The greatest surprise about Charles Krug wines is their price. Whilst at the winery in 1988, I tasted a 1985 California Chardonnay and a 1981 Burgundy — a Pinot blend. Both sold at around $3.50 and were extremely good wines. Even their Napa varietal wines and their "Vintage Select" Cabernets often up to ten years old when released, are very reasonably priced.

The Mondavis are involved in every stage of winemaking and taste everything before it is bottled.

Markham Winery has certainly made its mark in the Napa Valley since its inception over a decade ago. In fact it has just been acquired from Bruce Markham and his family by Japanese interests.

Markham Winery is housed in a creeper-clad stone building which was originally constructed in 1876 for the St. Helena Growers Co-operative.

In the mid 1970's, Bruce Markham began purchasing vineyards in the valley, acquiring interests in Yountville, Oak Knoll and Calistoga. With 300 acres of vines at his disposal, he decided to build a winery. Perhaps his highly visible site just north of St. Helena, on the main road had something do do with his years of success in the outdoor advertising business.

With the pick of his 300 acres to choose from (as two-thirds of the crop was sold to other wineries) Bruce's wines started to win acclaim. The chief varietals produced are Cabernet Sauvignon, Chardonnay and Sauvignon Blanc, although others, such as Johannisberg Riesling, Chenin Blanc and Merlot are also produced and, occasionally, a Muscat de Froutignac and a Gamay Blanc are made.

The Markham label features an antique cannon symbolising Bruce's four years as a gunnery officer in Korea.

Winemaker Robert Foley has taken on extra responsibilities since the takeover. He i a talented and energetic young man, who seems suited to management as well as his winemaking role at this well respected winery.

Robert Mondavi Winery

I f wine were a religion surely its "Messiah" would be Robert Mondavi — his mission to preach the gospel of wine. His message, a very clear one — "wine is an integral part of civilised living".

Much has been written about this extraordinary man who, I believe is today's most influential wine person world wide. His influence covers all continents, not only to winemakers but to all, he delights in sharing his knowledge and experience, even his dreams with. I often wonder whether Bob really ever experiences the peace and contentment his achievements and endeavours should richly reward him with, so restless is his need, in his own words: "To strive, to seek, to find", always looking for a better wine and a better way to spread the gospel. Now in his 75th year, he has more drive, enthusiasm and sheer zest for life than one man half his age could even aspire to.

Bob was born to Italian immigrants, his father Cesare having migrated in 1906, after two years of toil in the iron mines of north east Minnesota. He returned in 1908 with his bride Rosa, then only a teenager. Bob cannot remember his first taste of wine only that: "I had it from the beginning even with a teaspoon. My mother always used it". Although they struggled early in life, his mother took in young Italian boarders and there were never less than 15 male mouths to feed and clothes to wash.

Bob acknowledges it was from her his drive sprang. Always the best she could afford was never enough, there was always something more to strive for. Cesare, meanwhile, bought a saloon and later a grocery business.

With the onset of Prohibition a family was still allowed to make 200 gallons of its own wine per year. Cesare started supplying grapes, then in 1922 he moved his family to Lodi in the Delta region of California, where he set up a grape supply business. The family prospered, after repeal Cesare started making some wine at the Acampo Winery.

By then Bob and his brother Peter were at Stanford University and, they both expressed an interest in wine as a career. Bob actually changed his course to include some chemistry and took some private tuition from University of California professors.

In 1937 the family purchased the Sunny St. Helena Winery, in the Napa Valley, producing mostly bulk wine for bottling by others. Seeing the future in quality table wines the family purchased the historic, but troubled Charles Krug winery in 1943. Bob replanted its hundred acres of vines with classic varieties. Charles Krug grew to be one of the leading and most respected wineries in the Valley, winning many awards for its wines. Bob's drive and push brought him into some conflict with his brother Peter, and with a growing family, all interested in going into the business, Bob decided to leave and start his own winery in 1965. As his site he chose

the To-Kalon Vineyards near Oakville, made famous by Hamilton Crabb in the last century the winery however, had burnt down in 1939. Renowned American architect, Cliff May, was commissioned to design a winery, his California ranch house style with, its wide arch, bell tower and low verandahs, blends so well into its environment, almost as if it grew there!!

Robert Mondavi proceeded to replant the vineyards and the winery was opened in 1966. During the next decade with the situation at Charles Krug still not resolved, Bob still had to work as a consultant to other wineries, as well as selling 82% of the shares in his company to make ends meet. In 1978, with the settlement of the Krug issue, Bob was able to buy back a 50% interest a brewery held in his company.

The distinctive Robert Mondavi label, designed by wood engraver, Mallette Dean, features a line drawing of the winery. It is an ageless classic.

Bob is ably assisted in the business by his three children, Michael, the eldest and a science graduate from the University of Santa Clara and President since 1978 and in charge of planning and marketing. His other son Tim, a U.C. Davis graduate is Vice President in charge of production, whilst his daughter Marcia, is Eastern Vice President, spreading the Mondavi message out of New York.

Much of Bob's inspiration comes from his wife Margrit. Swiss born, she was employed by him to run his guided tour programme and public relations area. She speaks six languages and is one of the few people I have met who can keep up to Robert's energy level. She has created a wonderful complex at the winery beautifully balancing art, music and food with the joys of wine. The Sunny Vineyard Room is the focus of this effort. One of the highlights of the Mondavi cultural year is the annual summer jazz festival, which features leading jazz from around the world, but always highlighted by the Preservation Hall Jazz Band. Margrit still uses the name from her first marriage — Biever. It is a second marriage for both of them and one of the happiest one could witness.

The Mondavi wines, exciting from the start have developed a worldwide reputation. Bob however, is never satisfied with the status-quo, always seeking to improve on previous vintages. Bob is not necessarily wishing to say he has the best wine but rather each vintage is an improvement on its predecessor all his wines however, are world class and generally acknowledged as such.

"We've only scratched the surface we can learn forever . . . we are just beginning to understand what winemaking is all about".

Robert Mondavi has been responsible for many Californian and some world wine advances. He was first to introduce barrel fermentation in 1962 and in 1971 created a new wine style which carried a new name of "Fume Blanc" — a wood aged Sauvignon Blanc. Somewhat like a French Pouilly Fume, but in his own unique style, it saw the plantings of Sauvignon Blanc in the Napa leap from 700 to 10,000 acres in little over 10 years. The main wines produced at his Oakville winery are Cabernet Sauvignon, Fume Blanc, Chardonnay, Pinot Noir and Johannisberg Riesling. He uses a little Cabernet Franc and Merlot to balance his Cabernet Sauvignon and a touch of Semillion in the Fume Blanc.

On February 29, 1984 Bob pulled off the greatest wine coup in the world when the first "Opus One" wines were released, both the 1979 and 1980 vintages. This marked the culmination of 14 years of discussion between Bob and the recently deceased Baron Phillipe de Rothschild, from Mouton Rothschild in Bordeaux, far outshadowing any other joint venture in wine — it has been an outstanding success.

In the early 1970's, Bob helped start the significant "Leeuwin Estate" Winery in the south of Western Australia.

Bob continues with his family and fiercely loyal team around him — its like one big happy family, all totally committed to the mission — you must visit there. Bob also has the Woodbridge Winery at Lodi, but more of that in another chapter.

Robert Mondavi's mission is not only to sell Mondavi wine, but to sell the very idea of wine.

Monticello Cellars

Although only founded in 1980, Monticello cellars has already developed a formidable reputation for both its varietal and generic table wines.

Founder and owner, Jay Corley is a life long fan of Thomas Jefferson and his attempts to establish classic grape varieties 200 years ago. In fact, he has gone as far as building a replica of Jefferson's Virginian home ''Monticello'' on his 200 acre vineyard.

Jay's family came from Virginia and were also involved in agricultural pursuits there. Jay has certainly led a varied life and is an accomplished Italian linguist as well as having been involved in entrepreneurial and investment business in Southern California.

The winery and vineyard are situated just off the Silverado Trail in the southern part of the Valley. Jay selects the best of his crop for his Monticello wines and sells the rest to other wineries. Monticello also has several second labels: ''Cranbrook Cellars'' under which lower priced varietals are produced. ''Jefferson Cellars'' for generic wines at very affordable prices, such as his Claret and Vin Blanc and ''Chateau M'' for the exclusive and Private Reserve wines.

Quail Ridge

Elaine Wellesley comes from an interesting and varied background. She has gone through some tough times but has perservered and her wines are now highly repected and sought after.

Elaine was born in South Africa, but spent some time in England, then moved into a career in journalism and finally through an interest in wine ended up at U.C. Davis studying Enology.

She and her husband, Jesse Corallo, planted a vineyard on the slopes of Mt. Veeder in the Mayacama Mountains, then set up a winery on the opposite side of the Valley, in the abandoned century-old Hedyeside Distillery on Atlas Peak Road. When Jesse, who had been handling the sales and marketing, unfortunately died, Leon Santoro who has worked with Warren Wisniarski at the high profile Stags Leap Wine Cellars, joined the business. Leon has an engaging personality and has helped put Quail Ridge on the map. It is unusual for a small winery to have equally high billing for their red and white wines. Quail Ridge has been successful in this with their Chardonnay and their Cabernet Sauvignon.

Louis M Martini

The Louis M. Martini Winery is the quiet achiever of the Napa Valley having probably the greatest family involvement of any of the larger wineries. This involvement is best evidenced by the recent releases; "Los Ninos" — the children. Two wines, Reserve Cabernet Sauvignons from 1981 and 1982, have been released with labels featuring paintings by Shanna and Jessica, daughters of winemaker Michael and fifth generation members of this winemaking dynasty.

That the fourth generation Carolyn Martini was made President of the company whilst still in her 30's, is evidence of the increasing role and importance of women in wine.

It is a tribute to Louis Martini that all his vineyard sites are in regions which have lately become the focus of the industry. They also have varied soils and micro-climates which enable a range of grape varieties and, therefore, wines to be successfully made.

The wide viticultural base with over 15 grape varieties in seven regions enables many different wine styles to be produced.

Louis M. Martini offer a large range of excellent wines. Their prices are extremely competitive and represent some of the best values in Napa Valley. Both Louis M. and his son Louis P. have been awarded the rare and prestigious American Society Of Enologist's Merit Award, the current and future generations of the family look set to follow their example.

Newton Winery

One would expect the man chiefly behind the concept and building of the magnificent Sterling Winery to do something stunning when he set out on his own. English born Peter Newton has done more than that. Along with his charming Chinese wife, Su Hua, who has a doctorate degree in clinical psychology, they have created a veritable Xanadu on the slope of Spring Mountain.

The view of the Valley is breathtaking. The 560 acre mountain property was purchased in 1978, with 60 acres now under vine in the steeply terraced vineyard, which is meticulously kept. Some expansion is planned but much of the property is too steep to plant, elevations vary from 500-1,300 ft. The plantings are all Bordeaux red varieties chiefly Cabernet Sauvignon and Merlot, but with a little Cabernet Franc and Petit Verdot.

Above the Shangri-la like fermentation cellar a Chinese garden has been planted and a pagoda like tower perches on top, where winemaker John Kongsgaard can survey the whole domain with the Valley spread out before him.

John had some pretty big boots to fill, when he replaced Ric Forman, who came from Sterling to start the winery with the Newtons. A man of considerable physical stature and cultural refinement he has succeeded admirably. John's background includes time spent in leading wineries: Stony Hill and Stag's Leap as well as setting up and running Balverne Winery and Vineyards in Sonoma County.

John, who looks more like a football fullback, has a great interest in classical music and in fact is the impressario of a string quartet in San Francisco, for he is a musicologist by training and worked in this field in Europe.

John is also a great fan of Bordeaux and shares a love with me of Pichon Lalande. His wines, however, don't stand in any shadows. Tasting his 1985 Cabernet Sauvignon was one of the real pleasures of compiling this Atlas. A deep mauve in colour the bouquet was extremely penetrating with a distinct floral character along with rich berry aromas that are reflected on the palate. The wine has a subtle character from wood ageing.

The Newtons live in a spectacular home and garden they have built on the property. Dr. Su Hua lectures in wine marketing at the University of San Francisco, while Peter is still involved with the Sterling paper empire.

Newton Winery and its wines are literally the crowning jewel of the Napa. A visit is by appointment only, but for those serious about the ulitmate winery experience it is compulsory.

Napa Valley from
Newton Vineyard

The "Winged-Horse" is definitely leading the race to be Napa's most striking winery, according to the ancient legend: "Where his hooves broke the earth, a grotto emerged yielding the sacred spring of the muses and the god of wine became their favourite pupil".

The winery has more than a touch of Greco-Roman flavour in its post-modern style.

The design, by architect Michael Graves, was actually chosen in a competition held by the San Francisco Museum of Modern Art. Equally striking is owner Jan Shrem's house perched on top of the knoll, overlooking the winery. The Grecian pillars, porticos and grandeur of the building are offset by the muted terracotta colour and other earthtones enabling it to fit happily, if not subtly into the Napa environment.

Bringing the project to fruition has not been an easy task for Shrem with considerable resistance at local government level to the design mainly because Jan also planned the building as a museum to display his collection of surrealist art. Many locals and environmentalists are fighting a further invasion of tourists.

Jan Shrem's inspiration for the winery came partly from his many years living in France and some investments that brought him into contact with the wine industry. The winery is extremely well equipped and nothing has been spared, drives (caves) have been carved into the knoll behind the winery, providing ideal storage temperature and humidity for the ageing wines. There are ten

tall French oak vats from Demptos for use in the malolactic fermentation of red wine. These are aesthetically very pleasing and look at home in the main cellar.

The winery eventually went ahead but the first vintage was made at the Rombauer Winery under legendary winemaker, Andre Tchelistcheff's guiding hand in 1985. The second harvest, in 1986, comprising almost 60,000 gallons was crushed at the new winery and made by winemaker, Bill Pease, who had formerly worked at Konocti in Lake County. Prior to that he had made wine in Indiana and Kentucky. Clos Pegase is fortunate still to have the consulting services of Tchelistcheff.

Schrem himself is a somewhat retiring character, softly spoken and physically small in stature. But, don't be fooled. He loves a challenge and his voice picks up a sense of excitement as he describes some of the many he has faced in his time. He began publishing in Japan just after the Second World War, where the hunger for western knowledge was great, (his wife, Matzsuko is Japanese). He also became involved in real estate investment and lived in Paris for some years — investments in vineyards added to his growing interest in wine. He debated whether or not to enter the winemaking industry in France, but opted eventually for Napa with its wonderful climate and the opportunity to create a suitable home for himself, his art and his winemaking aspirations.

Clos Pegase is making three wines: a Sauvignon Blanc, Chardonnay and a Cabernet Sauvignon. Nothing has been spared in the pursuit of excellence. The 1985 Sauvignon Blanc, the first release. was in the crisp herbaceous style and well received. This was followed by the Chardonnay. The Cabernet has just been released early in 1988; it is in the elegant style now fashionable.

Jan is a quiet perfectionist who also has a deep belief in the role of wine in civilisation going back thousands of years. A large part of his gallery is devoted to this theme, which makes for an extremely interesting and enlightening visit along with the fine wines and the architectural marvel he has created.

Pine Ridge Winery

Gary Andrus' connection with wine came about in a most unusual way. As a member of the U.S. ski team, he met an Australian skier whose family had a small winery in the Barossa Valley in South Australia. On a subsequent trip to Australia, Gary visited her and became enchanted with wines.

Although his business interests stayed with skiing, including an involvement in a ski resort at Copper Mountain in his home state of Colorado, he still thought a lot about the wine industry and in 1977, he and his wife Nancy, started buying vineyard land near Stag's Leap on the east side of the Napa Valley.

Their first vintage was in 1978 and crushed at another winery and in 1979 they built a winery around an old home in a beautiful steep sided valley on the Silverado

Trail. The property had been owned by a Swiss Italian, connected with I.S.C., who had made wine in an underground cellar beneath the house even through Prohibition. Gary now uses this cellar for barrel ageing his Chardonnay, Cabernet and Merlot.

The winery is surrounded by steeply terraced vineyards and is named for the grove of pine trees that grows on top of the ridge.

Gary has taken classes at U.C. Davis and works very hard in the winery. His first assistant was New Zealander Grant Taylor, now at Domaine de Napa, while, Davis graduate Stacy Clark is assisting. The Merlot (with a little Cabernet Sauvignon, Cabernet Franc and Malbec) is a particular favourite of Gary's and an exceptional wine.

Robert Pepi Winery

Just off Highway 29 going northwards from Yountville is the Robert Pepi Winery. Housed in an attractive stone building sitting on top of a rocky outcrop, it looks most imposing and yet blends well into the terrain.

The Pepi family have a winemaking background in Italy. Robert A. Pepi moved to the Napa Valley and began growing grapes in 1966, after a career in San Francisco as a fur

dresser. After some 15 years, with his son Robert L. now involved, they decided to start a winery.

Having evaluated the various grape varieties on their vineyards over the years they decided to concentrate on Sauvignon Blanc and Semillon, but now they also produce a Chardonnay. The Pepis have been very successful with their Semillon, perhaps because of the cool climate of this part of the

valley.

The Pepi wines show the crisp fruit and grassy herbaceousness typical of this variety and pick up a lovely honey-citrus character as they age. Although not producing wines for long the Pepis have a great feel for what they do and are almost veterans compared with many winemaking operations in the Valley.

Raymond Vineyard & Cellar

The Raymonds have a genuine feel for wine, which has always been their sole livelihood. The wines they make are rich and complex, truly reflecting their thoroughbred creators.

RAYMOND VINEYARD & CELLAR
Address: 849 Zinfandel Lane, St. Helena, CA., 94574
Phone: 707/963 3141
Year of Establishment: 1974
Owner: Roy Raymond Snr., Roy Jnr., Walter
Winemaker: Walter Raymond
Principal Varieties Grown: Chardonnay, Cabernet Sauvignon
Acres Under Vine: 80
Average Annual Crush: 2,200 tons

Principal Wines & Brands	Cellar Potential (Years)
Napa Valley Chardonnay	2-4
California Chardonnay	2
Sauvignon Blanc	1-2
Cabernet Sauvignon	8-10

Trade Tours – Available by appointment only
Retail Room Sales – Available
Hours open to Public – Daily from 10am to 4pm
Retail Distribution – National

The Raymond family are down-to-earth, warm and friendly people for wine has been their life in the Napa Valley for five generations. Their ancestry goes back to Jacob Beringer, founder of Beringer Brothers Winery in 1876, where his grand-daughter, Martha married Roy Raymond. She died in 1986, but Roy Snr. is still very active in the Raymond operation, although in his mid 70's.

Roy Snr. made the wine at Beringer for 33 years until the Nestle takeover in 1971. Following the sale of Beringer, he began planting a 70 acre vineyard off Zinfandel Lane with his two sons Walter and Roy Jnr, but now this vineyard only supplies about 20% of their requirements. The Raymonds have long term relationships with 55 growers from all over the valley, some going back several generations. This ensures them of the right blend of grapes for each of their wine styles.

Walter is the winemaker whilst Roy Jnr. manages the vineyards. The brothers have also helped establish the Guenoc Vineyards and Winery in Lake County, for the Magoon family. This relationship developed through the Raymond's hunting excursions to the giant Guenoc ranch begun many years ago. When Orville Magoon took over, he met them and expressed his interest in recommencing winemaking, first undertaken there by the legendary Lillie Langtry. From 1981 until 1986, the brothers looked after the vineyard and made the wine until they became too busy with their own Raymond operations.

Some grapes are also obtained from one of California's most northerly vineyards, on the slopes of Mt. Shasta.

Walter is a very experienced and competent winemaker, having assisted his father at Beringer. Fifth generation member Terri, Roy Jnr's. daughter is now involved, having completed her studies at San Francisco State University.

Rombauer Vineyards

K oerner and Joan Rombauer were partners in the setting up of Conn Creek Winery. In 1980, they decided to establish their own winery, which they did, high on a heavily wooded hill overlooking the Silverado Trail, in the St. Helena area of the Napa Valley. Koerner is the grand-nephew of the famous author of the, "Joy of Cooking" Joy Rombauer and is also a pilot for Pacific East Airline.

Work on the large winery with all modern winemaking equipment started in 1982. Although the output of Rombauer Winery is substantial, only a small, but growing portion is marketed under the Rombauer label. Much of the grapes processed are custom-crushed for other vineyards and wineries, both large and small.

The design and efficiency of the facility are a tribute to Koerner's talent in this area and the reputation of Rombauer in their custom making capacity is extremely high. Many of the more illustrious of the new wineries of Napa had their first wines made here.

The main wines marketed by Rombauer are their Cabernet Sauvignon and Chardonnay along with a top Bordeaux blend of Cabernet Sauvignon, Merlot and Cabernet Franc. It's not easy to find this secluded winery, but worth the effort to buy some of their great wines.

Round Hill Cellars

With sales fast approaching 300,000 cases of premium wine and the accolade of "1986 American Winery Of The Year" (International Wine Review) under its belt, Round Hill has really "arrived" on the wine scene. Their exciting new winery on the Silverado Trail just beneath Rutherford Hill is the culmination of a market driven success story that goes back to 1977.

Ernie Van Asperen of "Ernie's Liquor Store" fame had become accustomed to searching out wines for bottling and selling at great value prices in his 85 stores through Northern California. He decided to start up a brand as a negociant and supply other stores. With his wife, Virginia, they went into a partnership with Charles Abela, a former fisherman, skilled in engineering and building. Jointly they leased an old stone winery near Freemark Abbey and named it Round Hill, after the Jamaican resort where the Van Asperens had honeymooned

The secret of their phenomenal growth has been giving the public very good varietal wines at value prices particularly under the "House" label. The Roundhill "House" Chardonnay released in 1983 was the first of the "fighting varietals" priced well under $5 per bottle.

Gradually Round Hill became less reliant on bought-in wines and today most of the wine is being made at the new winery, where winemaker Mark Swain presides, with a crush for 1988 of around 2,000 tons. Mark is highly trained in viticulture as well as enology and his infectious enthusiasm has created a dynamic atmosphere all his staff share in.

Round Hill also have a range of Napa Varietal wines positioned under $10 a bottle retail. A second label "Rutherford Ranch" is used for their most expensive reserve wines.

The new winery has come together in double quick time. The 10 acre property with some Cabernet vines already planted had a permit for a winery to be constructed as an Australian group, under Len Evans, had obtained one and planned to build on the property until his partner Peter Fox died in a car accident.

Round Hill have one of America's most striking wine labels recently updated under Virginia Van Asperen's watchful eye by design team Colonna and Farrell from St. Helena. The Royal blue with gold fold is most distinctive and classy.

The tasting room and visitors centre at the new winery will be run by Public Relations Director, Lee Hodor, a lady with a great sense of style and taste, who previously worked at the up-market Jordan Vineyards and Winery in the Alexander Valley.

Round Hill already a most significant winery is set to expand its horizons even further. Its "Quality plus Value" philosophy is never out of date.

ROUND HILL WINERY
Address: 1680 Silverado Trail, St. Helena, CA., 94574
Phone: 707/963 5251
Year of Establishment: 11 years
Winemaker: Mark Swain
Principal Varieties Grown: Cabernet, Pinot Noir, Petit Sirah, Chardonnay
Acres Under Vine: 107
Average Annual Crush: 1,100 tons

Principal Wines & Brands	Cellar Potential (Years)
Round Hill Reserve Chardonnay	
Round Hill Reserve Cabernet	
Round Hill Reserve Merlot	

Trade Tours – Available by appointment only
Retail Room Sales – Available
Hours open to Public –
retail sales 7 days a week 10am to 4.30pm
Retail Distribution – Nationally

Joseph Phelps Vineyards

Joe Phelps came to California in 1972 to construct three wineries for Pillsbury Mills of Minnesota including the Souverain Winery in Napa (now Rutherford Hill Winery). His Colorado construction firm Hansell-Phelps is still involved in heavy construction including bridges and freeways.

Joe fell in love with Napa and bought 250 acres just east of the Silverado Trail in the St. Helena area. The winery was constructed in 1973; set high above the vineyard it is an imposing building. There is a huge central pergola area, which was covered in blooming wisteria on the day of my visit. Joe's office sits right on top of the winery with a superb panoramic view of the vineyards with the centre of the Valley beyond the hills that encompass his main

Spring Valley Vineyard.

All in all, Joseph Phelps now has 672 acres of vines in the Napa Valley, the Spring Valley Vineyard of 177 acres around the winery, a further vineyard in the Stag's Leap area (mainly Cabernet Sauvignon) and a further vineyard on Manley Lane in the renowned Rutherford Bench area. Nine varieties are grown and all appear at Spring Valley, the first planted.

Two unusual varieties for Napa, which have proved very successful for Phelps are, first, Scheurebe, a Riesling cross from the Helmut Becker and his team at the Geisenheim Wine Institute in Germany. Phelps has made some superb late harvest wines from this variety. The other — Syrah, sometimes known as Shiraz, one of the main

varieties of the Cote du Rhone region of France (not to be confused with the Petit Syrah (Durif) variety, generally grown in California. The Syrah makes a peppery wine with strong berry aromas and flavours. Walter Schug became the first winemaker at Phelp's.

He came originally from Germany where he trained at Geisenheim. He arrived in California in 1961 and has worked at two previous wineries including Gallo.

Walter certainly made a name for himself at Phelp's particularly with his late harvest wines from Johannisberg Riesling and Scheurebe. However, his Cabernet Sauvignon from the Phelp's Vineyards on the Rutherford Bench and Stag's Leap has also developed quite a reputation.

An important member of the team at

Joseph Phelps Vineyards

Phelp's is Bruce Neyers, who virtually runs the winery on a day-to-day basis, as Joe is still involved in his construction business. Bruce is also in charge of the marketing.

In 1980 he had a desire to make wine again as it was in this area he was first trained and worked. On talking to Joe they decided to set up a partnership which included Bruce's wife Barbara. Bruce commenced winemaking in his spare time and Neyers Winery labels started appearing in 1982.

Joe Phelps is a big thinker whose vision and understanding goes well past the ordinary. He has invested heavily in winemaking equipment and numerous experiments in winemaking and ageing are carried out in a small pilot winery he has set-up. In looking

around his winery, I was struck by the thorough way everything has been done. There are many small tanks and vats as well as French barriques, which enables his winemaking team to separate wines made from the various grape varieties he grows and all the vineyards that he operates.

Joseph Phelp's vineyards purposefully maintains a low profile although a magnificent barrel room overlooking the vineyards is used for special functions. Everything is done by invitation or appointment. It is well worth the trouble to arrange a visit if you are in the Valley.

Rutherford Hill Winery

Rutherford Hill Winery has a magnificent location, its long building clad in creepers commands a panoramic view of the Napa Valley to the west, while, across the road, is the famous restaurant Auberge du Soleil.

The substantial building was built in 1972 by Joe Phelps for the Pillsbury Flour Milling Group from Minneapolis and called "Souverain of Rutherford", after a famous winery of the last century. In 1976, when Pillsbury sold their wine interests it was bought by a syndicate headed by Bill Jaeger and comprising mostly his co-owners of Freemark Abbey. The syndicate's view at the time was to create a second, higher volume label for Freemark.

Phil Baxter, the original Souverain winemaker, who joined in the partnership, had other ideas and has proceeded to make wines that have challenged the best in the Valley. His Cabernet Sauvignon and Merlot are two of the most impressive North American wines I have tried, both are rich in style with a superb berry fruit flavour, considerable wood, but very much in harmony with the rest of the wine, they have that hard to define velvety texture not often encountered. it has been a great pleasure for Milan and me to drink them on our frequent trips across the Pacific with Continental Airlines.

Much of the winery's grape intake comes from the vineyards of major partners Bill Jaeger and Chuck Carpy. This high quality fruit is not wasted by Phil Baxter, who is held in high regard by the winemaking community in the Valley and has trained a number of successful winemakers in his time.

Rutherford Hill make eight varietal wines in all, covering nearly all the classic European varieties plus a substantial Zinfandel from the Mead Ranch in the Atlas Peak viticultural area nearby.

This is a most attractive winery to visit and taste at. It also has a delightful picnic area for visitors. Although all their wines are of a very high standard, red wine lovers must try the Cabernet and the Merlot, I am sure they will put some down in their own cellars.

RUTHERFORD HILL WINERY
Address: 200 Rutherford Hill Rd, Rutherford, CA., 94573
Phone: 707/963 1871
Year of Establishment: 1976
Owner: Partnership managed by William Jaeger
Winemaker: Jerry Juper
Principal Varieties Grown: Merlot, Chardonnay, Cabernet Sauvignon, Gewurztraminer, Sauvignon Blanc
Acres Under Vine: 800
Average Annual Crush: 2,000 tons

Principal Wines & Brands	Cellar Potential (Years)
Chardonnay – Jaeger Vineyards	3 (to peak)
Merlot	7
Cabernet Sauvignon	10

Trade Tours – Available 11.30am; 1pm; 2.30pm
Retail Room Sales – Available
Hours open to Public – 7 days a week 10.30am to 4.30pm
Retail Distribution – National (50 states)
International: Japan, Canada, Switzerland, Sweden, U.K., Hong Kong, Denmark

V Sattui Winery

The V. Sattui Winery situated right on main Highway 29 in St. Helena, is a substantial stone building with a look of established wealth about it. That this is so is a tribute to Darryl Sattui because it was his vision and drive that created all this from nothing in less than a decade.

The beginning of the Sattui wine saga in California goes back to 1885, when Darryl's great grandfather Vittorio, founded a winery on Bryant Street in the heart of San Francisco, but closed up in 1920, when national Prohibition came into effect.

Darryl was a touch down on his luck in 1975, when he decided to revive his family's winemaking enterprise. He looked carefully and found a property to rent, leased all the equipment and started making wine, although he had no experience in the field.

His wisest choice was the site right on Highway 29. With the absolute necessity of creating a good cash flow immediately, he opened a large cheese shop in the front of the winery. Not only did this draw in many tourists to buy cheese and delicatessen goods, but it also provided an ideal accompaniment to his wines. Tables in an outdoor picnic area proved a huge success and suddenly fortune turned for Darryl.

After some eight or nine years it was time to expand and he built a very attractive solid stone winery, which honestly looks as if it has always been there, so well has it been designed and constructed. As part of the new winery, an underground cellar was also constructed to give an ideal maturation environment for the Sattui red wines, which are a large part of the production.

Darryl has been assisted through the whole venture by his blonde Finnish wife Mirja. A range of varietal wines is produced including Chardonnay, Sauvignon Blanc, Johannisberg Riesling, Cabernet Sauvignon and Zinfandel, some of which comes from grapes brought in from the Sierra Foothills.

Darryl Sattui has proved that with the right approach, a little ingenuity and a lot of hard work even a low budget winery can succeed. He deserves all the success he has achieved — the Napa Valley is richer for his enterprise.

Schramsberg Vineyards

Schramsberg exudes history for the many historical events that have happened at this beautiful secluded mountain vineyard and winery over its 126 year history, are not mere facts — you can feel them around you. There is an enchantment and one could easily imagine Robert Louis Stevenson with his new bride visiting on a beautiful summer's day that was only yesterday.

Jack and Jamie Davies have truly bestowed a wonderful gift on all Americans with the thoughtful and painstaking way they have restored and enhanced this national treasure.

Schramsberg's history goes right back to the beginning of commercial winemaking in the Napa Valley. Jacob Schramm, from the Rhineland in Germany emigrated to New York at the age of 14, made his way to California and became an itinerant barber. Perhaps it was the wine background of his youth or the need to settle down with his family, but by 1862 he had saved enough to buy a mountainside property. He planted vines, although still travelling plying his barbers trade for a living. His winery was second only to Charles Krug who started a year earlier in 1861.

Schramsberg has gained continuing notoriety from the visit of Robert Louis Stevenson and his wife on their honeymoon in 1880. Stevenson wrote at length and in glowing terms of his visit to Schramsberg: "... the picture of prosperity", and his famed saying : "... and the wine is bottled poetry".

Phylloxera dealt a telling blow to Schramm in the late 1880's and although his son carried on after his father's death in 1905, the winery closed down in 1911 and was sold as a summer house during Prohibition. Two unsuccessful attempts were made

to revive the vineyards and winery, one by Joseph Gargano in 1920 and the second by Catherine and Douglas Pringle in 1951. Both tried making methode champenoise, but did not perservere in this time and money consuming task. The market also was probably not yet ready.

After a previous venture into a "champagne making" with maverick winemaker Martin Ray, Jack Davies with his wife Jamie, bought the property in a very run down condition in 1965. Jack, a Harvard M.B.A., had held a number of top jobs in business, mostly in Los Angeles, but was still unsatisfied, searching for what he really wanted, in 1958 he had become the youngest member of the San Francisco Wine and Food Society and he talked a number of its members into coming in on the Schrammsberg venture. Jamie, who had studied at the Boston University and graduated from the University of California in Berkeley, had operated her own art gallery in San Francisco and both she and Jack had a great love for wine, food and nature. With two young sons and a third child (another son) on the way they decided to change their lives completely.

As amateur winemakers, they had some harrowing experiences. Jack nearly blew his legs off when a barrel he was sterilising blew up, he had mistakenly used a burning sulphur wick, not knowing it had contained brandy spirit before. Their ideas however, were correct and their vision true to this day. They speak highly of the wine people of Napa who offered them much invaluable help.

Schrammsberg revolutionised champagne making in America. They were first in many areas. They became the first to specialise totally in only making champagne (methode champenoise in the true French tradition) from the vine to the bottle. They introduced classic French grape varieties such as Chardonnay, Pinot Noir and Pinot Blanc into American Champagne-making for the first time. They pioneered early harvesting to achieve higher acid and crisper fruit flavours. Their "Blanc de Noirs" was the first "white" American Champagne made from red Pinot Noir grapes. They were the first to produce different champagne styles by using different grape varieties rather than just different levels of sweetness.

The Davies have faithfully restored the classic Schramm's homestead built in 1875 and have lived there since buying the property. All the original buildings have been restored including the stables and Jacob's first underground cellar, which carries the

California State Historical Site plaque.

The Davies have extended the underground tunnels for champagne ageing, these are carved deep into the hills made up of volcanic tufa.

Schramsberg Methode Champenoise have been lauded everywhere, often outside America. In 1972 the first presidential visit to China was celebrated with Schramsberg. There are five Methode Champenoise produced: the Blanc de Blanc from Chardonnay, a Blanc de Noirs from Pinot Noir, (seen when young, it has a slight pink tinge, but it turns into a rich burnished gold by the time it is released at 3-4 years old), the Reserve, blended from Pinot and Chardonnay it receives extra ageing, a Cuvee

de Pinot with some red colour and a unique Cremant Demi — sec from the Flora grape with some sweetness (Cremant means creamy, it has only half as much gas). Schramsberg's true products are often served at the White House as well as being available in all 50 States and a number of other countries.

Jamie Davies has a deep feeling for food and wine. She has studied with many of the world' leading chefs and has created an amazing number of wonderful dishes using methode champenoise. Schramsberg have spent a great deal promulgating this and other material which has been of great assistance to the whole industry and helped create the very solid and growing market.

Shown and Sons Vineyards

Dick Shown was involved in investment south of San Francisco and bought a Napa Valley Vineyard growing Cabernet Sauvignon and situated near the Silverado Trail, in Rutherford.

Realising there was more chance of making money from wine, than grape-growing, he built a small winery on the property in 1977. He specialised in making Cabernet Sauvignon. Changing tastes away from red wine and some other problems, caused the financial collapse of the enterprise and Joe Heitz bought the vineyard.

Dick Shown took this set-back in his stride and has set up Shown and Sons again, with a winery on the main Highway 29 in Rutherford, now making a larger range of wines. I am sure that, with his persistence and the good wines he is producing, success is close at hand. His son Chris is assisting in the vineyard and enologist, James Vahl, is overseeing the winemaking.

Sequoia Grove Vineyards

There are very few Californian Redwoods left on the rich soils of the Napa Valley floor but one can imagine the size of some of these giants before the Valley was cleared early in the 19th century. They are extremely slow growing and reach prodigious ages.

Hidden amongst a remaining Redwood grove and obviously named after the trees is the attractive enlarged barn that houses the James Allen family's ''Sequoia Grove'' Winery.

In 1978 after searching the inhospitable climates of Arizona, New Mexico and even Utah for a suitable place to grow vines, James and his wife Barbara bought a 22 acre property just north of the Robert Mondavi Winery on the east side of Highway 29. The property had a ten acre Chardonnay vineyard and they proceeded to turn the century old barn into a winery. Jim's brother Stephen has joined them and runs the vineyard. Jim and Barbara also have the help of their four children and Jim's mother.

The Allen family also have an involvement in the exciting new ''Domaine Carneros'' under construction in the Carneros district (the French Champagne house Taittinger are a major partner).

Sequoia Grove produce a number of Chardonnays including an estate bottled wine that is a little dearer. They also have planted Cabernet Sauvignon and other Bordeaux varieties, which they use in their Cabernet Sauvignon. Sequoia Grove is a happy and serene place amongst the bustle of today's Napa Valley.

Shafer Vineyards

John Shafer does not regret for a minute his decision to leave a successful text book publishing buisness in Chicago and become a vigneron in the Napa Valley. He chose as his site a neglected vineyard on the east side of the Napa Valley on the slopes of the famous Stag's Leap Mountain.

That was in 1972. The vineyard was neglected but this picturesque keyhole-shaped valley was ideal for viticulture. John his wife and their four children re-planted the vineyards. The first Shafer wines were made at the Round Hill Winery in 1978 and the following year at the Rutherford Hill Winery. By 1980 the family had constructed an attractive yet efficient winery at the top of the property overlooking the vineyards. The winery has been expanded gradually since.

John has been joined by his son Doug who graduated from U.C. Davis in 1979, but deciding he wanted to work with children left the valley and taught at Tucson Jnr. College in Arizona.

During his studies Doug had worked at Hanns Kornell's Champagne Cellars and at Robert Mondavi Winery and, in 1983 he decided to return to winemaking, commencing work at Lakespring Winery in Napa. He is now back at the family vineyards and winery.

Both Doug and his father take winemaking very seriously being extremely professional and meticulous in their approach. The vineyard is planted to Cabernet Sauvignon, Merlot, Cabernet Franc and Chardonnay, with reds making up two-thirds of the area under vine.

The Shafers have been working hard on developing and refining the style of their wines. The micro climate of their vineyards is cool, though the southerly and westerly aspects of the enclosed valley and the rocky mountain soil can create quite intense heat during the ripening period. This of course builds up strong flavours in the grapes.

Over recent years Shafer's have picked a little earlier and whilst still producing rich wines with a great intensity of flavour they have captured a superb elegance both in red and white. Doug has also been experimenting with barrel fermentation with his Chardonnay and, by careful handling and blending has created a style which, rich in flavour and texture, is crisp and elegant and a good food wine. Their Merlot is superb, usually blended with small proportions of Cabernet Sauvignon and Cabernet Franc to give it a little more spine. The Cabernet Sauvignon (with a little Merlot and Franc) is a substantial wine that repays bottle maturation while older vintages are held back and re-released when 5-6 years old, these are well worth looking out for.

The Shafers are quiet, no-nonsense sort of people always striving for perfection in their wines. The critics have applauded them and they deserve the praise.

Charles F Shaw Vineyard

Chuck Shaw would fit right in as the dashing army captain in an 18th century English novel — he is a gentleman with flair. Unlike some in the Valley he is unconcerned what other wineries are doing or what sort of wines they are making.

As it turns out Chuck was an army captain having graduated from West Point, went on to Stanford University. After leaving the army he spent two years in Paris as a banker. He and his wife Lucy, originally from Houston, fell in love with Burgundy and Beaujolais and dreamed of owning their own Burgundy Domaine. Lucy studied and graduated from the famous l'Ecole Cordon Bleu in Paris, mastering the grand French cuisine.

Chuck decided he would start a winery in California producing both a Cru and Nouveau style Beaujolais. Rumour has it he smuggled in some Pinot Noir cuttings from Clos Vougeot and some Gamay cuttings from a Cru vineyard in Beaujolais, both inside his raincoat! Who knows? certainly they are growing in his vineyards.

He and Lucy bought a property with a mile frontage on the west bank of the Napa river north of St. Helena. In 1978 they built a winery to match the turn of the century farmhouse they had restored, both have a Burgundy feel and style with their painted battened timbers.

Until 1983, they only produced Beaujolais from Napa Gamay, but with an increasing proportion of the imported vines Chuck "brought" in. In 1982 a Fume Blanc was produced but in future this will probably be labelled and marketed under the "Magnolia Ridge" label, a second brand of Charles F. Shaw.

In 1983 a Chardonnay was produced from vines on the home vineyard. Ric Forman one of the valleys foremost winemakers oversees the whole operation. Ric was formerly with Robert Mondavi and became the winemaker at Sterling Vineyards from its opening until 1978, when he joined his former boss at Newton Vineyards. Ric and Chuck between them

have bought the famous Star Vineyard, 41 acres of Chardonnay near Inglenook on the Rutherford Bench.

Chuck and Lucy also market under the Domaine Elucia label, Elucia being a combination of the names of their 3 beautiful daughters: Elizabeth, Lucille and Lydia.

The 1981 Reserve Gamay was served at the 1987 Summit Of Industrialised Nations in Williamsburg, Virginia, attended by President Ronald Reagan.

In 1981 the internationally famous singer, Luciano Pavorotti featured in a scene filmed at the Charles F. Shaw Vineyard and the special Gazebo built for the production now features on the label of the winery.

Chuck Shaw's wines appear in some of the world's leading hotels and restaurants.

They can feel right at home.

CHARLES F. SHAW VINEYARD AND WINERY
Address: 1010 Big Tree Road,
St. Helena, California, 94574
Phone: 707/963 5459
Year of Establishment: 1978
Owner: Charles & Lucy Shaw
Winemaker: Ric Forman
Principal Varieties Grown: Chardonnay, Gamay
Beaujolais, Pinot Noir, Sauvignon Blanc
Acres Under Vine: 14
Average Annual Crush: 500 tons

Principal Wines & Brands	Cellar Potential (Years)
Chardonnay Estate Bottled Reserve	10
Fume Blanc Estate Bottled	7
Gamay Beaujolais Estate Bottled	7
Pinot Noir	10+
Gamay Blanc	2
Gamay Beaujolais Nouveau	1

Trade Tours – Available by appointment only
Retail Distribution – Nation-wide, EEC Countries

Spottswoode Winery

Hidden in the cellar of what is undoubtedly the most beautiful old Victorian home in the Napa Valley is Spottswoode Winery, although it was only founded in 1982 (the centenary year of their home). Mary Novak has been growing some of the Valley's best grapes on her beautiful 40 acre vineyard, since she and her late husband moved to St. Helena in 1972.

Only two wines are made, a Sauvignon Blanc and a Cabernet Sauvignon. The wines are crushed and fermented at other wineries from the very best grapes from the Spottswoode Vineyard, which stretches out towards the Mayacamas Range behind the home, with its superb gardens and pretty outbuildings.

Mary is a vivacious and energetic woman; her sons and daughters have assisted in various ways in the vineyard and winery. The youngest Matthew is studying winemaking at present, whilst the oldest, Michael, who helped run the vineyard has now decided to follow his father's footsteps into medicine.

Silver Oak Wine Cellars

Justin Meyer was assistant cellarmaster of the Christian Brothers for many years. After leaving the order, he and Colorado oilman Raymond Duncan bought the Franciscan Winery out of bankruptcy in 1975, although they had already started Silver Oak as a maker of just one exclusive wine — Cabernet Sauvignon.

Sometimes several Cabernets are produced in one vintage, using grapes from different regions and acknowledging this fact on the label.

After selling Franciscan to its current West German owners in 1979, they concentrated their efforts at Silver Oak. In 1982, they built a new and bigger winery and, between them they own vineyards in both the Napa and the Alexander Valley in Sonoma County.

The Silver Oak Cabernets are not released until they are 5 years of age and are carefully made using extended maceration and a balanced use of barrel ageing which done properly takes time. The old adage that "the fewer wines you have the better job you can do" rings very true at Silver Oak Wine Cellars.

Silverado Vineyards

Sitting happily on top of a three hundred foot high hill amongst a sea of vines is the spectacular Silverado Vineyards winery built by Mrs. Lillian Disney, widow of the much loved Walt Disney, her daughter Diane and son-in-law Donald Miller.

Whilst not on the same scale as Disneyland, the winery is very aesthetically pleasing and commands some of the best views of the central part of the Napa Valley. There is certainly nothing contrived or make believe about the wines being produced by Jack Stuart, who runs the vineyards and winery. Indeed Jack travelled to London in late 1987 to collect the world's most prestigious wine award "Winemaker Of The Year", so successful were the Silverado Vineyards entries in the famed Bristol Wine Competition.

Jack learnt his lessons well at Robert Mondavi Winery and Durney vineyards while the wines are basically from estate grown fruit with 180 acres of vineyards planted.

Donald Miller heads production at Walt Disney studio so he doesn't have a lot of time to spare, but the winery and vineyards have received everything money could buy. Certainly there is no evidence of waste, it is a most successful operation in every way.

For those who like a rich style of white wine, Silverado whites are for you. The Sauvignon Blanc has a grassy herbaceousness with some full tropical fruit flavours coming on the palate, the wood ageing giving it a buttery vanilla overtone. Likewise the Chardonnay is an extremely full style with beautiful peach and apricot flavours again with some buttery vanilla in the background and a pleasant citrus finish. If their whites are good their reds are sensational. The 1984 Cabernet Sauvignon I tasted had a superb deep ruby colour with mauve highlights the wine showed strong cherry/berry aromas with a floral touch the palate carried on the berry fruit with some nice spice and mint characters. The wine had 7% Merlot, which was evident in the wine's early vitality.

Silverado Vineyards, only established in 1981, have already hit some high notes but one can be sure that many wineries are striving to pass them. I am certain though that their dedication and commitment to absolute quality will keep them at the top for sometime to come yet.

Spring Mountain Vineyards

S pring Mountain Vineyards is probably the world's best known winery not under its own name, but under its nom de plume "Falcon Crest" as it is here that the famous television series is set. As one might imagine, Mike Robbins, creator of Spring Mountain Vineyards is quite a character. In 1968 he bought a Victorian Mansion on the main Highway 29 near Freemark Abbey and started his winery. Six years later, he bought the old Miravalle Estate of Tiburcio Parrott high on Spring Mountain road and named for the marvellous view it has of the valley below.

Parrott built a classic Victorian home on the property in 1885, being somewhat influenced in its concept, if not design, by the Rhine House of his friends the Beringer Brothers. He made wine on the property until his death in 1894, being particularly proud of his red wine, made in the Bordeaux style. He called it "Margaux" and, amongst those who knew, it was a prized wine. From his activities and accomplishments he was obviously a man of style much like today's owner.

Michael Robbins graduated from Annapolis in engineering, flew fighter planes in the Korean War and came to the Napa Valley as a real estate investor, with a knack of seeing a property that was worth developing.

In 1976, he finished constructing a winery to match the Mirravalle Mansion, using as a base a hundred foot long underground cellar, dug out by Chinese labourers for Tiburico Parrot.

The long high building has a dome shaped turret some say came from Disneyland. If so it was certainly a premonition of things to come, but, in all seriousness, it is a superb winery building and the wines of Spring Mountain are certainly top class. In 1982 a Falcon Crest label was also introduced for obvious reasons, although the Spring Mountain label has remained the main premium label.

Tours of Spring Mountain are by appointment, as I am sure no work would get done if every interested onlooker visited. All the same, its worth the trouble. Michael Robbins has shown taste and style in the creation of his estate and the wines it produces, that are well worth experiencing.

Stag's Leap Winery

Somewhat tucked away from the Silverado Trail, nestled hard up against the steep slopes of Stag's Leap is the historic and beautiful Stag's Leap Winery, which has been lovingly restored by Carl and Joanne Doumani, who purchased the run down property, with 400 acres of vineyard land in 1970.

The winery had been burnt down and all that remained were its stone walls and a long tunnel dug into the hillside that was used to age the wines. The property also included the old Stag's Leap Manor Hotel which Carl and Joanne have restored as their residence.

The first wines under the Stag's Leap Winery label were made and bottled at the Rutherford Hill Winery, the 1979 vintage saw the initial crushing at the restored winery. After some legal problems involving their neighbours, the Stag's Leap Wine Cellars, some of the Doumani's products are labelled under the Pedregal label.

The restoration of this beautiful and historic property is a credit to the Doumanis and it is worth a journey off the trail to see it. Typical of the region, their wines are rich and full in style.

Stag's Leap Wine Cellars

Warren Wisniarski is one of Napa's highest profile winemakers. A man of great intellectual capacity, he came to the Napa Valley in 1964 after a career as lecturer in Political Philosophy at the University of Chicago.

He worked first at the original Souverain Winery, whilst waiting for the vineyard, he and his wife Barbara had bought in the Stag's Leap Valley, to reach maturity. Warren then spent some time at the Robert Mondavi Winery.

The first vintage at the new Stag's Leap Wine Cellars on the Silverado Trail, was in 1972. The 1973 Cabernet Sauvignon really put them on the map, when it won the famous Paris tasting in 1976, judged by French experts and up against the best Bordeaux wines. Since then Warren and his team have proved it was no fluke, as their wines continue to win international honours.

Stag's Leap also have an excellent second label, ''Hawks Crest'', made from various north coast regional grapes.

Stag's Leap Wine Cellars have helped position California well and truly at the top of the world wine ladder.

In 1969, James Spaulding, a reporter from Milwaukee, Wisconsin came west to California to teach journalism at the University of California, Berkley. He had already developed a love for wine and had in fact planted vines close to Milwaukee, but without success. At first he and his wife Barbara bought an 86 acre property on Diamond Mountain in the Mayacamas Range near Calistoga, and planted vines in this area. In 1973 they decided to build a winery on a small vineyard, owned by a partner in the venture, on the corner of Dunaweal Lane and Highway 29, a few miles south of Calistoga and right beneath the Sterling Winery.

In 1975, the partner was bought out and James has since been assisted by his son David, who has studied winemaking and taken over that role, as well as the marketing, in conjunction with his wife Kathleen. The two younger Spauldings are both also involved in other entrepreneurial wine ventures including a successful poster featuring a bottle of all Napa's significant wineries (over 100 wines appear on it). In full colour it is quite an eye opener.

Most of the grapes for Stonegate wines come from their hillside vineyards and those of their neighbours on Diamond Mountain, John and Fran Pershing. Interestingly enough,

the Diamond Mountain area was planted with wines prior to Prohibition but these gave way to prunes and walnuts.

Stonegate produce Sauvignon Blanc and Chardonnay in the white wine field. Both have extremely strong and well defined varietal fruit character; the Chardonnay has a little Carneros material blended with it adding an extra dimension.

Their Cabernet Sauvignon and Merlot are both outstanding and generous wines that age particularly well. Over 60% of Stonegate wines are sold to restaurants, but you can taste and buy at the cellars and should do so if you are in the Valley.

Stony Hill Vineyards

Although Joe Heitz sparked the major wine revolution in the Napa Valley the title of first boutique winery goes to Stony Hill Vineyards. Founded in 1951 it even pre-empted Hanzell in Sonoma by five years and was probably America's first such winery.

to 1943 when San Francisco advertising executive, Fred McCrea and his wife Eleanor bought a summer retreat hidden in the Mayacamas Mountains north east of St. Helena, over a thousand feet above the Valley floor. Some said the soil was too rocky and only fit for goats, but the McCreas

Chardonnay obtained from Herman Wente, one of few then growing the variety.

Fred died in 1977 but Eleanor continues the business. Stony Hill only produce about 4,000 cases and all is sold out each year to long time mailing list customers. Woe-betide anyone who gets their order in late!!

Sterling Vineyards

High profile takes on an extra dimension when one talks about Sterling Vineyards. The winery sits perched on a steep hill that rises alone from the valley floor. The bleached white, striking, almost space-age winery is reached via an aerial tramway that lifts one in a gondola to the wineries entrance.

Sterling had its founding in 1964, when

Peter Newton, the English-born president of the Sterling Paper Products company in San Francisco and his partner Michael Stone, a former Navy pilot, established a 400 acre vineyard near the current winery. In 1968, they built a makeshift cellar and, by the time the winery was completed in 1973, they were already successfully established.

In 1977, the Coca-Cola company, which had already bought Taylors Wine interests in New York State, purchased Sterling with the intention of turning it into America's largest Estate Winery. They purchased more vineyards including 100 acres on Diamond Mountain, in the Mayacamas Range. Seagrams bought Sterling in 1983, and have since expanded Sterling Vineyard's interests further, recently obtaining the highly respected Winery Lake Vineyard in Carneros.

One of Sterling's great strengths is the large vineyard acreage it controls within the valley, over 1,200 acres in total, involving eleven different locations all planted to

classic varieties. It is this spread, planted to suit individual grape types, that provides Sterling with an ideal estate base from which to work, vineyard manager, is Tucker Catlin.

Winemaker is Bill Dyer, formerly Theo Rosenbrand's assistant, who took over on Theo's retirement in 1985. The focus is very much on the estate bottled programme and vineyard designated wines. Chardonnay and Cabernet from Diamond Mountain. Chardonnay and Pinot Noir from the famed Winery Lake Vineyard and a newly released Red Table Wine – a Bordeaux-style blend of Cabernet and Merlot from the Three Palms Vineyard.

Bill ferments 100% of his Chardonnay in small oak casks an amazing commitment, which has been justly rewarded by his 1986 vintage, winning numerous double gold awards (including the California State Fair). Sterling also produce one of the best Sauvignon Blancs in this valley and an outstanding Merlot.

Sterling Vineyards

Sutter Home Winery

E very now and again a winery strikes the jackpot with a new wine style. Sutter Home have done this with their White Zinfandel.

Despite its detractors and those who said the wine was a fad and wouldn't last, this wine style is going from strength to strength. Although many others have come onto the market, Sutter Home have maintained their position at the top and may soon break the million case barrier. Perhaps there is some natural justice in the world after all as it was Sutter Home and the Trinchero family who first recognised the potential of the Zinfandel grapes grown in the foothills of the Sierra Nevada Mountains in Amador County and in 1968, released their first full bodied red wine made from the variety.

Zinfandel came to California around 1850. No-one is quite sure from whence, but it probably came first from a vine nursery in Eastern American and prior to that from south/eastern Italy. It is now California's most planted red variety, a very versatile grape making all kinds of red table wines from the palest blush through to the most dense and tannic wines you could imagine.

Zinfandel is also made into Port, Dessert styles and even into sparkling wine. It has a very positive fruit character often likened to wild berries; its secret when made into a pale blush wine like a white Zinfandel is that it produces a wine with good strong fruit aroma and flavour. Sutter Home understand the variety well from years of experience and have really mastered the White Zinfandel style, crisp, fruity and slightly sweet. Its a winner!

The history of Sutter Home goes back to 1890, when, John Sutter, a cousin to the Captain involved in the legendary Sutters Fort, started a winery in the Howell Mountain region east of Napa. Shortly after the turn of the century, he moved to the current location on the main Highway in St. Helena.

After he re-opened on the repeal of Prohibition, Sutter Home produced bulk wine mainly for other wineries. In 1946, John Trinchero bought the winery. He was well entrenched in the hospitality industry as his family had operated a resort hotel in up-state New York. He was joined shortly after by his brother Mario, whose son Louis (commonly called Bob) is now the winemaker, with his other son Roger now also involved. Sutter Home has gradually evolved from selling bulk wines, much of them to other wineries, to producing and labelling their own proprietary brands. This really started in the late 60's, about the time their first Zinfandel's were released.

Like Louis Martini, Sutter Home also make a Muscat Amabile. This delicious grapey wine has low alcohol and a slight "spritz" of gas on the palate.

Next door to the winery is the very pretty residence of President "Bob" Trinchero, a timber house which has just been totally renovated. With much work done on the fences and timber garden arbors, it looks like something out of a fairly tale, particularly when the lights come on at dusk.

The Trincheros are a hard working family dedicated to their Sutter Home Winery, this committment is sure to see them through many more years of successful winemaking.

SUTTER HOME WINERY INC.
Address: 277 St. Helena Highway South, St. Helena, CA., 94574
Phone: 707/963 3104
Year of Establishment: 1874
Owner: Trinchero Family
Winemaker: Louis R. "Bob" Trinchero
Principal Varieites Grown: Zinfandel, Cabernet Sauvignon, Sauvignon Blanc, Chenin Blanc, Muscat Alexandria
Acres Under Vine: 3,000
Average Annual Crush: total 49,500 tons

Principal Wines & Brands	Cellar Potential (Years)
Sutter Home White Zinfandel - California	1
Sutter home Zinfandel - California	4
Sutter Home Sauvignon blanc - California	2

Trade Tours – Available by appointment only.
Retail Room Sales – Available.
Hours open to Public: 7 days a week from 10am to 5pm
Retail Distribution: Broad National distrib.

Trefethen Vineyards & Winery

Trefethen Vineyards & Winery

In 1986 at harvest time there was quite a party at Trefethen. Passers-by would be forgiven for blinking once of twice to make sure they weren't seeing things. To mark the centenary of the winery the Trefethen family held a re-creation of the first crush complete with period costumes and using the original crusher/steamer driven by a team of Clydesdales from the Alexander Valley.

The Trefethens are very conscious and proud of their winery's heritage and have restored their winery in a most sensitive fashion. Much of the old equipment is displayed amongst the gardens, which repose under the Valley's most magnificent oak trees, some over 700 years old.

Built in 1886, by James and George Goodman, bankers in Napa, it was called Eschol after the biblical river valley where Moses' flock found a huge band of grapes. It was rather fitting therefore that when Eugene Trefethen, (then Chairman of Kaiser Steel) bought the 650 acre property, he first revived the vineyard. The vines today are the best looking in the entire Napa, and the long drive through the vineyard from the entrance off Oak Knoll Road, gives one a great sense of his dedication.

Eschol had been most successful in national and international competitions. In 1904, it was purchased by Napa farmer Clark Fawver, who made bulk wine both before and after Prohibition, the winery becoming a storage cellar for Beringer after Fawver's death, I am sure Nestle would give their right arm to own the property now.

Gene Trefethen started replanting in 1968 and today remains in charge of the vineyard. He is in the enviable position of only needing about one third of the grape for his own wines, the rest goes mainly to Domaine Chandon, who made their first Methode Champenoise base wine at the newly renovated winery in 1973. Trefethen grapes also find their way to other prestigious wineries such as Cakebread.

Gene's son John, a navy diver, was responsible with his wife Janet for the restoration of the winery and released their first wines in 1976. The Trefethen's really arrived in 1979 when their 1976 Chardonnay beat all French white Burgundies and a number of other Californian Chardonnays in a masked tasting held in the ''Burgundy capital'' of Beaune.

Today Trefethen make a Chardonnay, White Riesling (Johannisberg), Pinot Noir, Cabernet Sauvignon and two excellent non vintage wines, an Eschol Red and an Eschol White, which are blended from various varieties grown in the vineyard. They are top wines and excellent value for money.

The classic timber building with its old loft once housing the crusher but now Janet's office, is a monument to good taste and understated elegance. It has just been placed on the National Register Of Historic Places and rightly so. Good luck to the Trefethens — not that I feel they will need too much!!

TREFETHEN VINEYARDS
Address: 1160 Oak Knoll Ave, PO Box 2460, Napa, CA., 94558
Phone: 707/255 7700
Year of Establishment: 1886 - Revived 1968
Owner: Trefethen (Family owned)
Winemaker: David Whitehouse - winemaster
Principal Varieties Grown: Chardonnay, Cabernet Sauvignon, Pinot Noir, White Riesling, Merlot, Zinfandel
Acres Under Vine: 650
Average Annual Crush: 1,200 tons

Principal Wines & Brands	Cellar Potential (Years)
Chardonnay	10
Cabernet Sauvignon	15
Pinot Noir	5-7

Trade Tours – Available by appointment only.
Retail Room Sales – Available.
Hours open to Public: Daily from 10am to 4.30pm
Retail Distribution: National and International

Vichon Winery

Vichon has quite a reputation for its Chardonnay, often in the richer style made in a winery housed in a neat building situated on the Oakville grade with Panoramic views of the Valley.

Vichon came into being as the brain child of a number of hoteliers and restauranters, who formed a partnership. They made their first wines at the old Ehlers Lane Winery in 1980, the winemaker/partner being the very experienced Dr. George Vierra, who formerly worked with Robert Mondavi firstly at Krug and then at Robert's own winery. It is rather coincidental then, that after a disagreement between partners, Robert and his three children bought Vichon, retaining George as winemaker.

The wines of Vichon have already garnered quite a reputation. An interesting wine produced is their Chev Rignon a name derived from Chevrier, another name for Semillon, and Sauvignon Blanc. The wine is a blend of about 50% of each variety, a Bordeaux Graves style blend but with more wood-age and richness of flavour than its French counterpart. The winery's other red is a Cabernet Sauvignon, which has also reached great heights.

Vose Vineyards

For Hamilton Vose III, its been a long journey from beneath the sea in the navy seals, where he was an underwater demolition expert, to the top of Mt. Veeder, where he has carved out a vineyard and created a unique winery complex.

A desire to tackle a rural enterprise brought him back to California and he bought 300 acres on Mt. Veeder 2,000 ft. above the Napa Valley floor in 1970. Hamilton spent three years clearing the heavily timbered property and planted 95 acres of vines, Wines produced are Fume Blanc, Chardonnay, White Zinfandel called ''Zinblanca'', Cabernet Sauvignon and Zinfandel. All have lively crisp fruit characters common to the mountain grown wines and there are often real bargains by the case for those willing to take the four mile journey from the Valley up the Oakville grade.

Hamilton's family have been in America since 1620. Their original name, Deveaux, from Normandy France, was changed to Vose somewhere along the track.

Two delightful self contained cottages have been built at the vineyard which one can lease for a few days or a few weeks.

Villa Mount Eden Winery

ike McGrath is a fresh faced young man on a mission. It is one thing to have all the ingredients, it is another to mould them into truly great wine. In 1983, Mike took over from Nils Venge, who made the wine at Villa Mt. Eden since its rebirth in 1974. Judging from the last four releases 1983-86), Mike is thrusting himself forward as one of the young winemakers who will make a big impression on today's and future generations.

The Villa Mt. Eden Vineyard Estate goes back to 1881, with wine being made more or less consistently except for the Prohibition years. However, it was not until 1970 that anyone took much notice of this winery.

In that year the property with its 87 acres vineyard was bought by James and Anne McWilliams, he a San Francisco financier and she the grand-daughter of Bank of America founder, A.P. Giannini.

The plan was to use the property as a country residence, but once Jim started re-planting the vineyard, re-opening the winery seemed a logical idea. This they did with their first vintage being 1974, the Cabernet Sauvignon of that year won much praise

Nils Venge was winemaker and the winery slowly went ahead, until Mike McGrath took over in 1983. Trained at U.C. Davis, graduating in 1978, he first worked for Mike Grgich at Grgich Hills followed by a stint at Charles Krug. In since joining Villa Mt. Eden he really hit his straps. In fact, every single wine he has produced over four vintages has won a medal.

One of his stars has been the dry Chenin Blanc, crisp and packed with fresh fruit flavour, but refreshingly clean and dry on the finish. The other wines are a Chardonnay (a firm style that benefits from time in the bottle), a Cabernet Sauvignon, often with a touch of Merlot, which is made in the bigger style (the 1981 Reserve is still on the market and only a pup). The last wine is a very late harvest Sauvignon Blanc made from heavily Botrytised grapes, rich and luscious, having 18% residual grape sugar, but with lovely acid and rich flavours partly developed from barrel fermentation, the ideal drink by itself after a good meal.

Mike lives on the property with his French wife Isabelle and two young children. He is never far from his wines — night and day to him they are like part of the family.

Recently the winery and vineyard was taken over by the Stimson Lane group (Chateau Ste Michelle Washington State is their main enterprise) which has given Villa Mt. Eden access to capital to drive the vineyard and winery to even greater success. Mike McGrath is firmly in the driver's seat and knows where he's going.

VILLA MT. EDEN
Address: 620 Oakville Crossroads, Oakville, CA., 94574
Phone: 707/944 2414
Year of Establishment: 1881
Owner: Stimson Lane Wine & Spirits
Winemaker: Mike McGrath
Principal Varieties Grown: Chardonnay, Cabernet Sauvignon, Merlot, Cabernet Blanc
Acres Under Vine: 72
Average Annual Crush: 300 tons

Principal Wines & Brands	Cellar Potential (Years)
Chardonnay	
Cabernet Sauvignon	
Chenin Blanc	

Trade Tours – Available by appointment only.
Retail Room Sales – Available.
Hours open to Public: 7 days a week from 10am to 4.30pm.

Domaine Mumm

Domaine Mumm is aiming to be the ultimate statement in Methode Champenoise produced on the North American Continent. Under the Seagrams Wine Classics Group (Seagram also own the Mumm Champagne house in France), they are sparing no effort to produce the ultimate in quality.

Heading the organisation is Guy Devaux, Executive Vice President and General Manager. Guy has spent 40 years of his life involved in Methode Champenoise both in France and, since 1960, in the United States. His career began as a chemist at the Institute Enologique de Champagne in Epernay the heart of the Champagne district where he was born. It was here he learnt the working of the Champagne district with all its intricate techniques

In 1949 he was appointed Chief Winemaker of the Societe Marne at Champagne, one of the largest producers

in the champagne region and in 1960 came to the U.S. At Gold Seal, then America's premier producer of Methode Champenoise in Hammondsport N.Y. State, he worked closely with the legendary Charles Fournier.

In 1967 Guy took over Gold Seal and in 1979 Seagrams then owner of Gold Seal asked Guy to explore the possibility of creating Domaine Mumm in America. The project was top secret and labelled ''Project Lafayette''. After evaluating wine from New York, Washington State and Oregon, Guy narrowed down his search for the ideal location to California. He proceeded to make trial batches of Methode Champenoise from the various quality, coastal regions of California, from Mendocino to Santa Barbara, the only constant being the varietal make up, about 60% Pinot Noir, the balance being mainly Chardonnay with a little Pinot Blanc in some instances. After masked tasting with Mumm's French ''Chef de Caves'', Michel

Budin, Napa consistently came out in front.

In 1983, the final decision was made to proceed with ''Cuvee Napa'' and a facility was constructed near the entrance to the Sterling Winery. A new grand facility is opening on the Silverado Trail at Rutherford, which will also include some very up market entertaining areas and kitchen facilities. It will be a show place of the Valley.

Recently, Greg Fowler has been appointed winemaker. Greg has spent the last seven years as winemaker for Schramsberg Vineyards, pioneers of premium Methode Champenoise in America. This is a real coup for Domaine Mumm. Greg is basically in charge of the grape selection and the making of the base wines. Domaine Mumm's sister company, Sterling, has recently purchased the prestigious winery Lake Vineyard in Carneros, giving Greg access to perfect Pinot Noir and Chardonnay for Methode Champenoise.

Domaine Mumm

These grapes along with other selected vineyard crops are picked early and brought to the winery as whole bunches, then placed in the press whole. A special computer programme from Champagne, France ensures only the best free run juice is captured. All the various wines are kept separate (up to 60 in all). Blending the cuvee is done in December when, Michel Budin comes from France to join Guy and Greg.

So far there have been two Cuvee Napa releases. Both have received critical acclaim. They have a distinct bronze colour due to the high percentage of Pinot, with great depth of flavour and a superb creamy texture, much like the famous Cordon Rouge from France. Other releases are planned perhaps including even America's first vineyard designated Methode Champenoise. Quality and class is Mumm's message.

Inniskillin — Napa

Almost opposite Grgich Hills and just up the road from Beaulieu, is a 26 acre Chardonnay Vineyard, which will become the future site for one of North America's best vignerons.

Inniskillin pioneered vinifera wine growing and the boutique winery concept in Canada, on the Ontario Lake shore, near Niagara Falls.

Their Inniskillin wines particularly the Ice-wine, Chardonnay and Pinot Noir have become world recognised and they are regular wine show trophy and award winners on the international circuit. Their delightful boutique winery near the Niagara-On-The-Lake township has grown to a 100,000 case premium wine operation, as well as being a show place that runs culinary, hospitality and educational events.

Don Ziraldo is the Robert Mondavi of Canada. His winemaker and partner Karl Kaiser, is a perfectionist with his vineyards and wine. Together they form an awesome combination. In their Inniskillin operation they have built a strong and loyal team around them.

Inniskillin's new venture into California, will, in no way, diminish their efforts and winery status in Canada, but is sure to add an exciting new dimension, to Napa's wine industry.

Chateau Boswell

Looking like something out of a Hans Christian Andersen fairytale, Chateau Boswell vies for the title of Napa's prettiest winery.

Retired dentist, R. Thornton Boswell, built the winery in 1982 and the wines have just come on stream within the last couple of years. Set against the hills to the east of the Silverado Trial, it is certainly worth a visit and a phone call to see if a taste is possible.

Paso Robles San Luis Obispo

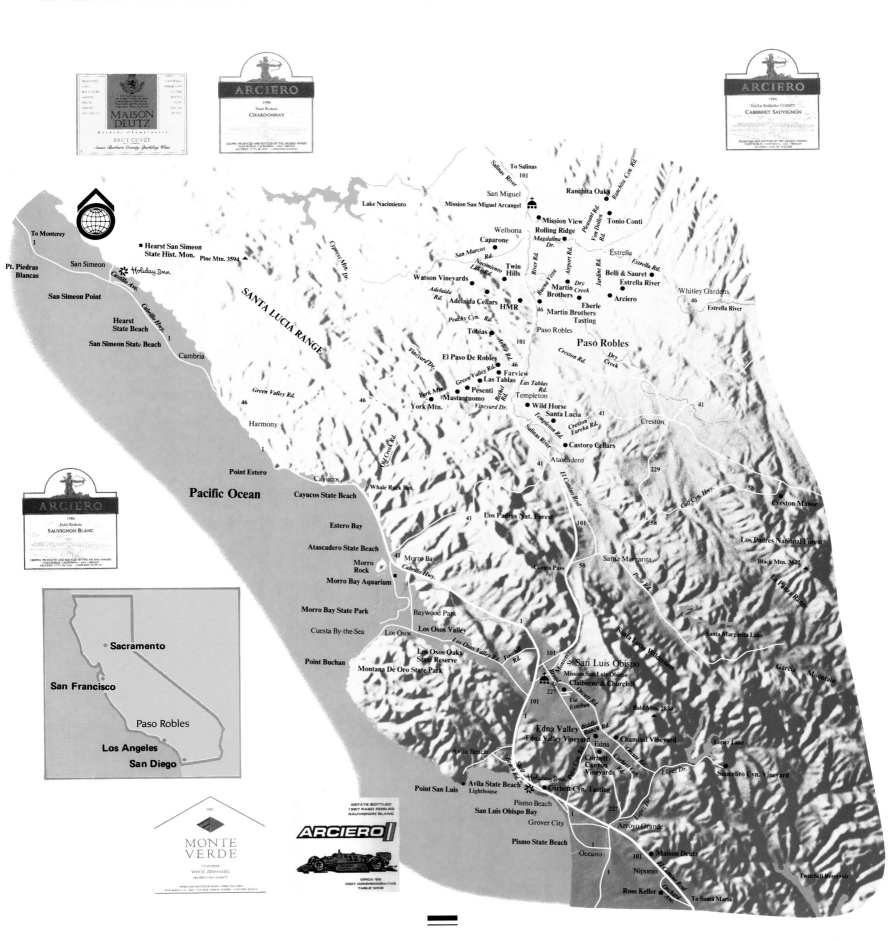

Pacific Ocean

Sacramento

San Francisco

Paso Robles

Los Angeles
San Diego

MAISON DEUTZ
BRUT CUVÉE
Santa Barbara County Sparkling Wine

ARCIERO
1986
PASO ROBLES
CHARDONNAY

ARCIERO
1984
SANTA BARBARA COUNTY
CABERNET SAUVIGNON

ARCIERO
1986
PASO ROBLES
SAUVIGNON BLANC

MONTE VERDE
CALIFORNIA
WHITE ZINFANDEL
PROPRIETOR'S RESERVE

ARCIERO
ESTATE BOTTLED
1987 PASO ROBLES
SAUVIGNON BLANC

CIRCA '88
INDY COMMEMORATIVE
TABLE WINE

Like most North American wine regions, the Paso Robles — San Luis Obispo region was established during the last century. It was not, however, until the 1960's that it really took off with the advent of the table wine boom. The climate is generally cool; the close proximity of the Pacific and its cold ocean currents, coastal fogs during summer and cooling sea breezes help moderate it still further. The hills above San Simeon — Cambria offer some of the world's most beautiful coastal vistas and a number of wineries have been established amongst them.

Most of the regions development has occurred east of Paso Robles with the large vineyards and winery of Estrella River, just purchased by the Nestle Wine division and close by the most impressive Arciero Winery, founded only in 1982, but already extremely well established by the efforts of the dynamic car racing and construction family.

The other main vineyard area is the Edna Valley, south of San Luis Obispo,

sporting the Corbett Canyon Winery and Shadow Creek Champagne Cellars which have grown considerably, partly through their promotion of a successful range of one litre varietals. This winery has been recently purchased by The Wine Group, owners of Franzia Winery. The Edna Valley Vineyard Winery, owned partly by the renowned Chalone Company, has been equally successful. A new venture backed by French Champagne House Deutz and Gelderman, along with the Nestle Company's "Wine World" and named Maison Deutz, has recently constructed a Champagne facility.

There is plenty of action in this viticultural area. With the shortage of suitable land in Napa and Sonoma counties and its high price vineyard development, the area around San Luis Obispo and Paso Robles will continue to develop at a rapid pace.

One of North America's most magnificent and exciting wineries is that called Arciero, built by the famous car racing, construction and big game hunting family. This is the Paso Robles region's largest winery, covering a massive 78,000 square feet, much of it unused at present. Brothers Frank and Phil are always looking ahead and

almost 600 acres of vines have been planted under Frank's watchful eye (he is certainly not too proud to jump on the heavy machinery either).

The brothers came to America in 1939 from Italy where Frank had already run the family farm in the Monte Cassino Hills, including grape vines, starting when he was only eleven years old. They joined their father in Detroit where he was working at Dodge Brothers and perhaps it was here the car racing bug struck. In 1945, Frank moved to California and started in the construction business. A few years later he talked Phil into joining him and Arciero Brothers Inc. started in the construction business. The brothers went on to build one of the biggest concreting companies in Southern California, undertaking projects others would not touch or could not handle. They built the Huntington beach harbour and the LAX

parking for the Los Angeles Olympics.

In 1980, they decided to get into the wine business. Over 12 million dollars and eight years later the enterprise is a show piece of the industry. Everything has been done in an absolutely ''no compromise'' style. The vineyards were ripped (using their construction skill) to 10 ft. giving the vines a chance to build a deep root system quickly. No pesticides or herbicides are used and their vineyards are a treat to look at. The winery built in an Mediterranean villa-style is not only functional, but aesthetically very pleasing to the eye, surrounded by five acres of landscaped rose gardens and manicured lawns. The visitors' centre is the best I have seen, boasting a superb delicatessen and a range of tasteful wine-related items, along with areas featuring displays of the brothers' other loves. Frank and his son Frank Jnr. (Butch) have three of their Indi and off-road

Arciero Winery

cars and Phil some of his big game trophies.

Despite their obvious wealth, the family are warm and very down-to-earth. They enjoy sharing their life experiences and winery with anyone who cares to ask. Betty, Frank Jnrs'. wife is also very involved.

As in their other successful missions in life, the Arcieros have built a strong and loyal team around them. Klaus Mathes, their winemaster and general manager is a big-thinking perfectionist, with a degree in engineering, viticulture and enology from his German homeland, where he ran the wine research station before he came to America in 1967. Joining the giant Almaden Winery of National Distillers, where he spent twenty years, a number of them as general manager, he introduced the Charles Le Franc range of premium wines.

The new winemaker who took over from Greg Bruni is Mike Loykasik, son-in-law of the famous Professor Singleton. Gaspare Cavazos runs the vineyard along with Frank Arciero while Lou Lombardi is their very personable director of sales and marketing.

The five varietal wines they produce are from the nine varieties grown and are of a consistently high standard, winning many awards. Their Monte Verde range of one litre varietals at bargain prices, has really taken off. Arciero is an object lesson to any aspiring vigneron.

Maison Deutz

Andre Lallier is the great great grandson of William Deutz who in 1838 founded "Champagne Deutz" in the small village of Ay, in the French Champagne appelation. In 1978, he travelled the world looking for the ideal place outside his native land to produce a Methode Champenoise of distinction.

South of Arroyo Grande, not far inland from the famous Pismo Beach, he found the place he believed was ideal. Morning and evening fogs and cool afternoon sea breezes keep the climate very temperate, the chalky limestone based soils and rolling hills reminded him of Champagne.

In 1981, the planting commenced. The classic Champagne varietals Chardonnay, Pinot Noir and Pinot Blanc have now become well established. The winery and champagne cellars, an architecturally striking building partly underground, were completed in 1984. The Cuvee (base wine) is made very traditionally by gently pressing the hand picked grapes in a "Coquard" basket press, the only one in the U.S.A. Eighty percent of the Cuvee is put through a malo-lactic fermentation as in France to give the wine added complexity and character.

Their first Cuvee, released in 1986, was a blend of 1983 and 1984 contained

Maison Deutz

approximately equal quantities of Pinot Blanc, Chardonnay and Pinot Noir. Andre Lallier personally oversaw the making.

The Nestle company's "Wine World" has been involved as a joint venture partner. Praise has flowed from all quarters and many have likened Maison Deutz to its French counterpart. It is refined and elegant as well as full in flavour. Salut Andre!!

Creston Manor Vineyard

In splendid isolation, high in the La Panza Mountains east of Templeton, is one of California's most promising vineyards. Situated some 1,700 ft. above sea level, Creston Manor Vineyards is part of the 479 acre "Indian Creek Ranch". First plantings were in 1981 and these have expanded to 95 acres. The soils vary, but are all well drained, being on a limestone base. About 150 acres are suitable for vines and all will be eventually planted.

The venture was founded by two families, David and Christina Crawford-Koontz, with Larry Rosenbloom and his wife Stephanie. Although from Los Angeles, Larry is very active in the vineyard's affairs and the

winery is expanding quickly. In fact, on my recent visit, the new extension to the winery, doubling its size, was nearing completion.

Victor Hugo Roberts, is certainly a suitable name for a winemaker. Victor is half French and a very talented young winemaker who takes his task very seriously. A graduate of Davis, he spent a short time in 1979 with I.S.C. and then the Brookside Vineyard in Southern California. Victor is assisted in the vineyards by Robert Vickery, whose wife, Doris, looks after the office and tasting room.

Creston Manor also has a second tasting room situated on Vineyard Drive at the Templeton exit off highway 101.

Whilst visiting the vineyard, I tasted their

first Estate bottled Sauvignon Blanc, a superb wine with a lifted tropical fruit character and pleasant herbaceouness. Another wine I found very impressive was a 1987 Pinot Noir, made in the Nouveau style by the whole berry (maceration carbonique) fermentation method. Their Chardonnay and Cabernet Sauvignon are very full wines and again impressive.

It is well worth the 17 mile drive to visit this pioneer winery. If you cannot get there, drop into the tasting room, right on the highway. Creston Manor, I am sure, has great things in front of it.

Corbett Canyon Vineyards

Founded at much the same time in 1978, the Corbett Canyon and Shadow Creek operations were bought by Glenmore distillers of Kentucky in 1981, who then merged them. In 1988, The Wine Group owner of Franzia Winery and Mogen David bought the group from Glenmore.

Corbett Canyon was one of the first to recognise the need for quality bottled varietals at affordable prices and came up with a one litre bottle under the "Coastal Classic" label. These wines still retail for around five dollars a bottle; in such popular varieties such as Chardonnay and Sauvignon Blanc they have become big sellers.

The Corbett Canyon Winery actually started its life as the Lawrence Winery, when James S. Lawrence, a Fresno State enology graduate, with two San Joaquim growers bonded the winery in 1978. The large mission-style building and equipment received a complete (1.5 million dollar) overhaul by Glenmore in 1983 and Gary Cott, the respected winemaker, formerly with Montevina in the Sierras, created an extremely good facility, greatly improving the wines and the fortunes of the operation.

The new owners are professionals in the business; they are sure to continue the good work and make the most of the quality grapes they have to work with.

Edna Valley Vineyard

E dna Valley Vineyard winery was built in 1983 by the Paragon Vineyard company, owners of a 600 acre vineyard in the valley set up in 1973 and the highly respected Chalone Company, owner of Chalone Vineyards in Monterey, Acacia Vineyards in Carneros and Carmenet in Sonoma.

The winery started off in a small way, with a low profile, but has grown quickly both in size and reputation. The wines are mainly Burgundian in style and all whites are barrel fermented, including their "Vin Gris", a salmon-copper coloured wine made as a white wine from Pinot Noir grapes. The Edna Valley Vineyard's Chardonnay and Pinot Noir are both complex wines, which spend considerable time in new French oak barrels imported from the Burgundy region.

Edna Valley also has a second label, Gavilan, which features other wine regions of the coastal counties, although always presented as a regional varietal wine. Chalone closely oversee the winemaking, whilst Paragon concentrates on the vineyards. The operation has a lot going for it and has quietly built an excellent reputation.

Pasquale, "Pat", Mastantuono was a home winemaker, who fell in love with the Zinfandel grapes from the Paso Robles Vineyards. Pat and his wife Leona decided to join the wine adventure as vineyard owners and bought their property in the hills, between the spectacular Cambrian coast and the main highway 101, in 1977.

They built a very attractive Mediterranean winery right on highway 46 and have since built their home on the property. Pat makes Zinfandel, Pinot Noir, Chenin Blanc and Chardonnay.

Mastantuono is one of the prettiest small wineries in America and is located in some of California's most beautiful country. With this inspiration it is no wonder Pat and Leona make such good wines.

Estrella River Winery

Estrella is fast justifying its name, which means "star" in Spanish. Recently this, one of California's most spectacular wineries, has been bought by the Beringer Wine World group of the Nestle Company. The chiefs at Beringer had obviously seen this rising star and were not only very interested in the brand but also in the large 875 acre vineyard property for supply of top quality fruit for their California blended varietals.

Estrella had its start in 1972, when Los Angeles businessman, Cliff Giacobine, looking for a rural investment, was advised to plant vines on his recently acquired cattle ranch. Cliff talked his younger half brother, Gary Eberle, into giving up his doctoral studies in cytology and to join him in the venture as viticulturist and winemaker. Gary went on to start his own winery nearby in 1983.

Cliff and Gary set up a large vineyard covering a full square mile and followed with a winery in 1977. They planted a number of varieties including the "trendy" Chardonnay and Sauvignon Blanc. They have been very successful with Muscat and Zinfandel. Tom Mayers recently took over from Gary as winemaker.

The winery itself is stunning, set on the top of one of the rolling hills of the region. It has observation towers with breathtaking panoramic views of the attractive countryside. Estrella wines have always been perceived as excellent value for money and am sure the new owners will be anxious to promote and further this positive image.

An Introduction to Santa Barbara & Santa Maria

Obviously from reading this atlas you have no doubt gained the impression that I take a very positive view of wine growing regions, their wineries, the people involved and the wines they make. I realise this is true but certainly if you take the time to visit wineries anywhere in North America, I am sure you will come to the same conclusion. The Santa Maria and particularly the Santa Ynez Valley have without a doubt some of the world's most beautiful countryside, unspoilt and, for California, very sparsely inhabited. You can drive for miles throughout these valleys carved out of the uplifted plateau and not see anything more than the odd deer quietly going about its business.

Vineyards were planted last century in this region, even in downtown Santa Barbara, but it was not rediscovered until the wine boom of the mid 1960's. The largest vineyard in the region, the 1,500 acre Tepesquet Vineyards has just been bought by a joint venture set up by Robert Mondavi and the Kendall-Jackson Winery from Lake County. Many other vineyards and wineries both large and small have sprung up. Two of America's finest are included; Zaca Mesa and Firestone, the brainchild of the cultured Brooks Firestone, one of the heirs of the tire enterprise. Vineyards now cover over 10,000 acres of the county which is all either region I or region II in climate, the most suitable conditions for premium wine growing.

One just hopes the happy balance between the vine and the environment can be maintained, so that this beautiful region can be enjoyed by future generations.

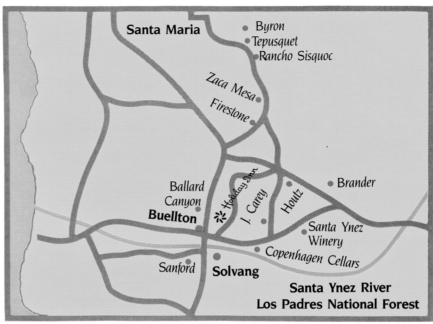

Santa Barbara & Santa Maria

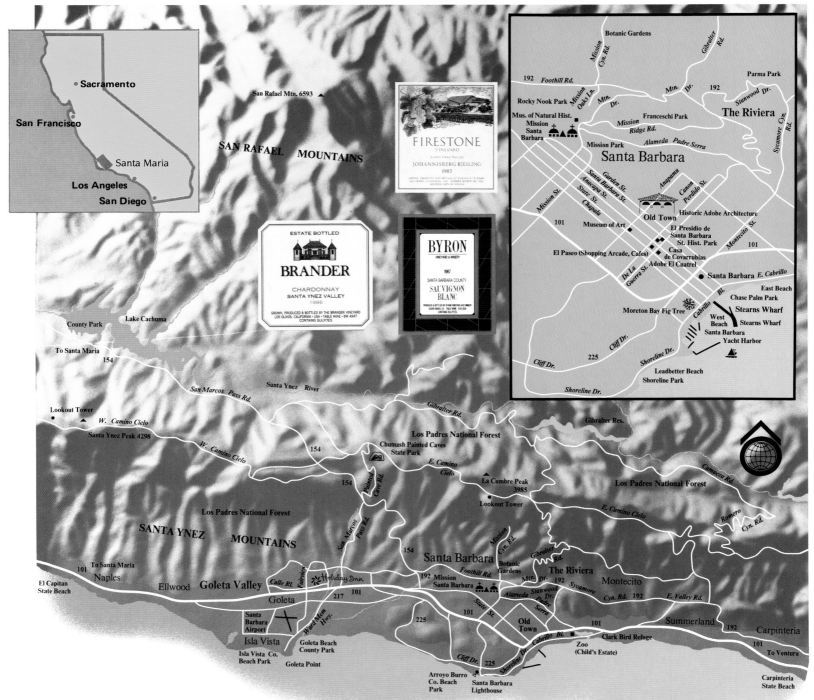

I t would be hard to find a better combination of people to run a wine business than Byron Ken Brown, his wife Deborah and Dale Hampton.

Ken's interest in wines developed when he was not long out of college, where he had obtained a degree in Business Administration. This was at the start of the wine revolution and he became involved in setting up the famous "Knights of the Vine" organisation. After a time with his father in property development, he decided wine was for him and went "back to school" at Fresno State and, by his last year, was running the college winery. Through his interests in Santa Barbara wine, he landed a job at Zaca Mesa in 1977 and made their acclaimed first (1978) vintage. Ken met his wife Deborah there —

she was managing the visitors centre — and they married in 1983. About this time he helped friend Dale Hampton, whose farming company manages over 4,000 acres of wines in the county, to set up his own winery.

Deborah and Ken became involved and the three are now the chief partners in the venture. The wines are made from grapes selected by Dale from the pick of the regions vineyards — Chardonnay and Pinot Noir from the cool region I, Santa Maria Valley and Cabernet and Sauvignon Blanc from the region II, Santa Ynez Valley.

Byron's winery built in 1984 is very attractively lined in timber and has been expanded in 1988. The blend of skills and enthusiasm at Byron shows in their wines.

BYRON VINEYARDS & WINERY
Address: 5230 Tepusquet Road, Santa Maria, California, 93454
Phone: 805/937 7288
Year of Establishment: 1984
Owner: Byron Vineyards & Winery Inc.
Winemaker: Byron "Ken" Brown
Principal Varieties Grown: Chardonnay
Acres Under Vine: 5
Average Annual Crush: 220 tons total

Principal Wines & Brands	Cellar Potential (Years)
Chardonnay Barrel fermented Reserve	1992
Pinot Noir Reserve	1991
Sauvignon Blanc	1998

Trade Tours – Available.
Retail Room Sales – Available.
Hours open to Public: Daily from 10am to 4pm, closed New Year's, Easter, Thanksgiving and Christmas.

The Brander Vineyard

F red Brander is somewhat reclusive and very much an individualist. In 1979, this Davis graduate set up a winery to produce classic Bordeaux style wines only. A Cabernet Sauvignon, blended with Merlot and Cabernet Franc and a Sauvignon Blanc blended with Semillon are produced along with various Blancs de Noirs, i.e. whites made from red varieties, in this case Merlot and Cabernet Franc. Fred has established a 45 acre vineyard and winery near Los Olivos and is building quite a reputation.

The Firestone Vineyard

Brooks Firestone's recipe for good living includes good fortune, good sense and more than just a little magic.

As grandson of Harvey Firestone, founder of the tire empire, Brooks has led an enviable life. With his wife Kate, a former soloist ballerina with Sadler Wells in England, Brooks left the security of the tire business for the excitement of pioneering a new wine region just north of Santa Barbara.

His interest began when his father Leonard, former Ambassador to Belgium, asked Brooks to investigate the possibility of planting vines on a property he had just purchased in the Santa Ynez Valley. Studies showed a grape surplus developing, so Brooks said, "Why not make wine, really top

wine, as well?" In 1975 the first crush took place.

The change of lifestyle has obviously suited him for he still has his boyish good looks as a grandfather in his early fifties.

Firestone Vineyard has 265 acres planted to seven premium varieties, primarily of their own vinifera root stocks. Cool ocean breezes and morning fog allow for a slow maturation of fruit to optimum colour, flavour and character. The winery is magnificently set up to produce the best wines possible. Cathedral-like rooms house row upon row of oak barrels. The latest equipment ensures all wine lots can be kept separate and their individual nature preserved, one of the most difficult things to do in many wineries.

Overseeing the vineyard and wine production is winemaker Alison Green, a U.C. Davis graduate. She had earlier worked in her father's Simi Winery in Sonoma and even spent time with the legendary Andre Tchelistecheff, who was then consulting to Simi.

Alison has been a part of the winemaking team at Firestone Vineyard since 1976 and from 1981 on has assumed the responsibilities of winemaker. One of her favourite aspects of the position is being able to continue working with Andre, who has

consulted for Firestone since the planting of the grapes.

There is a real sense of commitment and being part of the team among all at Firestone Vineyard. Brooks directs all vineyard and winery operation, but is frequently found in the cellar lending a hand. Kate plays an active role in public relations as well as managing Firestone's other winery, J. Carey Cellars. Alison lives a stone's throw from the Chardonnay vineyard for easy access. The rest of the staff is conscientious and dedicated, which makes for a warm family atmosphere at the winery.

All the classic varietals at Firestone are produced and rank in the top echelon of American wine. Although well known for rich velvety Merlots and Cabernet Sauvignons, the Johannisberg Riesling is what they are most noted for, an off-dry wine with generous flavours of apples, apricots and orange blossoms. And their late harvest Johannisberg Riesling is something else, heavily botrytised and rich, but so clean. I opened a half bottle of the 1985 prior to Christmas. It lay corked and less than half full for three months, by accident, and when opened again, it was still stunning.

If humanly possible visit this winery or at least try some of their wines.

FIRESTONE VINEYARD
Address: PO Box 244/5017 Zaca Station Road, Los Olivos, CA., 93441
Phone: 805/688 3940
Year of Establishment: 1972
Owner: A. Brooks Firestone
Winemaker: Alison Green
Principal Varieties Grown: Chardonnay, Gewurztraminer, Johannisberg Riesling, Sauv. Blanc, Cabernet Sauv., Merlot, Pinot Noir
Acres Under Vine: 265
Average Annual Crush: 1,200 tons

Principal Wines & Brands	Cellar Potential (Years)
Johannisberg Riesling	2-3
Johannisberg Riesling Select Harvest	6-10
Chardonnay	2-4

Trade Tours – Available
Retail Room Sales – Available
Hours open to Public: 7 days a week from 10am to 4pm
Retail Distribution: All States and also England, Denmark, Japan and Canada

Gale Sysock is one of the more inspired winemakers of North America. His competence and enthusiasm seem well matched. Gale has not had it easy for his family came from the Russian Ukraine area and he put himself through U.C. Davis, working 7 days a week as a cook and construction worker. He feels this experience has helped him a great deal with the practical side of winemaking.

Zaca Mesa is superbly located and suitably named; Zaca is Indian for "Peace and quiet" and Mesa for "hills".

Marshall Ream, an Atlantic Richfield executive, retired early and bought 1 800 acres in the Santa Ynez valley. He planted vineyards and had his first wines made at the Monterey Vineyard. Their success spurred him onto building a winery in 1977 and Ken Brown became the first winemaker (he now operates Byron Vineyards)

John C. Cashman III, bought the winery and the 235 acres of vineyard in 1987. His philosophy is to go to totally estate grown grapes at present Zaca Mesa is about 75% self-sufficient.

When I visited the winery late in 1987, Gale took me through an extensive barrel tasting of his 1987 wines. He has some stunning Chardonnays many different styles and plenty of options to blend them. Likewise, his 1987 Pinot Noirs have great colour and cherry/plum richness and some Shiraz, the grape of the Rhone Valley, grown extensively in Australia. The 1987 Shiraz showed raspberry flavours with some mint and was distinctly peppery, a very good wine only sold at the vineyard.

Zaca Mesa has brought back its production to 50,000 cases, to get quality to the zenith. I am sure the sales will quickly build up again with the wines they are making

Zaca Mesa

Sandford Winery

In 1981, Dick Sandford left a partnership he had set up with his U.C. Davis classmate, Michael Benedict and established his own winery just out of Buellton. Dick's main motivation in starting his own winery, was to get right back to the creative side and involve himself more heavily in winemaking.

The first Sandford wines were made at the Edna Valley Vineyard and the following year, they moved to a warehouse in Buellton. They are at present building a winery on a 760 acre ranch west of the town on Santa Rosa Road. Already Sandford have built up a big reputation for their Chardonnay. The distribution and sales of Sandford wine have mushroomed almost overnight and it is obvious Dick and his wife Thelma are very active in promoting the good wines they make. A lot more will be heard of this winery in the future.

Introduction to the Santa Clara Valley

I have already covered the eastern and northern portions of this area along with the Livermore valley. San Jose proper has had an association with wine ever since 1777, when the Franciscan Fathers bought the mission vines to the Santa Clara de Asis Mission. In the 1850's, commercial wine production commenced with French vignerons, Antoine Delmas and Etienne Thee, planting vineyards and starting wine production. Etienne's son-in-law, Charles Le Franc, succeeded him and, when his son Henry died in 1909, he was succeeded by his brother-in-law (then 50 years old) Paul

Masson. In 1896, Masson had started planting the mountain vineyard he called Cresta. He built the mountain winery later, incorporating part of St. Patricks Church, in San Jose, partly destroyed in the 1906 earthquake.

Masson had grown up in Beaune, Burgundy, before migrating to America at the age of nineteen. He became known for his grand entertaining and helped put Santa Clara on the wine map. Another famous winery in this rugged mountainous part of the region 2,500 ft. above sea level is the Ridge Vineyard established in 1960.

Almaden have just moved from their original home on Blossom Hill Road, the site of Etienne Thee's first vineyard in 1852. In fact it is the urban sprawl that has forced many of the larger wineries to search further south and north, for vineyard land and eventually to build their wineries. Many small boutique wineries have sprung up in Santa Clara County in recent years and some of the region south towards Monterey county is not under such urbanisation pressure.

Santa Clara is rich in wine history and well worth visiting.

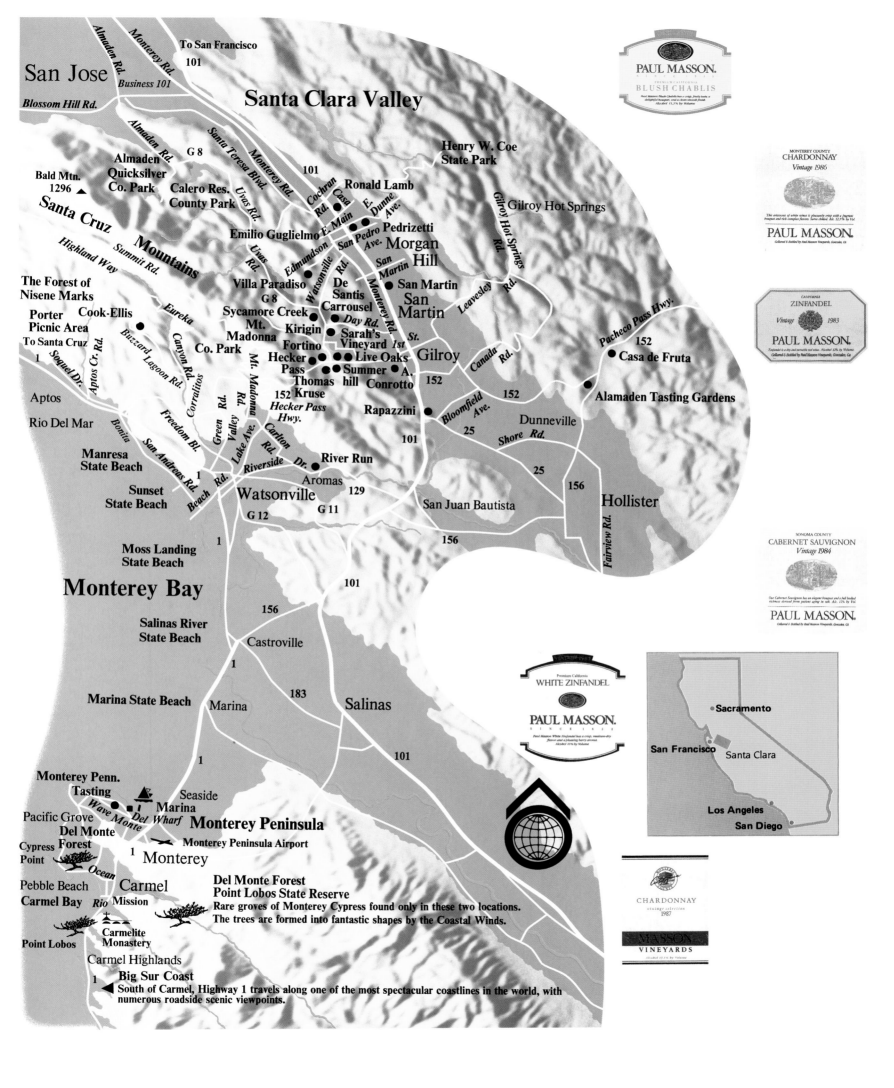

San Jose
To San Francisco
101
Monterey Rd.
Almaden Rd.
Business 101
Blossom Hill Rd.

Santa Clara Valley

Almaden Rd.
G 8
Santa Teresa Blvd.
Almaden
Quicksilver
Co. Park
Uvas Rd.
101
Monterey Rd.
Henry W. Coe State Park

Bald Mtn.
1296 ▲
Calero Res.
County Park
Cochran Rd.
Casa
Ronald Lamb
E. Dunne Ave.
E. Main
Gilroy Hot Springs Rd.
Gilroy Hot Springs

Santa Cruz
Mountains
Highland Way
Summit Rd.
Emilio Guglielmo
Edmundson
San Pedro Ave.
Pedrizetti
Morgan Hill
San Martin Rd.
Uvas Rd.
Watsonville Rd.
Monterey Rd.

The Forest of Nisene Marks
Eureka
Villa Paradiso
G 8
De Santis
Carrousel
San Martin
San Martin

Porter Picnic Area
Cook-Ellis
Canyon Rd.
Sycamore Creek
Mt. Madonna
Co. Park
Day Rd.
Kirigin
Sarah's Vineyard
Leavesley Rd.
Pacheco Pass Hwy.
152
Casa de Fruta

To Santa Cruz
1
Soquel Dr.
Aptos Cr. Rd.
Buzzard Lagoon Rd.
Corralitos
Fortino
Hecker Pass
Live Oaks
1st St.
Gilroy
Canada Rd.
Alamaden Tasting Gardens

Aptos
Mt. Madonna Rd.
Summer hill
A. Conrotto
152
152
Freedom Bl.
Thomas
Kruse

Rio Del Mar
Bonita
San Andreas Rd.
Green Valley Rd.
Lake Ave.
Carlton Rd.
152
Hecker Pass Hwy.
Rapazzini
Bloomfield Ave.
101
25
Dunneville Rd.

Manresa State Beach
Riverside Dr.
River Run
Shore Rd.

Sunset State Beach
Beach Rd.
Aromas
25
156
Hollister

Watsonville
129
San Juan Bautista
1
G 12
G 11
156
Fairview Rd.

Moss Landing State Beach
1
156

Monterey Bay
101

Salinas River State Beach
Castroville

Marina State Beach
1
Marina
183
Salinas

1
101

Monterey Penn. Tasting
Seaside
Marina
Del Wharf
Wave
Monte
Monterey Peninsula

Pacific Grove
Del Monte Forest
1
Monterey Peninsula Airport
Cypress Point
Ocean
Monterey

Pebble Beach
Carmel Bay
Rio
Carmel
Mission
Del Monte Forest
Point Lobos State Reserve
Rare groves of Monterey Cypress found only in these two locations. The trees are formed into fantastic shapes by the Coastal Winds.

Point Lobos
Carmelite Monastery
Carmel Highlands

1
Big Sur Coast
◄ South of Carmel, Highway 1 travels along one of the most spectacular coastlines in the world, with numerous roadside scenic viewpoints.

PAUL MASSON.
PREMIUM CALIFORNIA
BLUSH CHABLIS
Paul Masson Blush Chablis has a crisp, fruity taste, a delightful bouquet, and a clean smooth finish. Alcohol 11.5% by Volume

MONTEREY COUNTY
CHARDONNAY
Vintage 1986
This aristocrat of white wines is pleasantly crisp with a fragrant bouquet and rich complex flavors. Serve chilled. Alc. 13.5% by Vol.
PAUL MASSON
Cellared & Bottled by Paul Masson Vineyards, Gonzales, CA

CALIFORNIA
ZINFANDEL
Vintage 1983
Zinfandel is a dry and versatile red wine. Alcohol 12% by Volume
PAUL MASSON.
Cellared & Bottled by Paul Masson Vineyards, Gonzales, CA

SONOMA COUNTY
CABERNET SAUVIGNON
Vintage 1984
Our Cabernet Sauvignon has an elegant bouquet and a full bodied richness derived from patient aging in oak. Alc. 12% by Vol.
PAUL MASSON
Cellared & Bottled by Paul Masson Vineyards, Gonzales, CA

Premium California
WHITE ZINFANDEL
PAUL MASSON.
SINCE 1852
Paul Masson White Zinfandel has a crisp, medium-dry flavor and a pleasing berry aroma. Alcohol 10% by Volume

CHARDONNAY
vintage selection
1987
MASSON
VINEYARDS
Alcohol 13.5% by Volume

• Sacramento
San Francisco
Santa Clara
Los Angeles
San Diego

Paul Masson Vineyards

Paul Masson Vineyards

Paul Masson, like Almaden, claims the same birth year 1852. Paul Masson also claims to be "California's oldest continuously producing winery". Its history traces back as well, to the Bordeaux vigneron Etienne Thee, who poineered commercial wine growing on the original "Narvaez" land grant south west of San Jose, in 1857. Etienne was succeeded by his son-in-law, Charles Le Franc, also a French immigrant. Then Charles' son, Henry succeeded him, then along came Paul Masson in 1880 from Burgundy, France who married Le Franc's daughter, Louise and took over the operation on Henry's death in 1909.

In the meantime, Masson planted the mountain vineyard and built a striking winery in the sky, as he named it, just out of Saratoga in the Santa Cruz Mountains. He concentrated strongly on Champagne, but also introduced classic varieties such as Chardonnay, Cabernet Sauvignon and Pinot Noir, which he brought back from his regular trips to France.

After the 1906 earthquake had all but destroyed St. Patrick's Church in San Jose, Masson purchased the twelfth century Romanesque portal and other decorations which had been imported from Spain.

Although this property has been sold by the new owners, Vintners International, they continue to use it and the famous summer concerts which started in 1958, still attract over 60,000 music lovers each year.

Operations have now spread to Saratoga and the Salinas valley in Monterey county with 3,500 acres of wines and a very large winery.

Paul Masson pioneered the exporting of North American wines in 1960 and by 1969, was exporting to fifty countries and had received the Federal Government's "E" for export excellence award.

During Prohibition, Paul Masson was granted America's first permit to produce Medicinal Champagne. It was sold to Martin Ray in 1936, four years before his death and bought by Seagrams in 1942. European wine experts, Alfred Fromm and Otto Meyer, expanded the company to four wineries and around 35 million gallons capacity by the 1970's.

The Paul Masson philosophy "We will sell no wine before its time", well known to television viewers through the late Orson Welles and Sir John Gielgud, comes from the original vintner himself, who would not market any wine until he felt it was sufficiently mature.

Although Paul Masson has gone through many developmental changes, its philosophy and the quality and value of its wines, continue as number one priority. This is no different under the new, thoroughly committed owners, Vintners International, who are basically the staff who built it all up.

PAUL MASSON VINEYARDS
Address: 14831 Pierce Road, Saratoga, California, 95070
Phone: 408/741 5182
Year of Establishment: 1852
Owner: Vintners International
Winemaker: Larry Brink
Principal Varieties Purchased: Cabernet Sauvignon, Pinot Blanc, Pinot Noir, Chardonnay, Riesling, Chenin Blanc, French Colomard, Sauvignon Blanc

Principal Wines & Brands	Cellar Potential (Years)
Brut Champagne	2
Cabernet Sauvignon	4
Emerald Dry	2
French Colombard	

Trade Tours – Available by appointment only.
Retail Distribution: International

Almaden lays claim to be California's oldest producing winery dating back to 1852, when French immigrant Etienne Thee planted vines there. Almaden has, in fact, just moved out of their traditional home as part of a rationalisation plan.

The first wines under the Almaden label, were actually marketed around 1880, by Charles Le Franc. Following repeal in 1933, the winery was re-opened, by a syndicate headed by Charles Jones.

Louis Benoist, a wealthy San Francisco businessman, bought the property in 1941, as a weekend retreat to entertain his friends and he even brought famous chef, Louise Savin, to run his kitchen.

Benoist also brought in Frank Schoonmaker to advise him on what to do with the winery. Schoonmaker is credited with introducing premium Californian wine to the eastern markets. He found Benoist a winemaker, Oliver Goulet, who had previously worked for Martin Ray at Paul Masson. One of the innovative wines produced was America's first Grenache Rose, made in the French "Tavel" style. It became an instant success.

The vineyards in Santa Clara expanded, but, as suburbia infiltrated, Almaden gradually moved south and east, planting over 4,000 acres in San Benito county and 2,000 acres in Monterey county, with two large wineries. 1967 brought the departure of Benoist, when he was forced to sell after trouble with some of his other enterprises. Now Almaden also has wineries in Kern and Fresno counties.

The Charles Le Franc label was launched in the 1970's by wine master, Klaus Mathes, who spent twenty years with Almaden until he left in 1987.

Almaden is now under the ownership of the Heublein organisation of Connecticut. It has become one of North America's larges winemaking concerns and has been successful through building a quality and value image with all its myriad products from premium bottles, through to 28 litre "bag in the box" packages for restaurant use. This value concept continues strongly today.

An Introduction To Santa Cruz Mountains

In 1982, the Santa Cruz Mountains viticultural area appellation was established, taking in parts of San Mateo, Santa Cruz and Santa Clara Counties. During pre-Prohibition times, a number of small vineyards flourished in this region, producing some great wines. Its modern day development has virtually taken place only since 1961, when Robert and Polly Millen established their Woodside Vineyard on Kings Mountain Road. They also restored and use the Cabernet grapes from the La Questa Vineyard, famous during the last century.

The Santa Cruz region is one of the most picturesque and beautiful in California. Highway 17, which runs through the mountains from San Jose to Santa Cruz, has some awesome views. Situated high above the city of Los Gatos is the old Novitiate Winery founded in 1888 by the Jesuit order to supply altar wines to the Catholic church. In 1986, the winery and its classic old buildings were taken over by Domaine M. Marion, a wine negociants business, started by businessman and yachtsman, Dennis Marion, in 1979.

Ridge Vineyards, some 2,600 feet above sea level, near the summit of Black Mountain, has made a statement in North American wine over the last thirty years that is well in excess of its size.

The Santa Cruz Mountains are a viticultural jewel, but it takes a real commitment to succeed in this demanding region.

Santa Cruz Mountains

Domaine M. Marion

Dennis Marion is a man with considerable energy. An experienced wine retailer and marketer, he decided to open a wine negociant business in 1979. He commenced with a series of labels featuring artists floral paintings; business developed well and he decided he needed his own winery to expand. Having been associated with the David Bruce Winery at Los Gatos as its president, he approached the Jesuit order, who were operating the old Novitiate Winery at their monastery, to see whether he could lease the facility. Dennis succeeded and Domaine M. Marion was created. He has breathed considerable life into the magnificent old winery with a substantial production, as well as many events and tastings.

The Novitiate Winery had its beginnings over a century ago in 1888, when it opened to produce wine according to the Canon law of the Catholic church. These altar wines were the mainstay of the vineyards until 1967, when the training of Novices was moved to Montecito in Southern California. The winery's production slowed to a virtual standstill with the grapes being sold to other wineries such as Congress Springs.

Dennis Marion is to be congratulated in bringing this magnificent old winery back to life. It is well worth a visit to soak in the tranquility and beauty created by the monks and to taste some of Domaine Marion's fine wines.

Ridge Vineyards

character their fruit contributes to the wine. Ridge have worked a modern renaissance in making natural red wines, using the wild yeast present on the skins of the grapes and striving to maximise the fruit flavours and colour the grapes have to offer. This is achieved by long contact with the skins and judicious pressing of the skins. The wines are made from fully ripe grapes and are usually not fined or filtered. They also receive a comparatively long ageing in small oak barrels.

Ridge had its beginnings in 1959, right at the start of the wine revolution. David Bennion, a devoted home winemaker, interested three of his fellow Stanford Research Institute scientists in restoring an old vineyard and dilapidated cellar at the top of Black Mountain. In 1968, he quit his job and was joined by Paul Draper, the current winemaker, who had made wine in Chile and travelled extensively through France.

Some of the partners in Ridge have changed but, basically, the Ridge philosophy has remained constant. All wines are labelled with the region of their origin and their greatest are usually those from their Montebello vineyards around the winery.

Ridge's isolated and spectucular location on the Montebello Ridge, approaching the peak of Black Mountain, some 2,600 feet above the Santa Clara Valley, somehow seems to suit the statement they have made in North American wines - one which far outweighs their size as a vintner.

Their red wines, particularly, have set them apart from almost all other winemakers. The Ridge Cabernet Sauvignons and Zinfandels come not only from their own vineyards, comprising 50 acres around the winery, but from selected vineyards as far away as the Dry Creek Valley in Sonoma, Napa and the Sierra Foothills. The vineyards are selected for their old wines and the extra

Introduction to the Sierra Foothills

With some of California's richest historical heritage, gold of another sort is now coming out of the wine regions of the Amador and Eldorado counties, east of Sacramento.

In the years of 1860 to 1890, following the gold rush, many vineyards and more than one hundred wineries mushroomed, over a wide area of the foothills; then Prohibition caused the demise of the region. The newly originated and more easily managed land, with its high yielding potential in the central valley, forced a mass exodus from the Foothills.

The advent of the premium wine revolution and boutique wine estates caused a strong revival of the Sierras region during the 1960's. With its inland location and high altitude, frost can be a problem and therefore vineyard site with the correct aspect and air drainage is critical. All these factors suit small wine estates and around 30 of these have set up over the last 20 years.

U.C. Davis studies of wine made from Foothill grapes during the 1960's proved beyond a doubt, that high quality table wines could be produced. Zinfandel particularly does better in this region than anywhere else in California.

The D'Agostino winery in the Shenandoah Valley, dating back to 1865, is one of the few original cellars still in operation. The Shenandoah Valley now has a number of top wineries. Eldorado county has been a little slower to develop, but Greg and Susan Boeger have revived the old Lombardo-Possati Winery, dating back to 1860. Greg is the grandson of Napa wine pioneer Anton Nichelini. Richard Bush is also making excellent wines at his Madrona Vineyards.

The Foothills will probably never be a big wine region in terms of production but will, no doubt, support many new and interesting wineries, making characterful wines.

Sierra Foothills

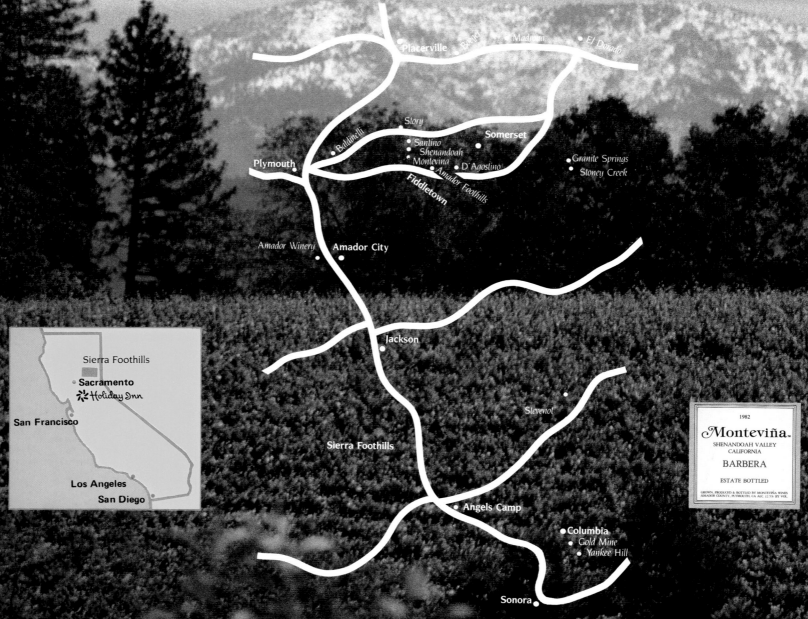

MontEviña
ESTATE BOTTLED

PREMIUM RED

TABLE WINE
SHENANDOAH VALLEY
CALIFORNIA

GROWN, PRODUCED & BOTTLED BY MONTEVIÑA WINES
AMADOR COUNTY, PLYMOUTH, CA ALC. 13.0% BY VOL.

1985
MontEviña

SHENANDOAH VALLEY
CALIFORNIA

FUMÉ BLANC

ESTATE BOTTLED

GROWN, PRODUCED & BOTTLED BY MONTEVIÑA
WINES, AMADOR COUNTY, PLYMOUTH, CA
ALC. 12.5% BY VOL. CONTAINS SULFITES

Placerville · Bueno · Madrona · El Dorado

Story
Baldinelli · Santino
Shenandoah · Somerset
Montevina · D'Agostino · Granite Springs
Plymouth · Amador Foothills · Stoney Creek
Fiddletown

Amador Winery · Amador City

Jackson

Sierra Foothills

Stevenot

Sierra Foothills
Sacramento
Holiday Inn
San Francisco

Los Angeles
San Diego

Angels Camp

Columbia
Gold Mine
Yankee Hill

Sonora

1982
MontEviña

SHENANDOAH VALLEY
CALIFORNIA

BARBERA

ESTATE BOTTLED

GROWN, PRODUCED & BOTTLED BY MONTEVIÑA WINES,
AMADOR COUNTY, PLYMOUTH, CA ALC. 12.5% BY VOL.

Baldinelli Vineyards

Ed Baldinelli retired from Kaiser Engineering to slow down a bit and took on a winery and partnership with John Miller, a Foothill grape grower, who had spent some time with the Amador county Department of Agriculture. The partnership is working well and the Baldinelli Winery is making some very good estate bottled Cabernet Sauvignons and Zinfandels. Ed certainly is not getting the rest he planned on, but is delighting in his involvement in producing quality wines. Their vineyard development started in 1972, but the winery's first wines were only made in 1979.

Boeger Vineyard

Greg Boeger's roots are well entwined with the vine. His grandfather, Anton Nichelini, founded a well known winery under his own name in the Napa Valley, in 1890.

Greg graduated from U.C. Davis with a master's degree, worked in wine research and then decided to go out on his own. He bought an old disused winery, then part of a pear orchard, a winery which had previously operated under the Lombardo-Fossati name, founded in 1860.

The painstakingly restored buildings are set in a pretty, sheltered valley and the vineyards are planted on the slopes in the rich, red volcanic soil. Greg makes excellent wines from the classic varieties, Chardonnay, Cabernet Suavignon, Merlot and Sauvignon Blanc, as well as two good value blended wines - Sierra Blanc and Hangtown Red. Greg and his wife Susan welcome visitors.

Madrona Vineyard

One of the highest altitude vineyards and wineries in California, at over 3,000 ft., Madrona Vineyards commands a panoramic view of the snow covered Sierra Nevada ranges. Placerville engineer, Richard Bush, established a 30 acre vineyard during the 1970's. After some trouble in selling his grapes, he decided to build a winery in 1980 and become a full time vigneron.

His estate bottled wines have developed a very sound reputation and in 1985, with business expanding, he took on Mark Foster, a promising young enologist. Madrona produce Chardonnay, White Riesling, Cabernet Sauvignon and Zinfandel. Many of their wines represent excellent value for money.

Montevina

Massoni house, which turned out well so Walter decided to build a winery, which he did in grand style in 1973. Gary has since left to pursue his career on the central coast.

The winemaker is now Jeffery Meyers, who joined in 1981, straight out of U.C. Davis, where he had received the Departmental citation for outstanding scholastic achievement. Jeff has turned out to be a very good practical winemaker also. His 1984

Zinfandel is the best I have seen, with strong cherry and plum fruit, overlaid with cedar and tobacco – deep, rich and complex. His 1987 vintage promises to be even better. A 1986 Botrytised Semillon with 10% residual sugar and 13.4% alchohol with lemon/grapefruit crispness and honey-like palate is just superb.

Montevina is one winery to definitely watch.

The Sierra Foothill's largest winery, Montevina, has also developed a reputation which many of the coastal counties wineries would envy.

In 1970, Gilroy banker Walter Field, bought two lots of Amador county land, the Massoni Ranch and the Brown Homestead. In 1972, Walter planted some 60 acres. His son-in-law, Gary Cott made some experimental wines in the basement of the

Santino Wines

Nancy and Matthew Santino fell in love with the beauty of the Amador Foothills. Their winery lies in a very pretty valley near Shenandoah vineyards and has a most picturesque outlook on the Sierras. In 1979 they sold their liquor store in the San Francisco Bay area and Scott Harvey, who had worked at two of the Foothill's leading wineries, Montevina and Story Vineyards, joined them. The wines have shone. Santino now distributes to all major states and Canada. Making a number of varietal wines and some vineyard designated Zinfandels, the Escher Vineyards special selection, being particularly good. Santino Winery has a happy feeling about it, which is reflected in its wines.

SANTINO WINES
Address: 12225 Steiner Road
Phone: 209/245 6979
Year of Establishment: 1979
Owner: Joseph Swhweitzer & Scott Harvey
Winemaker: Scott Harvey
Principal Varieties Grown: Zinfandel, Barbera, Muscat Canelli, Riesling, Rhone Varieties, Potugues Port Varieties
Acres Under Vine: Experimental vineyards only
Average Annual Crush: 450 tons

Principal Wines & Brands	Cellar Potential (Years)
Fiddletown Zinfandel (incl 3 others)	20
Sonoma County late Harvest Riesling	40
Muscate Canelli	5

Trade Tours – Available by appointment only.
Retail Room Sales – Available.
Hours open to Public: Daily from noon to 4pm
Retail Distribution: National

Shenandoah Vineyards

Shenandoah Vineyards has grown considerably in recent years and is challenging to be the Foothills' largest wine producer. Leon Sobon, formerly an engineer in Palo Alto, his wife Shirley and their six children pulled up stakes, selling all their property, moving to vineyard land in the Shenandoah valley. Since 1977, they have created one of the best managed and manicured vineyards I have seen, along with a winery that features many delightful human touches. All their work shows signs of love and care.

The Sobons, who had made wine at home in Palo Alto, have been helped by their children, who have pitched in and helped with the new vineyards and winery so that today it is a real picture. Shirley even went back to nursing for a number of years to make ends meet.

Today the Sobons' suffering seems to be over and the good wines being made and their reception assures their future is looking good.

Story Vineyard

In 1973, Sacramento vigneron, Eugene Story, followed his home winemaking experience by building a brick winery on a 55 acre vineyard. He and his wife, Ann, purchased just out of Plymouth, in the Shenandoah valley. When Gene died in 1981, Ann renamed the vineyard and winery "Story" (it had previously been known as Consumnes River Vineyard, for the river that forms one of its boundaries).

Ann has continued in partnership with Kevin Shannon and his Vin Information company based in San Francisco. Kevin assists in the managing, making and marketing of the Story Vineyard's wines. Their estate grown Zinfandel, is the chief wine produced.

Introduction to Sonoma Valley North

This region encompasses the largest wine growing area of Sonoma county, north of Santa Rosa. The area can be roughly divided into three separate regions, the Russian River Valley, The Dry Creek Valley and the Alexander Valley.

Although there were more than 100 wineries in the Sonoma Valley in the last century, it took the wine boom of the 1960's to re-establish viticulture on a wide-spread basis.

The early development of Northern Sonoma came about later than in the southern part of the valley around the town of Sonoma, which boasted some of North America's highest profile wine pioneers. Between them, General Mariano Vallejo and Count Agoston Horazathy stole the limelight in the 1850's and 1860's.

The Fountain Grove Vineyards and Winery, the remains of which lie on the northern outskirts of Santa Rosa, were home to one of the first major wine ventures of Northern Sonoma. In 1875, renowned poet Thomas Lake Harris moved his "Brotherhood of the the New Life" from New York state. Two of his followers were Missouri viticulturist, Dr. John Hyde and Japanese nobleman, Baron Kanaye Nagasawa. These two founded Fountain Grove and planted 400 acres of vines. Nagasawa took control of the enterprise in 1892, but, by the time he died in 1932, the winery had had its ups and downs. Hanns Kornell was involved for a while in the 1940's, but it was finally closed in 1951.

The old Martini and Prati Winery, west of Santa Rosa, dates back to the 1870's and has come back into the hands of the family. The Korbel family also founded their sparkling wine operation on the Russian River in 1886 and the Foppiano family started their winery in 1896.

The Italian Swiss Colony has a rich history and a classic old Roman-inspired winery. In 1880, banker Andrea Sbarboro, started a scheme to settle poor Italian and Swiss immigrants and give them work. He created the town of Asti and the Italian Swiss Colony Winery, built in 1887. Pietro C. Rossi, a pharmacist, became the first and very successful winemaker. In 1897, during a wine surplus he built, what was then the world's biggest underground wine tank with a capacity of 300,000 gallons. It was christened by holding a dance complete with a military band inside!!

Today, wine in Northern Sonoma county is booming, with close to 100 wineries and extensive vineyards. The climate varies from Region I, near the coast on Russian River through to Region III, in parts of the Alexander Valley. Many of North America's most respected wines and wineries are located within these beautiful valleys.

Introduction to Sonoma Valley North

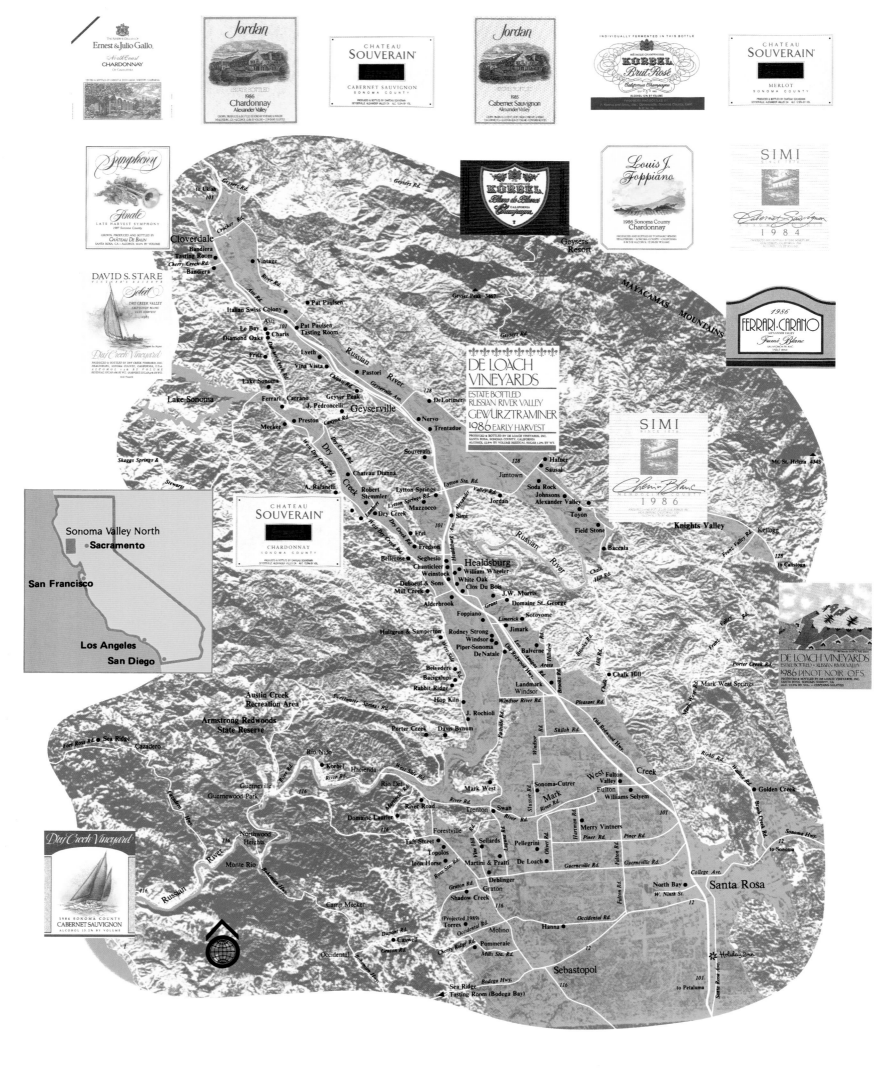

Belvedere Winery

In 1979, Peter Friedman an advertising executive who had created Rodney Strong's first personalised labels for Tiburon Vintners, decided he would go out on his own. He entered into agreements with some of Napa and Sonoma's most prestigious vineyards, Winery Lake and York Creek in Napa as well as Bacigalupi and Robert Young in Sonoma. The concept pushed vineyard designation one step further, with the vineyard name being the main feature on the label, the grape variety, appelation and the Belvedere name, being very much in the background. Peter built a winery in 1981 and has the support of partner Bill Hambrecht, an investment banker, also involved with Chalone Vineyards.

Peter has chosen his vineyard owners carefully. Charles Bacigalupi has 45 acres, mainly Pinot and Chardonnay; this vineyard is situated right behind the Belvedere Winery and, planted in 1964, produces grapes of rich and complex flavours. Winery Lake is, of course, one of the Carneros region's greatest vineyards, producing Pinot Noir and Chardonnay of distinction. Robert Young from the Alexander Valley, traces his Sonoma grapegrowing background back to 1860 and supplies some leading wineries, including Chateau St. Jean.

York Creek is a Mayacamas Mountain Vineyard, high on Spring Mountain Road and planted predominately to Cabernet Sauvignon. It is run by Fritz Maytag, who also owns the Anchor Steam Brewery in San Francisco. The Winery Lake Vineyard was owned by Rene and Veronica di Rosa and, in fact, Veronica's water colours are featured on the Belvedere labels. Sterling Vineyards bought Winery Lake Vineyards in late 1987 so the future of this label is a little unclear.

Belvedere also have another range under the Discovery label. These are affordable wines, with the district appelation on the label, as well as the variety. For these wines, Belvedere also buy in some of the wine, as well as the grapes. In fact, for their vineyard designated range from the up-market vineyards, they have just gone to a new label, which features Belvedere strongly. This is a good move as the wines are good and the winery is going in the right direction.

Bandiera — California Wine Company

In 1937, Emil Bandiera opened a small winery to make red wine, much of which, was sold in bulk and to visitors, who brought their own jugs and barrels. The next two generations of the family ran the winery until 1980, when it was sold to a syndicate of vineyard owners, headed by Adolf Mueller II. The old winery in Cloverdale was rebuilt and renamed The California Wine Company.

Bandiera has still remained the main brand name, varietal and generic wines are marketed under this banner, at very good value prices. The winery also runs two other brands: Sage Creek for the wines they produce from their Napa Valley vineyards and John B. Merritt, for their reserve wines chosen by their winemaker, John Merritt, who is the brother-in-law and former partner of Jim Bundschu, from the Gundlach-Bundschu Winery. The Seagrams Classics organisation now distribute the Bandiera wines and have gained footholds, right across America. Bandiera's wines represent excellent value and its always good to be able to find them in many places.

Davis Bynum Winery

Davis Bynum is a quiet, gentlemanly, ex-newspaperman, with a long standing interest in wine. This interest led him to start his own winery in 1965, at the back of a store in Albany, near Berkeley on the east side of the San Francisco Bay. In 1973, a grape grower friend, talked him into moving his enterprise, to an old premises, on West Side Road near the Russian River. Bynum relies for most of his grapes on local growers, who are also shareholders in the winery.

Davis Bynum Winery, has a real down-to-earth feel about it and has a large number of loyal followers, who often travel long distances, to taste and buy the wines. This says something, for the quality of the wines and the friendly attitude of Davis and his son Hampton, who is now also involved in the winery.

Chalk Hill Winery

Frederick Furth, one of America's leading anti-trust lawyers, is a man of great energy and many interests. Since he bought the 540 acre Donna Maria Ranch, situated high above the Northern Sonoma valley, in 1980, he has set about, putting his master plan together, to create one of America's most impressive wine estates, along with a show place facility for his other main love, giant Danish warmblood horses, especially trained for dressage events. At the top of the ridge, high above the vineyards and winery, he has created a magnificent park, under the large oak trees, complete with a gazebo, lawns and entertaining facilities, constructed out of local stone.

Coincidently, the Donna-Maria name which came with the ranch, fitted into his family rather neatly, as his wife's name is Donna and his mother's name is Maria.

Furth has decided recently that the Chalk Hill name is a better marketing proposition and is, therefore, now solely using it for the wines. Approximately 200 acres are now under vine and, in 1988, another large property across Chalk Hill Road has been bought with some acreage planted. The winery has recently more than doubled in size and sales of Chalk Hill wines are booming.

Furth has also built a beautiful home for himself on the property and large convention centre. Over the next few years, when it all comes together, his dream of a vinous paradise will be realised.

Chalk Hill make Chardonnay, Sauvignon Blanc, Gewurztraminer and a late harvest Botrytised Semillon along with, Cabernet Sauvignon and Pinot Noir. They are all in the top bracket of Sonoma wines. It is a real pleasure to sit and enjoy them and the stunning view of Mt. St. Helena from his Gazebo in the sky.

Chateau De Baun

In an industry where nearly everyone seems determined to improve on a theme, Ken De Baun has struck out with his own tune, Symphony. This grape variety is the result of 43 years developmental work by the highly respected Dr. Harold Olmo at U.C. Davis.

The parent varieties of this hybrid grape are Grenache Gris (a grey fruited red) and Muscat of Alexandria. The result is a white variety with intense fruitiness and complexity of flavours, a great improvement on the mono-dimensional and sometimes slightly bitter Muscat. Symphony is one of a number of successful hybrids developed by Olmo and certainly the most exciting in flavour terms as well as being high yielding. First known as J5-58, Symphony acquired its name at a masked wine tasting at Davis, when a respected winemaker, mystified but impressed with its wide array of aromas and flavours, likened it to a symphony. The name stuck.

Ken De Baun is a tenth generation American whose roots go back to the French Burgundy capital of Beaune, from where the sole surviving member of his family, Joost De Baun fled the bloody French revolution, firstly to Holland and then to New Amsterdam, New Jersey. Ken brought his family to Sonoma County and set up an industrial engineering complex in Santa Rosa where he still owns and operates four engineering firms.

Ken obtained a 116 acre vineyard in a business deal in 1982 and, about the same time, discovered Symphony and planted 96 acres of it on the property. His bold move has started to pay dividends with large crops of excellent fruit, being skillfully made into six different wines by winemaker Roland Shackelford. Four are table wines, starting with the dry Overture, through the sweeter Prelude, still sweeter Theme to the luscious Finale. Two Champagne styles are produced, a dry brut Romance and a demi-sec Rose style Rhapsody. A blush wine, Jazz - a blend of Symphony, Pinot Noir and Chardonnay - completes the range. Although wines are presently being made at a facility in Santa Rosa, a beautiful chateau-style winery will be built on the vineyard in 1989.

I found Symphony wines intriguing with their fruit aromas and flavours combining honeydew melon, orange peel and some apple characteristics, along with the spice of the Muscat, all thoroughly enjoyable - a musical orchestration of flavours and aromas.

Clos du Bois

I n June 1988, Clos du Bois' vineyards and winery were sold to Hiram Walker-Allied Vintners for a reputed $40,000,000. This handsome sum bought 540 acres of prime vineyard land in Sonoma's Alexander Valley, winery equipment, and a reputation. Observers were stunned at the price tag, as there was no winery building included; Clos du Bois is housed in several leased buildings in downtown Healdsburg, adapted to suit the needs of the fast-growing winery. The key to the sale was the solid reputation throughout the U.S. and abroad for consistently excellent wines and the brilliant job of marketing then done by founder and president Frank Woods.

Frank graduated from the Cornell University School of Hotel Administration, honed his skills in the marketing department of Procter and Gamble, and then ran his own marketing firm. In the early 1970's he began purchasing vineyards and brought out the first Clos du Bois wines with 8,000 cases of the 1974 vintage. In addition to producing vintage-dated varietal wines, Clos du Bois was one of the early wineries to push the vineyard designation concept strongly; they now produce Calcaire and Flintwood Vineyard Chardonnays, Briarcrest Vineyard Cabernet Sauvignon and Marlstone Vineyard, a proprietary red wine made in the Bordeaux tradition. In exceptional harvests, when the wines from their other vineyards are outstanding, they produce Proprietor's Reserve wines.

During the first decade, the top priority at Clos du Bois was establishing outstanding viticultural base vineyards, in the right micro-climates, using the most suited varieties, the best clones and disease-free and virus-free vines. Over the next decade, into the mid 1980's, the priorities were to set the wine

quality standard and establish markets for the various wines. John Hawley was hired as winemaker in 1981. His wines have made Clos du Bois into one of the top medal winners in the country.

In creating his winery, Frank Woods was always careful to point out that he was not trying to build a monument, but a winery that would do the job of making the best wine. For example, a huge investment was made in building the current inventory of over 10,000 small French oak barriques. The new president is Terrence Clancy, who has a long history in the wine business and will serve as president of Callawy Vineyard and Winery, in Temecula, as well as Clos du Bois. He is very candid in his admiration for the outstanding job done by Frank and in his absolute commitment to continuing, "improving, where possible", the quality of the wines.

Clos du Bois has grown into the biggest super-premium winery in America, one that does not have a jug wine of any sort. Both Frank Woods and Terrence Clancy believe that people are refining and developing their lifestyle in a quality direction. Premium wine fits into this picture and singles itself out from other alcoholic beverages as a civilised adjunct to life.

Dry Creek Vineyards

David Stare has a true zest for living, accompanied by enthusiasm and boundless energy. His love of sailboats is obvious when one sees his wine labels, which all feature sketches and paintings of classic yachts.

In 1985, David released a new range of Reserve wines under the David S. Stare label.

David was born in the mid west, but raised in Boston, obtained his engineering degree at M.I.T. followed by a masters degree in business administration from Northwestern University. His first job was the realisation of a boyhood dream when he commenced work at the Baltimore and Ohio railroads. Whilst working here he met retired newspaper editor, Philip Wagner, who had started Boordy Vineyards. David planted 40 of his own vines to make wine. Although he made some wine from bought grapes, another dream took him on a journey to

work in Germany, before his own vines matured. For two years he worked in market research for a German steel company, just outside Koblenz, in the heart of the German Rhineland. Again, his interest in wine was heightened.

On his return to Boston in 1964, he took a wine appreciation course and in 1970 went on a tour of French vineyards with some friends. During this trip he made up his mind to tackle winemaking as a career. The next year he moved to Davis in California and enrolled as a special post-graduate student in enology and viticulture and in 1972 launched "Dry Creek Vineyards". He bought the land the current winery stands on and made his first wines in a leased facility at Calistoga. 1973 saw the construction of the winery; a major addition was made in 1977 and it was enlarged again in 1985. Current plans are for more additions with a new facade and

Dry Creek Vineyards

tasting area.

David has an underground wine library, stocking all wines made at Dry Creek, along with his own wine collection containing many classic Bordeaux wines.

The 45 acre Dry Creek Vineyards supply about 25% of his requirements, the rest coming from selected growers in the Dry Creek and Alexander Valleys, including Robert Young, who suplied David's first grapes in 1972.

David has developed a high profile for his wines and winery; he is ably assisted in the winemaking by Larry Levin while his daughter, Kim Stare Wallace assists in the marketing. The whole team at Dry Creek are friendly, involved and committed.

The love David has for sailing has been integrally woven into his business. All wines, including the "David S. Stare" Reserves, have paintings or sketches of classic old yachts featured. David has his own yacht, a ketch "Fume Blanc" moored on the San Francisco Bay. It certainly does not take too much to talk him into hitting the water!!

In 1987, he sponsored Sonoma Valley high school students in a sailing course, run by the Nautical Heritage Society, on old classic yachts.

In 1986, he presented double magnums of his Reserve wines to Prince Albert of Monaco and Walter Cronkite, after the inaugural Monaco to New York Yacht Race.

David Stare works very hard and in many ways to make the best wines humanly possible and promote them well. The medals he has won and the success he enjoys are a tribute to him and his courage always to live out his dreams.

DRY CREEK VINEYARD
Address: PO Box T, Healdsburg, California, 95448
Phone: 707/433 1000
Year of Establishment: 1972
Owner: David S. Stare
Winemaker: Larry Levin
Principal Varieties Grown: Sauvignon Blanc, Chardonnay, Chenin Blanc, Cabernet Sauvignon, Zinfandel, Merlot
Acres Under Vine: 85
Average Annual Crush: 1,200

Principal Wines & Brands	Cellar Potential (Years)
Dry Creek Vineyard Fume Blanc	5-7
Dry Creek Vineyard Chardonnay	8-10
Dry Creek Vineyard Cabernet Sauvignon	10-15

Trade Tours – Available by appointment only.
Retail Room Sales – Available.
Hours open to Public: Daily from 10.30am to 4.30pm except major holidays.
Retail Distribution: Throughout the U.S., as well as England, Virgin Islands.

De Loach Vineyards

There is more than a little of the fire-fighter still in Cecil De Loach. Right on top of his cleverly constructed winery, he has built his own observation tower; he often goes up there just to think and get an overview of his fast expanding wine enterprise. From here he has, no doubt, devised many ways to put out any fires that threaten the progression of his business.

An ex-marine, Cecil also tried his hand as a race-track photographer, before his career as a fireman in San Francisco. In 1964, he was looking to invest in a rural property as a future retirement project, found a 24 acre vineyard and arranged with the owner, veteran grape grower Louis Barbieri, to stay on and teach him about vines.

Cecil decided it made more financial sense to make your own wine and sell it, so he built a winery in 1979 — after having started making wines from his grapes at other facilities in 1975. He finally retired from the San Francisco Fire Department, to concentrate fully on the wine business, in 1980.

Cecil has concentrated on making his wines very much to suit his own palate. His Chardonnay is big in fruit flavour with plenty of oak ageing. The wine judges and the public seem to agree with him as it has been a big hit. A Chardonnay Reserve is also produced under the label O.F.S. (Our Finest Selection), which is 100% barrel fermented and spends nine months ageing on the lees in the barrel, released each year on the 14th September, Cecil's birthday — it's great.

The De Loachs have a good team around them. Christine, Cecil's wife, is Vice President and spends a lot of time travelling, promoting and working with their agents, as does son Michael and Louise Orr, the winery's very capable director of public relations. Once a year Cecil takes the whole team to Mexico, Colorado or some other location for a whole week to review and plan for the future.

De Loach wines have built a very strong sales network involving 46 states. Cecil says he does not plan to expand much more, but his success may take care of that itself. The wines of De Loach are consistently at the top of the pack. Cecil and his team are proud of their achievements and are set to tackle even greater challenges.

DE LOACH VINEYARDS
Address: 1791 Olivet Road, Santa Rosa, Ca., 95401
Phone: 707/526 9111
Year of Establishment: 1975
Owner: Cecil O. De Loach Jnr.
Winemaker: Cecil O. De Loach Jnr.
Principal Varieties Grown: Chardonnay, Pinot Noir, Zinfandel, Gewurztraminer, Merlot
Acres Under Vine: 175
Average Annual Crush: 1,000 tons

Principal Wines & Brands	Cellar Potential (Years)
Chardonnay	2-5
White Zinfandel	
Fume Blanc	

Trade Tours – Available by appointment only.
Retail Room Sales – Available.
Hours open to Public: Daily 10am to 4.30pm
Retail Distribution: Nationwide, Canada, Japan, Scandanavia, Germany, U.K. and France

Ferrari-Carano Vineyards & Winery

Ferrari-Carano has everything going for it; very quickly it will come to be regarded as one of America's finest wineries.

Don Carano is a dynamo. He and his wife Rhonda are both second generation Americans — their families both emigrated from the same region of northern Italy. They were both also born and raised in Reno. Don studied at U.S.F. then spent two years as an officer in the United States Army before returning to University and gaining a law degree. Practising in Reno, he developed business interests in the hospitality industry and today owns The Eldorado Hotel/Casino, with 800 rooms, seven restaurants and a large casino area. Don's four sons and a daughter work with him.

Rhonda has a degree in nutrition and food journalism from the university of Nevada, Reno. She is director of advertising and public relations for the Eldorado, and is also heavily involved in the winery where she has overseen the design of an Italianate villa, soon to be built and to be surrounded by five acres of European gardens. Fresh produce will also be grown to be used in the Villa's demonstration kitchen and served in its hospitality area.

Since 1979, Don has acquired three vineyards situated in the Alexander and Dry Creek Valley's, a total of 350 acres in all, of which 250 acres are under vine. The winery is a state-of-the-art affair, put together and run by George Bursich, formerly with McDowell Valley Vineyards in Mendocino. George is fortunate to work with Barney Fernandez, Don's vineyard manager, formerly with Chateau St. Jean.

The 1985 Chardonnay, a first release, was hailed by many as one of the very best of the vintage. It sold out quickly; other varietal releases have received equally high praise. Ferrari-Carano have set their sights high and so far have more than reached their goals.

Foppiano Vineyards

This determined and resourceful family have turned their long established winery completely around in recent years and are now producing three ranges of top class varietal wines.

The family saga in North America goes back to 1894, when Giovanni "John" Foppiano arrived by ship in Panama. Walking across to the Pacific he took a ship to San Francisco, to join the gold rush, which took him to the Russian River at Healdsburg panning for gold. He found gold in another form, growing fruits and vegetables for the miners and local inhabitants. After five years he went back to Italy, chose a bride, Rosa, with whom he returned to Healdsburg, where they raised nine children. The eldest, Louis A., joined his father and they bought a winery and vineyard "Riverside Farm" on the banks of the Russian River at its current location.

In 1910, after some disagreements with his father, Louis A. bought the winery. In the same year his wife Mathilda had a son, Louis J., Prohibition struck and 110,000 gallons of wine were destroyed by the excise officers.

Louis J. was, and still is, quite an adventurer. Amongst other things, he struck up a strong friendship with famous aviator Walter Varney. At repeal, then 23 years old,

he started up the winery again. In 1937, the old winery was torn down and rebuilt, becoming one of the first wineries to do its own bottling. During the war years, sales to the east boomed and in 1946, Louis J. bought the adjoining Sonotoyme Vineyard, expanding his vineyard to today's 200 acres.

He also married in 1946 and the same year formed the Sonoma County Winegrowers Association along with 14 other wineries. He was also an early member of the Californian Wine Institute and a director from 1941-1986.

His son, Louis M, became involved in 1984, when his brother Rod tragically died. Louis M. is intense and, with winemaker Bill Regan, has pushed aggressively into the premium varietal market, under revamped packaging and excellent, complex wine styles. The top of the tree is the "Fox Mountain" reserve wines named after Louis J's ranch in Northern California, a Cabernet Sauvignon with Merlot and Cabernet Franc, full of style, complex with berry/fruit flavours and nice vanillan overtones; a Chardonnay is also being made. The "Louis J. Foppiano" varietal range has four different wines and the "Riverside Farms" selection six wines. Having tasted all of each range I can happily report Foppiano's have some of the best wines and value in northern Sonoma.

FOPPIANO VINEYARDS
Address: 12707 Old Redwood Highway, PO Box 606, Healdsburg, CA., 95448
Phone: 707/433 7272
Year of Establishment: 1896
Owner: Louis J. Foppiano/Louis M. Foppiano
Winemaker: William E. Regan
Principal Varieties Grown: Chardonnay, Sauvignon Blanc, Cabernet Sauvignon, Merlot, Cabernet Franc, Petite Sirah
Acres Under Vine: 160
Average Annual Crush: 1,700

Principal Wines & Brands	Cellar Potential (Years)
Louis J. Foppiano Chardonnay	5-7
Louis J. Foppiano Cabernet Sauvignon	6-9
Louis J. Foppiano Petite Sirah	10-15

Trade Tours – Available by appointment only
Retail Room Sales – Available
Hours open to Public: Daily 10am to 4.30pm
Retail Distribution: Restaurants & stores in 48 states, export to Japan, U.K. and West Germany

Hop Kiln Winery

D r. Martin Griffin is a man of many parts; a public health officer, he is also a wildlife conservationist, a lover of music, theatre and the finer things in life. In the 1960's, he bought a disused old, three towered, Hop Kiln, built in 1905. Whilst restoring it he planted vines on the property selling grapes to neighbouring wineries.

In 1975, he opened the Hop Kiln as a winery also moving a large ornate old Victorian timber home onto the property. He makes some unusual wines and "Hop Kiln" is a refreshing change from the stereotyped, state-of-the-art wineries. His white blend "A Thousand Flowers" contains Colombard, Riesling and other varieties; it is very dry and pleasant. He makes a red entitled "Marty Griffin's Big Red" from a number of unidentified varieties in his vineyard, a big, dark, rich wine, in its own style very good. Other varietal wines are also made including Chardonnay, Cabernet Sauvignon, Sauvignon Blanc, Zinfandel, Petit Sirah and Pinot Noir.

A delightful, if slightly eccentric, man Marty Griffin has added a much-appreciated extra dimension to the Sonoma Wine industry.

Fritz Cellars

J ay Fritz has a very successful freight forwarding business and he and his wife Barbara have built a striking and aesthetically pleasing winery into the hillsides of their vineyard on Dutcher Creek Road, between Dry Creek Valley and Highway 101.

The winemaking is in the capable hands of David Hastings, who arrived in 1983, after completing studies at Giesenheim in Germany. The winery was finally completed in 1981, although The Fritz 1980 Chardonnay was made there. David also has a degree from U.C. Davis and has worked in the Monterey region.

He is aiming for a refined style of wine with balance as well as flavour; certainly the Chardonnay and Fume Blanc I tried were excellent.

Frei Bros - E & J Gallo

Alittle known fact is that E. & J. Gallo, whose hub is in Modesto in the Northern Central Valley, is also by far the largest producer in Sonoma, crushing more Sonoma grapes than any other winery. Gallo is also a large purchaser of Napa grapes and wines.

In 1948, to strengthen their position and to ensure a supply of grapes of top quality, Gallo entered into a partnership agreement with the Frei Brothers Winery in Sonoma's famous Dry Creek Valley. Frei Bros. was established in 1885. In 1977, when the great-grandson of the winery's founder retired, Ernest and Julio became sole proprietors. Along with the historic winery and vineyards in Dry Creek, came a second vineyard property, the "Laguna Ranch" in the renowned Russian River viticultural area.

From the very outset, Gallo utilized the winery to crush and ferment grapes from Sonoma and Mendocino vineyards. Julio Gallo's criteria for quality demands that grapes be crushed quickly – within six hours of picking and that the grapes arrive at the crusher in as whole and as sound condition as possible. Another costly, but quality-oriented Gallo policy is that all North Coast fruit be hand picked. No machine-harvested grapes are accepted.

With the purchase of the winery and vineyards, Gallo brought to bear their extensive, long-term viticultural research which dates back to the 1940's. Julio Gallo and his son Bob, have personally created magnificent hillside vineyards at both Dry Creek and Laguna. In Dry Creek, 600 acres of classic premium varieties are planted (mainly Cabernet and Zinfandel); while in the cooler Russian River region, in Gallo's Laguna vineyards, the classic white varieties (Chardonnay, Johannisberg Riesling and Gewurztraminer) are now in their eighth leaf.

Having travelled the wine world extensively, Julio Gallo has come to believe that Sonoma is one of the world's great wine regions, especially the benchlands of the Dry Creek and Russian River Valleys. Here, on elevations above the valley floor, Gallo has re-contoured whole hillsides with heavy equipment creating new vineyards. These new vineyards are a real treat to the eye and produce superb fruit.

Never content, and always seeking a better way, blocks in both Dry Creek and Laguna have been set aside to continue Gallo's long-term commitment to viticultural research. Clonal selection, trellising and canopy management, irrigation and root stock studies are already underway.

Currently, all the wines produced at the Dry Creek winery are transferred to Modesto for further maturation and bottling. However, the Gallo family is committed to Estate Bottling at their Sonoma Winery and at some time in the future look for these super-premium Gallo selections.

Always careful and meticulous, it is good to see Gallo moving towards a much stronger statement of what has always been true; that they are one of the most respected producers of top quality premium table wines from California's world famous North Coast wine region.

Geyser Peak

Geyser Peak Winery has seen many changes of style in its century of existence. Built in 1880 by August Quitzow, who also constructed a brandy distillery, his old wood and stone buildings have been incorporated into today's cellars, beautifully structured and landscaped using local stone. The grounds are complete with a fountain, wrought iron gates and a large visitors centre with stained glass windows. Across the freeway and railway line is a further storage area, which is connected by pipeline to the main cellars. After the repeal of Prohibition, the winery, then owned by Dante and William Bagnani, also made vinegar under the Four Monks brand.

In 1972, the winery was bought by the Joseph Schlitz Brewing company, which spent a great deal on the upgrading of the winery

Geyser Peak

and its appearance. However, they lacked a proper understanding of premium wine; every package was produced including the "bag in the box" and even wine in cans.

In 1982, the Trione family, wealthy business people from Santa Rosa, bought the winery. They already had substantial vineyard holdings and Geyser Peak's vineyards now total around 1,100 acres. It seems to me that they are doing everything right.

They managed to get John McLelland, who had formerly run the giant Almaden company, to join them as chairman. John is extremely personable and has had a most interesting life, including being a radio announcer, a newspaperman and sometime spent at Charles Krug in Robert Mondavi's time, before becoming Almaden president.

John has rationalised the brands and sold the "Summit" bulk brand name to the Franzia Wine Group, as it spoilt Geyser Peak's chances to establish a premium reputation.

Only premium wines, mostly from estate-grown grapes are now made. John also works closely with winemaker Armand Bussone (whom he also employed at Almaden) in determining wine styles; much new equipment has gone into the winery.

John kindlly hosted me through an extensive tasting of the latest releases and some un-released wines. Exciting things are being produced. I tried an unfined and unfiltered Cabernet Franc from 1984, a beautiful wine, rich in cassis and raspberry flavours with pronounced wood overtones. The 1984 "Reserve Alexandre", a Cabernet Sauvignon, Merlot, Cabernet Franc blend

was sensational. With a glorious velvety texture and lively fruit, it will have long life.

Geyser Peak also produce some Methode Champenoise wines. The 1984 Blanc de Noir from Pinor Noir fruit had a fin bead (bubbles) and a nice creamy feel in the mouth; it is bottled and aged on tirage at Geyser Peak, then taken to Chateau St. Jean Champenoise facility for shaking down and disgorging.

Some of the Reserve wines are markete under the Trione label. The 1985 Barrel fermented Chardonnay I tried was just grea Geyser Peak has an air of quiet success about it. There is a feeling the winery is nov operating as it always should have.

Ironhorse Vineyards

There is something very special about Ironhorse Vineyards, something that only happens when people really care about what they are doing. Barry Sterling, his wife Audrey and daughter Joy, along with partner and winemaker Forrest Tancer, all have rich and varied backgrounds, which ideally suit them to creating a "perfect" vineyard and winery.

Barry and Audrey spent a good deal of their time in Fance when, for seven years from 1966, he was a partner in a Paris law firm. During this time they searched for a French winery to buy, even making an offer for a Bordeaux Chateau in 1971.

The Sterlings returned to California in 1974 and commenced searching for their ideal vineyard. In 1976, in a driving rain storm they first saw Iron Horse Ranch, then being developed as a vineyard by Rodney Strong. The property was only half

Ironhorse Vineyards

developed and complete with an 1876 Gothic style Redwood home with a distinct list to one side. Their guide on this visit was Forrest Tancer, cellar master for Rod Strong and also in charge of Ironhorse development. Forrest had been involved in his family's vineyards the TT ranch in the Alexander Valley. A political science graduate, he completed post graduate studies in viticulture at Fresno State, before spending two years in Brazil as an agricultural advisor with the Peace Corps. The Sterlings talked Forrest into continuing with the vineyard development with them, although he still worked as cellar master for Sonoma Vineyards for another two years. 1979 saw the Ironhorse Winery established as a partnership between the Sterlings and Forrest.

Ironhorse only process their own estate grown grapes, Pinot Noir and Chardonnay from their 110 acre vineyard on the rolling hills of the property and Cabernet Sauvignon and Sauvignon Blanc from Forrest's TT Ranch in Alexander Valley. As well as their varietal table wines, they also produce what is generally acknowledged as America's finest Methode Champenoise, the first vintage being a 1980. Three Cuvees in all are made, the "Wedding Cuvee", the first pressing of the Pinot Noir, the "Brut" a 75% Pinor Noir 25% Chardonnay blend and the "Blanc de Blancs" a 100% Chardonnay Cuvee aged longer on the yeast.

President Reagan and Mikhail Gorbachev have twice toasted with it at their summit meetings in Geneva in 1985 and in Washington in 1987.

Joy Anne, the Sterling's daughter, took over the sales and marketing in 1985, after a most distinguished career in the media, including eighteen months as Ted Turner's television news director out of Atlanta Georgia and being an assignment editor for A.B.C's 1984 Olympic coverage.

Audrey and Barry have restored the 1876 Redwood home, fitted it out with magnificent period furnishings and surrounded it with several acres of European style "informal" gardens, truly creating a paradise. Audrey is a hostess without equal. She spent four years as California's "Fair Employment Practice Commissioner", was the founder of the Los Angeles Art Museum and the Los Angeles Music Centre. She presides over the annual harvest lunches. Held every day during vintage time, in the gazebo by the winery they are a wonderful experience.

I can well understand why my Australian friend, Andrew Forsell, who is their assistant winemaker, is so reluctant to leave.

Tom and Sally Jordan have realised their dreams and created a vinous paradise in the Alexander Valley. Over the years Tom had become a fan of Bordeaux reds and in 1970, whilst on a visit to San Francisco he was dining at Ernie's restaurant. On chatting to the wine waiter about Bordeaux vintages, the waiter talked him into trying a Californian Cabernet, a first for Jordan. It was a 1958 "George de Latour" Reserve Cabernet, made by the legendary Andre Tchelistcheff.

Tom realised at this point his dream of owning a Bordeaux Chateau could be realised in a different way in California. He wasted no time in bringing two geologists to the Napa and Sonoma Valleys to search for his ideal vineyard, which he found on the banks of the Russian River in the Alexander Valley. Today, Jordan has 276 acres of vines, originally all was planted to Cabernet Sauvignon and Merlot but, in 1977, some

Tom's first move was to retain the service of Andre Tchelistcheff as winemaster, a position he retains to this day. In fact, the Jordans arranged a large surprise party for him in August 1987, to mark his 50th consecutive vintage in California. Andre was also charged with the job of finding a suitable winemaker. This he did, choosing not an experienced man, but young Robert Davis, top graduate from U.C. Davis. Between them they have formed an ideal master and disciple relationship and, at the end of each year, they travel to France together, courtesy of Tom Jordan.

Jordan's winery is the ultimate statement in the art and technology of winemaking. But it has added a process utilised by very few wineries — a cask hall with large, upright French oak vats, used to blend and age both the Jordan Cabernet and Chardonnay, for part of their lives, as young wines. I am sure

Jordan Vineyard & Winery

giving them a certain complexity and a refined and elegant structure. Of course, new small oak barriques are also used.

Jordan only make two wines, the Cabernet, the first vintage being a 1976 and the Chardonnay which followed in 1979. The Jordan Winery complex is much, much more than just a winemaking facility. It pays respect to wine in every way, in its context as part of gracious living. Sally, Tom's beautiful and gracious wife, has had a life long involvement with food and hospitality including studies at the famous Cordon Bleu school in Paris. She worked closely with the architects and interior designers and, between them, they have created a Chateau to match any of France's greatest.

It incorporates several superb hospitality suites with balconies looking out over the Alexander Valley. A glorious wood panelled dining room and entrance foyer commands views not only of the valley but back into the cask room, with its stunning cathedral ceiling.

With all this background, one might tend to think the Jordans are elitist. This is anything but the truth, as one can see in the relationship the family have with their staff, particularly the Mexican families, many of whom have a second generation now working for Jordan.

During the many dinners and lunches, the staff adopt other roles. The chief gardener is also the consummate Maitre d', the vineyard manager doubles as sommelier, in all a beautifully synchronised team. The Jordans have closed the winery for many a Mexican wedding banquet for their staff.

Tom Jordan was not phased when, at his first post vintage celebration, his table of first growth Bordeaux wines was passed over in favour of the beer keg. Judy Jordan, his daughter, also a geologist, has joined the winery, one of the most charming and genuine people you could meet.

JORDAN VINEYARD & WINERY
Address: PO Box 878, Healdsburg, 1474 Alexander Valley Road, CA., 95448
Phone: 707/433 6955
Year of Establishment: Founded 1972
Owner: Thomas N. Jordan Jnr.
Winemaker: Robert H. Davis
Principal Varieites Grown: Cabernet Sauvignon, Merlot (for blending into Cab. Sauv.), Chardonnay, (also small amount Cab. Franc for blending into Cab. Sauv.)
Acres Under Vine: 275
Average Annual Crush: 1,200 tons

Principal Wines & Brands	Cellar Potential (Years)
Cabernet Sauvignon	10
Chardonnay	6

Trade Tours – Available by appointment only
Retail Room Sales – Available
Hours open to Public: Mon to Fri. 8am to 5pm for retail sales (no appt. necessary); Mon to Sat. by appt. only for tours
Retail Distribution: All 50 states of the union, in add Bermuda, U.K., Guam, Hong Kong, Italy, Japan, the Carribean, Sweden, Switzerland, W. Germany and Tawain.

Korbel Champagne Cellars

It seems only fitting that the bucolic beauty and serenity of Sonoma County be the setting for Korbel Champagne Cellars, America's leading producer of classically-made Champagnes. Here, against a dramatic backdrop of evergreen-covered mountains, the Chardonnay and Pinot Noir grapes traditionally used in fine Champagnes flourish in the area's unusually temperate climate.

Korbel Champagne Cellars has been producing premium Champagnes in Sonoma County since the last century, when three brothers from Bohemia — Francis, Anton and Joseph Korbel — first arrived in the area. They brought with them a sense of tradition and history that was reflected in everything they did - from the planting of "noble" European grape varieties like Chardonnay to the construction of a Gothic-style winery that included a replica of the prison tower in Prague, where the young Francis Korbel had wrongly been imprisoned for participation in a political demonstration.

The Korbel brothers distinguished themselves early on by bringing over a succession of European winemakers to pioneer the production of traditionally-made Champagnes in America. Specifically, they used the "Methode Champenoise", the classic French Champagne-making process, to create a Champagne that both reflected and appealed to the generosity and frankness of the American spirit. Fruitier, less

austere and without the "yeasty" quality often associated with French Champagnes, it was a true American original and established, what has come to be known as the California style of Champagne.

Not surprisingly, Korbel soon became this country's leading Champagne brand - a position that it has occupied without interruption to this day. The brand's continuing success lies in the fact that it has consistently defined and even anticipated the evolution in American tastes.

In the late 1950's, for example, Korbel introduced its Korbel Brut. Although it was considerably drier and more expensive than most American Champagnes it would become America's largest selling premium Champagne, and helped pave the way for other U.S. Champagne makers to create their own "Bruts".

The man behind Korbel Brut was Adolf Heck who bought the Korbel winery in 1954. A third generation descendant of a winemaking family from Alsace-Lorraine, Adolf redefined the Korbel style through technical innovations and the development of classic Champagne cuvees, or blends, such as Korbel Natural, Korbel Blanc de Blancs and Korbel Blanc de Noirs. Even drier than Korbel Brut, these new cuvees nevertheless preserve the fresh fruitiness that is the hallmark of California Champagne.

Adolf Heck's legacy is carried on today by his son Gary, who took over the firm after his father's death. It was under Gary's leadership that Korbel first surpassed annual case sales of one million, reinforcing the brand's position as the dominant force in the American premium Champagne market in this country.

In addition to its Champagne making facilities, Korbel features a Champagne museum and a world-famous rose garden, which makes the winery tour one of the most impressive I have ever seen.

Winery tours are conducted daily.

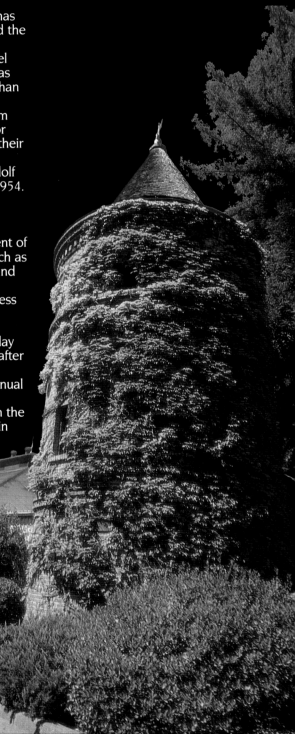

Martini and Prati

This large winery west of Santa Rosa, dates back to 1881, when two wine growing families built a facility to make wine. The Hiram Walker company later bought it and mainly supplied bulk wine to other wineries, particularly Paul Masson.

In a surprising turn around, almost exactly 100 years since it was founded, the Martini and Prati families brought back their winery.

When the Fountain Grove Winery closed in the 1950's, Martini and Prati bought the label and used it to introduce their own bottled wines. This has now become part of their business and they market some wonderful old dessert wines, as well as varietal table wines. Much of their wines are still sold in bulk.

It is worth a visit to this charming old winery to give one a glimpse of how large wineries of old operated. Like the winery, the wines are full of character.

Landmark Vineyards

Through an avenue of giant cypress trees just off Highway 101 in Windsor, is the Landmark Vineyards Winery. Bill Mabry III, became interested in winemaking, whilst still at school in the late 1960's. He helped his father, a retired Air Force Colonel, plant his vineyards in the Sonoma and Alexander Valleys and then took enology courses at U.C. Davis starting making Landmark wines in 1972, in leased space at another winery.

The winery was built in 1974 and now specialise in only three wines, a Chardonnay, a Cabernet Sauvignon and a white blend called "Petit Blanc".

Landmark have quietly grown to a sizeable enterprise, by concentrating on quality and building a solid reputation.

Lyeth Vineyards & Winery

One of the most up market wine ventures of the last decade has been the establishment of Lyeth. The winery is housed in a European style Chateau building, which also boasts an English flagstone entrance covered by a towering arch. Inside the winery (built around a courtyard) there are private accomodation suites, a library and a dining salon with appropriate kitchen facilities.

Only two wines are produced, each marketed with only one word, Lyeth, screened in gold onto the bottle. The first is a classic Bordeaux white blend, 70% Sauvignon Blanc and 30% Semillon. The 1985 had distinct spicy oriental lychee flavours, along with a herbaceous character and a crisp dry finish. The 1984 Lyeth red is a blend of 75% Cabernet Sauvignon, 20% Merlot and 5% Cabernet Franc, showing rich cassis and coconut flavours, with a superb silky texture, full and very Bordeaux-like in style - both easily rated gold medal status, in my view.

The winery was established by Monroe "Chip" Lyeth, a former air racing champion, restaurateur and long time Sonoma grape grower, who was tragically killed in an air crash, near the winery in early 1988. Absolutely nothing has been spared in its creation. Vin-Tech, a syndicate from Santa Rosa, has just bought Lyeth and will, no doubt, continue the good work done so far.

J. Pedroncelli Winery

The early part of the history of this winery is a little unclear but it was bonded in 1904 by wholesale grocer, John Canata and in 1927, during Prohibition bought by John Pedroncelli. John had migrated from Lombardy in Italy and settled with his aunt near Mt. Shasta in northern California, working for the railroad and in the dairy industry. In his travels he found the countryside around Cloverdale much like the vineyard land of his native country.

After buying the vineyards and winery, he struggled through the rest of Prohibition selling grapes to home winemakers. After upgrading the winery, most of the wine he made was sold to other wineries. However, one of his clients was a Bordeaux-born wine merchant, Henry Vandervoopt, who sold mainly to San Francisco restaurants, under their own special labels. At this time John Snr's. sons James and John had come into the business and, seeing the success of Vandervoot, started bottling and marketing their own wines. The first varietally labelled Pedroncelli wine was a Zinfandel in 1949.

In 1958, Pedroncelli released a Zinfandel Rose which became an instant commercial success. The Pedroncellis only use the grapes of their own and neighbouring vineyards and John jnr. has been winemaker since 1947. His son Michael and daughter Maureen are also involved. James is in charge of administration and marketing while his daughters, Cathy, Lisa and Julie are also working in the business.

The winery has just been updated and expanded again to include a beautiful new tasting and entertaining area. The Pedroncellis are a quiet, almost retiring, family, but the statement they make with their range of great value Sonoma wines speaks loud and clear for them.

Piper Sonoma

A nother first class Champenoise enterprise came into being in 1980, when in association with Rodney Strong, founder of Sonoma Vineyards. Piper-Heidsieck the French Champagne company, decided to commence production in California.

The winery was built in 1981, right next to Sonoma Vineyards Winery and opened in 1982, in order to release their first Cuvee, a Brut from 1980, which had been made at the Sonoma Vineyards facility.

Like its French cousin (which became famous in 1785, when Marie-Antoinette, made it the wine of the Royal court at Versailles), the Sonoma Cuvee is elegant and refined.

Originally Piper Sonoma obtained all their base wines for their Cuvees from Sonoma Vineyards, but now operate autonomously, carefully selecting and picking the grapes from various Sonoma growers' vineyards. Piper Heidsieck's Chef du Caves, Michel Le Croix, set up the facility and oversees the making with winemaker, Chris Markell.

The first Cuvee was a "Brut" blended from Pinot Noir and Chardonnay. Next released was a "Blanc de Noirs" with a light burnished copper colour; it spends an extra year on tirage and is fuller in body than the Brut. The most recently released has been a "Tete de Cuvee", which spends two and a half to three years on the yeast lees (tirage ageing). This full-flavoured, creamy-textured Champenoise, is made from Pinot Noir and Chardonnay and is in fairly short supply.

The appointments at Piper Sonoma are suitably elegant and tasting is conducted in these delightful surroundings. The Cafe du Chai serves lunch and The Marquis Room, with its outdoor terrace, can seat up to 250 people for banquets and receptions. Piper Sonoma is a successful and enriching addition to Sonoma's wine industry.

Seghesio Winery

The Seghesios are now in their fourth generation as Sonoma wine growers. Eugene and Edward, grandsons of founder Edoardo, have taken the company from a bulk wine producer into the premium bottled wine market.

Edoardo worked for Italian Swiss Colony in the latter part of the last century and in 1902, bought a 350 acre ranch owned by I.S.C. and built a winery. The office now situated on the vineyard was actually the Chianti Railroad station until they bought it and moved it to the property.

In 1940, the Seghesios bought the old Scatena Bulk Winery, on Grove Street, in the town of Healdsburg. 1982 was the first year they bottled and labelled their own wines, including a Chianti using the classic Tuscan blend of Sangiovese, Canaiola, Malvasia and Trebbiano. Ted is the winemaker and is making some of the genuine wine bargains of Sonoma Valley.

Soda Rock Winery

Life began for the Soda Rock Winery in 1880 as the Ferrari Winery. For many years following Prohibition it remained dormant but, in 1978, Transylvanian born Charles Tomka and his son Charles Jnr., bought the old facility and set about restoring it. Charles Snr. is somewhat of a genius when it comes to innovative restoration and he put much of the old Ferrari equipment back together again.

The winery is now producing a considerable amount of wine for bulk sales to other wineries as well as a range of wines under "Charlies Country Wines labels". Charlie Snr. prides himself on making completely natural wine without chemicals, much as he did for the nobility in his native Hungary.

This winery is quite an eye opener to visit with its refreshing down-to-earth owners and premises.

Simi Winery

S imi Winery has been blessed by the guiding hand of a number of strong and resourceful women in its 112 year history. Founded in 1876 by brothers Guiseppe and Pietro Simi, who were San Francisco wine dealers, the winery was named Montepulciano, after their Italian home town.

The two brothers both died in 1904, Pietro or Guiseppe leaving a sixteen year old daughter Isabelle. Somehow she met the challenge of running the winery for six decades, until she sold in 1969. The new owner was Russell Green, who had an oil and gas company in Los Angeles and vineyards in Sonoma county.

He renamed the winery ''Simi'', but in 1974, it was bought by an Englishman, Michael Dacres Dixon. He later sold it to a New York distributor, which has since been bought out by the Moet-Hennessy conglomerate, while Michael has stayed on as President.

Mary Ann Graf became America's first female college-trained head winemaker when she joined the winery in 1970 under Russell Green, adding another chapter to the female connection at Simi. In 1969, Michael Dixon, in a real coup, hired Zelma Long from Robert Mondavi, to become Simi's chief wine maker. Zelma's wines have been nothing short of sensational.

Simi have a large acreage of vines on the top of Chalk Hill Road. Much of this attractive estate has been planted in the French way with extremely close row and vine spacing. The vineyards are immaculately kept and the Cabernet grapes I have seen from here are without equal; small berries with intense flavour and a herbaceous quality. Zelma is particularly happy to work with this fruit.

The winery was originally built by Chinese labour, using local stone. The 1981 additions have been beautifully integrated into the old cellars. Michael Rolland, a French consultant from St. Emilion, has worked with Zelma on the master blend of the Simi Cabernet, which also contains Petit Verdot, Cabernet Franc and Merlot. Simi have the runs on the scoreboard but, I am sure, they are more interested in future challenges than in past achievements.

SIMI WINERY
Address: 16275 Healdsburg Avenue, Healdsburg, California, 95448
Phone: 707/433 6981
Year of Establishment: 1876
Owner: LVMH/Moet-Hennessy, Louis Vuitton
Winemaker: Zelma Long
Principal Varieties Grown: Cabernet Sauvignon, Chardonnay, Sauvignon Blanc, Cabernet Franc, Merlot, Petit Verdot
Acres Under Vine: 170
Average Annual Crush: 2,000 tons

Principal Wines & Brands	Cellar Potential (Years)
Chardonnay	5
Cabernet Suavignon	10
Sauvignon Blanc	3

Trade Tours – Available.
Retail Room Sales – Available.
Hours open to Public: Daily from 10am to 4.30pm except New Year's day, Easter, Independence Day, Thanksgiving Day and Christmas Day.
Retail Distribution: Throughout the U.S. and several Foreign markets

Sonoma-Cutrer Vineyards

S onoma-Cutrer Winery reminds one of something out of a James Bond movie, the space-age technology and architectural design giving one a distinct impression that perfection is the goal.

This impression is well founded and a reflection of the owner Brice Cutrer-Jones's single-minded approach. Brice was a fighter pilot during the Vietnam war and from there went on to get his M.B.A. at Harvard.

In 1973, with Kent Klineman, he put together a limited partnership of 25 people with the express purpose of making one wine – Chardonnay. His judgement was spot on and he has left no stone unturned in his quest to make the best. During the last 15 years, Sonoma-Cutrer has established almost 800 acres of Chardonnay in several different Sonoma locations. This acreage is more than enough to supply their own needs (production at present is about 80,000 cases). This excellent vineyard base allows

winemaker Bill Bonetti to select absolutely the best grapes possible to work with.

It is when you enter the winery that the perfectionist mentality becomes obvious. Bill Bonetti draws on the experience of 38 harvests, 13 in Italy and the balance in California. Over the years he has pioneered many new techniques including the first barrel fermentation of Chardonnay in America, in 1962, during experiments he ran alongside Robert Mondavi at the Charles Krug Winery.

Winemaking techniques at Sonoma-Cutrer very markedly from many used in other wineries. The grapes are hand picked into shallow plastic bins to prevent them juicing under too great a load. When they reach the winery they do not go into a crusher stemmer, but onto a continuous belt, where any leaves, stalks or faulty bunches are removed. This belt takes the grapes through a 25 yard long cooling tunnel, where they are

brought down to 45 F, in ten ton batches. After this process, the grapes go into a membrane press where, just like Champagne no crushing takes place.

The Chardonnay is then fermented in new or near-new French oak barriques, again temperature-controlled at all stages. When the wine is moved, including bottling, air is excluded by inert gas cover. Part of the large temperature-controlled cellar, where the wine barrel ages is earth and sprayed with water periodically to keep humidity high.

Sonoma-Cutrer produce four superb Estate Chardonnays. The Russian River Vineyard is a lean style with citrus overtones, the Cutrer Vineyards, still delicate but with toasty cashew flavours and stone fruit in the background, the "Les Pierres" (meaning the Rocks), coming from a stony vineyard, is richer in fruit flavours, while a Founders Reserve is also made from time to time.

Chateau Souverain

There must be some truth in the old adage that one must suffer for something that is really worthwhile. Tom Peterson, Chateau Souverain's extremely competent winemaker, must feel as if he had died and had been reborn in heaven.

The environment for the first two years of his time there was a winemaker's hell. The top executives changed like the wind and the grower-owners of the winery dumped whatever fruit they could not sell elsewhere on Tom. He had to struggle through with the wrong varieties and often with grapes in poor condition — of course the owners expected top wines as a result. The winery, although well set up by the perfectionist Bill Bonnetti in the early 1970's, was in need of some updating and the small oak cooperage was so old as to be virtually useless. Tom is a very persistent person and his reward came with the purchase of Chateau Souverain by

the Wine World arm of the Nestle Company also owner of Beringer.

Tom joined Souverain in 1984 from The Monterey Vineyard, where he had spent six years with Dr. Richard Peterson (no relation), one of the great enologists of the modern era. Tom, a San Francisco native, earned a B.A. degree in anthropology from Stanford paying his way through by working in the kitchen of the campus canteen. He also worked close by at the large Beltramos wine shop and it was there that his interest in winemaking began to flourish.

After a back-packing trip through the Alaskan wilderness, he returned to California and got a job with the Vinifera Vineyard Company, developing new vineyards and maintaining old ones. His understanding of and empathy with the grape grower has been of great help to him at Souverain. As a mature-age student, he went back to studies,

240

Chateau Souverain

this time in enology, where he obtained his master's degree at U.C. Davis in only two years, this impressive work landing him the job at Monterey Vineyards.

Chateau Souverain had been built in 1972 by a group of Napa growers, but purchased during construction by Pillsbury Flour Mills (who also built a facility in the Napa Valley). They sold to a group of 300 growers from Sonoma, Napa and Mendocino in 1974, after heavy losses.

Wine World's purchase in 1986 brought immediate changes. They have spent two million dollars on new refrigeration, a range of new small stainless steel tanks and much needed imported small oak cooperage.

They also gave Tom the ability to set up grape supply contracts with some of Sonoma's leading quality growers. Illustrious names such as Wasson from Alexander Valley, Sangiacomo from Carneros (Sonoma),

Hafner from Chalk Hill are but a few. Already the wines have turned around. The wine market is just starting to sit up and take notice. Compared with other prestige Sonoma labels. Souvrain's prices are very reasonable.

The Chateau buildings are also in the process of receiving a two million dollar re-design and restoration. The impressive facade, which is French influenced, also incorporates a typical "Sonoma Hop-Kiln" look. The restaurant additions and renovations have been completed, creating one of the wine country's most classy, quality eating establishments.

Chateau Souverain is now enjoying the care and attention it has always deserved. Tom Peterson and his team should be proud of the great renaissance they have accomplished.

Rodney Strong Vineyards

Rodney Strong Vineyards

Rodney D. Strong has had an interesting and exciting life to say the least. A school athletics champion, he went on to study dance in New York City with George Balanchine and Martha Graham. Following his dance studies he went to Paris and opened in the first show at the famous "Lido". He then returned to New York to dance in a number of Broadway productions and at this stage, started to look to the future. In his own words; "I didn't want to be an old dancer".

Whilst in Paris he had developed an interest in wine and when he moved to California he worked for several years at various wineries. Rod, with his wife and former dancing partner, Charlotte, opened a bottling cellar and tasting room, under the Tiburon Vintners banner, housed in an old Victorian residence on the waterfront at Tiburon.

In 1961, Rod bought his first vineyard 160 acres in Windsor and also the Old Windsor Winery originally opened in 1898. The Windsor label developed a large mail order and a special personalised label business, partly through Rod's Tiburon Vintners business contacts. To meet demand, Rod bought and planted more vineyards, building up to 5,000 acres.

In 1970, he started the Sonoma Vineyards brand and became one of the first to pioneer the vineyards designation concept. During the 1970's, Piper Heidsieck were searching for a suitable location to set up a Methode Champenoise operation in North America. In 1979, they and their distributors, Renfield, went into a partnership and apppointed Rod Strong to build and run the Piper Sonoma company. A winery was built adjacent to his own Sonoma Vineyards and the first release, a 1980 "Brut", was a huge success. Rod has seen Piper Sonoma off to a successful start and is now back full-time in his own winery.

In 1984, with so many wineries and vineyards in Sonoma county (about 100 whereas in 1960, when Rod started, there were only 12), it was decided to change the Sonoma Vineyards name to Rodney Strong Vineyards; all packaging and marketing since then has reflected this change.

Rod still maintains a number of vineyards and vineyard designated names such as Alexander's Crown, River East, River West, Charlotte's Home, Claus and Chalk Hill, which appear on his labels. As well he has the vintage varietal wines and the Windsor Vineyards names continues, particularly in the mail order and personalised label field.

At present Rod and Charlotte are building a stunning home on the slopes of Alexander's Crown, commanding majestic, panoramic views of the Alexander Valley.

Many activities, music festivals and so on, take place at the winery, which is built like a giant flat-topped pyramid, not only making it attractive, but very functional. Rodney Strong Winery draws from some 1,600 acres of its own vineyards and user skill and long experience, to make several excellent ranges of wine. Rod has helped put Sonoma well and truly on the wine map.

Trentadue

Leo and Evelyn Trentadue have a warm and friendly family winery with an extraordinary gift shop and tasting room, which features a large collection of glassware and china. The Trentadues grew grapes in the Santa Clara valley before moving to a 200 acre vineyard property, in the Alexander Valley, in 1958. The winery was built in 1969 and the son Victor is now involved. They planted some unusual varieties such as Golden Chasselas and have an area of 90-year-old Carignane vines. They also made America's first varietal Sangiovese (one of the classic Chianti grapes); the 1986 is superb with a spicy, lively, wild berry character.

Another Trentadue wine I found intruiging was their Botrytised Chenin Blanc, which showed delightful fig and pear flavours. One of the most unusual wines I have seen was their 1986 Aleatico (an Italian variety), a red wine which had been slightly fortified with grape spirit and retained 5% grape sugar, a very grapey wine with cherry and cassis flavours and very well made.

Trentadue also use the number "32" on some labels, which is "Trentadue" in English. Certainly different, a visit to Trentadue, is an experience.

William Wheeler Winery

Very much the country squire, Bill Wheeler with his partner and wife Ingrid have led fascinating lives. Bill was born in Missouri, but grew up in Santa Barbara. His schooling was at the Thatcher school in the Ojai valley where each boy was required to have a horse; here Bill's love of the land began. He studied history at Yale and went on to the London School of Economics, then to the Sorbonne in Paris, finally obtaining an M.B.A. from Columbia University.

Bill worked in the State Department of Foreign Aid in Argentina and Brazil and it was in Rio de Janiero he met Ingrid. She had been born in Hong Kong to a Scottish mother and Norwegian father. As a one year old, her parents took her on a 103 day escape march across China, during World War Two. She went on to study in England, Switzerland and France, and on a visit to her brother in Brazil, met Bill. They were married in England, then spent a time in Brazil and Columbia.

On their move to California, they decided to buy a 175 acre ranch in the Dry Creek Valley where they planted Cabernet

Sauvignon and, after a time as grape growers, started making their own wine in 1979. Two years later they completed a winery on the property and moved there to live.

In the meantime, they had restored an old warehouse building into a charming French-style wine facility with blending, ageing and bottling facilities, just off the plaza in the town of Healdsburg, where they also have a tasting room.

Julia Iantosca is their young and capable winemaker. They make Sonoma county varietals and vineyard designated wines from the "Norse" ranch, named for Ingrid's family background. A Monterey Chardonnay is also produced.

Bill and Ingrid do things with a lot of style and class.

Italian Swiss Colony

One of the most significant early developments of the Californian wine industry, was the establishment of the Italian Swiss Colony Vineyards and Winery, in Northern Sonoma.

I.S.C. began as a philanthropic farming venture, started by San Francisco banker, Andrea Sbarboro in 1880. His concept was to set up a large commercial farm where poor Swiss and Italian immigrants could work planting and tending grape vines. Room, board and wine were provided and a wage of $35 per week. From this, five dollars was deducted each week for a share-holding in the colony. Eventually after 25 years, the worker would own his own vineyard. The town they established was called Asti, after its Italian counterpart.

The workers, however, prefered the cash and the whole venture became a private company. In 1887 the winery was completed but the first vintage was a disaster. Next year Pietro Rossi, a San Francisco pharmacist, took over and successfully ran the winery until the turn of the century. The colony expanded, buying a number of vineyards and wineries in several Californian counties. In 1897, Rossi constructed the world's largest underground cement tank, to hold 300,000 gallons of surplus wines. In a pre-vintage celebration, a dance complete with a military band, was held inside this tank!

Rossi and Sbarboro both erected classic Italian villas behind the winery. Rossi persuaded Charles Jordan from France's Loire Valley to come to Asti, as a sparkling wine maker; immediately it was released, his Golden State extra dry Champagne took the grand prize at the Turin exposition.

Colony also started making and selling a Chianti in a traditional raffia-covered bottle. After the Italian government objected, in 1910, the word Chianti was dropped and the brand name "Tipo" kept. So successful was it, in both red and white versions, that it became the American generic term for Chianti or other wines in a raffia-covered bottle.

Pietro Rossi died in a buggy accident in 1911 and in 1913 the Californian Wine Association took over the company. It was bought back by Edmund and Robert Rossi (Pietro's twin sons) and Enrico Prati (the vineyard manager), during Prohibition.

National Distillers bought I.S.C. during the war years, then Allied Grape Growers took over followed by Heublein in 1968. In 1983, they closed the large tasting room and, with the threat of the winery being closed, Allied Grape Growers in a different form as I.S.C. wines (now The Beverage Source) again acquired the winery.

A range of premium table wines under the Colony Classic label was created by Edmund Rossi Jnr., grandson of Pietro.

In July 1988 in a surprise move, the Nestle Wine World group, also owners of Beringer and Chateau Souverain, bought the I.S.C. Winery. They plan to plant much of the 540 acres around the winery and are formulating plans for the restoration of the estate.

Topolos at Russian River Vineyards

The Topolos family, brothers Michael and Jerry and sister Christine, not only have one of the best, small wineries in Sonoma county, but also a charming and beautiful restaurant.

The original building was an old manor house erected in 1879, and now the cobblestoned patio outside has a bubbling pond. The surrounding gardens contain northern California's, largest collection of native plants. In summer, it is a delight to sit under the pergola, between the restaurant and winery and enjoy a Greek-influenced brunch, complete with a Greek musician and his bazouki. In winter, the garden room and sunset room indoors are warmed by a wood burning stove.

The Topolos have 27 acres of vineyards around the winery and Michael has his own ranch and vineyards in the Sonoma Mountain appelation. The Topolos' winery is a striking building, cleverly integrated with the old manorhouse. It features the Fort Ross and Hop Kiln styles of architecture common in Sonoma architecture, of the last century.

Michael's wines are hand crafted and very individual in style. He makes them using natural methods, with no filtration or fining for the red. He also finds time to lecture in winemaking at the Santa Rosa junior college.

I found the Topolos' whites, Chardonnay and Sauvignon Blanc, to be crisp, fruity with some floral highlights — both were lightly wooded. Their Cabernet Blanc was very refreshing with raspberry flavours and a touch of herbaceous character. The reds were all in the big, deep-coloured and rich-flavoured styles, reminiscent of days gone by. Zinfandel and Petit Sirah are Michael's favourite varieties.

Topolos' Russian River Winery, is a compulsory stop in the Russian River wine road.

Introduction to Sonoma Valley South

The high profile pioneer vignerons of the 1850's and 1860's General Mariano Vallejo and "Count" Agoston Harazathy, really put Sonoma on the wine map. Although not the first region in California to make wine commercially (as it was preceded by both Los Angeles and Santa Clara), it certainly made the most impact and a lasting one at that. Vallejo was the Mexican Commandant of Northern California and, when the Sonoma Mission (established in 1823) was abandoned in 1834, Vallejo took over its vineyards.

The Mission, San Francisco Solano de Sonoma, lies in the centre of the picturesque town of Sonoma and has been restored over recent decades. Vallejo's brother, Salvador, also established vineyards and it was, in fact, his vineyard that the legendary "Count" Harazathy bought on a visit to Sonoma in 1856. Harazathy was, in fact, not a "Count", but a political refugee from Hungary. He was a genius at launching promotional ventures, particularly those associated with wine. Harazathy had tried establishing vineyards in Wisconsin, where he also established a town in his own name (now called Sauk City). He is often credited as being the father of Californian wine, but this is not really true as

this honour most properly belongs to Jean Louis Vigne (suitably his name means Vine) a Frenchman who brought European vines to his El Aliso Vineyard in Los Angeles in the 1830's.

However, it was Harazathy who shared the good news, when he returned from a Californian government sponsored trip to Europe with 100,000 vines featuring 300 varieties. He became the unwilling sponsor of the industry, when the state failed to pay him! He started the Buena Vista Society, named after his Pompeiian villa, in 1863. The large sandstone winery, had ageing tunnels going into the hills but unfortunately, it was not a financial success and a depressed Harazathy headed to Nicaragua, where he disappeared on his sugar cane plantation, in 1869, apparently taken by alligators.

His son Arpad carried on for a while, but Buena Vista was wiped out by phylloxera in the 1870's. Nothing was heard of Buena Vista until the early 1940's, when it was revived by Frank Bartholomew, a San Franciscan journalist.

Harazathy's sons, Arpad and Alilla had married Vallejo's two daughters and today the Vallejo and Harazathy names have been resurrected by the great-great-grandson of

the two pioneers, whose name is suitably Vallejo (Val) Harazathy. He is M.C. Vallejo's winemaker, in a joint venture with Glen Ellen Wines. Part of the proceeds from the sale of the wines are going to the restoration of the Old Vallejo Winery, Qui Qui Ri Qui, behind his historic and restored home Lachryma Montis, near the Sonoma plaza.

Another early vigneron was Jacob Gundlach, a German winemaker, who established the Gundlach-Bundschu Winery in 1858 — Jim Bundschu is the current owner and operator.

Southern Sonoma stretches up 20 miles through the beautiful Sonoma Valley to Santa Rosa. Vineyards now stretch up into the Mayacamas Mountains and the Mt. Sonoma region, climate is basically Region II. Modern wineries such as Glen Ellen, Kenwood and Chateau St. Jean have become large and important and many small prestige winemaking concerns have commenced starting with the prestigious Hanzell in 1957, which is credited with introducing small imported oak cask maturation to California.

Southern Sonoma is not only historically significant, but a fast developing prestige vineyard region.

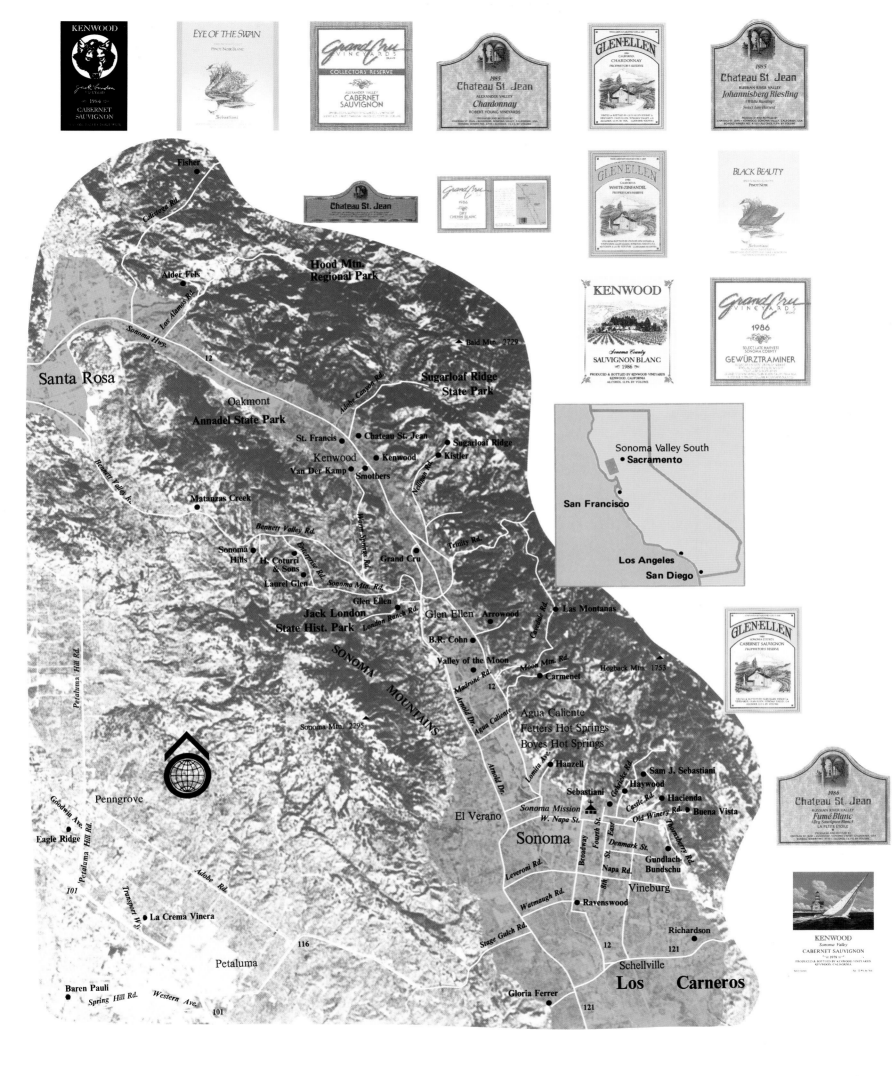

Grand Cru Vineyards

Walt and Tina Dreyer had already had an association as part owners in the Grand Cru Winery, when they brought out their partners in 1981. The wine operation was recommenced at Grand Cru in 1970 where original winemaker Bob Magnani is still in charge of the wine production.

The winery is based around the century old Lemoine cellars and much of the barrel ageing is done inside the old vaulted cement tanks, which have been cut open, forming a series of arches, stacked with French oak barriques.

The Dreyers also have agricultural interests in the Visalia region of the central Valley and in 1978, started looking for a suitable vineyard and winery. They found Grand Cru and started developing the winery immediately. Its capacity has trebled, with sales expanding to around 60,000 cases per year from a 10,000 case base.

Chenin Blanc has long been a strength of the winery and a dry version has just been produced. 1987 marks the first Chardonnay from Grand Cru and their collectors Reserve Alexander Valley Cabernet Sauvignon 1982 is absolutely superb.

Tina and Walt met at Stanford University. Tina has a strong interest in the culinary arts, which closely ties in with their developing wine styles. They have three sons, Dan, Matt and John, who all show some interest in becoming involved. New vineyards are planned and I am sure a solid future is in front of Grand Cru.

Carmenet Vineyard

The Chalone Vineyard company must have a penchant for developing mountain vineyards for the Garmenet Vineyard is situated high above the valley, on Moon Mountain Drive in the Mayacamas ranges. Whereas the Chalone, Acacia and Edna Valley Vineyard, all also owned by the Chalone Vineyards company, are Burgundy-oriented, Carmenet is a totally Bordeaux-style operation and, in fact, the name is a classic French word embracing all the grape varieties of Bordeaux.

The two flagship wines are first, a red blend of approximately 85% Cabernet Sauvignon, 10% Merlot and 5% Cabernet Franc. The first vintage, a 1982, was a knockout, made from Carmenet Estate fruit, but at the Edna Valley winery. The other wine produced is a typical Bordeaux white blend of Sauvignon Blanc (90%) and Semillon (only 10%).

The Carmenet Winery was partially completed for the 1983 vintage. It is quite something, state-of-the-art equipment and rare, but effective floating head tanks under a

wooden dome, with an octagonal sky light. This "winery in the round" is also very efficient. Carmenet have also blasted tunnels into the hillsides behind the winery and created a typical Bordeaux Chai, for maturing their red and white, in French oak barriques. The winery was set up by "Mac" McQuown and a syndicate including Dick Graff of Chalone. The listed company, Chalone Vineyards Inc. now owns it.

Wine director from the start has been Jeff Baker. He and his very able assistant, Pam Starr, a U.C. Davis graduate, who spent some time at Sonoma-Cutrer, use very traditional methods, hand plunging the red two to three times a day during fermentation and giving it an extended maceration. The wine is then racked from barrel to barrel every three months and fined with egg whites. All white wines are barrel fermented and aged "sur-lie" (on the yeast lees) and all go through a malo-lactic fermentation. As well as the Sauvignon Blanc — Semillon blend, a barrel-fermented French Colombard, from 50 year old Napa vines is

made — an interesting style indeed.

Carmenet know exactly what they want and are well on their way to achieving their goals.

Chateau St. Jean

In 1973, three influential growers from the Joaquin valley, Robert and Edward Meraoian plus Kenneth Sheffield, came up with the idea of starting a French-style Chateau, based on the vineyard designation concept, then only in its infant stages in America. In 1973, they chose as their site a 124 acre property stretching up into the Mayacamas Mountains, just north of Kenwood.

The choice of their first employee, Richard Arrowood, has turned out to have been a brilliant one. A Sonoma local who had worked for Korbel, Italian Swiss Colony and Sonoma Vineyards, Dick made the first Chateau St. Jean wines, at the Sonoma

Vineyards facility in 1974. Right from the start, vineyard designation, has been a strong feature of the winery and in some years up to nine separate Chardonnays have been produced in a single vintage.

The winery which was named for Jean Merzoian, one of the partner's wives, was first operational for the 1975 vintage and is now one of the most spectacular in north America. The original home on the property is a grand Mediterranean villa, built around 1920 by Ezra Goff, a lumber and mining magnate. It has been restored and incorporates a magnificent tasting room.

In 1980, Chateau St. Jean launched into Methode Champenoise production, at a new facility west of Santa Rosa at Graton. Edgar (Pete) Downs, a U.C. Davis graduate, who had worked three years at Korbel, was employed as maker of the sparkling wines.

The St. Jean Cuvees, spend a long three years on tirage being made from the classic Pinot Noir and Chardonnay varieties. A vintage dated Brut, is produced along with a vintage dated Blanc de Blanc from Chardonnay; both have been received with acclaim.

Dick Arrowood has a bachelor of arts in organic chemistry from California State in Sacramento and undertook post graduate studies in fermentation science at California

State in Fresno. His reputation, after his 15 years at St. Jean, is second to none.

In 1984, the Suntory International company from Japan bought Chateau St. Jean, long serving President, Alan Hemphill left in 1987 and former Sterling Winery's President Greg De Lucca took over.

As well as vineyard designated Chardonnay, Johannisberg Riesling, Sauvignon Blanc (labelled Fume Blanc), Gewurztraminer and Pinot Blanc, Chateau St. Jean also make some of America's greatest late harvest wines from Gewurztraminer, a Sauvignon Blanc/Semillon blend and, of course, Johannisberg Riesling. Until 1978, they had used T.B.A. on a very late harvest Botrytised Johannisberg Riesling to signify it would qualify as Trokenbeerenauslese, under German wine law. After the German government complained, this designation was no longer used. The wine, nonetheless, is outstanding. At the winery only, you can buy their vintage Vin Blanc an excellent and very affordable wine.

Chateau St. Jean, have carved a unique niche in the premium wine field and are jealously guarding it, with a continuing stream of outstanding still and sparkling white wines.

Glen Ellen Winery

No winery or wine brand has experienced the dramatic growth of Glen Ellen Winery, since its establishment in 1981. Perhaps it was the fact that the Benzinger family, under patriarch Bruno had long looked after the wine distribution in New York State. The Benzingers read the market to perfection. They could see the publics insatiable thirst for premium varietal table wines, but they could also see the wineries pricing these out of the markets' reach. They therefore introduced, their Glen Ellen Proprietors Reserve range, all varietal wines, but blended from various Californian coastal and central wine regions. The packaging was attractive, the quality good and the prices extremely competitive. With their distribution skill the results were sensational. Glen Ellen is fast approaching two million cases of premium varietal wines per year in 1988. Considering their goal of 30,000 cases by 1990, they are certainly well ahead!!

The Glen Ellen vineyards are situated in a beautiful, hilly part of the original Jack London Ranch. The Benzingers also produce a range of Sonoma county and estate bottled varietals, using deliberate viticultural techniques in the vineyard. These methods, when combined with the different soil types and depths, plus the various aspects of their hilly vineyards combines to achieve the wine styles they want.

Helen and Bruno have seven children, most of whom live on the property and are involved in the business. Mike is the winemaker and the others are involved in the vineyards, wine production and sales. The whole place has the air of a great big

Glen Ellen Winery

extended family. On our visit during harvest we were invited to join the family and winery workers in the kitchen for lunch.

The old Victorian timber home, now their national headquarters, is an historical landmark, dating back to 1868, when it was built by a German carpenter, Julius Wegner, who also planted vineyards. Wegner was the master carpenter, for the General Mariano Vallejo.

The Benzingers have a very important member of their team in Bruce Rector. Bruce is a winemaking consultant and a U.C. Davis graduate. He joined Glen Ellen at the beginning in 1981 and is responsible for sourcing the growers, for the Proprietors Reserve range, a massive job today and one he should be justly proud of, considering the unbelieveable success they have had. Bruce became a partner in the business in 1985.

Even the daughters Patsy and Kathy are involved along with their five brothers. Glen Ellen is indeed one big happy family producing the wines at both ends of the scale that are like themselves — warm, friendly and approachable.

GLEN ELLEN WINERY
Address: 1883 London Ranch Road, Glen Ellen. CA., 95442
Phone: 707/996 1066
Year of Establishment: 1981
Owner: The Benziger Family
Winemaker: Mike Benziger
Principal Varieties Grown: Cabernet Sauvignon, Sauvignon Blanc, Merlot
Acres Under Vine: 80
Average Annual Crush: 670 t on property; 38,000 t on property & various other locations

Principal Wines & Brands	Cellar Potential (Years)
Proprietor's Reserve Chardonnay	3
Proprietor's Reserve Sauvignon Blanc	3
Proprietor's Reserve Cabernet Sauvignon	3-4

Trade Hours – Available.
Retail Room Sales – Available.
Hours open to Public: 7 days a week from 10am to 4pm
Retail Distribution: 50 states

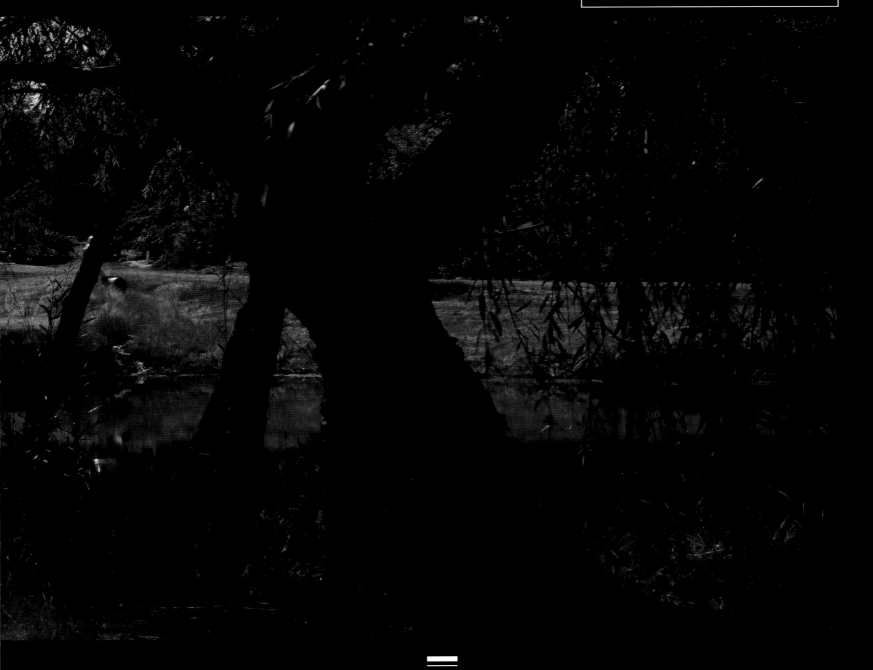

Valley of the Moon

Under a magnificent 400 year old, spreading, Bay Laurel tree, lies a delightful, low profile family winery, Valley of the Moon, called as such, because of Jack London's coining of the name for the region. The 200 acres around the winery are part of what was once Senator Hearst's Madrone Vineyard. Harry Parducci and his two sons, Harry Jnr., the winemaker and Gerard, in charge of marketing plus vineyard operations, run the winery between them and a few long time employees. Over recent years, they have been planting the red varieties, Zinfandel, Pinot Noir and Cabernet Sauvignon, a wise move, considering the renaissance of premium red table wines. These new plantings are mainly in the Mayacamas Mountains and the Parduccis are very happy with the resulting wines. Their delightful old winery is a pleasant reminder of a by-gone era, but their winemaking is certainly up to todays high standards.

Their Semillon is a most impressive wine, showing some tropical/oriental fruit flavours and their Zinfandel is complex and full in flavour, without being heavy.

Harry Snr's. father, Enrico, founder of the winery in 1941 and also creator of the Columbus Sausage and Salami Company, would surely be happy with the wine enterprise, his family have built up.

Haywood Winery

One of the prettiest winery settings one could imagine is the Haywood Winery location, dug into a rock outcrop under spreading Californian oaks surrounded by a native garden, resplendent with wildflowers. Peter Haywood and his wife, began growing vines in 1974. Six years later, a neighbour, who had built a small winery, wished to sell so Peter took over. Gradually he is utilising his grape crop and hopes eventually to supply all his grape production to Haywood. At present he still sells about half to other wineries. Haywood Chardonnay has been consistently good. Other interesting wines have been made including a late harvest Merlot in 1980, from raisined fruit and with some sweetness. The Haywood Rieslings have also shone. This is a very pleasant winery to drop into for a tasting.

Hacienda Wine Cellars

Hacienda Wine Cellars were founded in 1973, by Frank Bartholomew, at the tender age of 75 years. Frank was a modern day wine pioneer for, in 1941, whilst a San Francisco journalist (he went on to head U.P.I.) he purchased a piece of land on the outskirts of Sonoma. Two large decaying stone buildings on the property turned out to be Agoston Harazathay's old Buena Vista Winery, which Bartholomew re-established and subsequently sold, in 1967.

Frank retained much of the vineyard land and opened Hacienda in a Mediterranean building there which was once a hospital. Crawford Cooley a grapegrower friend of Bartholomew, joined him as a partner in 1976, Frank died in 1987, but Hacienda goes from strength to strength under the Cooley family. Two interesting wines I tried, were their Moonlight Dessert wine, a fortified blend of Cabernet, Merlot and Black Muscat with 10% residual sweetness, it is spicy with chocolate and mint flavours — delicious. They also make a vintage port from Merlot and Cabernet fortified with pot still brandy, a unique product in America, well worth seeking out and which will age very well. A range of varietal table wines is also made.

On a hill near the winery, a replica of Agoston Harazathay's Pompeiian villa is being built, a suitable tribute to his role in the North American and Sonoma wine industry.

Gundlach Bundschu Winery

1988 marks the 130th consecutive vintage at this historic vineyard, known originally as Rhinefarm, with its "Bacchus" brand established by Jacob Bundschu, a German wineman, in 1858. He and his son-in-law Charles Bundschu built huge underground wine vaults in San Francisco, which were unfortunately destroyed by the 1906 earthquake.

Athough this finished their winemaking activities, the Bundschu family continued as grapegrowers and in 1973, Jim, a fifth generation family member rebuilt the winery and resurrected the brand.

Jim and his marketing chief, dry humoured Jim McCullough, form quite a characterful combination. Their marketing approach is novel, to say the least, playing heavily on the unpronounceable name and a large cult following has developed. One poster depicts Mary, Jim's mother "lecturing" to a police officer pulled up beside her car. "If you can't pronounce Gundlach Bundschu Gerwurztraminer you shouldn't be driving".

257

Sebastiani Vineyards

The name Sebastiani is synonymous with both wine and the town of Sonoma. Outside Gallo's crushing facility at Frei Brothers, this is Sonoma's largest winery. Many of the town of Sonoma's public facilities, have incorporated the name of this long active family.

Samuelle Sebastiani arrived in San Francisco in 1895 from Tuscany. He made cobblestones for San Francisco streets and saved up enough money to buy the old Milani Winery in 1904. The site of the stone buildings he purchased dates back to the first vineyard north of San Francisco where vineyards were planted by the Franciscan Padres, from the Sonoma Mission, in 1825. Samuelle built the business, mainly around bulk wine sales, both to the industry and the public. When he died in 1944, Samuelle was succeeded by his son, August, who became one of the industry's most innovative, as well as respected, wine makers. He began bottling and marketing Sebastiani wines, under their own name. August introduced America's first 1.5 litre premium wines, with generic styles under the August Sebastiani name and then varietal wines under the same name, with the addition of the word "country".

August died in 1980, but his widow, Sylvia is a real dynamo and still chairperson of the winery. Her cooking book, Magniamo (Let's eat), has been a hit, selling at the winery and many other places. Son Sam took over and invested heavily in upgrading the winery and pushing harder into the premium varietal market. He has now gone out into his own Sonoma winemaking venture. Sylvia's younger son, Don, is now at the helm after being called back from campaigning for his fourth term in the California legislature in 1986. In 1980, he had become the second youngest member ever of the Californian Assembly.

Don, in his own words, is "Striving for style and quality". Sebastiani have cleverly aimed, not only different wine styles and packages at various segments of the wine market, but completely different brand names. The recently released Vendange (French for grape harvest) range gets right away from the Sebastiani name and is aimed at the value, premium, varietal market. They still have their traditional Sonoma Valley varietal range and have their proprietors' reserve wines. Probably the most exciting development are the vineyard designated wines just being released. Their labelling is completely different from anything previously done by any winery, with the vineyard name,

being the only wording on the elegant label in bold type. Five 1986 Chardonnays and two 1985 Cabernet Sauvignons were released, in 1988. All seven wines, are from different vineyards within the Sonoma Valley.

Sebastiani Winery situated within the town of Sonoma, is a beautiful and historic old facility, which has been lovingly cared for. It is, by far, the Sonoma Valley's most popular tourist destination. Many of the casks carry intricate carvings, executed by the late Earle Brown and are well worth seeing.

In 1987, Sebastiani bought the large Woodbridge Growers Winery in Lodi, to help supply their fast growing sales, for they are now America's 8th largest winery, with quality consistently good through all their ranges. A recent addition has been the Richard Cuneo Methode Champenoise, named after brother-in-law and director, Dick Cuneo.

Sebastiani have had a number of firsts in the industry. Their 1972 Gamay Nouveau became America's youngest ever released dry red, contrasting with the company's policy of always having some 5-15 year old, red wines available, a noble philosophy they still hold onto. The Eye of the Swan Pinot Noir Blanc, was one of America's first blush wines.

Mary Sullivan has taken on the chief winemaker's position after 12 years with Sebastiani. She works closely with the company's many contracted growers to ensure the premium wine boom at Sebastiani is well grounded. As Samuelle's favourite saying, carved into one of the barrels in his beloved cellar goes: "When the first glass of wine invites a second, the wine is good". At Sebastiani the current generation, seem to have the formula worked out pretty well!!

Kenwood Vineyards

In 1970, six wine enthusiasts banded together and bought the historic Pagani Brothers Winery, built in 1906. It is now run as a partnership between brothers Marty and Michael Lee and brother-in-law John Sheela. Marty runs the marketing strategies of Kenwood and came up with a brilliant artists series of Cabernet Sauvignons, starting with the 1975 vintage. Each year the best Kenwood Cabernet Sauvignon, is chosen to carry a label featuring a famous American artist. Some controversy hit the first release, when the B.A.T.F. in Washington D.C., declared the painting (a Californian art nouveau scene, with an impressionistic nude female featured) to be obscene. The artist, David Goines, whose work appears in the Louvre, Paris, as well as the Museum of Modern Art in New York, was inspired to do a similar scene, but with a skeleton of the girl's form. Again the B.A.T.F. said "no". Despite this, the series has been very successful and the current 1984 release sells for around $30 per bottle.

Marty lives in Jack London's original home and Kenwood buys all the grapes from the London Ranch, run by London's descendant Milo Shepard. Mike, Marty's younger brother, makes the wines, and has learnt his trade well from Bob Kozlowski, the renowed wine chemist and a previous partner at Kenwood. John Sheela looks after administration, grower liaison and finance. All together they have a good team at Kenwood.

The Kenwood Sauvignon Blanc, has been somewhat of a trend-setter for the variety. Kenwood's other wines are all in the upper echelon as far as quality is concerned, but prices are very reasonable.

The winery has produced a large range of prints, posters clothing etc. based on their art series as well as their annual Jack London Cabernet release, with its striking ceramic printed bottle. This clever and imaginative promotional strategy, conceived by Marty Lee, provides the wine lover with some excellent and artistic wine appointments for their home or work place.

Kenwood have been a worthy addition, to the noble and historic wine industry of the Sonoma valley.

Introduction to Temecula, San Diego and Mexico

This portion of the southern part of the west coast, stretching 200 miles south of Los Angeles, into Mexico, has a long and colourful winegrowing history.

Mexico, of course, has the oldest wine industry in North America, dating back to the time of the Conquistadores in the 1500's. The last 25 years have seen the development, from very few wineries and small production to over 60 wineries with wine production, in nine main wine districts. The best wines are coming from the Baja California peninsula, where the rich alluvial, irrigated coastal valleys are cooled by ocean breezes and morning fogs that sweep in from the Pacific. The other region that is making a name for itself, is situated in the province of Zacatecas, at the extremely high altitude of around 7,000 ft., which obviously cools the climate considerably. The Mexican wine industry's fortunes have fluctuated with its volatile political climate.

Over the years, a number of prominent Californian vignerons have helped the Mexican industry. First in 1889, James Concannon, from the Livermore Vineyard bearing his name, travelled to Mexico and convinced legendary "strong man" President Diaz, that a successful commercial wine industry was possible in Mexico. Concannon shipped in several million cuttings of vinifera from California and, with his brother Thomas, was successful. In 1910, with the industry booming, Antonio Perelli-Minetti from California, arrived to try and re-make the fortune he lost in a wine venture in San Francisco. He successfully established a 900 acre vineyard near Torreon, but had to leave quickly during the civil war in 1916. He went on to make another fortune in California.

The Baja California has some good vineyards and in 1962, Dimitri Tchelistcheff, son of the famous Andre, did some pioneering of his own, with the Bodegas de Santo Tomas Winery, in Ensenada. He planted classic varieties and introduced modern technology into the winery. The Spanish Domecq company also has a large modern winery, north-east of Ensenada. Baja California now has some 25,000 acres of vines.

The San Diego region had some 5,000 acres of wines in the 1930's but the Ferrara Winery and the Bernardo Winery, both near Escondido are the only survivors. They have been joined by the San Pasqual Winery, established in 1973, south of Escondido. However, most development has been in the Temecula region, north near Rancho California. The Callaway Vineyards and Winery, founded by the former president of Burlington Industries, Ely Callaway, in 1974 began a mini boom in this area. There are now 4,000 acres of vines and over 10 wineries. Cooling breezes from the Pacific through the Rainbow Gap keep this region quite temperate. Callaway only makes whites and most successful ones at that. Hiram Walker bought this winery in 1982.

Southern California will no doubt see vineyards springing up in new locations over the next few decades.

Temecula, San Diego and Mexico

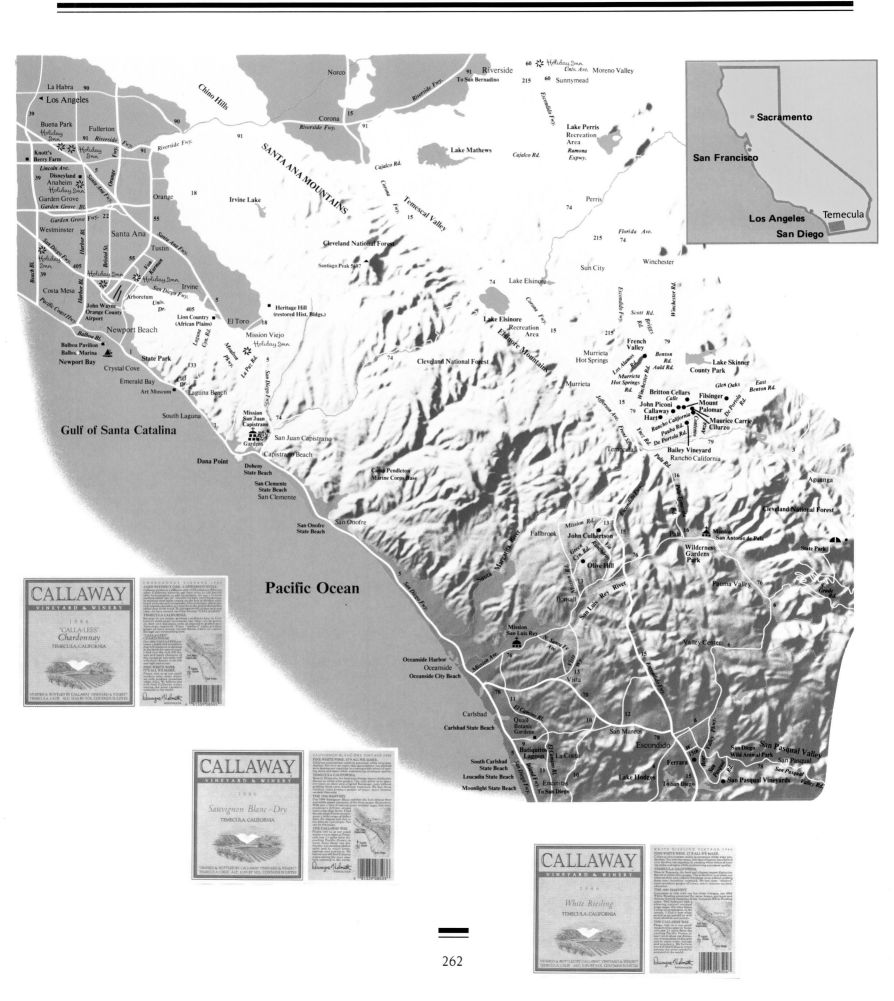

Callaway Vineyards and Winery

In 1969, after searching for the ideal climate for a number of years, Ely Callaway planted a 134 acre vineyard in the Temecula district of Southern California, where he planned to retire several years later. At the time he was president of the world's largest textile company, Burlington Industries.

Ely had studied the climatic conditions closely for some years and found Temecula to his liking. Temecu is actually an Indian name, meaning "the land where the sun shines through the white mist". The Rainbow gap runs through the coastal mountains to the Pacific; the morning mists and afternoon sea breezes it brings to Temecula give it ideal, moderate climatic conditions for viticulture. The soils are sandy with a granitic base and the vines have been planted on their own vinifera roots.

Callaway has not only been successful with his winemaking, but also in promoting the vineyard as a tourist attraction. Handy to both Los Angeles and San Diego, an elaborate visitors centre, which also runs wine appreciation courses and dinners, has been established.

The first Callaway wine was a Botrytised Chenin Blanc from the 1973 vintage, named Sweet Nancy, crushed and fermented at a Napa Winery.

The Callaway Winery was built in 1974 and Karl Werner, former winemaster at Germany's famous Schloss Vollrads, became the first winemaker, succeeded by Stephen O'Donnell, who unfortunately died in 1983. Current winemaker is Dwayne Helmuth, who introduced their successful Calla-lees, a Chardonnay fermented in stainless steel, but left to age "Sur-lies" on its yeast lees, as is done in the Chablis region of France.

Callaway strive for fruit flavour in their wines, only whites have been made since 1982, Sauvignon Blanc, White Riesling, Chenin Blanc and of course Chardonnay, being the main products.

Callaway wines have been highly acclaimed and received countless awards and gold medals. In 1976, the first Callaway Riesling, a 1974 vintage, was served to Queen Elizabeth and Prince Philip, by the Pilgrims Club at their American Bicentenary luncheon, in New York.

Callaway's viticulturist, John Moramarco, has been there from the start and must take much of the credit for the success of the venture.

Bodegas de Santo Tomas

The history of Bodegas de Santo Tomas, the Mexican Baja California State's largest and oldest winery, dates back to 1888, when Italian immigrant Francisco Andonegui gave up gold mining and built a small adobe winery, near the site of the original Santo Tomas Mission. Towards the end of his life Andonegui, sold the vineyards and winery to the then governor of Baja, General Abelardo Luis Rodriguez, who owned the business for the next forty years, although he was too busy to be much involved in its operation, as his political career took him on to be president of Mexico. The general moved the winery north from the beautiful Santo Tomas Valley to Ensenada, where it is still located today, covering several city blocks off the Avenida Miramar. He also planted more vineyards in the Rancho Guadalupe area, north/east of Ensenada.

In 1962, General Rodriquez hired Dimitri Tchelistcheff, the 32 year old son of the famous Russian-born enologist Andre, who came to California in 1937 and is North America's pre-eminent winemaker. In his position as technical director, Dimitri worked some miracles, first in the vineyards, with his introduction of classic varieties and modern viticultural techniques, then in the winery, where he brought in refrigeration, closed fermentation, small wood maturation and a host of other technical advances, all at reasonable costs. After 15 years, Dimitri left in 1977. The winery passed from the General's widow in 1967 to the Elias Pando wine firm of Mexico City. They remain the current owners and their vineyards have expanded to cover over 1,000 acres in the Guadalupe, Santo Tomas, San Vicente and San Antonio de Los Minas Valleys of the Baja. They make many different wines, some for the local market and many of their styles are Spanish-influenced. Their varietal, Cabernet Sauvignon, Chenin Blanc and blended wines I tasted, showed some influence of the warm climate, but were remarkably good. A visit to Bodegas de Santo Tomas, is not too difficult as it can be reached, by only two hours driving, along the stunning coast line, south from San Diego.

Bodegas de Santo Tomas

Yolo, Solano and the Sacramento Valley

Yolo and Solano county are part of the Sacramento valley, which stretches some 200 miles northward from San Francisco.

Prior to Prohibition there was a total of over 40,000 acres of grapes in the nine counties covered by this river valley. By the start of the wine revolution in the mid 1960's, only a few hundred were left, but now nearly 10,000 acres have been replanted, mainly to premium table wine varieties. Some old wineries still operate around Sacramento, including the 3 million gallon Gibson wine company's, Elk Grove Winery, producing largely fruit wines. Most of the development has been in the Sierra Foothills in Eldorado and Amador counties (more of this is covered in chapter 16). Yolo and Solano counties have also had their share of exciting wine growing development and one in particular, the R.H. Phillips Vineyards, in the new Dunnigan Hills, 30 miles north-west of Sacramento, has added an extra dimension, to the North American wine industry. The area around Clarksburg, fifteen miles south of the State capital, in the Delta region, is also being used as a grape source, for many leading Chenin Blancs, often made in coastal county wineries. The R & J Cook Winery is a successful new and growing winery in this region. West of Sacramento near Davis, the home of the University of California, Davis with its world renowned wine school, there are several wineries, including the interesting Satiety Winery of Sterling and Elaine Chaykin, with its strong culinary connection. In Solano county, the grape is also having a renaissance, near its eastern border in the Suisuin Valley, only 15 miles as the crow flies from Napa. Several quite large vineyards and wineries have been established here in the early 1980's, including the Cadenasso Winery and Wooden Valley Winery, both near Fairfield.

The North counties of the valley played a big role in the early history of Californian wines, particularly Senator Leland Stanford's (founder of Stanford University) Vina Vineyard and Winery (now only a storage shell used by the Trappist monks, who have built a monastery next door). Stanford planted the world's then largest vineyard of 5,000 acres and, in 1881, was also the world's largest brandy producer. Captain John Sutter of "Sutter's Fort" fame, established a vineyard in Sutter County near Yuba City in 1848. It was in Sutter County that the ubiquitous "Thompson Seedless" variety was first grown, by farmer William Thompson.

It went on to dominate the California grape industry and caused indirectly, the demise of the Sacramento valley as a wine region. Lack of autumn rains further south in the central valley, where the grapes could be dried in a surplus year without risk, caused a shift of vineyards out of the higher risk Sacramento Valley.

A modern, suitably named, wine venture is the "Renaissance Vineyard", in Yuba County, just launching onto the market. Its 360 acre vineyard and winery have been created by a religious sect one of whose members, Karl Werner, is in charge, formerly with Callaway Vineyards in Temecula. Before that held the prestigious position of winemaster at the Schloss Vollrads Winery in Germany. More of this and other new wine developments, is sure to be heard of in these counties before the end of the century.

Yolo, Solano

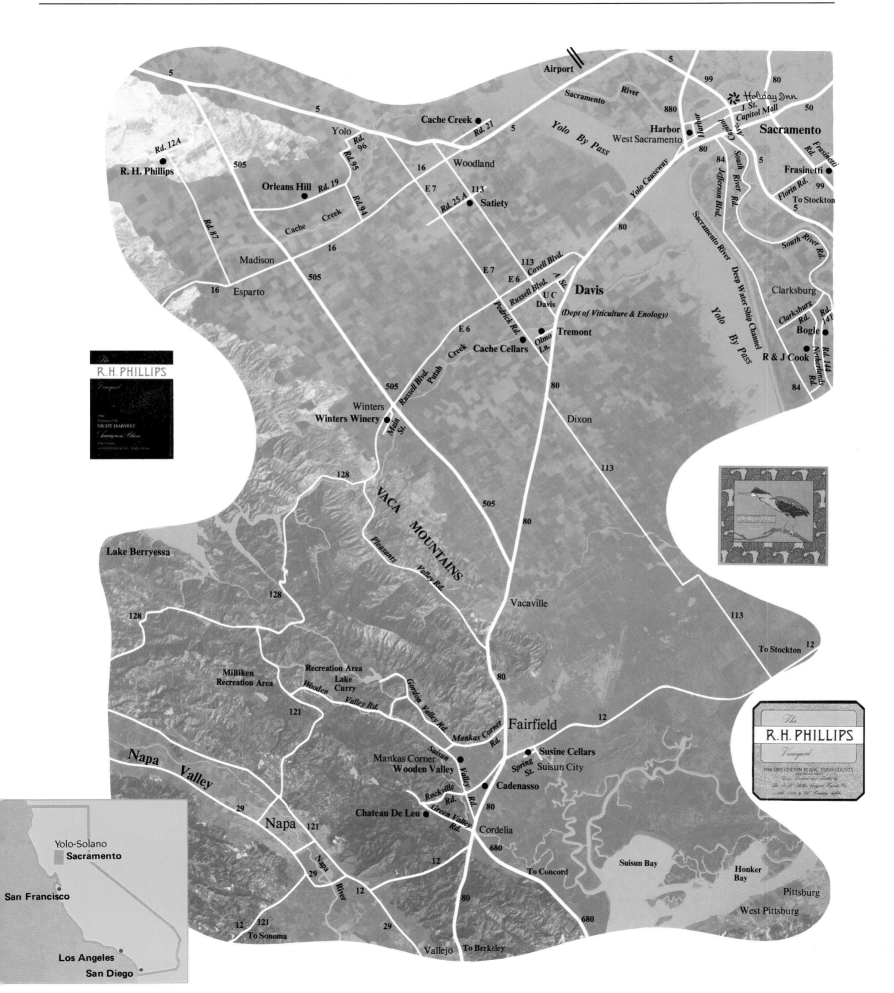

Airport

5

99   80

880   Holiday Inn
J St. Capitol Mall   50

Harbor   Sacramento
West Sacramento

Sacramento   River

Yolo By Pass

Cache Creek   Rd. 21
5

Rd. 96

Yolo

Rd. 12A

R. H. Phillips

505

Rd. 95

Orleans Hill   Rd. 19

Rd. 94

Cache   Creek

16

505

Madison

Woodland

16   E 7

Rd. 25 A   113
Satiety

84

South River Rd.   5

Jefferson Blvd.

Yolo Causeway

80

Frasinetti

Frasinetti Rd.

Frasinetti

Florin Rd.   99
To Stockton
5

South River Rd.

16   Esparto

E 7   113   Covell Blvd.
E 6   A St.   Davis
Russell Blvd.   U C
Davis   (Dept of Viticulture & Enology)

Clarksburg

Clarksburg
Rd.   Rd. 141

Bogle

Rd. 144

Netherlands Rd.

R & J Cook

84

Deep Water Ship Channel

Sacramento River

Yolo   By Pass

E 6   Pedrick Rd.
Cache Cellars   Olmo
Ln.   Tremont

Russell Blvd.   Putah   Creek

505

Winters
Winters Winery

Main St.

Dixon

80

128

128

128

VACA

MOUNTAINS

Pleasants   Valley Rd.

Lake Berryessa

505

113

Vacaville

80

113

To Stockton   12

Milliken
Recreation Area

Recreation Area
Lake
Curry
Valley Rd.

Wooden

Gordon   Valley Rd.

121

Napa

Valley

Mankas Corner
Wooden Valley

Mankas Corner Rd.

Suisun

Fairfield

12

Susine Cellars

Spring
St.   Suisun City

R.H. PHILLIPS
Vineyard

1986 DRY CHENIN BLANC YOLO COUNTY

29   Napa

121

Chateau De Leu

Rockville Rd.

Green Valley Rd.

Valley Rd.

Cadenasso

Cordelia

80

680

12

To Concord

Suisun Bay

Honker
Bay

Pittsburg

West Pittsburg

Napa   River

29

12

12   121

To Sonoma

29

Vallejo   To Berkeley

80

680

Yolo-Solano   Sacramento

San Francisco

Los Angeles
San Diego

The
R.H. PHILLIPS
Vineyard

1986
Dominga Hills
NIGHT HARVEST
Sauvignon Blanc
Yolo County

The R. H. Phillips Vineyards

The R. H. Phillips Vineyards and Winery have opened up an entirely new chapter in the history of North American wines.

The Giguiere family had been farmers in the Dunnigan Hills, some thirty miles north-west of Sacramento, for many years, raising sheep, dry farming cereal crops and sunflowers. The family originally came from the French Basque region and their maternal grandfather R. H. Phillips had come down from Washington State to settle the property. In 1980, they were looking for ways to better utilise their 2,600 acre property. Vines do not require too much precious water, so they commenced grape growing. They decided to make some wine themselves, using another winery's facilities, just to see what sort of wine could be made. They were pleasantly surprised, so a winery was quickly planned and John Giguiere's college friend, Clark Smith came in to make it all happen. Clark is an extremely intelligent young winemaker, who has thrived on the challenge of this new viticultural region. The decision to plant Semillon grapes has been a most fortuitous one, as some of the best wines I have seen from this classic Bordeaux variety, have been produced, by Clark, who had long experience in the retail wine trade before going onto U.C. Davis and obtaining a masters degree, in enology and viticulture.

The Dunnigan Hills have some of the most beautiful rolling landscapes of the North American continent and are part of the Eastern foothills of the coastal range, over whose hills only 40 miles away is the Napa Valley. The terrain and soils are ideal, but supplementary irrigation is necessary as the region is in a rain shadow. One of the great advantages, is that land in this region is only hundreds of dollars per acre, not tens of thousands of dollars as in the Napa Valley and some other recognised Californian regions. The open nature of the land makes planting easy and relatively inexpensive. All the Phillips vines are on their own vinifera rootstocks. These facets, combined with the ideal region III climate and the Bordeaux and Loire varieties planted lead to great wines at bargain prices. Wine drinkers are just starting to discover this.

The Reserve Semillons from Phillips are stunning. Semillon grown here in the warmer

climate produces lovely honey, citrus and pineapple flavours that develop beautifully with age. The reserve also receives some limousin oak ageing in French barriques and about a year and a half of bottle age, before release. The 1985, 1986 and 1987 vintages I have tasted are great wines all with ageing potential. Sauvignon Blanc and Chenin Blanc have done well, and the first estate Chardonnay, a 1987 barrel fermented wine, to be released shortly, is very impressive.

R. H. Phillips have huge potential, for virtually their whole ranch could become a vineyard. Their moves have been innovative all along the way — the hand harvesting at night, with its beneficial effects on the wines, has led to a striking label. This rising star of wine will shine for many moons to come.

Satiety

Sterling Chaykin's view is that wine is a wonderful adjunct to the enjoyment of life, his wish is to satiate the visitors to his winery, by giving them a complete experience, with the enjoyment of food, wine and hospitality.

He and Elaine his wife, have set up a country style food and wine complex in a neat and functional winery building, south of Davis near Woodland. Over the next few years they plan a restaurant and other developments to create a haven, where their wines can be truly enjoyed at their best.

R & J Cook

Roger and Joanne Cook were substantial grape growers near the attractive town of Clarksburg, in the Sacramento delta area. Roger's family had been involved in grape growing for four generations.

Roger set out in his own vineyard venture in 1971, but after marrying in 1978, realised that to make it pay, he and his bride Joanne would have to make wine as well. They gradually set up a winemaking facility as funds permitted. With its success, they have now invested in new buildings and equipment, concentrating largely on white wines, particularly Chenin Blanc and Sauvignon Blanc. An unusual, but highly successful wine they also produce is a Blanc de Noir from the Merlot variety, with the lifted floral aroma and fruit of the Bordeaux grape, usually used as a blending variety for red wines.

The Cooks are happy with their move and welcome visitors.

Introduction to North and South Carolina

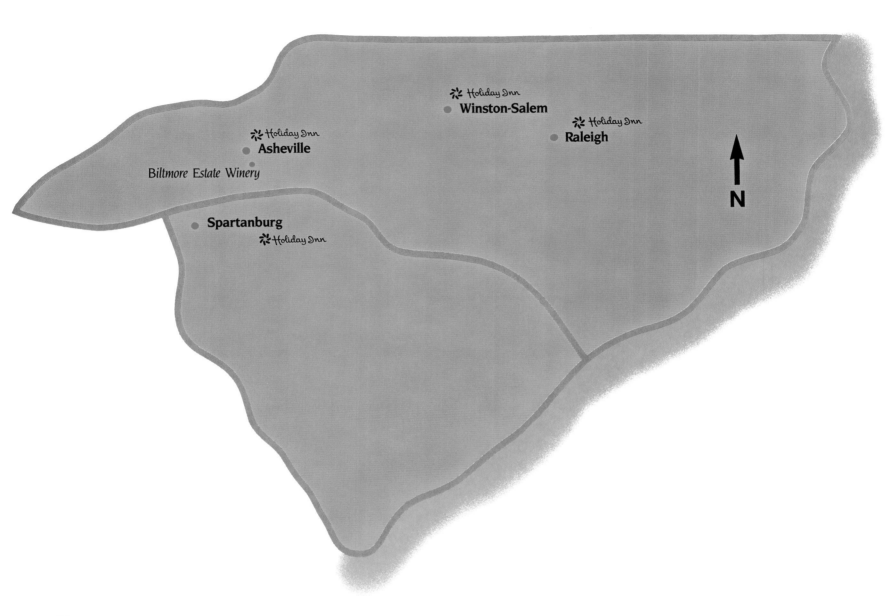

A lthough not exactly the states that spring to mind when one thinks about American wine, it was in fact in North Carolina that America's most popular pre and post Prohibition wine, Virginia Dare, was conceived. The legendary "Captain" Paul Garret had a vision that was half a century before its time - that wine could be sold as food, like other farm products and that it could be consumed in moderation with meals and help employ many people in its production.

His wine enterprises started with the turn of the century and, by the time National Prohibition struck in 1920, he had seventeen wineries in six states. He battled on through Prohibiton with several novel ideas, including the brilliant "Vin-glo" concept, to bring canned grape concentrate to the home with full winemaking and bottling equipment as a package. These ideas did not succeed but, on repeal, he once again recouped his fortune through the success of Virginia Dare, whose unique flavour was based on the Scuppernong variety, native to the Southeast of America and a member of the "Vitis Rotundifolia" family, sometimes known as the Muscadine varieties. These grapes, in fact, made North America's first wine in the hands of the French Huguenots in Florida in the 1560's.

Many of the counties in the Carolinas were declared dry as early as 1908 and have remained so until recent years. New farm wine laws and government grants supporting viticultural research have seen a resurgence of winegrowing in the last decade and North Carolina sports one of America's grandest wineries, The Biltmore Estate, completed in 1985, standing on a 8,000 acre property near Asheville N.C. Here George Washington Vanderbilt constructed a magnificent chateau, late in the last century, which would not be put to shame by the palace at Versailles.

Vines look set to become a much more common sight in the heart of tobacco country.

In the last years of the 19th century, philanthropist George Washington Vanderbilt decided to create an estate and chateau to rival the splendid chateaux of the Loire Valley of France. Anyone who visits the 8,000 acre Biltmore Estate today can attest to the fact he was successful.

William A. Vanderbilt Cecil, grandson of the founder, decided around 1970 that it would be fitting that, as in France, his chateau should have its own vineyards and make its own wines. His thinking was obviously influenced by the fact the wine boom had started and tourism was already a vital part of the Biltmore Estate operations.

Firstly, a 12 acre experimental vineyards of French hybrids and old world vinifera were planted. The location is in the foothills of the Blue Ridge Mountains, some 2,600 feet above sea level. It proved most suitable and the vines thrived. A small winery was then constructed in the basement of the greenhouse. Much has happened since and there are now 125 acres planted and, in 1985, an imposing winery, built around the dairy barn, was opened.

French winemaker Phillipe Jourdain was

hired from the south of France and has made
wines in the new multi-million dollar winery
since it opened.

The Biltmore Estate also includes a
superb restaurant, the Deerpark, where
much of the wine is sold. The Biltmore Estate
and Winery is truly an eye opener and doing
a wonderful job to promote quality wine and
its benefits to those in the south.

Introduction to Florida

Holiday Inn

Tallahassee   **Monticello**

Alaqua Winery   Lafayette   Vineyards & Winery

Holiday Inn   **Portland**   **Panama City**

Fort Walton Beach   Holiday Inn

N

Although Florida is not one of the main wine producing states in the union, it was here that the first American wine was made, around 1563, by the French Huguenots near the present site of Jacksonville. In fact, when the British Admiral, Sir John Hawkins, relieved the starving Huguenots in 1865 he found they had plenty of wine - some twenty hogsheads in all - made from the Muscadine wines.

The Muscadine vines do not have bunches of grapes like the "Vinifera" of Europe or the Labrusca of the Northern States, but clusters of large individual grapes and are very resistant to all diseases. The climate of Florida can be extremely hot and humid and the native Muscadines are much more suited to it than bunch-bearing varieties.

In 1979, the Florida legislative encouraged grape growing again by dropping its high tax entirely on all Florida-grown wine, also setting up grape wine research programmes at the Gainesville and Tallahassee universities. The results are some interesting hybrid bunch varieties such as "stover", which have started a winegrowing renaissance during the last decade.

Lafayette Vineyards & Winery

Florida's most impressive winery, without a doubt, is the Lafayette Vineyards and Winery, located in the more temperate climate of the panhandle in the North-west of the state.

The Tallahassee region has a long viticultural history, with its rolling hills and native oak trees reminding one of parts of France. Perhaps it was this similarity which drew the Marquis de Lafayette to the area. Following the American civil war, some 130 years ago, he was rewarded for his country's assistance with a land grant. In 1882, another Frenchman, Professor Emile Dubois, arrived to test the region for grape growing potential. He experimented with over 150 grape varieties, built a winery and in 1900 won both gold and silver awards for his wines at the Paris Exposition.

The modern day Lafayette Winery is housed in a most attractive French- inspired Chateau, surrounded by 35 acres of wines, 13 of which are vinifera and French hybrids. Lafayette was founded in 1982 by C. Gary

Cox, a native Tallahassean, who had planted his own hobby vineyard in 1980. His experience in building, accountancy and agricultural pursuits suited him ideally for the job. He was joined by a number of investors including his winemaker, Jeanne Burgess. Jeanne obtained her bachelor's degree in physical education in 1976 and, after several years teaching, helped her father establish a 10 acre vineyard in 1980. Her interest in wine was sparked and she went on to obtain a post-graduate degree in enology and viticulture from the Mississippi State University, working in the university's pilot winery.

She assisted in the establishment of a central Florida Vineyard and winery before joining Lafayette in 1983. Wesley Cox, a graduate of the Abraham Baldwin Agricultural College in Georgia, is the vineyard manager for Lafayette.

The wine I found most impressive was the newly released Blanc du Bois, from a newly released Florida hybrid. This had a beautiful floral aroma and fresh tropical fruit flavours, with a nice spicy dry finish. The Stover Special Reserve and a Methode Champenoise - Marquis de Lafayette, also from the Stover hybrid, were also very impressive. Some Muscadine varieties, namely Welder and Magnolia, are grown and make very acceptable wine, if somewhat unusual to the inexperienced palate. Another white hybrid, Suwannee, is also grown, whilst a red from the native "Noble" muscadine variety was very pleasant. Lafayette are showing the way to succeed in this challenging viticultural region.

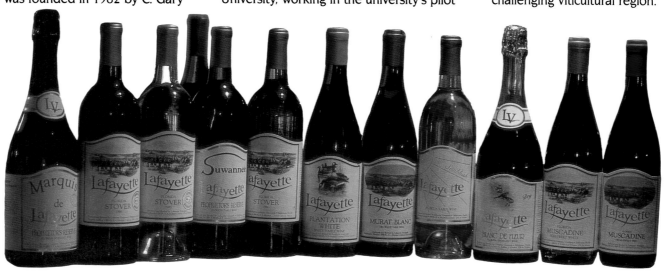

Introduction to Georgia

Georgia had an early start in winegrowing when the founder of the state, General James E. Oglethorpe, made a declaration in 1733 that all settlers must grow grapes for wine and mulberries for silk. By 1880, Georgia had become the nations sixth largest wine producing state, with almost a million gallons of wine coming from 3,000 acres of vines.

Prohibiton hit Georgia in 1907 and winemaking collapsed. Apart from some Muscadine vineyards in the south and a few wineries making peach wines, Georgia's vinous renaissance did not start until 1983, when four significant wineries opened in the cooler northern Piedmont area.

By far the most significant is Chateau Elan, some 30 miles north east of Atlanta, part of $20,000,000 development. A French Chateau of truly grand proportions houses the winery and a magnificent French wine and food market. Over 100 acres of vines are already planted largely Vinifera. With this sort of lead growth in Georgia's wine industry looks set to explode.

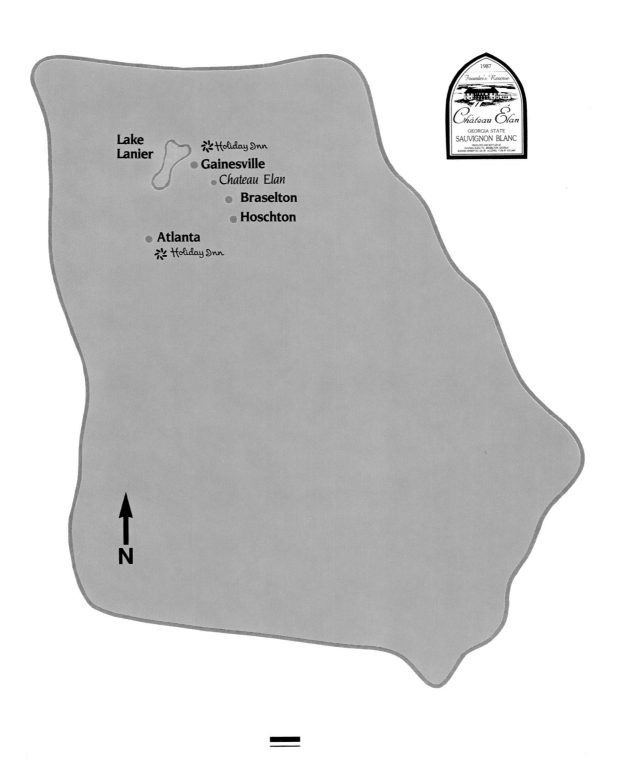

W hen the modern history of North American wine unfolds, surely Chateau Elan will figure prominently. No stone has been left unturned in creating a superb Chateau-style winery, surrounded by a food and wine complex that defies the imagination. On top of all this the 1,000 acre property will boast a 27-hole golf course, health spa and residential community. One hundred acres of vines are now planted and a further 150 acres about to be added. The winery's total production will soon amount to half a million gallons annually.

The wine and food complex is intriguing, all located in the main Chateau building and modelled after a French street market, complete with three huge wall murals, two typical French street scenes and the other depicting the history of winemaking. The complex also includes a wine museum, a

bistro-style restaurant and banquet facilities. Probably most fascinating is the recreation of the true French street scene. Quarry stone pavers lead to wrought-iron fences and street lights that could come straight out of Paris. Much of the produce is presented on Parisian street carts and a touch of grandure is encompassed by the floating staircase with the arched palladian windows filled with stained glass.

Who would have such a vision to put this all together? The gentleman concerned is Donald Panoz, who has built a giant pharmaceutical company based in Ireland but spanning the globe. Donald established his American headquarters in Gainesville just north of Chateau Elan. The countryside so captivated him he just had to do something more. An inveterate wine lover, the terrain reminded him of the great French wine

country around Bordeaux and the Loire Valley, so he decided to establish vineyards and a winery.

In Jean Courtois, their winemaker, Chateau Elan have a real asset, a fifth generation member of a French winegrowing family, who have a 75 acre vineyard and a winery very close to Chateauneuf-du-Pape. Donald Panoz met Jean at his family's winery and immediately offered him the job. In fact Jean goes back each year for a short time to oversee the making of their Cotes du Rhone Village Vinsobres.

Jean, to me, has one of the healthiest and most sound philosophies of winemaking I have seen. He firmly believes North America and other new world wine producing countries are beginning to overhaul the old world wines, due to their innovative approach and desire to create

Chateau Elan

even better wines.

He in fact recently took some Chateau Elan wines back to France, where they received critical acclaim. His approach to making subtle elegant and fruity wines appears to be working, as he has already won 55 awards (as of 1988) in wine shows around the world.

Chateau Elan is a showpiece of the North American wine industry and deserves all the success it is currently achieving.

An Introduction to Indiana

Winegrowing in Indiana goes back to 1804, twelve years before it became a state. Swiss immigrant, Jean-Jacques Dufour, planted vines at Vevay in 1804, naming the town after his hometown of Vevey in Switzerland, where his father cultivated vines. Dufour wrote one of America's first wine books, "The American Vine Dressers Guide", published in 1826. Indiana's next wine development came in the far south-west of the state, in 1814, when the Trappist monks formed a winegrowing colony calling it Harmonie, taken over 11 years later by Robert Owen who renamed it New Harmony. Today the St. Wendel Winery with its Hindu winemaker, Murli Dharmadakari, stands near this site. By 1911, Indiana was a major wine producing state with 11,000 tons of grapes being crushed.

In 1971, Indiana's wine industry was all but dead, but a new farm winery law was enacted that year, leading to a number of small wineries opening throughout the state. Largest and most significant of these is the Huber Orchard Winery, founded in 1978, by Gerald and Carl Huber on their large ranch, which specialises in fruit production.

N

Holiday Inn

Bloomington
Holiday Inn
Oliver Winery

Huber Orchard & Winery

● **Starlite**

Borden ●

New Albany
Holiday Inn　　**Louisville, Ky.**

St Wendell Cellars

Huber Orchard Winery

Industrious, friendly and outgoing would best describe the Huber family, now into their seventh generation on their ranch, situated in the rolling hills known as "The Knobs of Starlite", just across the border from Louisville, Kentucky. The 540 acre ranch boasts 100 acres of apples, 25 acres of strawberries, 35 acres of vegetables, 10 acres of vines plus many other fruits. Not to be content with this, the family lease two other farms. Apart from the winery built in 1978, when they converted an old dairy, the Hubers have added a cheese factory, in which they also make their own deli meats, a gift shop and a restaurant. All the enterprises are based around their own home grown produce. Gerald and his son Ted run the winery, Gerald's wife Mary-Jean runs the gift shop, whilst their Uncle Carl and Aunt Linda run the farm.

The Huber wines come in 18 different types from seven French hybrids and three native grape varieties, a few fruit wines are also made. I was most impressed with their overall quality particularly the Seyval Blanc and the de Chaunac. Their raspberry wine was also excellent.

An Introduction to Michigan

Michigan is an impressive wine state, currently ranking sixth in the Union in wine production, with some 20 wineries operating within its borders. Most of the Michigan vineyards are near to the shores of Lake Michigan, where the climate is moderated by this huge deep body of water.

During the last century, most of the wine growing was being conducted in the east of the state on the shores of Lake Erie. However, in the early years of the twentieth century, the famous Welch Grape Juice company began to source its grapes from the Michigan shores in the south-west of the state, sparking a vine planting spree. The depression years proved a boon for Michigan grape growers with the huge demand from home winemakers.

Michigan winemakers received some tax protection for their wines but were slow to react to the change in wine tastes towards light premium table wines. Since about 1982, however, much improvement has occured in both the varieties planted and the wines being made; much of this improvement has come from the larger wineries such as Warner and St. Julian but smaller wineries are also making some great wines. Gradually the French Hybrids and Vinifera wines are taking over from Labruscas, such as Concord, and the future looks bright, as many areas of the state are suitable for winegrowing.

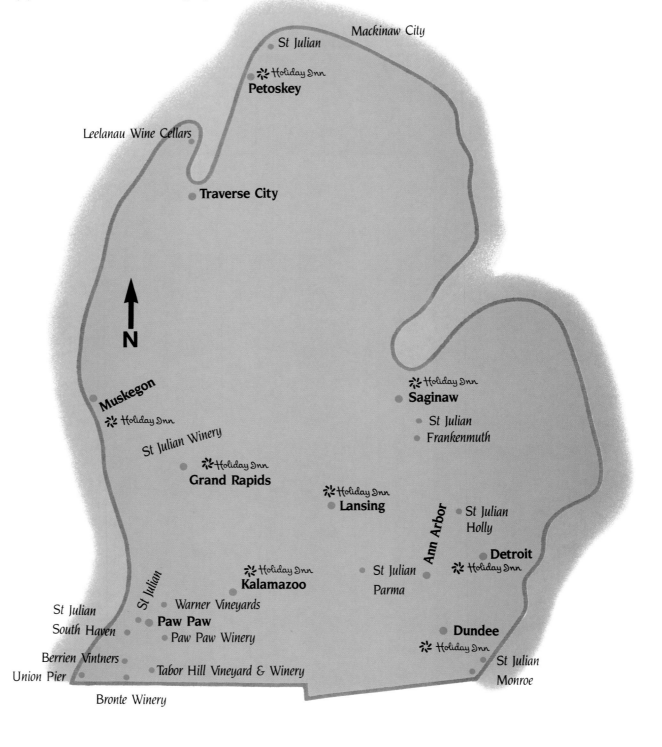

St. Julian Vineyards

In 1921, Mariano Meconi started the St. Julian Wine Company in Windsor, Ontario, under the name of the Italian Wine company. No doubt, many of his products found their way over the border during Prohibition. On repeal in 1933 he moved the business to Detroit and, in 1938, to its current site in Paw Paw.

St. Julian was the patron saint of Meconi's home town, Falaria, in Italy, hence the name. David Braganini, the founder's grandson, now runs the business. St. Julian make a large range of wines in many varying styles and, over the last few years, have opened seven large and striking tasting and sales complexes around the state. In addition, the winery at Paw Paw has an excellent tasting complex, the first in Michigan and rebuilt in grand fashion following a fire in 1971. The St. Julian Champagne particularly impressed me.

Tabor Hill

When the Tabor Hill Winery and Vineyard opened in 1972 it was the first new Michigan winery in more than 25 years. The vineyard planting was started by Leonard Olson and Carl Bahnholzer, in 1968. They concentrated only on premium vinifera and French hybrid varieties. Bahnholzer left to start his own winery, just over the border in Indiana, and, by 1976, an under-capitalised Olson was in trouble. To the rescue came businessman David Upton, whose father and uncle started the Whirlpool Corporation. David also owns the only ''Abstract and Title'' company in Berrien County.

The winery is set in on a ridge in beautiful rolling countryside, everything is superbly presented and a delightful and innovative restaurant has wonderful views over the vineyards. The wines are absolutely top quality. The 1976 White Riesling easily rated a gold medal in my estimation, the Chardonnay was out of stock, but their Hartford Cream Sherry, an olorosso style with up to 25 year old wines in the blend, really ''took the cake'', a superb wine. David and his winemaker, Rich Moersch, can be justly proud of their efforts and have deservedly had their wine served at the White House several times. Tabor Hill also have tasting rooms at Richmond and Saugatuck.

Warner Vineyards

I n 1938, farmer and banker John Turner, started a business producing grape products of all sorts including wine. He was joined by his son-in-law James Warner who, with a great deal of hard work, built a business that today produces three and a half million cases of grape products per year.

Over the last decade, James has been joined by his three sons, Jim the eldest, general manager, Bill in charge of marketing and the youngest, Pat, involved in many aspects of the Company's operations.

Warner have made a strong move into the premium table and sparkling wine area and are now producing varietal wines from Michigan grown vinifera and hybrid grapes, some of which are grown on their 900 acre land holdings. Warner also bring in some Californian juice, which is made into wines correctly labelled as "American Varietals" and blends; a few of these "Warner West" wines come from specific appelations such as Napa and are labelled as such.

The area around the pretty and rather quaint, old, red brick tasting room named "Ye Olde Wine Haus", on the banks of the Paw Paw River, a fast flowing trout stream, has been beautifully landscaped and outdoor picnic lunches are served.

Warner also have a fermentation cellar at nearby Lawton and a tasting room in Mackinaw City.

An Introduction to Missouri

I n 1866, Missouri surpassed Ohio as the second largest wine producing state of the Union. The stalwart of this amazing grape boom in the state was Professor George Husmann, who, in the same year, wrote his first book, "The Native Grape and The Manufacture of American Wines". Later, in 1881, he went to California where he was instrumental in halting the spread of phylloxera and assisting in the implementation of its preventative cure, the grafting of vinifera onto American native rootstocks. By national Prohibition in 1920, the Missouri wine industry had ground to a standstill.

Things were slow to start following repeal, but some wineries, notably Bardenheiers in St. Louis, re-opened. Much of Missouri was still "dry" until recent years. Now, over 30 wineries operate in more than a dozen Missouri counties.

The chief wine regions are at Hermann on the banks of the Missouri River, the Ozark highlands plateau around the towns of Rosati and St. James, as well as the south-western and south-eastern corners of the state which are seeing a rebirth in winegrowing.

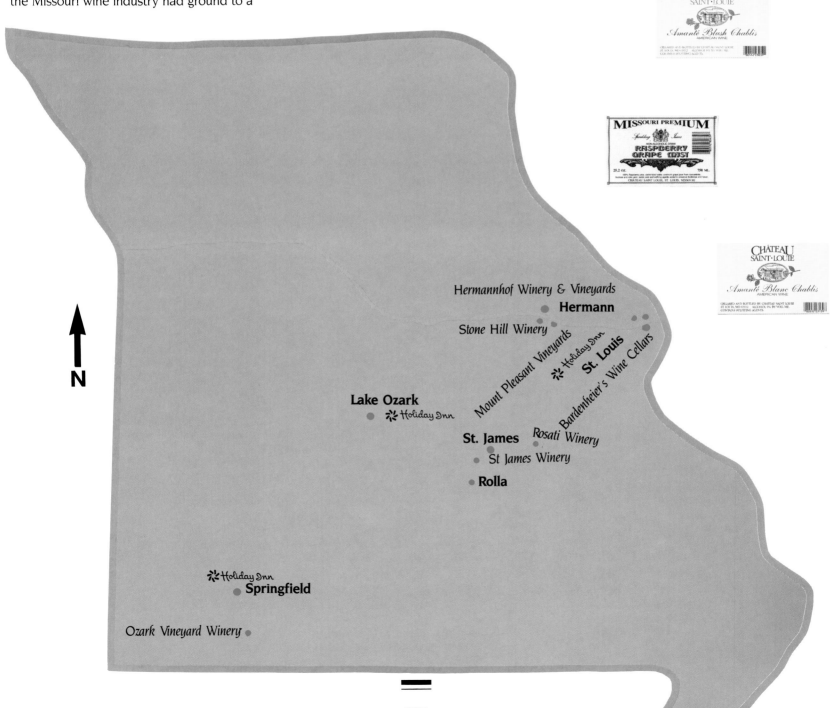

Chateau St. Louie

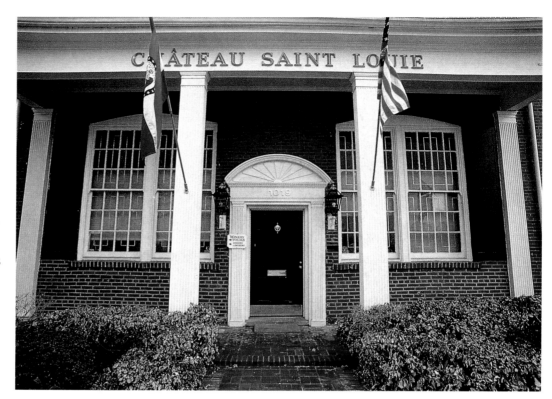

Chateau Saint Louie recently became the new name of the Bardenheier's Wine Cellar established way back in 1873. This is a large winery, with its cellars holding almost one million gallons of wine, closed during Prohibition but re-opened by Joseph Bardenheier upon repeal. Joseph, the son of the founder, moved the winery a number of times each year to a larger premises. The winery was finally settled at its current location in the heart of the city of St. Louis.

Upon Joseph's death in 1962, his son, John, and more latterly John's son John Jnr., have continued on the business. In 1970, they started growing grapes for the first time, planting 50 acres of French hybrids on their Lost River Ranch, near Thayer in South-central Missouri. In 1983, the Futura Coatings Company, whose business includes the coating of steel wine tanks throughout America with epoxy linings, bought the business. Some vinifera varieties have also been planted recently by the new owners on their Thayer Ranch.

Mt. Pleasant Winery

One of the oldest wineries in Missouri is Mount Pleasant Vineyard near the town of Augusta. This complex of old buildings has been lovingly restored by Lucian Dressel and his wife, Eva, who bought the property in 1967.

Lucian, a young graduate of Harvard and Columbia Universities, decided on winegrowing as a career whilst travelling Europe, rather than the accounting profession he had trained for.

The buildings and cellars he bought, he later discovered, were the remains of the Mount Pleasant winery made famous last century by Lutheran minister and vigneron, Frederich Munch, who also wrote, "School for American Grape Culture".

Lucian has planted some of the early American hybrids cultivated by Munch. His dry white varietal, Rayon D'or, of which he is the only grower in America, impressed my greatly. He also makes a very good port, recently awarded a bronze medal in a London international wine competition.

Stone Hill Winery

The town of Hermann, Missouri is home to a number of wineries, the oldest and most impressive of which is the Stone Hill Winery, built in 1847 by Michael Poeschel. Over the next 20 years, it grew into the third largest winery in the world. Today, the old cellars are operating under the careful guidance of Tim and Betty Held, who took them over in 1965. Both are direct descendants of founding families who arrived in Hermann in 1837.

Stone Hill's arched underground cellars, known as the Apostle Cellars, because of the twelve huge casks carved with a likeness of each the disciples. Unfortunately, during Prohibition these 15,000 gallon casks were dismantled and sent to Germany. The Helds are now trying at present to get them back.

In 1979, the Helds opened a restaurant at the winery, naming it ''Vintage 1847''. The venture is a joint one involving the Held's vineyard manager, Gary Buckler and his wife Debbie. The ''Old Stable'' which they have renovated for the purpose has come up superbly. Gary and Debbie have both attended the Culinary Institute in Hyde Park, New York and Gary has won the prestigeous ''Courvoisier Culinary Classic'' for professional chefs. In 1987, they published a very elegant 64 page book outlining their best recipes, available at the restaurant.

The Norton grape does particularly well at Hermann and the Helds use some grapes from 115 year old wines they cultivate to make an excellent red wine, strong in wild berry flavours. Their Seyval Blanc is also a very good wine.

Stone Hill is a great winery to visit and to soak up the glorious old world atmosphere as well as to have a meal in their restaurant. It is all a credit to the Helds.

289

An Introduction to New England

The famous resort island of Martha's Vineyard off the Massachusetts coast and its neighbouring island, Nantucket, both supported vineyards and wineries over two hundred years ago. The industry, however, fell into obscurity and was not revived until 1965, when pharmacist John Canepa planted 800 French and American hybrid vines on his New Hampshire property. Today, some fifteen wineries operate in the New England states of Connecticut, Massachusetts, Rhode Island and New Hampshire, whilst some vineyards exist in Maine and Vermont.

Although the climate of much of this general region is not too hospitable to the vine, a number of micro-climates exist where even vinifera varieties such as Chardonnay, Johannisberg Riesling and others are now being successfully grown. A number of successful wineries are now producing in excess of 10,000 cases each per year, a good reflection of the vinous development taking place.

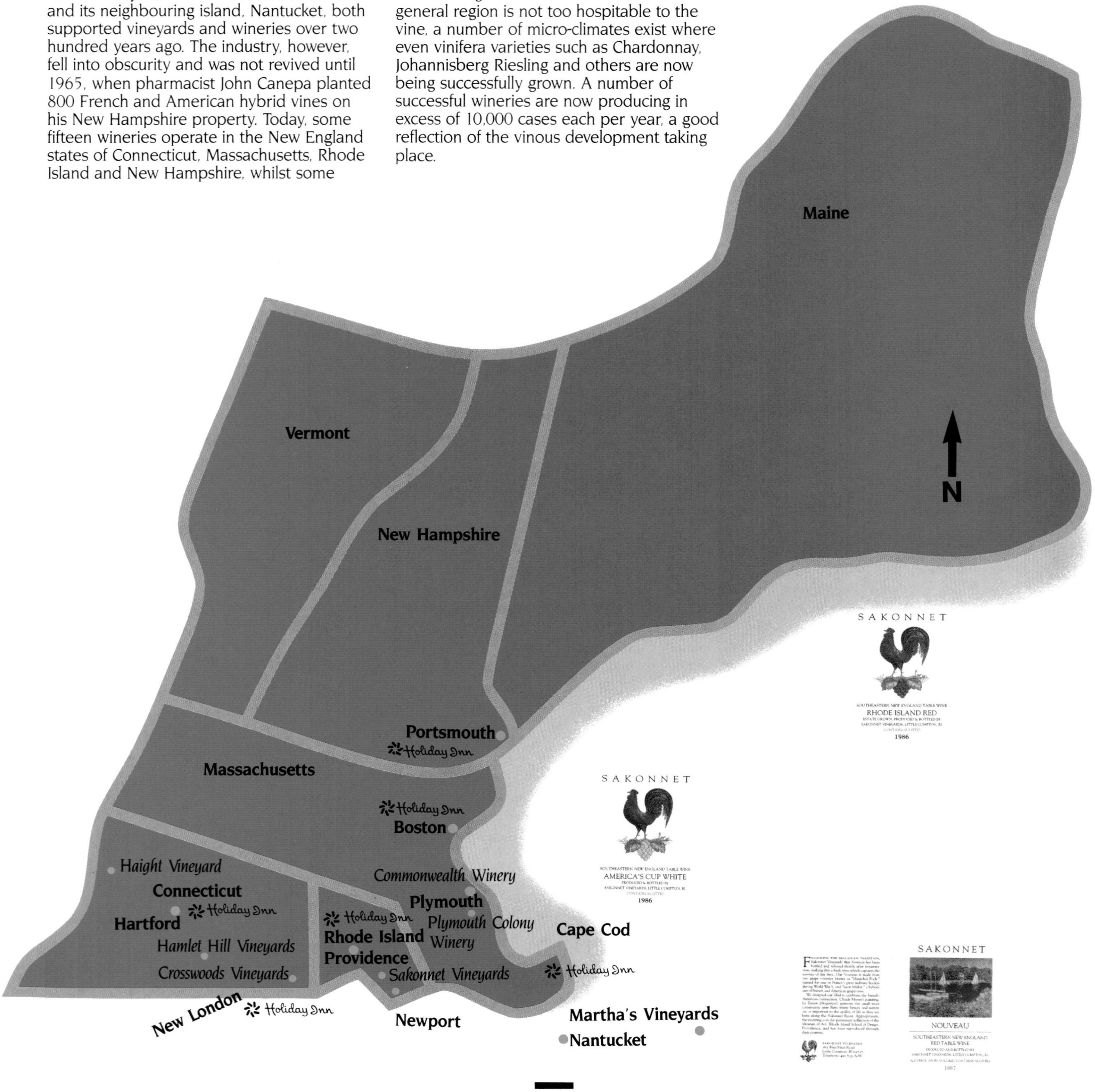

Maine

N

Vermont

New Hampshire

SAKONNET

SOUTHEASTERN NEW ENGLAND TABLE WINE
RHODE ISLAND RED
1986

Portsmouth
Holiday Inn

Massachusetts

SAKONNET

SOUTHEASTERN NEW ENGLAND TABLE WINE
AMERICA'S CUP WHITE
1986

Holiday Inn
Boston

Haight Vineyard
Commonwealth Winery
Connecticut
Plymouth
Hartford   Holiday Inn   Plymouth Colony   Cape Cod
                Rhode Island   Winery
Hamlet Hill Vineyards
Providence
Crosswoods Vineyards   Holiday Inn
                Sakonnet Vineyards

New London   Holiday Inn   Newport

Martha's Vineyards
Nantucket

SAKONNET

NOUVEAU
SOUTHEASTERN NEW ENGLAND
RED TABLE WINE
1987

Plymouth Colony Wines

Surrounded by a shallow lake near its historic namesake city, lies a very picturesque, small winery founded by Charles Caranci. Plymouth Colony also makes a number of fruit wines and recently won the best of show wine award from 99 other wines, including grape wines, entered in the eighth annual New England Wine Council's competition, the winning wine being made from cranberries and raspberries.

The Plymouth Colony is well set up to provide a pleasant visit for the many tourists who visit historic Plymouth.

Commonwealth Winery

The first modern day Massachusetts winery was the Commonwealth Winery founded in 1978 by David Tower, in the historic city of Plymouth, landing place of the Pilgrim Fathers. David had studied enology at U.C. Davis in California and also worked for two years in German wineries.

The first vintage was made in an abandoned library building with equipment hastily put together to accomodate the 50 tons of grapes David had ordered from New York State. The winery has expanded quite dramatically and is now situated near the water in Lothrop Street. Whilst still using some out of state grapes, Commonwealth are

making wine from local grapes supplied by growers with when they have contracts. A

Massachusetts Chardonnay and a Riesling are being produced.

Haight Vineyard

Sherman Haight had a 165 acre hobby farm near Litchfield in Western Connecticut. Not satisfied with his other crops, he planted vines in 1975. Inspired by the legendary, late Dr. Konstantin Frank, Sherman planted Vinifera vines. When the Connecticut state legislature passed a farm winery law in 1978, he converted a hay barn on the property to a winery. Sherman's daughter, Katie, has studied enology and worked at wineries in other countries. I remember meeting her at Best's Winery in Australia in 1986; she still assists in Haight Vineyards and Winery at various times. Haight also run a number of popular events each year at the winery.

Hamlet Hill Winery

enry Maubert first visited Pomfret in Connecticut in 1949, shortly after World War II, during which he had been interned by the Nazis for his work with the French underground. Understandably, he wanted to put Europe as far behind himself as possible. The Pomfret area reminded him of Beaujolais in France and he made his mind to come back someday.

After studying at Harvard and a career in marketing, he and a New York advertising executive, John Spitz, bought the seven year old Hamlet Hill Vineyards and Winery in August 1986. In less than two years the output has doubled and the short term aims are to double output again to 25,000 cases by 1990.

Hamlet Hill is an innovative building of quite striking architectural design. On entering the balcony landing inside, the winery looks a little like a theatre in the round, an automated voice-guided self tour is provided and an attractive tasting room is attached. The winery was built in the late 1970's by August W. Loos, a wire and cable manufacturer with a passion for modern renaissance architecture. The winery he created is a real show piece, but also an excellent winemaking facility, due mainly to his winemaker Dr. Howard Bursen's involvement. Howard formerly worked at Walter Taylor's Bully Hill Vineyard with Walter's then winemaker, Herman Weimer.

Henry Maubert's son has quit his commission as a Marine Captain to assist his father in achieving his ambitious plans. They have recently employed a French winemaker from Bordeaux. Hamlet Hill have just achieved the impossible by shipping 5,000 cases to France!!

America's smallest state, Rhode Island, is home to a fine winery, Sakonnet, which has been recently taken over by Earl and Susan Samson from the founders, Jim and Lolly Mitchell, who first planted vines on their farm in 1975.

Jim Mitchell, a chemical engineer, had worked in thirty-three countries before becoming a winegrower on Rhode Island, in fact it was whilst working in Libya, with time on his hands that he first began making wine. Jim chose Rhode Island because of its similarity in climate to Bordeaux, France. Like Bordeaux, it is surrounded by water and has a milder winter than much of the Eastern Seaboard.

Over the thirteen year period that the Mitchells ran Sakonnet, they built up a 38 acre vineyard comprising 40% vinifera vines, namely Gewurztraminer, Johannisberg Riesling, Chardonnay and Pinot Noir; the rest of the vineyard being planted to French hybrids.

Earl Samson, the new owner, moved in just in time for the 1987 harvest with which he is particularly happy. Conditions were dry and warm during ripening and the harvest was plentiful. Earl is a native New Englander but spent a number of years in California. During the early 1970's, he assisted retired Air Force Colonel William Mayberry plant his Sonoma Vineyards and ran the Landmark Winery for the Mayberrys for some years.

Apart from their viniferas mentioned above, Sakonnet make a very good Nouveau Red, a "Rhode Island Red" (blended from hybrids and "America's Cup White", a blend of hybrids) and "Eye of The Storm", a Blush. Sakonnet wines are regular wine show award winners.

An Introduction to Arizona and New Mexico

The Desert states have a winegrowing history going back to the seventeenth century. The Spanish Franciscan Missions set up in the Rio Grande Valley first brought wine to this isolated part of North America. By 1880, New Mexico ranked fifth in the Union in wine production with almost a million gallons of wine vintaged annually from over 3,000 acres of vines. As in most states, Prohibition wiped the industry out and, although a dozen or so wineries re-opened on repeal, they could not adequately compete with the nearby Californian wines. By 1977, only three remained. The 1980's have, however, seen a mini-boom in vineyard planted in both states, much of it in the higher altitude and therefore cooler areas of each state. Low land prices have also had much to do with this new development as vineyard properties in California are obviously now getting very expensive.

New Mexico, particularly, is seeing some large vineyard developments involving the planting of thousands of acres and some foreign investors particularly European wine firms are involved.

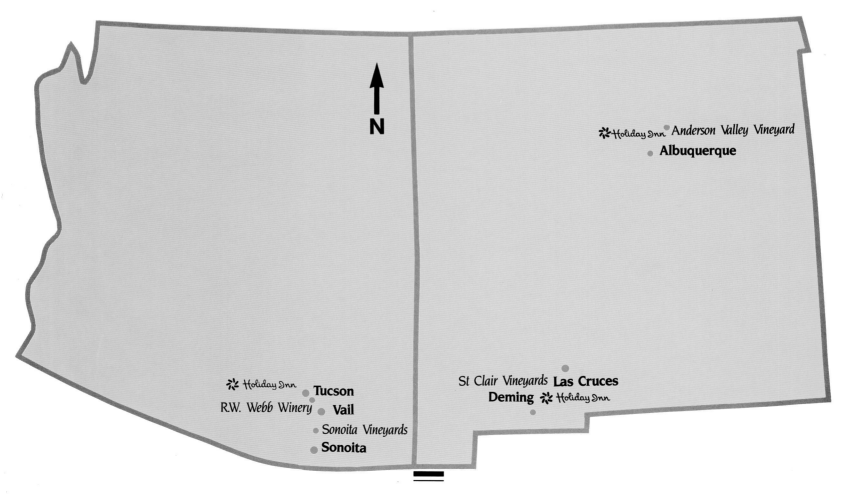

Anderson Valley Vineyards

Although the Anderson Valley Winery was not built until 1984, the vineyards have been established since 1976. Maxie Anderson made his name famous as the first to fly a balloon across the Atlantic. He also ran Rancher's Exploration, a silver mining firm in New Mexico. Maxie had a deep and long-standing interest in wine and food, which led him to planting a vineyard on the outskirts of Albequerque. Unfortunately, in 1983, just as the vineyards were coming into full bearing, Maxie was killed in a ballooning accident during the World Cup races in Germany. Fortunately his son, Chris, continued with his father's plan and built the winery. He used his experience in the building trade as an electrical engineer to full advantage and has built a most serviceable, attractive winery and tasting complex.

R. W. Webb Winery

Robert Webb was the first to open a new winery in Arizona since 1915. Robert had his own winemaking supplies business and saw a need to establish a new winemaking industry. He planted vines on his own mountain property in south-eastern Arizona and also persuaded a number of other farmers to plant vines, now buying grapes from 24 of them.

Robert comes from the third generation of an Arizonan farming family, but spent some time as a Navy pilot before opening his hobby and winemaking shop. The winery was firstly located in an industrial area of Tucson in 1980, but moved in 1986 into a new, beautiful Spanish adobe-style premises a few miles out of town. Robert only uses Arizona-grown grapes and makes exceptional wines. His 1986 Cabernet Sauvignon and the 1987 Sauvignon Blanc I found to be excellent.

R.W. WEBB WINERY
Address: 13605 E., Benson Highway, PO Box 130, Vail, AZ., 85641
Phone: 602/629 9911
Year of Establishment: 1980
Owner: Robert W. Webb
Winemaker: Robert W. Webb
Principal Varieties Grown: Cabernet Sauvignon, Sauvignon Blanc, Johannisberg Riesling, Petit Sirah, Merlot
Acres Under Vine: 20
Average Annual Crush: 120 tons

Principal Wines & Brands	Cellar Potential (Years)
Am. Cabernet Sauvignon Reserve	20
Az. Cabernet Sauvignon	30
Az. Johannisberg Riesling	3

Trade Tours – Available.
Retail Room Sales – Available.
Hours open to Public: Mon thru Sat. 10am to 5pm; Sun. 12 noon to 5pm; closed Easter, Christmas, New Year & Thanksgiving
Retail Distribution: State of Arizona

An Introduction to New Jersey

New Jersey has had periods in its history where it was a major wine producing state, mainly due to the large wineries close to New York City. These, sadly, closed in the 1970's. The 1980's, however, have seen a rebirth of the industry and the establishment of a number of boutique wineries producing outstanding premium table wines, in a number of areas within the state. The largest winery is the Renault Winery close to Atlantic City, dating back to 1864, purchased by newspaperman, Joseph P. Milzal in 1976 and totally resurrected. Today it entertains well in excess of 120,000 people per year.

The New Jersey grapegrowing industry's history is probably most famous for the contribuion made to it by Dr. Thomas Bramwell Welch, who started the Welch's grape juice business near Vineland in New Jersey in 1868. Welch's grew into what is today a huge business based in many states.

Many boutique wineries have sprung up near the Delaware River in the northern part of the state, since the farm winery law was enacted in 1981.

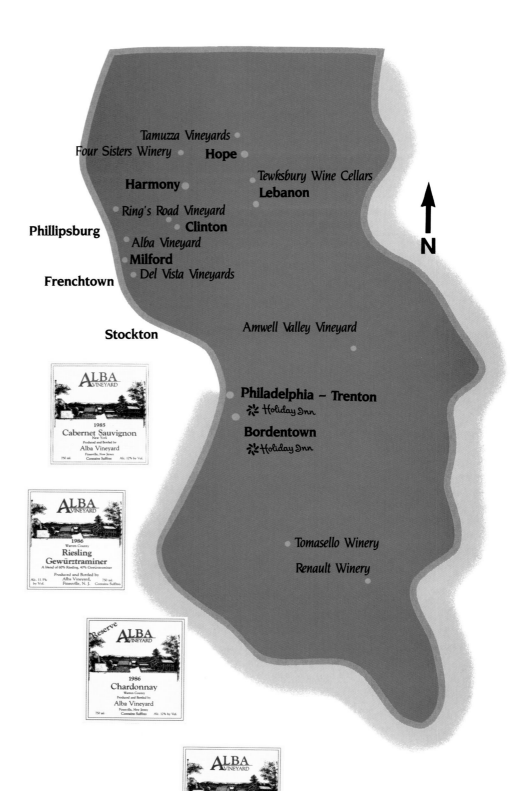

Alba Winery

Rudi Marchesi is an energetic young man, a big jovial fellow with a bushy red beard, just as much at home driving his tractor in the vineyard or appearing on a television talk show.

Alba is situated close to the Delaware River near Phillipsburg. It was only established in the early 1980's, but has already made a big mark in the eastern wine shows with a number of medal successes.

In 1988, Alba played host to the Hunterdon Winegrowers Festival. Hunterdon County has seven wineries and a number of vineyards all doing an excellent job to promote the good wines they are making. Alba's wines are a prime example of the style and quality this new region is capable of producing.

ALBA VINEYARD
Address: R.D. 1 Box 179AAA Milford, N.J., 08848
Phone: 201/995-7800
Year of Establishment: 1983
Winemaker: Rudolf C. Marchesi
Principal Varieties Grown: Cabernet Sauvignon, Chardonnay, Riesling, Gewurztraminer, Vidal Blanc
Acres Under Vine: 34
Average Annual Crush: 1988 estimated - 130 tons

Principal Wines & Brands	Cellar Potential (Years)
Cabernet Sauvignon, Warren County	10
Chardonnay Reserve, Warren County	5
Vidal Blanc, Prop. Reserve, Warren Co.	1-5

Trade Tours – Available; after hours tours by appointment only.
Retail Room Sales – Available.
Hours open to Public: Tues to Friday 1pm to 6pm - Sat 10am to 6pm - Sun 12noon to 5pm.
Retail Distribution: New Jersey and 7 other states.

Renault Winery

New Jersey's oldest and largest winery was founded in 1864 by Louis Nicholas Renault, who was sent from France by the Champagne house of the Duke of Montebello to promote their Champagnes in the New World. He was also responsible for making Egg Harbour City, near his own and other wineries, famous as "The Wine City".

Louis was succeeded by his son in 1913.

John D'Agostino bought Renault in 1919 and produced "Renault Wine Tonic" during Prohibition, turning it into a nationally-sold product. After some decades of neglect, after his death in 1948, the winery was bought by Joseph P. Milza in 1976. Joseph, a newspaper publisher, cleaned up the winery and added

a restaurant and tastings/sales complex. Today, the winery plays host to a huge number of tourists. The winery surrounds are superb, with a lake and landscaped gardens. Joseph has also added French hybrids and Vinifera vines to the vineyards and is making some very good quality table and sparkling wines.

An Introduction to New York State

Next to California, New York has more wineries (around 80 in all) and produces more wine than any other state in America, producing over 30 million gallons.

Overall the quality of these wines made in New York State has improved dramatically, mostly due to the extensive new plantings of vinifera and hybrid vines over the last decade replacing much of the labrusca varieties hitherto planted there.

New York has five principal vineyard districts. Half the vineyard acreage is in the Chatagua region on Lake Erie near Michigan. Next is the Finger Lakes region, in which most of the wineries are situated. Then there are the Niagara County vineyards, eastward of Niagara Falls. Another area is the Hudson Valley and Cascade Mountains region, just north of New York City, followed by the fast expanding vineyards situated at the north end of Long Island.

New York State winegrowing goes back over 300 years to plantings on Manhattan by the then Governor of the State, Peter Stuyvesant.

The Hudson Valley became the first commercial wine growing district when in 1839, the Brotherhood Winery (America's oldest continuously operating winery) was founded in Washingtonville.

In 1976, a farm wineries bill was passed by the state legislative lowering the minimum license fee for a winery to $25 and boutique wineries blossomed. New York State has many varying climatic and soil conditions, some ideal for the vine, with Long Island proving particularly suitable. Premium winegrowing in New York State is set to expand dramatically.

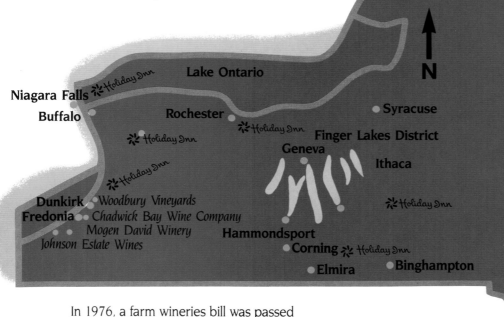

The Wine Group Cellars - Mogen-David

One of the largest wineries in New York is the Mogen-David Cellars of The Wine Group, owners of the Franzia Winery in California, who bought Mogen-David, when they took over both companies from the Coca-Cola company, in 1981.

Mogen-David actually had its start in Chicago through rather unfortunate circumstances. In 1947, The Wine Corporation of America run by Max Cohen and Heryn Marcus, had a problem. 40,000 gallons of their Californian Port and Sherry, their biggest selling wines, spoiled and had to be destroyed. Their only other wine was a sweet Kosher wine, Mogen-David made from the Concord grape under supervision of a Rabbi, being mainly consumed by the Jewish community. To save the company, they had

to promote it to all and sundry and, to their surprise, sales surged upward and an entirely new market developed.

They moved the winery to the Chautaugua grape belt on the shores of Lake Erie, where the world's greatest concentration of Concord grapes are grown, to be near their source of grape supply. Today the range has expanded with white Kosher wines and other drier Kosher products. The unique Concord Kosher wine style is really an American invention and it is now sold world-wide.

An Introduction To The Finger Lakes

The Finger Lakes are a series of long, narrow and deep lakes, carved out of the land by glacial activity during the Ice Age. The largest lake, Cayuga, is about 40 miles long and up to 3 miles wide. These dozen or so lakes and the steep slopes leading to them, have created a beautiful landscape and a popular tourist destination, covering twelve counties. The Lakes, also because they hold large bodies of water, have a moderating influence on the climate and the steep slopes, also have good air drainage decreasing the risk of spring frosts. Most vineyards are planted on the hillsides, although viticulture is possible around any of the lakes. The main vineyards and wineries are centred around Keuka and Seneca Lakes, the exceptions being Canandaigua and Widmers, which are situated on lake Canandaigua.

The town of Hammondsport is the wine capital of the Finger Lakes. The three large wineries located at Hammondsport are all now under the same ownership, that of Vintners International, a company formed mainly by the executives of the former owner, Seagrams Wine Classics, who staged a leveraged buyout of much of their former employer's wine empire. The oldest of these three wineries is the Great Western Winery,

founded in 1860 as the Pleasant Valley Wine Company, by Charles Davenport Champlin and some other growers in the region. Built with hand-cut local stone and with solid oak archways, it is a wonderful old winery to visit, involved chiefly in sparkling wine production. Further down the hill from Great Western is the Taylor Wine Company, which in fact took over Great Western in 1961. Taylors is the largest North American winery outside California and, including the Great Western Winery, its capacity is over 30 million gallons.

Walter Taylor, a cooper, came to Hammondsport in 1880 and two years later bought a 27 acre vineyard on Bully Hill, just

An Introduction To The Finger Lakes

out of town. His five children all assisted in the business and it grew quickly. During Prohibition, they made and marketed grape juice. In 1919, they bought the Columbia Winery, their current site.

Gold Seal Winery is the other one of the three Vintners International properties while the classic old winery on the shores of lake Keuka is currently up for sale as production has been transferred to the Taylors Winery. Charles Fournier, a French Champagne master made this winery famous. Vintners are keeping the brand, although not the winery.

There are about 35 wineries in the Finger Lakes region. The other large group is the Canadaigua Wine Company which includes Widmers Wine Cellars, and the Batavia Wine Company. Another leading winery is Vinifera Wine Cellars, founded by Dr. Konstantin Frank, who emigrated to America in 1951. Frank succeeded in introducing vinifera vines to Eastern America. For three centuries, others had failed, but he had been brought up in Russia and learned there techniques for protecting vines from the killing winter cold.

After working at the New York Agricultural Station at Geneva, for a few years, he teamed with Charles Fournier at Gold Seal. Between them they found a hardy root stock from native vines in Quebec, Canada and propagated these to get them started. Their experiments worked and vinifera vines are slowly taking on, although much of the Finger Lakes wine industry is still based on Labrusca and French Hybrid vines. The Finger Lakes region particularly with sparkling wines, but lately with Germanic Riesling styles and Chardonnay in the French mold, is set to tackle any other North American wine region.

Finger Lakes

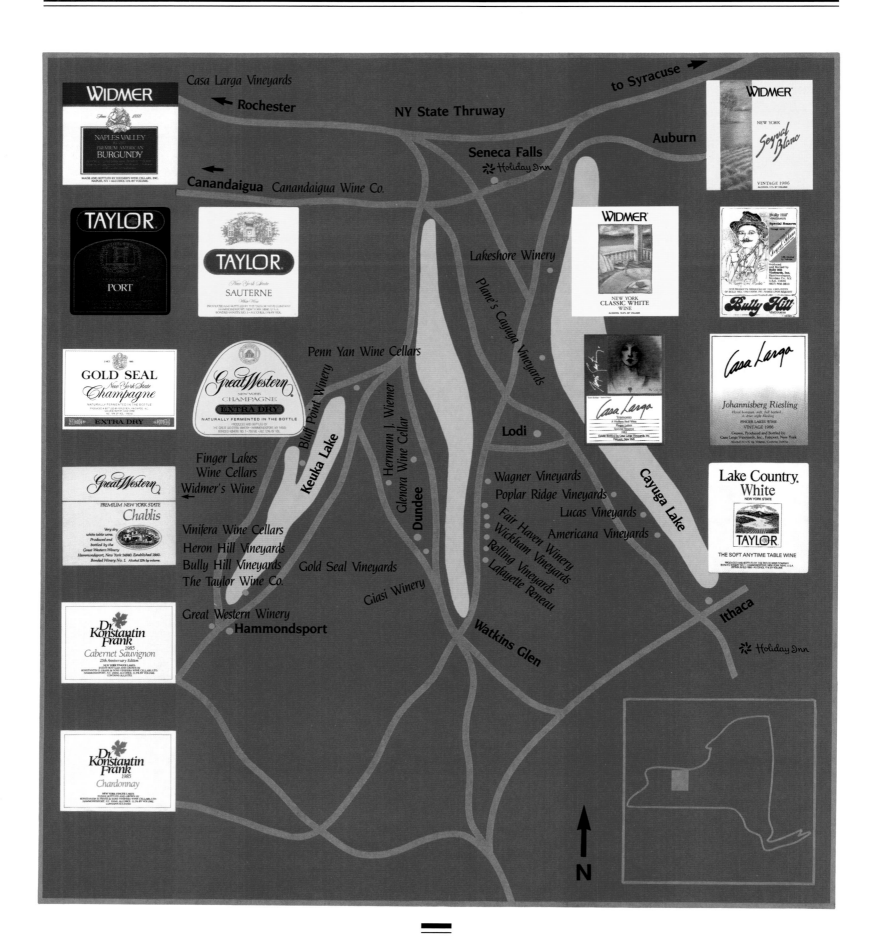

Casa Larga Vineyards

← **Rochester**

to Syracuse →

NY State Thruway

WIDMER

Auburn

WIDMER NEW YORK Seyval Blanc VINTAGE 1986

NAPLES VALLEY PREMIUM AMERICAN BURGUNDY

Seneca Falls
Holiday Inn

← **Canandaigua** Canandaigua Wine Co.

TAYLOR PORT

TAYLOR New York State SAUTERNE White Wine

Lakeshore Winery

WIDMER NEW YORK CLASSIC WHITE WINE

Bully Hill VINEYARDS Special Reserve

Bully Hill VINEYARDS

GOLD SEAL New York State Champagne EXTRA DRY

Great Western NEW YORK CHAMPAGNE EXTRA DRY NATURALLY FERMENTED IN THE BOTTLE

Penn Yan Wine Cellars

Casa Larga

Casa Larga Johannisberg Riesling FINGER LAKES VINTAGE 1986

Bluff Point Winery

Lodi

Great Western PREMIUM NEW YORK STATE Chablis

Finger Lakes Wine Cellars
Widmer's Wine

Hermann J. Wiemer

Glenora Wine Cellar

Dundee

Keuka Lake

Wagner Vineyards
Poplar Ridge Vineyards
Lucas Vineyards
Fair Haven Winery
Wickham Vineyards
Rolling Vineyards
Lafayette Reneau
Americana Vineyards

Cayuga Lake

Lake Country White NEW YORK STATE TAYLOR THE SOFT ANYTIME TABLE WINE

Vinifera Wine Cellars
Heron Hill Vineyards
Bully Hill Vineyards
The Taylor Wine Co.

Gold Seal Vineyards

Giasi Winery

Dr. Konstantin Frank 1985 Cabernet Sauvignon

Great Western Winery
Hammondsport

Watkins Glen

Ithaca

Holiday Inn

Dr. Konstantin Frank 1985 Chardonnay

N

Canandaigua Wine Company

Canandaigua has one of the largest wineries in the nation. It has just completed some extensive renovations, but maintains an extremely low profile. The winery is situated within the city limits of Canandaigua, a beautiful city at the northern end of Lake Canandaigua, the western-most of the four main Finger Lakes of New York State.

Canandaigua has one of the most beautiful tastings rooms in America. It is not located at the winery, but in the Sonnenberg gardens, 50 acres of America's most magnificent late Victorian gardens, created in 1887.

Mary Clark grew up in Canadaigua and married Frederich Ferris Thompson, whose father and brother helped found the Chase Bank. Frederich and a partner founded the First National City Bank of New York.

Frederich bought a large estate in Canadaigua in 1863, naming it Sonnenberg (Sunny Hill). In 1887, the grand 40 room mansion was built and, between 1902 and 1916, his widow (he died in 1899) created the magnificent gardens in his memory.

In 1931, the U.S. government bought the estate to construct the Veterans Medical Centre. In 1972, however, 50 acres, including the mansion and gardens were conveyed to a non-profit educational trust and in 1973 the gardens were opened to the public for the first time since Mrs Thompson's days.

In 1979, the Canandaigua Wine Company converted what was the former Canning Cellar for the estate into a wine tasting room. The setting is superb, as is the building, with its Old English Tudor-style. A splendid stained glass window suitably entitled "Abundance", and a number of old casks from the winery, adorn the interior. The wines featured include some of Canandaigua's most famous — the J. Roget Champagnes and sparkling wines, the Richards Wild Irish Rose and the Bisceglia table wines.

The Canandaigua Wine Group also own Richards Wine Cellars in Petersburg, Virginia Tenner Brothers Wine Company in Patrick, South Carolina, Bisceglia Brothers Winery in Madera, California, as well as Widmers Wine Cellars in Naples, New York and The Batavia Wine Cellars in Batavia, New York.

This large group of wineries has been brought together by the Sands family. Marvin Sands made the first moves in 1954 and his son, Richard, now executive vice president of the company under his father, has carried on the good work.

Bully Hill Vineyards

W alter S. Taylor is a man for all seasons, without a doubt the most colourful character in an industry abounding with such people. Walter was born into the third generation of a Wine dynasty, founded by his grandfather, also Walter, a master Cooper.

The Taylor Wine Company was founded in 1880, at the very site now occupied by Bully Hill. In 1886, the Taylor Wine Company moved closer to Hammondsport purchasing the larger Columbia Wine Company. Later they bought the Pleasant Valley Winery next door and, in 1961 renamed it Great Western, when Walter S. joined his father and uncles in the business. He helped usher Taylors and Great Western into the modern era of table and French Hybrids, rather than the traditional Labrusca grape varieties.

Always outspoken, Walter stretched a little further than his uncle and the board at Taylors could cope with. He found himself dismissed from the company but, full marks to him, he launched straight into the creation of a new winery, housed in the barn at his grandfather's Bully Hill property.

Bully Hill has become enormously successful, mainly due to Walter's uncanny sense of promotion; but one should not underestimate his wines, particularly the reds, which are big, generous-flavoured wines and most enjoyable. Watler is anunabashed champion of the French Hybrids, believing them more suited to the Finger Lakes harsh climate and capable of making better wine than vinifera varieties there.

Walter has not only created a winery, but a superb wine museum honouring his late father Greyton, who died in 1970. The museum contains not only many winemaking and vineyard relics, from over 50 wineries previously operating in the region, but also Walter's own artistic impressions of the industry and many historically significant documents, wine advertisements and so on. The Greyton S. Taylor Wine & Grape Museum is a fitting tribute to his father and an enriching addition to America's wine history.

In 1977, Walter had a testing time, when the Cola-Company took him to court to restrain him from using his own name. Although they won, the moral victory was very much Walter's and he has certainly captialised on his "misfortune", particularly in the marketing of his "no-name" wines.

Walter even trotted out his pet goat with his slogan "you can take away my name but you can't take away my goat". It became quite a famous animal and Walter still has some of its offspring on his 2,000 acre property, of which 150 acres are under vine.

Many of Walter's paintings appear on his labels. He has painted over 800 works in all, including several of the N.A.S.A. space shuttle launches. He is in fact the only artist to have painted those live (not from photographs). Walter's poems have also gained fame and he is joint author of the "Home Winemakers Handbook".

Along with his Yugoslav-born wife, Lillian, a former Olympic skier, he runs a very good restaurant in his grandfather's old winery site. Building is afoot at present to convert his grandfather's former home to a bed and breakfast inn.

As if all this were not enough, Walter still indulges in his favourite pastime, flying. He has several planes in the hanger on his own airstrip, including an ultra-light plane he has just built himself.

Walter is a little saddened that he was forced by a court order to return to the company in 1977 much of the Taylor Company papers. These were then publically burnt. Still, through all this he has maintained his sense of humour and Taylors under new ownership have developed and prospered.

Winemaker at Bully Hill is Greg Learned, who has been with Walter a number of years succeeding Hermann Wiemer, who has started his own winery.

Aside from Bully Hill, Walter has a small separate winery on the hill, where he makes a reserve red called St. Walter de Bully, a French Hybrid blend which spends some time in small oak. A big, rich style, I found it very good indeed. All the Bully Hill wines are very reasonably priced.

Walter seems almost content with his life now, but with him who knows what is around the corner? One thing that is beyond doubt however, is his committment to quality wine.

═══

A ndrew Colaruotolo was carrying on a long standing family tradition, when he planted his 14 acre vineyard, just outside of Rochester, near Lake Ontario. His family had long had vineyards in the Frascati district of Italy and Andrew had tended them in his youth.

Andrew arrived in New York around 1950 and established a successful home building business. He is still active in this field with his company, Anco Builders.

Many years ago, he bought a 98 acre plot of land at Fairport, on the outskirts of Rochester, planning to develop it into a housing estate in the future. The site is superb, situated on a hill with panoramic views of the Rochester skyline and the rolling hills of the region. Andrew has knowingly sacrificed a small fortune by his decision, in 1974, to plant vineyards on this land.

following his family tradition.

The winery was completed in 1980, although the first wines were produced in 1978. Casa Larga means "large house" and was the name of his family vineyards in Italy. The winery is actually somewhat like a large house, with a spacious glass walled entertaining area, built over the vineyard with views of the city.

Andrew's son, John, is general manager and has a degree in construction engineering. Between them, father and son, they built the winery with painstaking attention to detail. Their wines have also been carefully and lovingly crafted. The vineyard has expanded to 20 acres with plans to go to 35, managed without chemicals through Andrew's skill and experience.

Casa Larga have built quite a reputation for their wines over the last ten years. Their vineyards are largely vinifera-based and they produce a fairly large range for a small winery, with their Gewurztraminer, Chardonnay and Cabernet Sauvignon all being gold medal standard by my ranking. A Reserve Cabernet under the Tramonto label is absolutely outstanding as is their Reserve Chardonnay, Pallido, much of which is barrel fermented.

Casa Larga have had the assistance of Ernst Fischer, now at Montravin Cellars in Ontario, Canada. Ernst has a winemaking background covering three continents, including eight years in Turkey. He is also skilled in Methode Champenoise production. Casa Larga have just released two Champagnes, a Blanc de Blanc Chardonnay with two and a half years age and one from Muscat Ontenelle, a rare Italian variety, obtained from Dr. Konstantin Frank, the renowned vinifera champion of the East.

Pinot Noir and Johannisberg Riesling have also been successful for this dedicated, hardworking family, who have gained the success they so richly deserve.

CASA LARGA VINEYARDS INC.
Address: 2287 Turk Hill Road, Fairport, New York, 14450
Phone: 716/223 4210
Year of Establishment: 1978
Owner: Andrew Colaruotolo
Principal Varieties Grown: Johannisberg Riesling, Chardonnay, Gewurztztraminer, Cabernet Sauvignon, Pinot Noir
Acres Under Vine: 25+
Average Annual Crush: 120 tons

Principal Wines & Brands	Cellar Potential (Years)
Chardonnay	10
Johannisberg Riesling	5
Pinot Noir	10+

Trade Tours – Available.
Retail Room Sales – Available.
Hours open to Public: Year round Tues to Sat 10am to 5pm; Sun 12 noon to 5pm; Closed Mondays and Public holidays.
Retail Distribution: directly from winery throughout N.Y. State.

In a series of magnificent old bluestone buildings above the Taylor Wine Company lies the Great Western Winery. It started its life in 1860 as the Pleasant Valley Wine Company, when Charles Davenport Champlin and his farmer neighbours built the winery to process the grapes they were growing, naming it after the narrow valley stream feeding Keuka Lake flows through.

New York's first Champagne was made here, just in time to celebrate the end of the Civil War in 1865. The grape used in this initial sparkling wine was Catawba, the same one celebrated in the Ode by Nicholas Longworth. The French brothers, Joseph and Jules Masson, were hired as winemakers by Champlin.

The name "Great Western" was coined by Colonel Marshall Wilder, a famed Boston horticulturalist. Whilst attending a tasting at Pleasant Valley and sampling a new Champagne from Delaware and Catawba, he commented, "Truly this will be the great Champagne of the West". No doubt he meant "west of the true Champagne region in France". The name stuck. A number of wine judges must have agreed with him, because Great Western Champagnes won many gold medals at wine competitions, including America's first in Europe, at the 1873 Vienna Exhibition.

No one is quite sure when, but the township around the winery became known as Rheims, no doubt inspired by the French Champagne capital Reims. The name Rheims was also borne by the post office and the station on the railroad built by the Pleasant Valley Wine Company to transport their wine from Hammondsport to Bath.

During Prohibition, Great Western obtained the first permit to produce a "sacremental" sparkling wine for the clergy.

When Champlin, the founder's grandson died in 1950, the winery was sold to a syndicate of investors.

In 1961, a new chapter for Great Western opened when the large Taylor Wine Company, situated adjacent to Great Western, acquired a controlling interest in them. Greyton Taylor took over the reins and introduced varietal table wines to its portfolio. In 1964, he introduced the first Finger Lakes varietals made from French-American hybrid grape varieties.

The Great Western cellars also serve as the head office for the Taylor Wine Company. Much work has been done on them restoring them to their grandeur of old with facilities to entertain visitors.

In 1980 Great Western pioneered the making of Ice Wine in North America, emulating the great German wine by leaving the grapes on the vine until the first freezing

temperatures of winter, usually late December or sometime early January, when frozen grapes are crushed. The water remains in the skins as ice crystals, leaving a concentrated amber nectar. The wines made from this nectar have an incredible lusciousness and concentrated fruit flavour. The Vidal grape used by Taylors has proved ideal for the purpose.

Great Western have introduced Vinifera into their Champagnes and are constantly developing in all wine fronts.

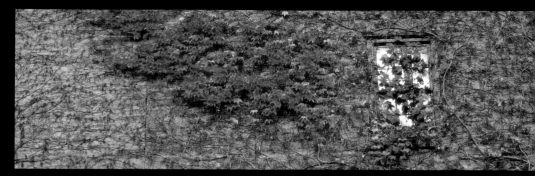

Chateau La Fayette Reneau

S ituated close to, but high above, Seneca Lakes eastern shore is the pretty La Fayette Reneau, established in 1985. It is the region's newest winery, built with an old world feel and in very good taste. It has become a popular stopping point on the scenic drive around this very attractive lake shore. The tasting room also commands an impressive view of their vineyards and the Seneca Lake.

Heron Hill Vineyards

N ew York advertising executive, Peter Johnstone, saw an opportunity when the New York Farm Winery law was passed in 1977 and started a winery. The Heron Hill Winery is built into the side of Bully Hill and its long building with its sun-deck commands a panoramic view of Lake Keuka. Peter was joined in the venture by grapegrower John Ingle. Between them, they planted the third vinifera vineyard after Dr. Konstantin Frank and the Gold Seal Vineyards. I have tasted a number of Heron Hill wines and have enjoyed their Chardonnays and Rhine Rieslings very much. They also make a Cabernet Sauvignon. The name ''Heron Hill'' is one that the imaginative Johnstone coined. It certainly appeals on a wine label; the vineyard also markets a second label, ''Otter Spring''.

Gold Seal Vineyards

The grand old stone buildings which sit on the lake shore at Hammondsport and which housed the Gold Seal Winery are currently in the process of being sold as, in 1984, wine production was moved to the Taylor/Great Western complex which had recently been acquired by Gold Seal's then owners, the Joseph Seagram Organisation.

Gold Seal Wines, however, are going on from strength to strength. It was this winery which pioneered the planting of vinifera vines in Eastern America, succeeding where, for over 300 years, others had failed. Gold Seal's first vinifera wines produced under their legendary winemaker, Frenchman Charles Fournier, were released in the late 1950's.

Fournier was one of a number of French winemakers employed by Gold Seal over the years. The first was Charles Le Breton from the Roederer Champagne Cellars; he was succeeded by Jules Grance from Moet et Chandon in 1921 and, finally, Charles Fournier in 1934, lured from his poisition as chief winemaker for the Veuve Clicquot House by the challenge of the New World of Wine.

Gold Seal changed its name several times. Starting as the Urbana Wine Company in 1865, it changed its name to Gold Seal in 1887, then back to Urbana in 1933, finally returning to Gold Seal in 1957.

Probably the most significant of the many positive moves made by Fournier was his hiring of Dr. Konstantin Frank, the Ukranian-born and Russian-trained viticulturist, in 1953. Frank went on to prove beyond any doubt that vinifera vines could survive, indeed prosper, in the east, with proper care and protection from disease.

Gold Seal make a number of very good Champagnes, along with varietal and generic wines of many styles. Both Charles Fournier and Konstantin Frank have died in recent years, but their contribution to the North American wine industry and their association with Gold Seal will always be remembered.

Taylor Wine Company

Through many changes the Taylor Wine Company has gone from strength to strength. In 1880, Walter Taylor, a master cooper, arrived in Hammondsport. Wineries were thriving and there was plenty of work for a man of his trade. He bought himself a seven acre vineyard and, in 1882, a 70 acre farm on Bully Hill. Walter and his wife, Addie, planted half the area with white and half with red varieties. They were joined in this venture by his father, George with his wife.

Walter and Addie's five children went into the business and Taylor wines began to be sold far and wide. During Prohibition the Taylors, not to be thwarted, began producing and selling grape juice mainly to home winemakers, also acquiring the larger Columbia Winery at the current site of the Taylor complex. After purchasing the Great Western Winery in 1961, Taylors became a public company, the first American winery to make this move. The family still maintained control and ran the company until the last of the brothers died in 1976.

1977 brought a major move in the industry, when the Coca-Cola Company bought Taylors, following this with other major wine industry purchases, becoming America's third largest vintners. By 1983 though, they had incurred considerable losses in their wine enterprises and sold all their wine interests. Taylors became a part of Seagrams and the Seagram owned Gold Seal's production was transferred to Taylors, further enlarging the already huge winery, also incorporating the Great Western Winery.

In 1987, in a courageous leveraged buyout, a number of Seagram employees, headed by Michael Cliff, bought the Taylor Wine Company, incorporating Great Western and Gold Seal, plus Paul Masson Vineyards in California, along with the Taylors California Cellars and the Monterey Vineyards.

The Taylor Winery along with the Great Western Cellars aesthetically blend into the hillsides behind Hammondsport — their buildings seem to stretch for miles.

The main visitors' centre at Taylors has a superb museum, along with a historical tour that takes one from the beginning, through the fascinating history of Taylor and its associated wineries, Great Western and Gold Seal. A 35,000 gallon vat has also been converted to a 40 seat theatrette, where a wine educational film is shown.

Taylors cultivate a large 1,243 acre vineyard holding and historically have made a large range of wines including Champagnes, red and white table wines, both generic blends, plus varietal wines from French hybrids and Vinifera varieties. They also make higher strength sherries and ports, aperitif and dessert wines.

Whilst at the winery, I tasted their newly-released Blanc de Blanc under the Great Western label. It had a beautiful fine-lasting bead (bubbles), a creamy texture with subtle melon and cashew nut flavours. It is a crisp, dry finish and elegant Champagne which could hold its head up high in any company.

Taylors do things well under the watchful eye of president Michael J. Doyle, who has

Taylor Wine Company

seen a number of ownership changes during his time there.

THE TAYLOR WINE COMPANY
Address: Route 88 Hammondsport, New York, 14840
Phone: 607/569 2111
Year of Establishment: Taylor 1880; Great Western 1860; Gold Seal 1865
Owner: Vintners International Company Inc.
Winemaker: Snr. winemaker - Steven D. Coon
Principal Varieties Grown: Catawba, Aurore, Concord, Chardonnay, Elvira & 5 other varieties
Acres Under Vine: 1,200

**Principal Wines &
Brands**
Lake Country White
Taylor Cream Sherry
Taylor Port
Taylor Extra Dry Champagne
Trade Tours – Available.
Retail Room Sales – Available.
Hours open to Public: Jan thru April Mon to Sat 11am to 3pm; May thru Oct. Mon to Sun 10am to 4pm; Nov & Dec. 11am to 3pm

Willy Frank is carrying on a proud tradition started by his father Dr. Konstantin Frank, a Ukrainian-born and German-trained viticultural and enological scientist. Following his emigration to the United States, Frank had more impact on winegrowing outside California than any other person in North America's 400 year old vinous history.

In 1951 when already 52 years old, Konstantin Frank decided the New World was for him. His interest in the grape went back to his youth when he studied agriculture at the Polytechnic Institute of Odessa in his Russian homeland. He followed this by further studies in enology and viticulture; prophetically his thesis was entitled "Studies in the Prevention of Winter Frost Damage to the Grape". Konstantin then went on to plant many thousands of acres of vinifera vines in the Ukraine for the State-owned Winery. In 1943 he and his family escaped to Austria before the German occupation. Following the war, he ran farm properties for the American occupation forces.

He arrived in New York in 1951 with his wife and three children, virtually penniless and speaking no English (although he spoke seven other languages). The Agricultural Station at Geneva in upstate New York gave him some manual work and, after two years, he landed a job with Charles Fournier at Gold Seal Vineyards. During his ten years there he pioneered vinifera planting and, experimenting with dozens of rootstocks and grape varieties, he grafted over 250,000 vines and became the first person to succeed with vinifera in North America's eastern wine region. Konstantin's strong belief was that, if it could be done in Russia with temperatures going down to minus 40 F, it was very possible in New York State.

In 1959 he bought his own farm above Hammondsport and planted 70 acres of vinifera. His wines became the first viniferas outside California to receive critical acclaim. Not only did Konstantin Frank pioneer vinifera, but he was most generous with his time and energy to assist any winegrower in the East to do likewise. The establishment of a truly world class wine industry in the East has been mostly his doing.

Willy, Konstantin's son, is carrying on the family tradition, taking over on his father's death in 1985, after a career in New York as a press photographer. Willy, however, always helped at vintage time and started planting his own Finger Lakes Vineyard in 1980.

Aside from installing top winemaker, Eric Fry, formerly with Robert Mondavi and Jordan in California, he is now launching into Methode Champenoise under the "Chateau Frank" label. A unique wine of the Vinifera Wine Cellars is their "Rkaziteli", a Russian variety dating back 5,000 years to Mt. Ararat the reputed resting place of Noah's Ark.

The Vinifera Wine Cellar's Chardonnay, Pinot Noir and Cabernet Sauvignon wines I tasted with Willy would be worth gold medals in my opinion.

Wagner Vineyards

The first winery to be built since Prohibition on the rise between Seneca and Cayuga Lakes was Bill Wagner's Wagner Vineyards. Bill, a long time grapegrower in the region, was inspired to build a winery after the New York Farm Winery legislation came into effect in the early 1970's. Bill is a perfectionist in all he does and felt the need to make his own wine, from what he was confident were the best grapes grown in the region.

The winery he built is a striking octagonal building, overlooking Lake Seneca. Next door he has built a cafe named after his grand daughter "Jenny Lee", open for lunch during the summer months. The whole structure has been constructed from pine and local hemlock timbers and the shape makes for a most efficient winery-in-the-round.

Winemaker is John Herbert, who has worked for Bill since 1974, two years before the winery was opened. An extremely pleasant gentleman, John has proved a very competent winemaker and has the good fortune to be able to pick the best grapes from Bill Wagner's extensive vineyards. The remainder are sold to eager wineries in the region.

Wagner use some oak from the Wisconsin and Minnesota region. The tight-grained timber from these cool areas has proved very suitable for the wine maturation programme. The Wagner 1987 barrel-fermented Chardonnay is rich and complex — I awarded it over 19 points out of a possible 20. The Gerwurztraminer, Riesling and Pinot Noir were not far behind. Seek out Wagner Vines; they are worth finding.

Herman J. Wiemer Vineyards Inc.

The tall, dark and handsome Hermann Wiemer is undoubtedly producing some of North America's best vinifera wines.

Hermann was born in Bernkastel, the famous wine town on Germany's Mosel River. His family had made wine there for over 300 years, but, in 1968, he left for America and became winemaker at Walter Taylor's Bully Hill Vineyards, making quite a name for his hybrid wines over the next decade.

In 1980, Hermann left Bully Hill to further develop his own 140 acre property near Lake Seneca, which he had bought in 1973. His greatest desire was to succeed with the European vinifera varieties he had grown up with in Germany.

Hermann bought a run down but quaint Victorian villa with a huge barn next door. The villa has been faithfully restored and the barn has been converted into a beautifully equipped winery, with an innovative and architecturally striking loft, where Hermann's guests can stay.

The Eastern Seneca Lake shore has a milder climate than most of the Finger Lakes region, being at a lower altitude and near the extremely deep body of water that moderates the winters substantially. The soils are also deeper here than in the surrounding regions and traditionally peaches and cherries grow best in this area.

Hermann also runs a vine nursery at the vineyard and supplies vinifera vines as far afield as New Mexico and Texas. His winemaker, Dana Keeler, is a local from Corning and worked with Hermann at Bully Hill. He is right in tune with his employer and they make a very good team together.

Hermann's training under the famous Dr. Helmut Becker at the Geisenheim Wine School in Germany is obvious in his wines, which all show superb retention of fruit flavours. A new release I tasted, a 1987 barrel fermented Chardonnay, had superb stonefruit flavours, overlaid by a sweet vanilla oak character, one of the finest wines from the variety I have seen. Hermann has made quite a reputation with his Johannisberg Riesling, which has become the first New York State wine to be served on an International airline. The winery also produces a good Methode Champenoise from the Riesling grapes; it is crisp and dry. A little red is grown, namely, Pinot Noir and Gamay. The vineyard's Gamay in the Beaujolais style, usually sells before it is bottled. The piece-de- resistance is certainly the "Individual Bunch late Harvest Johannisberg Riesling" luscious and rich, but like all Hermann's wines scrupulously clean and fresh.

Widmers Wine Cellars

Nineteen eighty-eight marks the centenary celebrations of Widmers, now owned by the giant Canandaigua Wine Company.

The region was pioneered viticulturally by German Vinedresser Andrew Reisinger in 1852, but it was not until thirty years later, when John Jacob Widmer came to the local town of Naples and set up in opposition to Maxfield wines, owned by the powerful Naples banker, Hiram Maxfield, that things started to happen.

John and his wife Lisette were very hardworking and established a healthy enterprise. In 1910, they sent their son .Will to the German wine college at Geisenheim. He was the first to introduce Spatlese and Auslese styles to the American wine scene and the first New York winemaker to make varietal and vintage-dated wines.

The Widmers survived Prohibition making grape juice and other grape products. After Prohibition, Widmers took over their fierce competitor, Maxfield Wines.

A long standing trademark of the Widmer Winery is its huge sherry solera of barrels in stacks four deep, covering the entire roof area of the large winery. Sherry matures faster and better when exposed to great temperature changes, which it certainly gets on Widmers' roof, where it is exposed to winter snow and century degree summer heat.

Today, Widmers still make a large range of good quality and reasonably- priced wines. The winery is large and attractive and well worth a visit.

An introduction to the Hudson Valley

North America's oldest continuously operating wine region is situated only an hour or so's drive north of New York City.

Wine making in this very scenic area dates back to 1677, when French religious refugees settled at New Palz, making wine from the local native grapes. New York State's first large commercial vineyard was planted on the banks of the Hudson River at Crotan Point, just over 30 miles north of New York City.

The Hudson Valley also sports America's oldest operating winery, "Brotherhood" at Washingtonville presently going through a real rejuvenation.

A number of small high quality boutique wineries such as Rivendell (formerly Chateau George) and Cascade Mountains have joined the larger older wineries such as The Hudson Valley Wine Company, the Royal Winery and of course Brotherhood. In all there are now 24 wineries in the region.

Visitation from New York has obviously had a big impact on the development of wineries in this region and their number and size is bound to expand even further.

Impressive wines are coming from vinifera vines recently planted in the area.

Brotherhood - America's oldest winery

It seems rather ironic that our last port of call on the final research trip for this Pictorial Atlas was America's oldest continuously operating winery. We had been in the region several times before, but each time nightfall had beaten us.

We arrived half expecting a totally tourist oriented place not really interested in quality wines. To our surprise and delight, we found a rebirth taking place, some great innovative wines and a fresh and vibrant attitude throughout this splendid old winery.

During 1987 a consortium, headed by a truly international winemaking genius, Caesar Baeza, took over. Development in a short period at Brotherhood has been spectacular — not that a lot of money has been spent — but the grand old place in now being properly utilised and equipped to make excellent wines, as well as providing the visitor with a memorable experience.

Caesar Baeza grew up visiting his family's winery just outside Santiago in Chile. He studied wine there and went on with a scholarship to Madrid, following this with further studies in Montpellier, France. Here he met noted Napa winemaker, Bernard Portet. He went to California and worked for Bernard and studied at U.C. Davis before joining the giant United Vintners. In 1974 he went to Brotherhood as assistant winemaker, staying there for two years, leaving after the much-respected owner, Frank Farrell, died. He went back to California to join the large

Lamont Winery and became one fo the first to make white wine from red grapes, helping the winery solve a big problem.

His inventive nature brought him a job offer from Pepsi Company's international wine division and over the next ten years he made wine in countries such as Yugoslavia, Romania, Russia, Spain, Bulgaria, Germany and France to name a few. He was responsible for quantum leaps in quality style and presentation of wines in these places, but a part of his heart was still at Brotherhood. When Pepsi Company looked at the possiblity of buying Brotherhood, it was Caesar who checked it out. Pepsi said "no", but Caesar still dreamt of it. Some months later, a syndicate formed and

approached Ceasar; his time arrived at last. He came with two conditions. First, to have a free hand to convert it into a premium winery and second, to make his own wine. In his words "Wine is not a commodity" and "A bottling line is not a winery".

Brotherhood had its humble beginnings in 1839, when Frenchman Jean Jacques decided with his previous grape harvest only netting him a pittance that he would make wine himself. In 1886 the Jean Jacques winery's distributors, Emerson & Co., took over and in 1921 a Mr. L.L. Farrell bought Brotherhood. His nephew Frank took control in 1952 and revitalised the winery and its wines. Unfortunately, following his death in 1976, it went downhill but is now totally revamped.

The winery also has a very good restaurant, "The Hors d'Oeuverie" and a cafe "The Cheeserie". The cellars have been totally renovated including the mile of underground tunnels.

One of Caesar's new wines is "Mariage", a blend of 80/ Cabernet Sauvignon and 20/ Chardonnay, a most unusual marriage, but, following the tradition of red/white blends of the Rioia in Spain and the Rhone Valley in France, many other vinifera varietals and other wines are being added to the Brotherhood range.

Wine and wineries have their cycles. Fortunately, Brotherhood's time has come again.

Hudson Valley Wine Company

The setting of the Hudson Valley Wine Company, in a cluster of stone buildings high above the Hudson River is almost perfect. The ``village'' containing the winery is surrounded by vines on the 315 acre estate.

The winery was started in 1907 by retired New York banker, Alexander Bolognesi, who found the delightful rolling countryside much like that around his hometown of Bologna in Italy. Alexander concentrated on estate-bottled wines from the native Labrusca vines which he grew on the property. Following his death, the winery was run by his widow, Valentina. The Bolognesi's were very private people and their pretty wine village was never open to the public.

Things changed when the winery was purchased by Herb Feinberg, a wine importer, who with his three brothers started the ``Monsieur Henry'' wine label. Herb opened the winery to the public as an ideal picnic spot for the New Yorkers day out. He runs hay rides through the vineyard and the village now has a restaurant for groups as well as tasting facilities and other attractions.

Hudson Valley Winery with its attractive setting and numerous activities makes for a pleasant place to while away a few hours.

Rivendell Winery

North America is full of enthusiastic and energetic winemaking families, none more so than the Ransoms of Rivendell Vines in the Hudson Valley.

Sallie and Jack Ranson and two their sons, Fred and Bob, are positive, dynamic and make one feel right at home the minute one steps inside the door of the winery; another son runs a nearby Westchester Restaurant.

The Rivendell Winery is situated on a 450 acre farm formerly known as the ''Gardiner Vineyard and Farm Company'', an enterprise founded by building contracter, George Nutman, who named it ''Chateau Georges''.

Nutman planted 30 acres of French hybrids and built a winery in a building that was formerly a summer camp facility. George Nutman died in 1986 and the Ransom family bought the property from the estate early the next year.

Winemaker is Jim Moss, a former research chemist, who, apart from making wine, has his own wine merchants business, Paramount Wines.

Whilst visiting, I was fortunate enough to try some of his 1987 wines straight from the fermentation cellar. The Chardonnay, which had been barrel fermented, was really excellent, with big upfront flavours of apricot, melon and grapefruit.

The Ransoms have travelled extensively through wine areas of the world, particularly Australia, and with ideas gained from these sojourns, are in the process of converting another charming old building on the estate into a restaurant and tasting area, complete with a massive stone fireplace as well as a balcony shaded by huge trees, looking out over their valley of vines.

Sales have expanded enormously and Rivendell looks set to grow at an even faster rate. Rivendell wines have won a swag of medals over the last two years and its easy to taste why.

Long Island has the most temperate climate of any part of New York state and "Moses the Frenchman" Fournier planted a large area of vines there prior to 1640.

Although the climate is quite mild enough for any grape variety, it is also moist and humid, encouraging vine diseases. This appears to be the reason extensive vineyard

holdings on the island never eventuated. With the ability to control these pests and diseases by the use of modern sprays, Long Island has seen a vine planting boom since 1973. The first new winegrowers were Alex and Louisa Hargrave, who planted their vineyard and built a winery in the "Old Potato Cellar" on their sixty-six acre former potato farm.

Other significant wineries have started on the north fork of the Island, some 70 miles from New York City, including Long Island's largest winery, Pindar, established in 1979 by Dr. Herodotus Damianos. Recently planting has also begun on the south fork.

Long Island had twelve bonded wineries and almost 1,000 acres of vinifera vines by 1988.

Lenz Vineyards

Westhampton Beach restaurant owners, Patricia and Peter Lenz, had a deep and abiding interest in wine and boasted a very comprehensive wine list of American wines.

When thinking of retiring from the restaurant, they decided they would enjoy the lifestyle of the vigneron. With winegrowing starting nearby they did not have far to go to live out their dream. In 1978 they bought a potato farm and planted 30 acres of vines, turning the large barn into a winery.

By the time of our visit in spring 1988, they had added a second building incorporating a tasting room. The whole complex is particularly attractive and their wines, which include a Gewurztraminer and Merlot as well as Chardonnay are of exemplary quality. A classic Bordeaux red blend of Cabernet Sauvignon, Merlot and Cabernet Franc is also put out in good years.

Hargrave Vineyard

Alexander and Louisa Hargrave were both Harvard graduates, he in Chinese, she in education. Together they enjoyed their summers in the French Bordeaux region and also shared a common interest in the culinary arts. With their interest in wine becoming overpowering, they decided to set up their own vineyards and winery, but where? The Hargraves searched the east and west coasts of North America, even looking near Alex's home town of Rochester, in upstate New York. It was, however, to Long Island (Louisa's home) they eventually came, spurred on by a Cornell Professor friend, who had just successfully planted some vines on the Island. They commenced planting a 66 acre potato farm in 1973 and later built Long Island's first post-Prohibition winery. Today they have approximately 84 acres, 55 being under vine. Their Chardonnay has been particularly successful but they also produce Cabernet Sauvignon, Riesling, Sauvignon Blanc and Pinot Noir.

Pindar Vineyards

D r. Herodotus Damianos has named his exciting vineyard and winery after the ancient lyric poet, Pindar, from his Greek homeland. With 200 acres planted to classic Vitis Vinifera varieties and an annual production of 50,000 cases, it is already Long Island's largest winemaking operation. Plans are to expand further to a 100,000 case capacity.

Planting started in 1980 and the winery was completed in record time to be ready for the 1982 crush. Grape varieties include Cabernet Suavignon, Merlot, Petit Verdot and Cabernet Franc, the classic red wine varieties of Bordeaux. Pinot Noir, Chardonnay and Pinot Meunier, natives of Champagne, are also planted along with the Germanic Gewurztraminer and Johannisberg Riesling.

At the time of our visit, the winery was being run by cellarmaster, Mark Fritzlowski, a native Long Islander. Aside from straight varietal wines from the above varieties, Pindar are producing a super-premium Bordeaux red blend under the name "Mythology".

The winery and cellars at Pindar are well set-up and certainly have the potential to handle the planned increase in production. The Pindar wines I tasted, particularly the Chardonnay and Merlot were of outstanding quality; they gave me a very pleasant surprise. The Chardonnay exhibited strong melon and tropical fruit aromas combined with a rich feel in the mouth and pleasing complexity from barrel fermentation and ageing. The Pindar Merlot had spicy cherry and wild berry flavours with some floral highlights while the palate had a mouthfilling velvety texture — a superb wine. Two Methode Champenoise are also made, a straight Pinot Meuniere and a Pinot Noir/Chardonnay Cuvee.

With their outstanding award winning wines and their proximity to New York City, Pindar Vineyards seems assured of a very rosy future.

An Introduction to Ohio

Ohio enjoyed the position of America's largest winegrowing state, in 1859 when almost 600,000 gallons were produced there, accounting for over a third of the nation's production. Chief amongst the wine pioneers responsible for this was Nicholas Longworth, who arrived in Cincinnati from New Jersey in 1803, the year Ohio became a state.

Longworth arrived with nothing, but quickly made a fortune through his legal practice and land development. His interest in wine drew him into becoming first a grapegrower and then a winemaker. He introduced the "Catawba" grape and made a worldwide reputation with his still white wine, which he followed with a Champagne (America's first). The famous poet Longfellow was inspired by this very drink to write his "Ode to Catawba Wine". Longworth at one stage had over 1,200 acres under vine in Cincinatti. Unfortunately, a vine blight virtually wiped Ohio off the wine map in the 1860's, when over 10,000 acres of vines were killed by it.

Winegrowing moved to Northern Ohio, on the Lake Erie shore, and also to the Lake Erie Islands just off Sandusky and Put-In-Bay. Prohibition retarded this rebirth, but today a large wine industry is centred there. The "modern Longworth" is Bob Gottesman, who in the mid-seventies, bought and rejuvenated the state's largest four wineries, Lonz on the Middle Bass Island, Mon Ami and Firelands (formerly Mantey) on the lake shore, and Meiers in Cincinnati. Ohio is once again one of the largest winegrowing states outside California, with over 50 bonded wineries.

Ohio

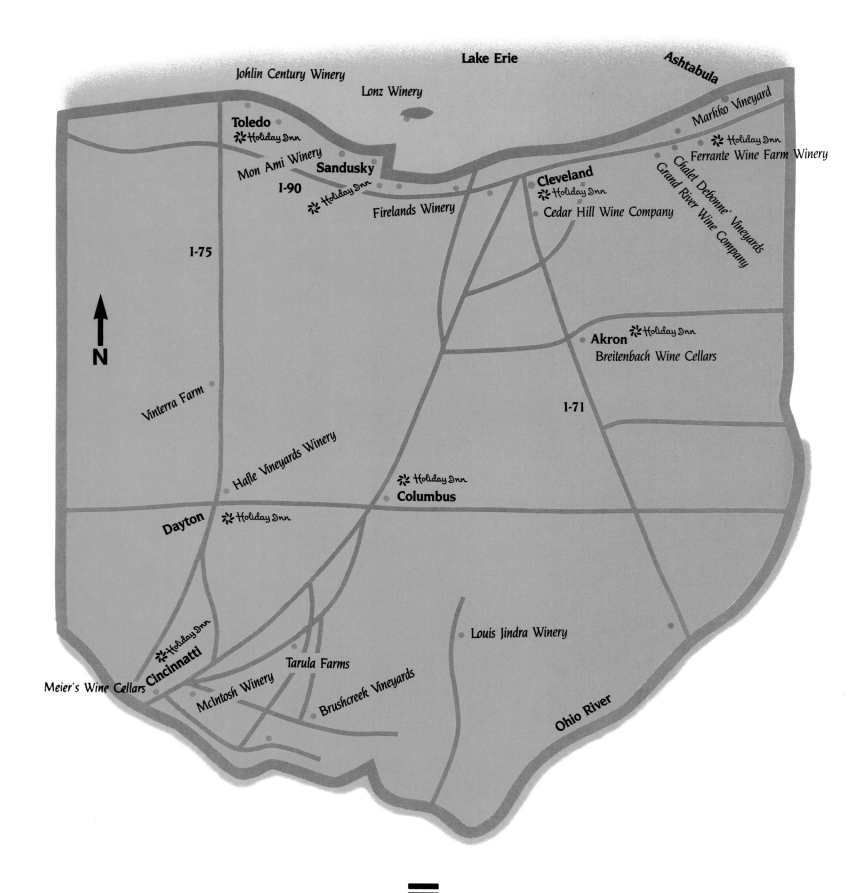

Lake Erie

Ashtabula

Johlin Century Winery

Lonz Winery

Markko Vineyard

Toledo

Holiday Inn

Holiday Inn

Mon Ami Winery

Ferrante Wine Farm Winery

Sandusky

Cleveland

Chalet Debonné Vineyards

I-90

Holiday Inn

Holiday Inn

Grand River Wine Company

Firelands Winery

Cedar Hill Wine Company

I-75

Holiday Inn

Akron

Breitenbach Wine Cellars

Vinterra Farm

I-71

N

Hafle Vineyards Winery

Holiday Inn

Columbus

Holiday Inn

Dayton

Louis Jindra Winery

Holiday Inn

Cincinnatti

Tarula Farms

Meier's Wine Cellars

McIntosh Winery

Brushcreek Vineyards

Ohio River

Markko

Arnulf Esterer is a modern-day winegrowing pioneer. In 1968 he left his good job as an industrial engineer to tackle a rural life with his wife, Kate, and family, plus partner Tim Hubbard.

Markko was named for the Finnish ex-policeman from whom they bought the property. Arnulf has prepared himself for the task by working two vintages for no pay with Dr. Konstantin Frank at his Vinifera Wine Cellars in New York State. First, Chardonnay and Riesling were planted — Ohio's first modern-day vinifera plantings, and then Cabernet Sauvignon.

The Markko wines I found were outstanding, reflecting the character, heart and soul that Arnulf, his family and partner have put into their vineyard and winery.

MARKKO VINEYARD
Address: RD 2, South Ridge Road, Conneaut, OH., 44030
Phone: 216/593 3197
Year of Establishment: 1968
Owner: Arnulf Esterer & Thomas Hubbard
Winemaker: Arnulf Esterer
Principal Varieties Grown: Chardonnay, J Riesling, Cabernet Sauvignon
Acres Under Vine: 14
Average Annual Crush: 16 t Chardonnay, 14 t J Riesling, 4 t Cab. Sauv.

Principal Wines & Brands	Cellar Potential (Years)
Chardonnay Reserve	10
Johannisberg Riesling Reserve	10
Cabernet Sauvignon	25

Trade Tours – Available
Retail Room Sales – Available
Hours open to Public: Monday thru Saturday 11am to 6pm
Retail Distribution: Within 200 miles California, Washington D.C.

Chalet Debonne

Anthony Debevc graduated in Pomology from the Ohio State University in 1970, having been brought up on a fruit and grapegrowing property planted by his grandfather, Anton, near Madison on the Ohio Lake Shore. On Anthony's return, he planted vinifera and hybrid varietals to add to his father's Concord grapes. The following year, the father and son team opened the winery.

The Chalet building is pretty, neat and houses a very good, small restaurant. The cellars and winemaking facilities are underneath the building. The equipment is excellent but the oak barrels are intriguing as the have been constructed from oak timber felled on the property and made into barrels by one of America's few remaining cooperage firms, A.N.K. from Missouri. The tight grain, derived from the oak's slow growth in this cold climate, makes them ideal for wine maturation.

The Debevc's make several ranges of wine. The top of the line are their Debevc Vineyards varietals and many have won trophies in wine competitions.

The family all pitch in. Rose, Anthony's mother with Beth, his wife, look after the restaurant, gift shop and tasting room. It's a great stop for the wine traveller.

Firelands Wine Co-operative is housed in a striking modern building, completed in 1987, equipped with the very latest in winemaking technology, to make wines for the wine empire put together since 1976 by Robert Gottesman, owner of Paramount Distillers in Cleveland. Bob is a visionary person and started his acquisitions with the Meiers Wine Cellars in Cincinnati, with their vineyards on the ``Isle of St. George'' just off the coast from Firelands. He followed this by buying the century-old Mon Ami Wine Company at Port Clinton and the Lonz Winery on Middle Bass Island.

Firelands was known as Mantey Wines when Gottesman purchased it in 1980, its centenary year. The new facility has been cleverly and aesthetically blended into the old Mantey Winery and now crushes over 4,000 tons of grapes each vintage. The Firelands role as a cooperative, to process for itself and its sister wineries, has an historic parallel, as this is just what the Mantey Winery did when it was first established, being set up to make wine for various German immigrant vineyardists in the region.

The winery is run by Bob Gottesman's nephew, Ed Boas, a very personable and competent young man. In charge of winemaking is Claudio Salvadore, originally from Italy, where he made wine for the large Zonin company, travelling with them to their Barboursville Winery in Virginia, where he made wine for two and a half years prior to joining Firelands.

Three vinifera wines I tasted at the cellar impressed me a lot: a 1986 Chardonnay, a 1986 Johannisberg Riesling and a 1985 Cabernet Sauvignon. The grapes for these wines came from the large vineyard holdings Fireland's have on North Bass Island, which has one of the mildest climates in Ohio. Another wine I found unusual, but appealing and certainly well priced, was their Pink Catawba, spicy, with some grapefruit flavours, a lively and refreshing wine to serve chilled. Another good wine is the Gerwurztraminer.

Firelands have an exceptionally good film on grapegrowing and winemaking, which is shown to visitors, who are certainly treated very well indeed.

Lonz Winery

The historic Lonz Winery, situated on the shores of Middle Bass Island, first opened in 1863, during the Civil War. Andrew Wehrl, a German immigrant, commenced making wine under the name of the Golden Eagle Winery. He carved underground cellars into the limestone at today's Lonz Winery location. By 1875, Golden Eagle had become America's largest Winery and boasted two 16,000 gallon wine casks, then America's largest.

Andrew was a man of enormous energy, serving also as postmaster from 1866 to 1895. He also owned several of the Island freight and passenger vessels.

After some turbulent financial times, the winery was sold to a Mr. August Schmidt in 1907. Several other owners came and went and, in 1923, the winery burnt to the ground. In 1926, George and Fannie Lonz bought the residence and burnt-out winery.

The Lonz family had been making wine and grape juice since 1884, when Peter. George's father, commenced production. George rebuilt the winery in 1934, following the repeal of Prohibition, modelling it after a Bavarian Wine castle. In 1942, disaster struck, when the winery burnt down again. Lonz rebuilt it straight away, this time adding a tower complete with a copper dome.

George Lonz died in 1969 and the winery lay idle for three years before being purchased by real estate promoter, Phillip Porteous. He had major plans to develop the winery, but none came to fruition. The winery was auctioned in 1976 and, after lying virtually dormant, was bought by Robert Gottesman in 1979. Much work has been already done to restore the grand old building and the yacht marina. Much has also been done in terms of rejuvinating the range of Lonz wines. The "Isle de Fleurs" Champagne, made famous by George Lonz, is now a 50% Pinot Noir and 50%

Chardonnay based Cuvee and beautifully packaged. I am sure it would have inspired George's legendary violin playing at the winery. I also tasted an exquisite 1987 Cabernet Sauvignon, not yet released along with a 1987 Johannisberg Riesling, a 1987 Gewurztraminer and a 1987 Chardonnay, all wines being of exemplary quality. Lonz draw largely on the Gottesman-owned vineyards on North Bass Islands. Most wines are made on the mainland, but some, like the "Isle de Fleurs" Champagne, are produced at the winery.

During 1988 and 1989 extensive renovations and restoration work is being undertaken to this classic old winery, ensuring it will be a showplace of the future and happily host festive days such as the 1988 Memorial day weekend, when 3,000 people enjoyed a fun, but orderly, day's entertainment at the winery.

Meiers Wine Cellars

I n his first foray into the Ohio wine industry in 1976, Robert Gottesman bought Ohio's largest winery, "Meiers", situated in the city of Cincinnati. In the 1950's Robert had bought the distilling and wine importing firm of Paramount Distillers, following a career at Schenley Distillers. After his purchase of Meiers, over the next two years he bought three major, century-old wineries on the Ohio lake shore, namely Mon Ami, Lonz and Mantey (now Firelands). To his credit, he has invested heavily in all of them, reviving some of the grandure of the Ohio wine industry of the last century.

Meiers is set in delightful gardens. These, and a large and very pleasant under cover tasting and entertaining area, play host to many thousands of visitors every month of the year. Most of the grapes used to make the Meiers wines come from the Isle of St. George, situated on Lake Erie only two miles from the Canadian border. The moderate climate here ensures a long 200-day growing season, where classic vinifera and French hybrid vines thrive.

Meiers began in the 1850's as a grape juice plant. In 1928 Henry Sonneman bought it and began making wine following Prohibition. In 1941 he bought the Isle St. George Vineyards and had expanded the winery to two million gallons capacity by the early 1960's.

Meiers produce a large range of wines, inlcuding premium sherries as well as table and sparkling wines made from hybrid and vinifera varieties. The cellars are very old with some casks of 100 years of age. A visit if you are in Cincinnati is a great idea.

Mon Ami Wine Company

The ivy-covered stone cellars of the Mon Ami Winery and their surrounding gardens are a joy for the eye to behold. Suitably enough, the peninsula containing the winery and jutting out into Lake Erie is called Catawba Island. The Catawba grape was first introduced to Ohio by Nicholas Longworth in 1825 and he proceeded to make an enviable reputation for the Champagnes he made from it.

Mon Ami's mainstay has been Champagne. Two floors of the beautiful old building's four floors are underground and devoted to Methode Champenoise production by the traditional process, using some of the pre-Prohibition equipment, fine for quality. However, for efficiency's sake, new equipment is being installed.

Mon Ami was founded in 1870 as a winery cooperative by a number of local growers on the Island. Norman Mantey, a third generation grapegrower, took over the winery and installed a fine restaurant on its ground floor. In 1980, he sold the property, along with his own Mantey Winery (now Firelands), to Robert Gottesman's Paramount Distillers.

Robert Gottesman has a very strong commitment to the Ohio wine industry and to the Ohio lake shore and Lake Erie Islands vineyards, in particular with his four major wineries and large vineyard holdings. Along with his other properties, a major investment in restoration work is being made at Mon Ami over the next few years.

Year-round, the winery presents a pretty face and a welcome is always extended to the wine traveller. Our visit was in the heart of winter and, with snowflakes falling on the building and gardens, Mon Ami truly looked like something out of a fairy tale.

Johann Schiller, a retired German soldier, is generally credited with being Ontario's first vigneron. He planted vines on 20 acres near what is now Mississauga, in 1811, going on to make wine from these Labrusca vines. Some 50 years later, the property was bought by Count Justin M de Courtenay and his vine growers' association whose wines were marketed under the Clair House label.

In the 1860's, the Concord grape made its way to the Ontario wine industry, from the north-eastern United States. This vine is hardy and disease resistant, ideal for the grape farmer. Unfortunately, it makes foxy, unpleasant wines. The Catawba, another

native Labrusca, was the next planted on Pelee Island in Lake Erie most of the grapes went south to Ohio wineries, but Brights began purchasing some in 1893. These pioneer vignerons from Kentucky also built a winery on Pelee Island called Vin Villa. The new Pelee Island winery (actually situated on the mainland) planted Canada's largest vinifera vineyard here in 1980.

Major J. S. Hamilton bought much of the Pelee Island wines and helped the growers set up a winery in Brandford, which he bought in 1909. London Winery absorbed this operation in 1949.

The Niagara grape was introduced in

1882 and widely planted. By 1890, there were 35 wineries in Ontario, mostly in Essex county, which remained the premier Ontario wine region until 1920. Barnes Wines, in St. Catherines, the best known original winery of this era, was founded in 1873 by George Barnes. In 1874, Thomas Bright and his partner F. A. Shirriff opened a winery in Toronto. In 1890, they moved to Niagara Falls and in 1911 changed the name to T.G. Bright and Company. By the turn of the century there were 5,000 acres of vines along the Niagara peninsula.

In 1916, Prohibition struck Ontario, however it was still legal to make wine. The

number of licensed Ontario wineries grew from 10 to 67. Poor wines and unscrupulous operators prospered. After Prohibition ended in 1927, the State monopoly systems took over and, at least quality was regulated.

In the 1930's, Brights brought a French winemaker to Ontario, Vicomte Adhemar de Chaunac de Lanzac. He started making some table wines of quality from the Delaware and Catawba varieties. At that time, nearly all wines being made were high strength, sweet, fortified wines de Chaunac persuaded his employers that better grape varieties were needed and in 1937, went to France, to study the new hybrid varieties. The war

interrupted, but in 1946, de Chaunac brought in 40 varieties of hybrid and vinifera vines, opening a whole new chapter of Canadian wine. Many acres of native wines were uprooted and replaced by hybrids and a few vinifera varieties.

The sparkling wine boom, headed by Andres Baby Duck, led the industry into the seventies. At least it was introducing many people to wine! The mid seventies brought with them the German Liebfrau wine imitations, such as Schloss Laderheim and Alpeniweiss.

The most significant and positive move came in 1974, when Niagara nursery man

Don Ziraldo and partner Karl Kaiser, talked the Ontario liquor board into issuing them a license as an estate winery, the first new winery license since 1930. Inniskillin, their winery, became very successful and spawned a number of estate and boutique wineries, along the Niagara peninsula plus south and western Ontario. Better grape varieties mainly vinifera, have been planted and winemaking has improved out of sight. The bigger companies have had to re-address the market place and Canadian wine has been the winner. Ontario has shown it can produce world class wines.

Southern Ontario

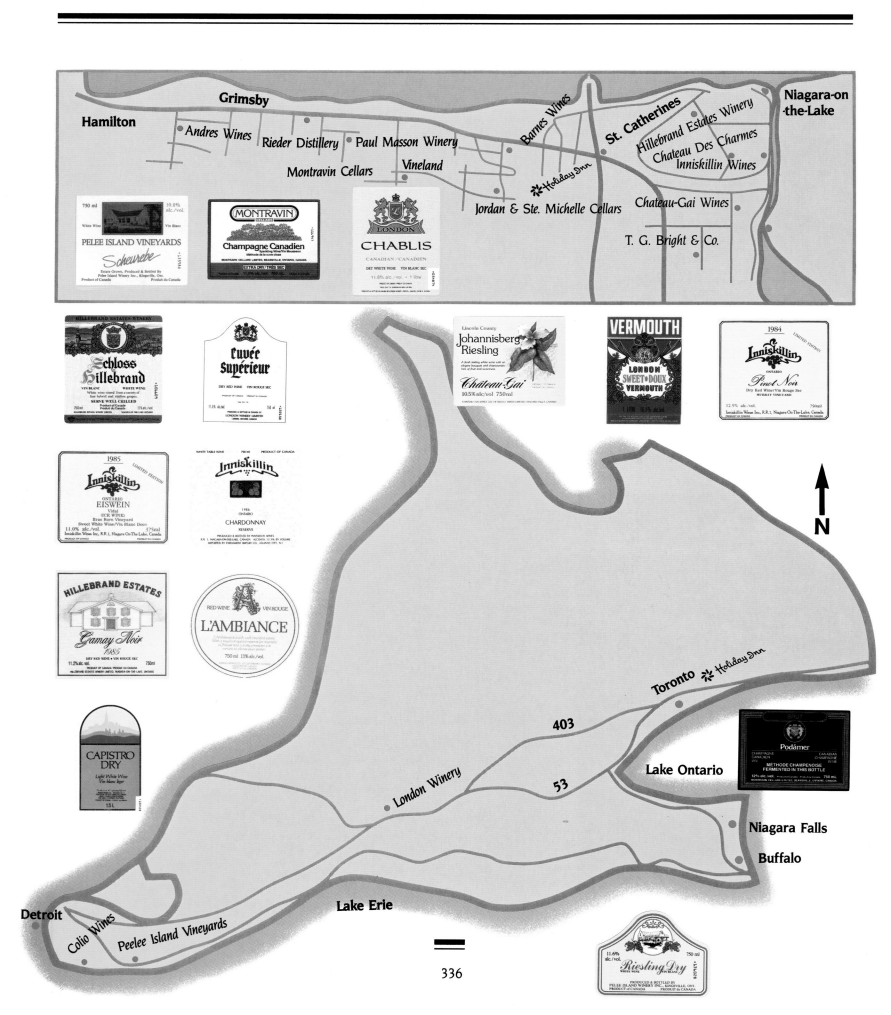

Barnes Wines

The oldest operating winery in Canada is Barnes Wines, on the banks of the Welland canal in St. Catherines. George Barnes bought the property in 1873 and built a classic old, cut stone building, which still stands today. Many of Barnes' cellars are still underground.

Barnes is the only Canadian winery that has continuously operated since the last century. Most of the wines it produced before the early 1970's were fortified Sherry and Port styles made from the native North American grape varieties.

In 1973, the winery was purchased by Reckitt and Colman. After examining the market, they decided that table wines were the way to go and Barnes took a new direction. In 1981, Keewhit, a private company, bought Barnes and in 1982, the Gilbeys-I.D.V. Group, a British distiller, wine producer and hotelier, bought a large share of the business.

Barnes have experienced a total revolution and are now producing 90% table wine, much of which is in the varietal wine field. 1986 marked the last vintage where they crushed a Labrusca grape and now they are totally dependent on hybrid and vinifera grapes — a far cry from 90% Labrusca and a similar percentage of fortified wine of a few decades ago.

Nicholas Opdam is their very positive, young director of enology, who previously spent five years with Andres. His attitude is "What can I get out of this grape?" and he is really packing some fruit flavour into the wines. I must admit, the 1985 Gerwurztraminer I tasted is one of the best wines from the variety I have seen anywhere.

BARNES WINES LIMITED
Address: 206 Martindale Road, St. Catharines, Ont., Canada, L2R 6S4
Phone: 416/682 6631
Year of Establishment: 1873
Owner: Gilbey Canada (IDV) Keewhit Investments.
Winemaker: Nicholas Opdam
Principal Varieties Purchased: Seyval Blanc, Vidal, 23512, Marechal Foch, De Chaunac, Riesling, Chardonnay, Gewurztraminer
Average Annual Crush: 3,000 tons

Principal Wines & Brands	Cellar Potential (Years)
L'Ambiance White/Red	2
Adagio	1
Heritage Estates Chablis	2

Trade Tours – Available; group tours by appointment only, public tours.
Retail Room Sales – Available.
Hours open to Public: Winter: group by appointment, Summer: group by appointment; Public daily except Sundays and holidays from 11am to 1pm and 3pm.
Retail Distribution: All Canadian provinces via Liquor Boards & own retail stores in Ontario (currently 14)

Andres Wines

Andrew Peller founded his company in British Columbia in 1961. (I have talked about his winery in Chapter two). Andres now have wineries in six Canadian provinces of which the Ontario winery was one of the later ones to be established, even though Andrew Peller has lived near Hamilton most of his life after migrating from Hungary in 1927.

After difficulty obtaining a license going back over 15 years, Andrew bought the Beau Chatel Winery in Winona in 1970.

Aggressive and innovative, Andres introduced a new low alcohol (7%) sparkling wine called Baby Duck onto the market in 1973. They also introduced the "bag-in-the-box" concept, pioneered in Australia, with a four litre cellar cask range in 1975.

Andrew's son Joseph left his successful career in medicine to take over the company in 1965. Over recent years, Andres have concentrated more heavily on table wines – their non vintage Domaine d'or red and white blended wines, show good structure and fruit flavour and are very good value for money. They are also moving into the varietal wine field, both with hybrids and vinifera wines.

Another product range, released a few years ago, is their Auberge line in litre bottles; again value is the message. Andres became Canada's largest winemakers by the mid 1980's, but have recently been overhauled due to the merger of Brights and Jordan Ste. Michelle Cellars.

Andres keep a very keen watch on the pulse of the market place and I am sure many new and interesting premium wines, are just around the corner.

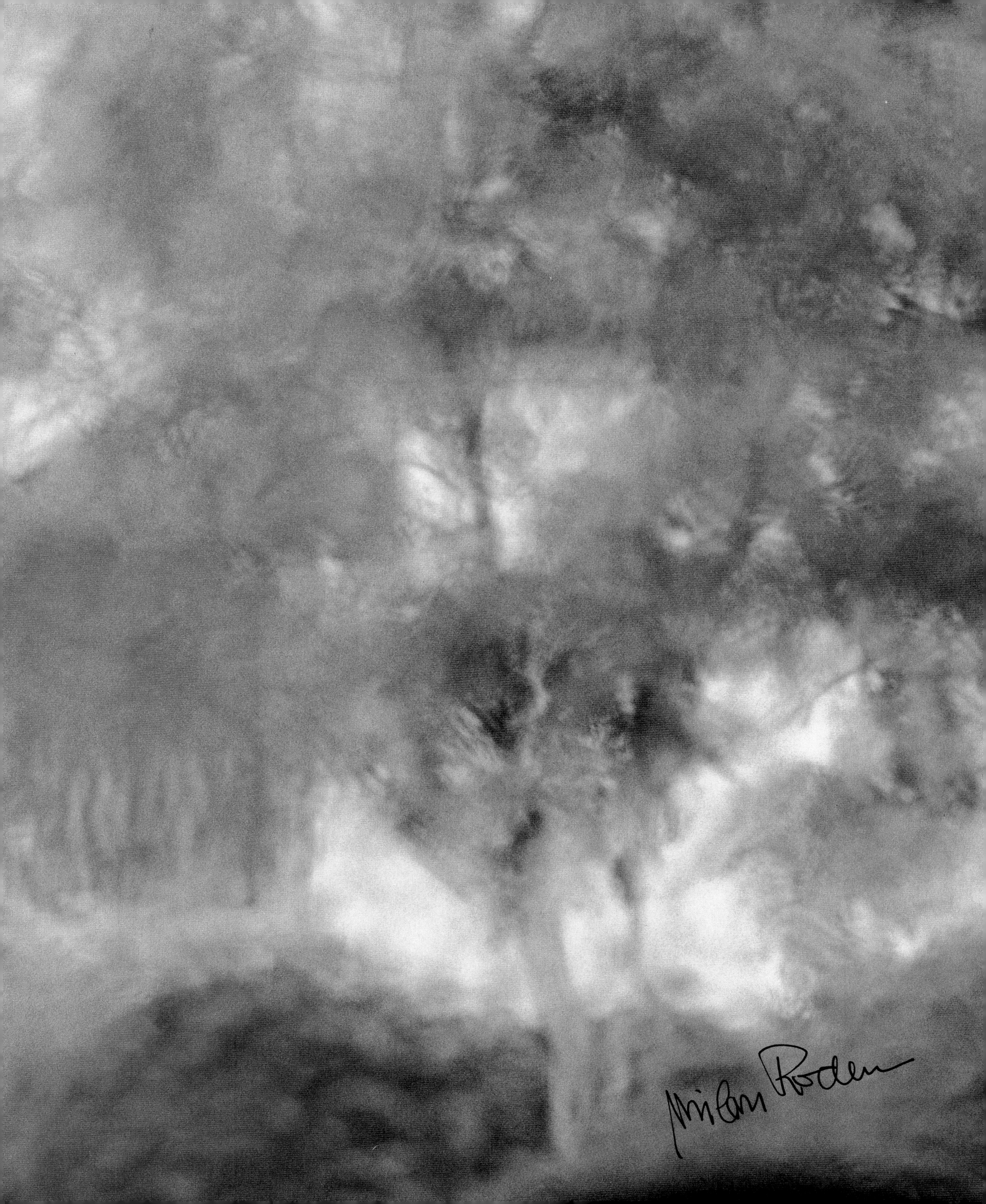

Brights Wines

Canada's largest winery T.G. Bright and Company Limited, had its humble beginnings in 1874, on Front Street in Toronto, when lumberman, Thomas G. Bright and his partner F.A. Shiriff formed a wine company.

In 1890, with business expanding, they moved to the current location in Niagara Falls to be nearer to their grape supply and the firm's name became, the Niagara Falls Wine Company. T.G. Bright bought out his partner in 1911 and changed the company name to his own. By 1933, Brights had become the world's largest privately owned winery with a capacity of over four million gallons. In 1934, Harry Hatch who controlled The Hiram Walker distilling operation, bought Brights from the family.

Hatch wasted no time in upgrading Brights. He brought in Dr. John Eoff, a wine chemist, who had worked in California and a young French wineman from the nobility, Viscomte Adhemar de Chaunac. Between them they revolutionised the Canadian wine industry, introducing new hybrid vines and European vinifera replacing the Labrusca

wines over a number of years. Since 1934, Brights has spent a staggering 6 million dollars on research. de Chaunac made two trips back to France, one in 1937 and another in 1946. In 1972, he was honoured by the industry, when one of the hybrids he introduced, which became the mainstay of the Ontario red wine industry, was named after him. Brights have had a number of firsts in the Canadian wine industry: the first bottle fermented sparkling wine, Brights President Champagne, in 1949 which still leads the market, in 1953 Winette Canada's first low alcohol sparkling wine, at 7% (long preceeding Baby Duck), also Canada's first Chardonnay in 1956 and its first nouveau from Gamay de Beaujolais in 1980. Bright's long time director of research George Hostetter retired in 1986, after 46 years of service. The following year, he was awarded the Order of Canada for his work in developing new, improved grape varieties and clones that have benefitted not only Ontario wines, but have had world-wide relevance.

In 1986, Brights purchased the Jordan

Ste. Michelle group, to form Canada's largest winemaking concern, a merger which has gone smoothly, to the benefit of both companies.

Chief winemaker is Herman Gras, a Chilean by birth, who joined Brights in 1974 intending to stay only a year or two. He is doing an excellent job and has recently released a superb premium blend, Avant Premiere, a red of Merlot and Baco Noir, winning a gold medal at the Monde Selection competition in Belgium. There is also an Avant Premiere white blended from Riesling and Chardonnay, both of which carry Herman's signature.

Brights have a number of vinifera varietals in limited quantities along with their "Entre-Lacs", French-style red and white wines. They also have table wine under a Brights House label varying in sizes from 1 litre through to 20 litres which are Canada's biggest selling dry wines.

Brights truly have something for everyone. A visit to their "winewood" tasting room, lined with the staves of two 70,000 gallon casks, is well worthwhile.

Chateau Gai Wines

Chateau Gai has had long and involved history, dating back to 1857, although these connections are too obscure to justify this year as their founding date. Achilles Rougemous opened a winery in 1857, in Cooksville near where Johann Schiller began the Canadian wine industry. In 1926, the Canadian Vine Growers Association took over. Under the banner of Canadian wineries, they had bought five small wine companies, including the Stanford Park Wine Company, on Chateau Gai's current site, started by the Marsh family, at Niagara Falls in 1890. The name was changed to Chateau Gai in 1941 by Alec Sampson an ex-newspaperman with considerable flair, who upset the French somewhat, however, by promoting his Canadian Champagne in the streets of Paris, fuelling a long enduring legal challenge, still a bone of contention between the two nations. Alec introduced the Charmat method (a French bulk, but natural way of making sparkling wines) to Canada in 1928.

Things at Chateau Gai languished for a number of years, until the brewing giant, John Labatt bought them out in 1973. After evaluating the market scene, Labatt decided to enter the modern wine era and in 1978 spent some 8 million dollars replacing the outdated equipment and much of the old wooden cooperage, with stainless steel.

Chateau Gai now has a revamped product list, fairly heavily biased towards white and including their attractive Lincoln County label, featuring Ontario's provincial symbol the Trillium flower. They produce a Pinot Chardonnay, Johannisberg Riesling, Gamay Rose plus Merlot. Alpenweiss is their German wine style and a light low alcohol white Capistro is also made. Chateau Gai Canadian Champagne is still the biggest seller for them.

After coming to terms with the wine market during the last decade, the future looks bright for Chateau Gai

Colio Wines

Colio is Canada's most southerly winery, enjoying a relatively mild climate, on the same latitude as Northern California. The vineyards they draw on are located on the shores of Lake Erie, which warms them in winter and cools them in summer.

Wine growing in the Essex and Kent counties goes back over a century and is on the increase again, with vinifera vines playing a big role.

The concept for the establishment of Colio was conceived in 1977, when a group of Italian businessmen from Windsor visited the Italian city of Udine in Friuli, in search of wine to import. It became too difficult, so they decided to build their own winery, which they did at Harrow, opening in 1980. There have been some changes in the partners and the company is today 100% Canadian owned. The first winemaker was Carlo Negri from Northern Italy who created wines with fresh, fruity flavours which remains the style under current winemaker Colin Pearson. Value for money is an integral part of the Colio philosophy. Only vinifera and French hybrid grapes are now used. The supplying growers are closely supervised by Colin and his staff.

Two of the top blended selection of the winery are their Riserva Bianco and their Riserva Rosso. Colin also makes a Chardonnay, Seyval Blanc, Vidal and Baco Noir along with some other blended wines as well as two sparkling Charmat wines, a Brut and a Spumante.

Colio have secured good distribution through southern Ontario in quick time and are now making progress in the Toronto area, and in other provinces. Colio have a unique "wine line," a telephone wine advisory service.

Colio have a simple philosophy: good wines with plenty of fruit flavour, at very affordable prices.

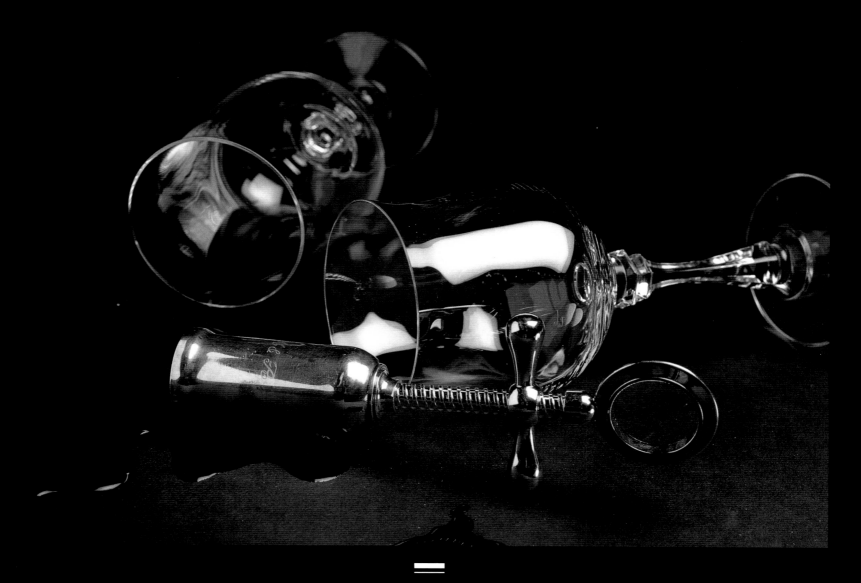

Little did Joe Pohorly realise when he started his modest winemaking facility, Newark Wines in 1979, that within eight years it would be Canada's largest estate winery (outside of the big long established players). Joe, a school teacher, had a 35 acre vineyard he established on his family's property in the 1960's. In 1982, the German company, Scholl and Hillebrand, winemakers in the German Rhinegau, near Rudesheim, bought Newark Winery, changing its name to Hillebrand Estate Wines. Their growth rate has been nothing short of amazing, helped along by the large number of neighbourhood stores they have setup. These stores only sell Hillebrand wines; at present there are 26 and plans are afoot to increase this number to 40 in 1988.

The company is in the capable hands of the dynamic and enthusiastic John Swann. His winemaker since 1987 is Frenchman Benoit Huchin, who spent three years at Jordan Ste. Michelle Winery. He looks after an annual production of some 200,000 cases of premium wine up from only 6,000 in 1982. The winery is extremely well set up with a definite German precision evident. It also sports Canada's first "Europress", which utilises a soft inflatable bag to press the skins gently, giving all the flavours, plus a clean juice with no bitterness. Although they only have 35 acres of their own wines, Hillebrand buy from 60 growers. Vineyard manager, Greg Bertie, is very active in research, working hand in glove with the University of Guelph. He is leading the growers into premium varieties and modern viticultural techniques.

The Hillebrand range of wines is extensive with vinifera and hybrid varietals featuring strongly. Hillebrand also make a Canadian Champagne, a Blush and a Rose under the Elizabeth label plus two sherries from an out-of-doors Solera. In 1982, they produced Canada's first Eiswein from frozen vidal grapes which has been a great success, emulated by others.

The winery has an attractive tasting area with a pleasant ambience that makes Hillebrand an exciting winery to visit.

HILLEBRAND ESTATES WINERY LIMITED
Address: Hwy 55, Niagara On The Lake, Ontario
Phone: 468 3201
Year of Establishment: 1983
Owner: Underberg Canada Inc.
Winemaker: Benoit Huchin
Principal Varieties Grown: Chardonnay, Riesling, Vidal, Cabernet Sauvignon, Merlot, Pinot Noir, Seyval Blanc, Gewurztraminer
Acres Under Vine: 26 - experimental
Average Annual Crush: 2450 tons

Principal Wines & Brands	Cellar Potential (Years)
Eiswein	18
Chardonnay	5
Riesling	3

Trade Tours – Available by apppointment tel: 468-7123.
Retail Room Sales Available.
Hours open to Public: Mon to Sat 10am to 6pm other tours by arrangement.
Retail Distribution: Liquor stores in Can. & own 24 retail wine stores

Inniskillin Wines

Inniskillin is an object lesson to anyone aspiring to start an estate winery. This picture book winery, is situated on the beautiful Niagara Parkway, a few miles north of the pretty town of Niagara-On-The-Lake, famous for the annual "Shaw" Festival.

The establishment of the winery was born out of the frustration of two brilliant men. Donald Ziraldo's family had been involved in farming and had a nursery near the Parkway. Don was dissatisfied with the vine varieties used in Canada and had propagated a number of varieties for quality vine making, following his studies in Agronomy at the University of Guelph. Karl Kaiser was unhappy with the wines then available in Canada, compared with his homeland in Austria, where he had helped his grandfather make wine. Karl bought some vines from Don and came with a bottle of wine he had made, in Don's words, "It was terrific". The two got together and decided to start a winery. A big stumbling block was the

fact that no new winemaking license had been granted in Ontario since 1929. Don, however, loves a challenge and using his deft negotiating skills, approached the then head of the Liquor Control Board, General George Kitching, whom he impressed with the idea, of a cottage winery. Don and Karl submitted a sample of a 1974 varietal Rose and got the green light — Inniskillin became Canada's first boutique winery.

The winery commenced operations in an

old tin shed on the Ziraldo Nurseries, the Inniskillin name coming from the original name of the property. In 1978, Inniskillin moved into their new winery, an attractive white washed structure, reminiscent of the upmarket Californian wineries. The tasting, sales and seminar complex is housed in the original barn, a weathered, but charming building they call their "boutique".

Inniskillin, under the direction of events and public relations manager, the extremely

Inniskillin Wines

competent and gracious Debi Pratt, run many educational functions, dinners, receptions, exhibitions etc., and have become closely associated with food, art and music, entertaining many well known international identities, as well as being ambassadors for all things of quality that are Canadian.

It is in the light of the driving desire of president, Don Ziraldo, to put Canadian wines on the world stage, that Inniskillin have participated, not only in many international wine competitions (winning many awards including the Diamond Award for its Icewine, after three successive vintages have received gold awards at Intervin), but also being the first Canadian winery to participate in prestigious overseas shows, such as Vin Expo in Bordeaux, (the world's foremost wine show, held bi-annually).

Karl Kaiser's range of wines began with hybrids in the seventies and, gradually, vinifera wines as their own and other growers' grapes became available. His plan is

to be all vinifera within the next decade.

Karl's Chardonnay has been outstanding, but he also makes excellent Gerwurztraminers, Johannisberg Rieslings, Cabernet Sauvignons and a Pinot Noir, which he believes can become a classic in this region. Vineyard designation is used by Karl, the main vineyard being Seeger, which he planted, but has been sold to the Seeger family to help Inniskillin fund their winery, and Montague. Two blended wines, Brae Rouge and Brae Blanc (named after the farm Brae Burn, the winery is situated on) have been good mainstays for the company. Karl and Don also put out a proprietors' reserve label and two Methode Champenoise wines, including a Chardonnay Blanc de Blancs.

Inniskillin wines have enjoyed some considerable success on the export market to the United States, England, France, Japan, Germany and Switzerland. Their wine boutique, where Karl's charming wife Sylvia, also works, is great and in Toronto they have

two wine boutique stores one in First Canadian Place and another on Yonge Street. If one cannot get to the winery to get their product, distribution is now widespread after many years of perseverance, particularly with leading restaurants, to overcome the negative image of Canadian wine.

INNISKILLIN WINES INC.
Address: R. R. Niagara Parkway, Niagara-On-The-Lake, Ontario, Canada
Phone: 416/468-2187
Year of Establishment: 1974
Owner: Karl J. Kaiser; Donald J.P. Ziraldo
Winemaker: Karl J. Kaiser
Principal Varieties Grown: Chardonnay, Pinot Noir, Riesling, Marechal Foch
Acres Under Vine: 60
Average Annual Crush: 800-1200 tons

Principal Wines & Brands	Cellar Potential (Years)
Chardonnay	4
Pinot Noir	5
Riesling	1-2

Trade Tours – Available.
Retail Room Sales – Available.
Hours open to Public: Mon - Sat 10am to 6pm; public tour & tasting 10.30am daily only (incl. Oct.); closed January.
Retail Distribution: Canada, U.S.A., Denmark, England, Hong Kong.

London Winery

Through the acquisition of J.S. Hamilton and Company at Brantford in 1945, London Winery can lay claim to being Canada's oldest winery with a founding date of 1871. The London Winery itself was built in 1925, whilst Ontario was still under Prohibition.

The winery was founded by two brothers A.N. and J.C. Knowles, who had come from Nassau in the Bahamas. A.N. Knowles was an electrical engineer and his brother had some winemaking experience in Ohio, firstly and then at his father-in-law's winery, in Oakville, Ontario.

When Prohibition was repealed in 1927, London were prepared with mature wines. Although still strongly based on Sherries and Ports, London launched into table wines, as long ago as the 1950's, when they introduced two white table wines, Windsor Castle and Green Gables, both made from the Niagara Labrusca variety.

London Winery bought eight smaller wineries within their region and consolidated them at their main premises. The company is still heavily involved with sherry and was the first in Canada to use the revolutionary, new Flor process of Sherry making, invented by Ralph Crowther of the Vineland Horticultural Research Station, on the Niagara peninsula.

In the early 1980's, London launched hybrid table wines, with Marechal Foch, Baco Noir and also a generic Chablis blend.

London Winery have an extensive range of Meads after taking over the Strawa Honey Company in 1965. Neville Knowles, son of the founder, is in charge, having spent over forty years with the winery.

LONDON WINERY LIMITED
Address: 560 Wharncliffe Road South, London, Ontario, Canada, N6J 2N5
Phone: 519/686-8431
Year of Establishment: 1925
Owner: Knowles Family
Winemaker: Jim Patience; Peyrt Knowles
Principal Varieties Grown: Vidal, Seyval Blanc, Riesling, Marechal Foch, De Chaunac, Baco Noir
Acres Under Vine: 60 - Cedar Springs Farm
Average Annual Crush: 4,000 tons

Principal Wines & Brands	Cellar Potential (Years)
London XXX Sherry	
London 410 Port	
London Cuvee Superieur Red	
London Chablis	
London Sweet Vermouth	
London Dry Vermouth	
London Honey Wine	

Retail Distribution: Products sold through government stores nationally in every province except Quebec; and own 21 retail stores.

Montravin Cellars

Around the same time Inniskillin were obtaining their license and starting off, another significant wine venture also got their start.

Karl Podamer, a Champagne master, had four decades of experience in Methode Champenoise production, firstly with his father Ferenc at the family cellars in Hungary, when young Karl was only nine years old and then in France. After coming to Canada as a refugee and working as a butcher, he put together a syndicate of Niagara businessmen and set up the Champagne cellars in Beamsville.

Karl was joined in the Champagne making by enologist Ernst Fischer, then head winemaker at Chateau Gai. In his own words, Ernst was, "tired of being involved in big wine companies". Ernst has had a rich and varied life, including sparkling wine making in many corners of the globe, he spent eight years in the industry in Turkey some time in Germany and then eight years at Gold Seal, in New York state with the legendary Charles Fourmier, before coming to Canada. He has now taken over at Montravin and is particularly happy and in control, he still consults in New York state to the exciting Casa Larga vineyard in Rochester. Montravin have a number of beautiful, large, Slovanian oak casks, which they use to mature their cuvees for the Podamer range of Methode Champenoise wines. The grapes are all Ontario grown, mainly Chardonnay and Riesling.

In 1983, the name was changed from Podamer Champagne Company to Montravin Cellars, although the name Podamer remains on the premium Methode Champenoise wines, a Brut Blanc de Blancs solely vinifera based, a Brut, Extra Dry and the Special Reserve with longer on the yeast lees are produced as well, all are fine wines.

Montravin also have a Champagne Canadien range an Extra Dry and a Pink/Rose, made by the Charmat Method.

This worthy addition to the Canadian wine industry is an enjoyable and informative place to visit.

MONTRAVIN CELLARS
Address: 1233 Ontario Street, Beamsville, Ontario, Canada, L0R 1B0
Phone: 416/563 5313
Year of Establishment: 1973
Owner: Partnership
Winemaker: Ernst J. Fischer
Principal Varieties Grown: Riesling, Chardonnay, Seyval Blanc, Vidal, French American Hybrids
Average Annual Crush: 300 tons

Principal Wines & Brands	Cellar Potential (Years)
Podamer Champagne (4 varieties)	3-4
Montravin Champagne Canadian (2 varieties)	2
Concerto White - table wine	2
Concerto Red - table wine	4

Trade Tours – Available by appointment only.
Retail Room Sales – Available.
Hours open to Public: Mon to Fri 10am to 12noon and 1pm to 4pm. Evening tours for groups over 15.
Retail Distribution: L.C.B.O. and Liquor Boards in other provinces.

Pelee Island Vineyards

The most beautiful winery in Canada is the Pelee Island Winery, built on the shores of Lake Erie, looking out towards the islands, where Canada's largest vinifera vineyards are established.

Pelee Island has an illustrious wine history having been the site of Canada's first commercial winery, Vin Villa, founded by two Americans from Kentucky, who made table, fortified and sparkling wines. At the turn of the century, the Island supported three wineries, Prohibition saw the demise of these operations, but the remains of Vin Villa are still visible.

Pelee started planting 100 acres of vinifera vines of the Island in 1980 and obtained their license in 1982. Varieties planted include Johannisberg Riesling, Chardonnay, Gerwurztraminer and Pinot Noir. Austrian winemaker, Walter Strehn, oversaw the initial years, and has been succeeded by another Walter, Walter Schmoranz, a real character and a most enjoyable man to spend some time with. He is a most competent winemaker and is assisted in these endeavours by Alex Bomben, whose family in Germany have a Schnapps making business going back to 1480. Pelee also have some German vinifera crossed varieties such as Zweigeltreb and a

Scheurebe, I found particularly attractive.

Pelee's wines are all top quality, Walter is particularly pleased with his 1987 vintage. I must admit, on seeing his barrel fermented Chardonnay with its nutty, almond, cashew and stone fruit flavours and depth of character, I have to agree with him. His 1986 Pinot Noir is also a wine of complexity with delightful lively strawberry and cherry flavours.

The winery's tasting room and audio-visual presentation are very professionally put together, making Pelee a popular stop for Detroit day trippers and Windsor residents.

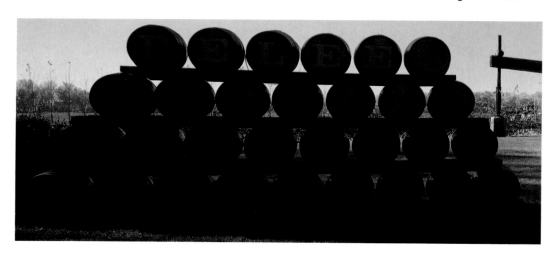

PELEE ISLAND WINERY & VINEYARDS INC.
Address: 455 Highway 18 East, Kingsville, Ontario, Canada
Phone: 519/733 6551
Year of Establishment: 1982
Owner: Private Corporation
Winemaker: Walter Schmoranz
Principal Varieties Grown: Riesling, Chardonnay, Scheurebe (Prof. Dr. Becker), Gewurztraminer, Pinot Noir
Acres Under Vine: 190
Average Annual Crush: 550 tons

Principal Wines & Brands	Cellar Potential (Years)
Eiswein	10
Late Harvest Riesling	8
Pinot Noir	6

Trade Tours – Available.
Retail Room Sales – Available.
Hours open to Public: Mon to Fri 9am to 6pm - Sat 10am to 6pm
Retail Distribution: Liquor Control Board of Ontario

Oregon

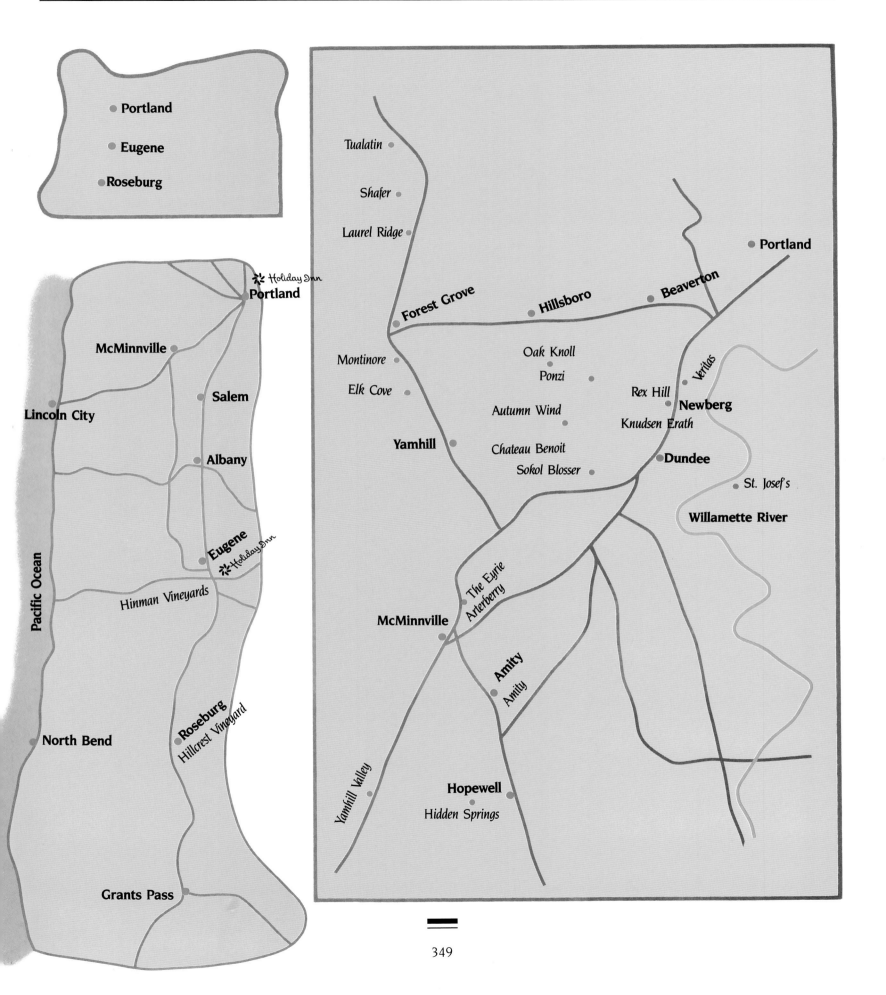

Portland

Eugene

Roseburg

Holiday Inn
Portland

McMinnville

Salem

Lincoln City

Albany

Eugene
Holiday Inn

Hinman Vineyards

Pacific Ocean

Roseburg
Hillcrest Vineyard

North Bend

Grants Pass

Tualatin

Shafer

Laurel Ridge

Portland

Forest Grove

Hillsboro

Beaverton

Montinore

Oak Knoll

Veritas

Elk Cove

Ponzi

Rex Hill

Newberg

Autumn Wind

Knudsen Erath

Yamhill

Chateau Benoit

Dundee

Sokol Blosser

St. Josef's

Willamette River

The Eyrie
Arterberry

McMinnville

Amity

Amity

Yamhill Valley

Hopewell

Hidden Springs

Miriam Roden
Coast of Oregon

An Introduction to Oregon

Today there are over 50 wineries actively making wine in Oregon. The vine was first brought to the state in the 1850's by settlers from the east travelling over the Oregon trail. Just prior to Prohibition, around 40 small wineries flourished in the state. Some remained after repeal but gradually they ceased business.

When Richard Sommer, who had studied viticulture under Professor Maynard Amerine at U.C. Davis, planted his Hillcrest Vineyard in 1961 he became Oregon's first winegrower. A year later, David Lett began growing Pinot Noir in the Willamette Valley near Portland, and became the state's second winegrower.

The majority of vineyards commenced business in the 1970's and 1980's. The Willamette Valley near Portland is the most popular area, followed by the Umpqua Valley and the Rogue River Valley of Southern Oregon. New plantings have also commenced in the Columbia River Valley in North-eastern Oregon.

The cool climate and the often rich red soils have proved very conducive to producing great Pinot Noirs and sparkling wines. Oregon is already making a mark in the world of wine with these products.

Rex Hill Vineyards

Paul Hart is a determined and patient man. His aim is to produce North America's best Pinot Noir and Chardonnay. He certainly knows his sums and the long-term thinking it takes to achieve his lofty goals. Paul sold his actuarial consulting business in 1981 and has invested over one and a half million dollars, mostly his own money, in the winery and vineyards, since then.

A good example of his willingness to accept the cost of his decision is the fact that he has stripped the grapes from his 13 acres of vines. During the last four years he has not used them or even sold them, as he believes the vines and his future wines will benefit from this action.

Rex Hill, in fact, has made and released wines, although they have not been sold until at least two years old. The first vintage was in 1983, when a Chardonnay and Pinot Noir were produced to Paul's specifications at other wineries, a year before his own winery was completed.

The winery is a real showpiece with some of the old arched tunnels remaining from the days when it was a fruit and nut drying shed. Everything is absolutely pristine and no amount of cash has been spared in installing the best possible equipment as well as new French Burgundian oak barriques. The Rex Hill stainless steel tanks all have floating heads, meaning the wine nevers sees even a breath of air.

The Rex Hill winemaker is Lynn Penner-Ash, Oregon's first woman winemaker. Her experience at Stag's Leap Wine Cellars for four years, as well as Domaine Chandon and Chateau St. Jean whilst she was studying at U.C. Davis, have stood her in good stead.

The wines are all made from fruit of vines more than 12 years old. During our visit, I tasted the 1985 Oregon Chardonnay, a 1984 Pinot Noir, a 1984 Pinot Gris and a 1987 White Riesling which was just being bottled. They were all excellent. One could only wish there were more wines around like Rex Hill.

Paul Hart was going to complete a doctorate in philosophy, not mathematics as he finally did. Perhaps he did the right thing as his philosophy, as far as wine is concerned is right on.

Knudsen-Erath Winery

The third winery started in Oregon was Knudsen-Erath, which had its beginnings in 1967, when Richard Erath bought some grapes from Richard Sommer and took them back to California to make some wine at home. A year later, the Eraths bought 50 acres in the Dundee Hills area, just outside Portland. In 1972 the winery commenced business.

A short time later, Seattle lumber executive Calvert Knudsen became involved, firstly by commissioning Richard Erath to plant a vineyard for him and secondly by buying a share in the winery. It is now one of Oregon's largest wineries and its reputation is steadily growing.

Hinman Vineyards

South-west of Oregon are the very attractive Hinman Vineyards and Winery, built by former school teacher Doyle Hinman and his partner David Smith, assisted by their wives Betty-Lou and Annette. Doyle fell in love with wine, planted his own vineyard and took off for the Geisenheim Wine Institute in Germany, where he spent six months, back in 1972. In 1979, they completed the winery and a superb tasting room. Production has increased quickly and the quality of their wine has proved excellent, particularly the Gewurztraminer and White Riesling, perhaps owing something to Doyle Hinman's time in Geisenheim.

Hillcrest Vineyard

Richard Sommer was responsible for the rebirth of the Oregon wine industry, a staunch individualist, who is possibly a touch eccentric as well. He went travelling north from California in 1961 in search of a perfect place to plant White Riesling vines. His studies under Maynard Amerine at U.C. Davis had taught him that cooler climates were best for many vinifera varieties to make the ultimate wine. Never

one to be limited in his thinking, Richard gradually travelled north testing any grapes that were growing. In Roseburg in Central Oregon he found his place and bought 40 acres there.

The winemaker at Hillcrest in now Philip Gale. I found all the wines of good quality, but the Rieslings really excellent, particularly the Late Harvest.

Oak Knoll Winery

The Vuylsteke family have built themselves a thriving wine business, not only producing excellent, premium varietal wines from classic grape varieties such as Chardonnay, Pinot Noir and White Riesling but other fruit and berry wines as well.

The winery has been built in a converted barn on the property to which Ron Vuylsteke moved his family after leaving his electronical engineering job at Tektronix. The winery, vineyards and orchards are situated about 20 miles west of Portland. Ron has been assisted in establishing the business by his five sons, wife and daughter. They have also opened a tasting and sales complex on the coast at Lincoln City, some 40 miles away and called it "Shipwreck Cellars".

Oak Knoll also put on an annual "Bacchus goes Bluegrass" festival each May at the winery.

Sokol Blosser

Rating as one of the largest wineries in Oregon, Sokol Blosser is certainly still quite small with a strictly limited production of around 25,000 cases. The very attractive and well-equipped winery is largely built underground near the peak of a rocky knoll. The innovatively designed tasting and function area has delightful views in many directions over the vineyards.

Sokol Blosser put a great deal of store by the quality of the grapes from their own Sokol Blosser, Hyland and Durant vineyards, 140 acres in total and with the same owners as the winery. The soil around Dundee is rich, red and volcanic, which the world over seems suited to Pinot Noir.

Bill Blosser is a retired urban planner and his wife Susan Sokol-Blosser a history professor, who is very active in the community and political arena.

The wines of Sokol-Blosser, particularly Pinot Noir, have consistently won praise as some of America's best. Joseph Drouhin, the French Burgundy house, is establishing vineyards next door confirming the Sokol-Blosser good choice of a vineyard location.

Tualatin

In 1973, former chief chemist with the Louis Martini Winery, Bill Fuller, teamed with San Francisco businessman, Bill Maulkmus and started a vineyard and winery in some striking hill country 30 miles north-west of Portland. The 85 acre vineyard is an absolute picture and producing excellent fruit.

The former strawberry packing shed has

been turned into a very modern winery. The large complex also caters for banquets and even weddings. The picnic ground under the cherry trees too is very attractive.

Tualatin make a delicious Gewurztraminer as well as Chardonnay, Riesling and Pinot Noir.

An Introduction to Pennsylvania

Commercial winegrowing in North America began in Pennsylvania at Spring Mill on the Susquehanna River, northwest of Philadelphia, when the Pennsylvania Vine Company started there in 1793. Wine was made from the Alexander grape, which was discovered growing wild by Thomas Penn's gardener, James Alexander, in the mid 1700's.

Vines then, as today, are grown all through the state. However, much of the over 9,000 acres are planted to Concord vines, used for grape juice, jam and so on.

Wine development, following the repeal of Prohibition was slow to start, as the state own and controls the liquor distribution system. After much lobbying, in August 1968, a farm winery law allowing production and sale by wineries led to many small wineries starting around the state.

The greatest concentration of vines and wineries is on the short Lake Erie shore of Pennsylvania, but about 50 wineries mostly small operate throughout the state.

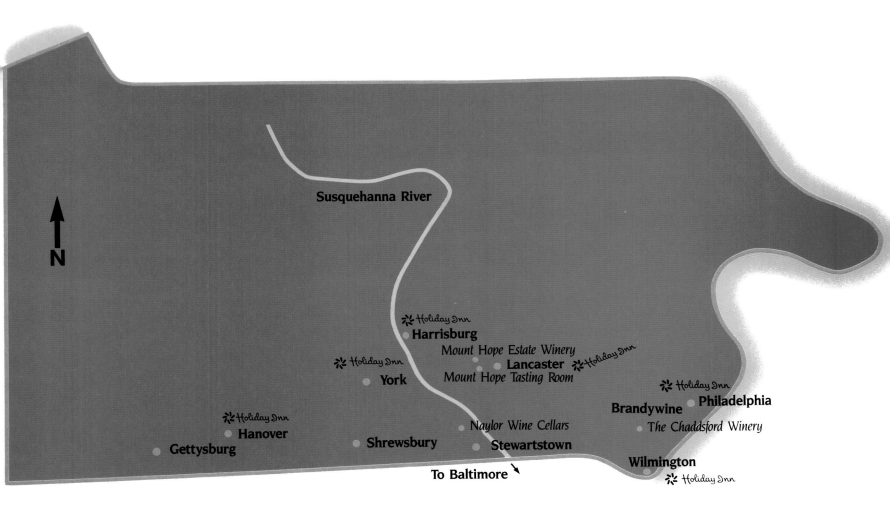

Chaddsford Winery

Eric Miller grew up with wine. His family lived in Europe during his youth spending much of their time in the small Burgundy village of St. Romaine. His father Mark was an author, illustrator and wine lover, putting on a weekly wine tasting where Eric had to guess the wines correctly to earn his weekly allowance. Small wonder, with this motivation, that he went on to know wine well.

On the family's return to New York State, their belongings were packed in wine barrels, not suitcases, and Mark, with Eric's help, opened the Benmarl Winery in the Hudson River Valley.

In the late seventies, Eric met Lee at an eastern wine conference, his proposal of marriage was quite unique — a label on one of his specially selected vintages, printed in small type at the bottom was "This wine celebrates the marriage of Eric and Lee on January 1, 1978".

The couple badly wanted their own winery and searched the Eastern states. They fell in love with a small property at Chadds Ford, ironically situated in the historic brandy wine area.

Lee has a degree in journalism from Pennsylvania State and started the wine magazine, "Wine East". She is also author of the first book on Eastern Wineries "Wine East of the Rockies".

The winery buildings are about to be doubled in size; they have also opened a wine store at Reading Terminal Market in Philadelphia.

Mount Hope Estate and Winery

In 1800, Henry Bates Grubb built a superb Georgian mansion from sandstone. Much work was done to it over the next century, resulting in a grandeur only the Victorian era could create, with a grand ballroom, greenhouse, solarium and exquisite appointments.

The theme of the whole estate is now very much Elizabethan with an annual "Renaissance Fair" featuring such things as Jousting competitions, Shakespearian plays in the Globe Theatre, constructed on site. This

fair lasts 15 weekends Sunday through Monday in the months of July, August, September.

All year round, tours with costumed guides can be taken of the 32 room mansion, its outbuildings and gardens which feature a 200 year old boxwood maze.

The winery is in the barn. I found their Chardonnay and White Riesling of very high quality and a red hybrid blend under the Renaissance Faire label an extremely pleasant Beaujolais style.

Naylor Wine Cellars

In Southern York County, not too far from where commercial wingrowing in North America began, Richard and Audrey Naylor commenced making wine in a converted potato barn in 1978.

Dick's connection with the vine went back to 1967, when he looked after a run down three acre Labrusca vineyard for a friend, receiving the crop as compensation. In 1975, he and Audrey bought a 1,000 acre property and planted some vines. In the early 1980's, they built a new winery just up

the road from their old one and now have 27 acres of vines comprising Labrusca, French hybrids and some vinifera.

Reds are Naylors real forte and the various Chambourcins and Cabernet Sauvignons I tasted impressed greatly as did their Johannisberg Riesling.

Dick and Audrey also operate two wine shops in York, one at the Queensgate shopping centre and one at the Burlington North Malls.

An Introduction to Tennessee

Today Tennessee has over a dozen active, small wineries making wine from bunch Labrusca, hybrid and vinifera varieties, as well as the Cluster Muscadine types. Commercial winemaking in Tennessee goes back at least until the mid nineteenth century, but little was heard of winemaking for almost a century until a new farm winery law was enacted in 1977. It still has its faults, although sales and distribution by local wineries was made easier by amendments in 1983.

The first new winery was opened by retired air-force sergeant major Fay Wheeler in 1977, using grapes from vineyards of Labrusca hybrid and vinifera he had planted in the early 1970's. This winery, near Jamestown, was named ''Highland Manor''. There is no specific vineyard area in the state, with vineyards dotting the countryside from the Smokey Mountains in the east to the Mississippi River in the west.

An interesting and novel winery, Laurel Hill, is situated in a pretty old Victorian villa, in an inner suburb of Memphis, Raymond Skinner processes grapes here grown on his ''Laurel Hill'' Vineyard in Lawrence County.

Tennessee is unlikely to become a major winegrowing state, but is producing some good premium wines and the industry is sure to expand.

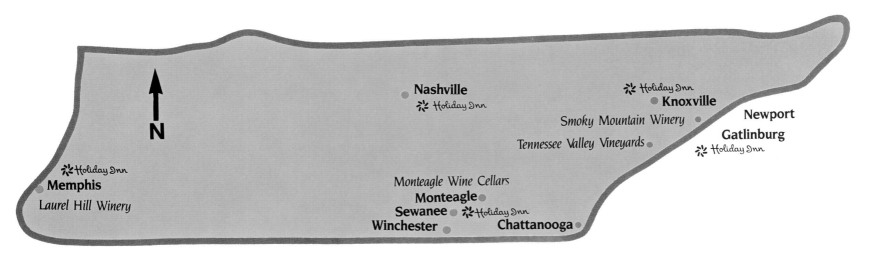

Smokey Mountain Winery

I n 1981, Everrett Brock and his wife, Miriam, who were producing handmade toys and other handicraft products, opened a small winery in the Brookside shopping centre in the tourist town of Gatlinburg. As the winery was situated at the entrance to the Smokey Mountains National Park, they took the name.

Most of the grapes come from the Little River Vineyards near Townsend, although a number of independent growers are used. Winemaker is Patrice Fischer-Johnson, a biologist from Maine, who has worked at wineries in California and New York State.

The top of the line are the Lecomte White, a Chardonnay blended from Tennessee and California wines, and a red from De Chaunac variety.

They also make a Brookside range. The white is made from Johannisberg Riesling and is a good wine. Under the ''Mountain'' label, they bring out wines made from native varieties and round off a large range with a Scuppernong white and a Muscadine red from these native south-eastern cluster varieties. Some fruit wines such as strawberry, raspberry and blackberry are also produced.

Laurel Hill

O nly a couple of miles from the downtown area of Memphis, on Madison Avenue, is situated the Laurel Hill Winery of Raymond Skinner.

The building containing the winery is a superb old Victorian villa with several levels, which has been lovingly restored and makes a very suitable home for the making of wine

and also for the tasting and sales areas.

Raymond has planted a 12 acre vineyard of hybrid and vinifera vines in nearby Lawrence County, and this forms the basis of his small, but excellent wine production. Production and sales are growing slowly and Raymond is certainly enjoying the lifestyle.

Tennessee Valley Wines

Jerry Reed, a Delta Airlines pilot, has bought out the Tennessee Valley Winery in which he started out as a partner back in 1984 with two other families. Jerry is assisted in the winery by his sons, Chris on the winemaking side, and Tom in the vineyards.

John Watkins assists in the winemaking as a consultant. Although the winery is in a simple building without embelishments, it is functionally very good and the Reeds have invested in some new oak cooperage. Plans are afoot to triple the size of the winery with

a two floor addition.

The winery started with hybrid varieties, but Jerry has planted some Chardonnay, the first vintage being 1987. The barrel sample I tasted had a rich peach/apricot flavour with a nice cashew/vanilla character from the wood ageing a very fine wine indeed. The Reeds also have some Cabernet Sauvignon planted — the 1986, their first vintage, also not yet released, is a fine wine.

Tennessee Valley appear to be making the best wines in the state and take a lot of pride in their flourishing business.

Monteagle Wine Cellars

Monteagle, one of Tennessee's newest wineries, was only finished in time for the 1986 crush. The winery, a southern bungalow-style building, was designed and constructed by the owner, Joe Marlow, who also has large farming interests near Hillsborough.

The winery is situated on the slopes of Monteagle Mountain, on the Cumberland plateau, an area settled in the 1870s by

Swiss immigrants, who introduced the grape and wine to the area. Winemaker is Bob Burgin, a graduate of the Enology course at Mississippi State College.

I tasted vinifera, hybrid and Muscadine wines and found all of good quality. The White Muscadine impressed me greatly with its floral aroma, tropical fruit flavours and a touch of pepper and spice; a very enjoyable, clean wine, the best of its type I have seen.

An Introduction to Texas

In 1974, Texas had a single century-old winery at Del Rio on the Rio Grande. About this time, a study undertaken by the Texas A.M. University was released, showing that wines could thrive in most parts of the state. A wine boom ensued, leading to major planting and today almost twenty wineries are in operation.

Three main areas have emerged; one is in the west of Texas on the Pecos River, the main operation being a joint venture between Cordier the Bordeaux wine and spirits firm and Richter a Montpellier nursery business, both French interests, and Texas businessman, Richardson Gill. He had helped start Llano Estacado, the largest winery in the Central High plains area near Lubbock. The third region is in the rolling hills around Fredricksburg.

Aside from these main regions, several significant wineries such as the ''Fall Creek'' operation of Ed Auler and his wife Susan at Tow, help make up what is a growing industry. Texas, with its huge areas of suitable land and climate could one day be a major winegrowing state.

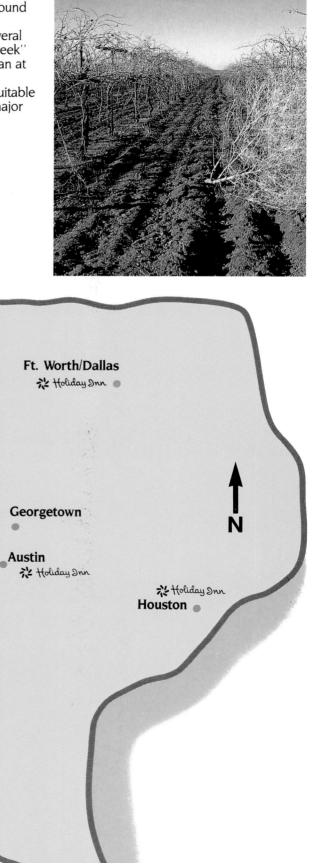

PHEASANT RIDGE

AWARD-WINNING WINES / FROM THE HIGH PLAINS OF TEXAS

CABERNET SAUVIGNON — LUBBOCK COUNTY
PROPRIETOR'S RESERVE RED — COX FAMILY VINEYARDS
CHARDONNAY — LUBBOCK COUNTY
SAUVIGNON BLANC — COX FAMILY VINEYARDS
SEMILLON — TEXAS
DRY CHENIN BLANC — COX FAMILY VINEYARDS

Holiday Inn
● **Amarillo**

Pheasant Ridge Vineyards
Lubbock ❄ Holiday Inn
Llano Estacado Winery

Ft. Worth/Dallas
❄ Holiday Inn

● **Odessa**
❄ Holiday Inn

El Paso

Fall Creek Vineyards
Tow ● **Georgetown**
Oberhellmann Vineyards
Fredericksburg ● **Austin**
❄ Holiday Inn

San Antonio ●
❄ Holiday Inn

❄ Holiday Inn
Houston ●

N

Llano Estacado Winery

The high Plains of North-western Texas have rich and deep red soils that gently undulate for hundred of miles. It's certainly not too pleasant there in a summer dust storm. The climate in the winter can be quite cool, however, and during our visit in February there was some snow on the ground.

Three professors from Texas Tech University got together in the early 1970's to experiment with grape varieties, planting a 15 acre vineyard of 75 different grape types. One of the three, Robert Reed, had been experimenting with vines since the mid 1950's. In 1975, they organised their own winery naming it Llano Estacado, after the name of the high plains which was coined by explorer, Francisco Coronado. He drove high stakes in the tall buffalo grass, to provide him with a marked path back from his exploration of New Mexico in 1542.

The winery has done very well in wine competitions, including winning a double gold for its 1984 Chardonnay at the 1986 San Francisco Fair. Production is now approaching 50,000 cases of premium wine per annum.

Fall Creek Winery

Ed Auler, an Austin lawyer and businessman, also operates a beef cattle ranch of several thousand acres in the Hill County north-west of Austin. Whilst in France, during the early 1970's, he noticed the terrain, soil and climate in many of the wine regions which he visited were remarkably like those on his own ranch. In 1975, he decided to experiment by planting some vineyards. He was pleasantly surprised by the quality of the grapes and the resulting wine so, in 1979, he went commercial, constructing an elegant ranch house winery near his vineyard and homestead on the banks of Lake Buchanan, a feature which helps moderate the climate for his vines.

The Fall Creek Vineyard has now expanded to 65 acres, all planted on Champanal rootstock, which is resistant to the cotton root rot problem, common in Texas. Ed has invested heavily in the best equipment and plenty of French oak barriques. He is a demanding perfectionist and his wines have always sold out well before the next vintage release.

At the 50th Presidential Inauguration, the 1983 Fall Creek Sauvignon Blanc and the 1983 Chenin Blanc were served, a real feather in Ed's cap.

Ed is helped by Tom Barkley, his vineyard manager and assistant winemaker and by his wife, Peggy, his laboratory technician.

Oberhellmann Vineyards

O ff highway 16 north of Fredricksburg in the rolling hill country, near the state capital of Austin, lies the 30 acre vineyard and winery of food-broker, Robert Oberhellmann. Robert's training in food technology has equipped him well to handle the complex task of winemaking.

The first plantings were made in 1976 and, after four years of making wine, experimentally, Robert and his wife, Eveyln, began building their Swiss chalet-style winery, which is not only very functional, but most pleasing to the eye. The buildings are surrounded by landscaped gardens, where many outdoor functions and an annual wine festival are held.

Many of the wines produced are Germanic in style and all are made from their own vineyards, which are totally planted to vinifera varieties.

Pheasant Ridge Winery

C harles Robert (Bobby) Cox III has established one of the best-looking vineyards in North America, healthy and very well tended by himself, his sister Shelley and wife Jennifer. Part of the reason for his success with the vines is, I am sure, his experience working at the Texas A & M University's experimental station for Fruit and Vegetables.

The vineyard, planted in 1979, is producing superb fruit which Bobby is turning into remarkable wines. The climate at Pheasant Ridge can get quite cool as it is located at an altitude of 3,500 ft. The only

risks, aside from a fairly low rainfall that must be supplemented, are spring frosts and hailstorms.

Bobby's father helped him start the business and it is a real family affair. The vineyard has expanded to 47 acres of vinifera vines only, and supplies 95% of the winery's needs. Every wine so far released has won a medal in wine competitions.

The 1982/1983 Proprietors Reserve Red I tasted had deep colour and immense flavours accompanied by a velvety texture easily worthy of a gold medal.

An Introduction to Virginia

Virginia was the first American colony to cultivate the vine. Attempts to grow the noble vinifera vines of Europe began in 1619, under Lord Delaware. None, however, survived more than a few years. Some notable Americans such as George Washington and, later, Thomas Jefferson went to great lengths to succeed with vinifera. Jefferson, in fact, spent 30 years and considerable resources in this battle, even importing soil from the grand chateaux of Bordeaux in France to help him.

Many things were blamed, soil, climate and so on. However, the real culprits were vine diseases and pests, which the native American vines are immune to, but which attack the more delicate vinifera. With modern day viticultural knowledge and chemicals, these can be controlled and vinifera vines are now grafted on to American rootstock. These factors plus the growing interest in premium wine and American wines in particular has led to a vinous explosion in Virginia, where over 40 wineries are now operating.

A number of European investors have ventured into Virginia including Jean Le Ducq's. striking Prince Michel Winery and museum at Culpepper and his sister winery Rapidan River Vineyards nearby. The giant Zonin family Winery in Italy has started the Barboursville Vineyard near the historic ruins of the Jefferson-designed Governor's residence.

Virginia's new wine industry is just finding its feet, but is looking at a bright future.

Robert Harper has led a wonderful, rich and exciting life. For many years Robert raced Porsche cars and went on to manage the world racing interests of the Dunlop Company.

In 1976, Robert and his wife Phoebe bought a truly beautiful property on the easterly slopes of the Blue Ridge Mountains in northern Virginia, where slopes of the amphitheatre-shaped vineyard help to draw off any spring frosts. Robert has also trained his well-kept vineyard onto high V-shaped trellises to minimise the risk of disease and to provide maximum leaf exposure to the sun, which helps develop flavour in the grapes.

The winery has been built on the top of the hill and commands a spectacular view of the vineyard and valley beyond. The top floor of the winery is a large area with a polished timber floor wood panelling, large windows and a huge stone open fireplace, always burning in winter.

With this idyllic setting and Robert's perfectionist attitude in the winery and vineyard, it is not surprising that his wines are top flight. Of the three wines I tasted, two had won first place prizes in the Annual Virginian Wine competition. The 1986 Naked Mountain Chardonnay had generous flavours, reminiscent of peaches and apricots, with just a touch of oak to give it complexity — a real winner which will also age well. The other trophy winner was a 1986 Riesling, which had spicy pineapple and other tropical fruit flavours, with just a hint of sweetness, a great wine. The third wine I tasted was a 1985 Sauvignon Blanc, which had a grassy herbaceous character, overlaid with beautiful fruit — again a superb wine.

Robert and Phoebe have constructed the winery with their own hands and Robert runs it whilst Phoebe works as a security officer at the Federal Court in Washington D.C., which is only 50 minutes drive. They have just employed their first staff member to help with the increasing business.

In their idyllic setting, the Harpers have created a wine Mecca, which is very well positioned (just off highway 66) for Washington and Baltimore wine lovers to visit. I am sure they are all pleasantly surprised with what they find.

Naked Mountain

La Abra Farm & Winery

When hurricane Camille struck in 1969, with 40 inches of rain in two hours, turning Al Weeds serene Valley, aptly named La Abra (the cove) into a raging torrent, Al must have wondered why he had left the investment banking world to become a farmer. Not to be daunted, he went on to plant a vineyard to add to his other rural interest.

Al, assisted by his wife and mother-in-law, have rebuilt the old building on the property, mainly using stones collected from the vineyard. They have created a real haven by themselves and are obviously enjoying the lifestyle.

Al's wife still works part-time as an operating nurse, but, since 1981, Al has been a full-time man of the land. La Abra produce a number of hybrid wines, as well as apple and peach wines from their own orchards. Many wines are marketed under the "Mountain Cove" label, which has proved easier for people to pronounce and relate to.

Barboursville Vineyards

Barboursville exudes a feeling of history and the timeless nature of wine. Statesman James Barbour, who was Governor of Virginia from 1812 to 1814, built a grand mansion on his plantation to a design of Thomas Jefferson. The building was gutted by fire on Christmas Day 1884, but the picturesque ruins still remain.

The estate was bought by the Zonin Family, Italy's largest privately- owned vignerons with a history in viticulture going back to 1821. The 830 acre property now has 50 acres under vine planting having commenced in 1975, with the first vintage three years later.

History has certainly repeated itself, as Thomas Jefferson brought out an Italian Filippo Mazzei in the latter part of the 18th century to plant vinifera and make wine. In charge of the vinifera vineyard and winery now is Adriano Rossi, an Italian and a graduate of the Oenological Institute of Alba in northern Italy.

Having tasted a number of his wines, I found his Gewurztraminer, Chardonnay and Cabernet Sauvignon particularly impressive.

Montdomaine

Thomas Jefferson, former President and one of the authors of the Declaration of Independence, was more than a little preoccupied with the cultivation of the wine grape. In 1774, he persuaded Italian wine expert, Filippo Mazzei, to come to Virginia to plant European vinifera vines and make wine. The project was interrupted by the American Revolution, the vineyards being destroyed in the battle. Jefferson did not give up, but was, of course, absent for much of his life on political business including a time in France as Ambassador.

Jefferson also had to battle with the unseen enemy, vine diseases and a bug

which mysteriously nibbled at the roots of the vine eventually killing it (one hundred years later this bug, Phylloxera, would destroy the vineyards of France). Jefferson eventually settled for native vines.

In 1977, Mike and Lynn Bowles, Pan American Airways employees with a love for wine, revived the Jefferson dream, planting vines as a joint venture with wealthy wine lover, Bob Carter, owner of the old Mazzei Vineyard site. They also revived the old "Monticello Wine Co" label and are now producing excellent Chardonnay, Cabernet Sauvignon, Merlot and other classic varietals.

The Prince Michel Vineyard, built by Parisian, Jean Le Ducq and his American partner, Norman Martin, is a real showpiece. Superbly equipped, it has a great wine museum and a separate luxurious tasting area. The building has been modelled after a Bordeaux Chateau and looks most impressive, set high above the passing road. The museum also has a theatre, where a multi-projection audio-visual wine educational presentation is run.

Winemaker is Joachim Hollerith, who formerly worked for Rapidan River Winery and advised on the Prince Michel location, also assisting in the design of the winery.

Rapidan River is also now under Prince Michel's ownership. Joachim is assisted by Alan Kinne, who had 10 years experience in the Michigan and Long Island wine industries before coming to Virginia.

Prince Michel have 110 acres of vines planted and are concentrating on Chardonnay and Cabernet Sauvignon.

Jean Le Ducq, also has an interest in a Spanish winery and is a member of the French St. Emilion wine order. His love of wine is obvious in the winery he has created

Rapidan River Vineyards

Jean Le Ducq first bought Rapidan River Vineyards before building Prince Michel. Whilst the wine varieties, style and philosophy behind Prince Michel is totally French, Rapidan River concentrates on Germanic styles. Coincidentally, the region was settled by Germans and, as early as 1710, vineyards flourished in the region.

Joachim Hollerith, from a German family, studied at the Geisenheim Wine Institute in his homeland. The winemaker on the spot (as Joachim also runs Prince Michel) is Fernando Franco from El Salvador, a graduate in horticulture and viticulture from his own country. Fernando was pretty happy whilst we were there, as he had just won the only gold medal awarded to a Virginian winery at the International Easter wine competition in New York.

Rapdian concentrate on their Gewurztraminer and White Riesling, but also make a Chardonnay and a Methode Champenoise.

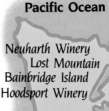
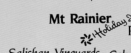

Prohibition in the 1930's bought a boom in wineries and, by 1937, there were over 40 in operation. Their number however, gradually dwindled as California developed a virtual monopoly on wine.

In 1967, the legendary Andre Tchelistcheff travelled to Washington State and began advising the "American Wine Growers" wineries, a forerunner to the large Chateau Ste. Michelle and Columbia Crest wineries of today. The revolution had started. Tchelistcheff still consults to them and innumerable small and medium sized premium wineries have sprung up. By the turn of the century, Washington State will, I am sure, will outdistance all but California in wine production.

W ashington State has had a explosion in grape and wine production in the last two decades. In 1982, it became the second-largest grape producing state after California.

There are now well over 10,000 acres of vinifera vines growing in the state and over 50 producing wineries, a far cry from the three wineries and virtually no vinifera vines of 1968.

Grapegrowing in Washington goes back to the 1860's, when vineyards were planted in the Walla Walla and Puget Sound regions. The first winery appears to have been at Frank Orselli's property in Walla Walla.

Just after the turn of the century, irrigation water became available in the huge Yakima Valley, transforming it from a semi-desert to a rich fruit-growing region. Post-

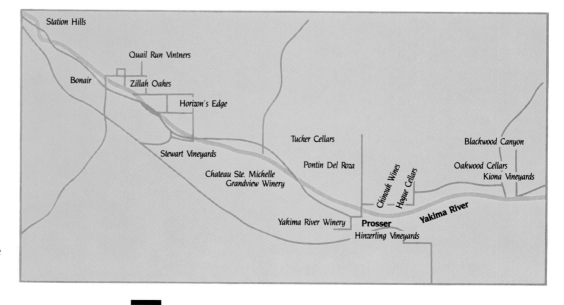

Quail Run Vintners

High on a hill above the Yakima River at Zillah is situated the Quail Run Vintners Winery, making a range of wines under the "Covey Run" label that have impressed enormously, right from the winery's first vintage in 1982.

Stan Clarke was a viticulturist for the large Chateau Ste. Michelle Winery. Several growers in the Yakima Valley convinced him to start a winery for them and eighteen investors, mostly growers, came in on the project.

The wines made include Chardonnay, Johannisberg Riesling, Chenin Blanc, Gewurztraminer, Merlot and Cabernet Sauvignon. The winery is equipped with function rooms and a large sun deck, where visitors may picnic.

Just near Seattle at Kirkland, on the picturesque Moss Bay, Quail Run have a second tasting room.

Preston Wine Cellars

Like a giant ship in a sea of vines, the Preston Winery has a unique tasting and viewing area. Perched atop the winery building, Preston Wine Cellars have gradually expanded as success has brought Bill and Joann Preston extra capital. They are among the early pioneers of the modern era of Washington winemaking. In 1972, they planted 50 acres of vinifera vines at their Pasco location, increasing this to 180 acres in 1979.

The winery was built in 1976, in time for the 190 ton crush of that year. The Prestons have been joined by their daughter, Cathy, who looks after sales and public relations. The tasting area also has a large gift shop, and outside, amongst the beautifully landscaped gardens, is a "conversation piece" picnic area, where cooking facilities are available.

Preston run many special events such as their annual Kite Festival and have won many awards for their wines, which include almost all the classic vinifera varieties.

C hateau Ste. Michelle's history goes back to the 1930's when, under the banner of the "American Wine Growers", it began making wine from Washington-grown fruits, berries and grapes.

In 1967, with increased interest in premium table wines amongst American winedrinkers, the then manager, Victor Allison, talked famous winemaker, Andre Tchelistcheff, into advising on the making of wines from the company's vinifera vineyards, which were quiet small at that stage. Tchelistcheff carefully made wines from the 1967 vintage and, on evaluating them two years later, was astounded by the quality. Plantings were quickly increased and today Chateau Ste. Michelle own over 3,180 acres

of wines in the Columbia Valley in Eastern Washington and control three large wineries. Supplementary irrigation is used, as although the temperature and soil is ideal (being on the 46th parallel, which passes between the great French region of Bordeaux and Burgundy), the region is semi-arid. An irrigation scheme only provided this missing ingredient early this century. Due to the sandy soils and isolated location, Phylloxera is not a problem, enabling the vinifera vines to be planted directly into the soil without costly grafting, that some say slightly affects quality as well.

With a huge area to choose from for vineyard planting, Chateau Ste. Michelle's viticulturists have chosen different

microclimates and soils best suited to each variety.

The first winery built was Grandview in the 1940's, Washington State's oldest bonded location in the town of Grandview and near the state's first vineyard, Hahn Hill. The second winery is the stunning "Chateau Ste. Michelle", set on 87 acres of landscaped gardens and parks, complete with lakes, at Woodinville on the outskirts of Seattle. This Chateau, built in 1976, is on the Estate formerly owned by timber baron, Fred Stimson, used as his summer residence, designed by New York's "Central Park" designer and called Hollywood Farms. Their last winery constructed was the River Ridge — now renamed Columbia Crest Winery,

Chateau Ste. Michelle

near the banks of the Columbia River and surrounded by 2,000 acres of vines.

Each winery specialises, with its own winemaker in charge. All red wines are made at Grandview, all the delicate, Germanic whites and Chenin Blanc are produced at the Columbia Crest Winery. At the Chateau Ste. Michelle Winery at Woodinville, all the wood-matured whites, such as Chardonnay, Sauvignon Blanc, Semillon, as well as the Domaine Ste. Michelle Methode Champenoise sparkling wines are made.

Cheryl Barber is the chief winemaker. She joined Ste. Michelle in 1976 as a laboratory assistant, after gaining her degree in Food Science and Technology from Washington State University. She has enjoyed

and benefitted enormously from working with Andre Tchelistcheff. 1982, saw Cheryl appointed assistant winemaker and, the following year, head winemaker.

No group of wines from one winery has impressed me as greatly overall as those from Chateau Ste. Michelle. The 1980 Reserve Benton County — Cold Creek Cabernet Sauvignon, just released, is out of this world. One of the really good things about Chateau Ste. Michelle wines is that they are also widely available and reasonably priced.

CHATEAU STE. MICHELLE
Address: 14111 N.E. 145th, Woodinville, WA., 98072
Phone: 206/488 1133
Year of Establishment: 1937
Owner: Stimson Lane Wine & Spirits
Winemaker: Cheryl Barber
Principal Varieties Grown: Cabernet Sauvignon, Pinot Noir, Sauvignon Blanc, White Riesling, Chenin Blanc, Semillon, Chardonnay, Gewurztraminer, Merlot
Acres Under Vine: 1,000
Average Annual Crush: 10,000 tons
Principal Wines &
Brands
Cabernet Sauvignon
Chardonnay
Semillon
Trade Tours – Available
Retail Room Sales – Available
Hours open to Public – 7 days a week from 10am to 4.30pm
Retail Distribution – National and International

Columbia Crest Winery

In 1981, one of America's biggest premium wine developments began with the breaking of ground at the Columbia Crest Winery, site of the Stimson Lane/Chateau Ste. Michelle wine goup's vineyards. Situated on the Columbia River in south-central Washington, this impressive winery and its 2,000 acres of surrounding vineyards has seen 26 million dollars of investment since that time.

The winery has been constructed with 90% of the production areas underground, helping to keep an even cool temperature and steady humidity level in this region, where temperatures from night to day and from winter to summer vary enormously. The winery is in the centre of the vineyard, which is great from a wine quality point of view, as the grapes are only minutes from the crushing facility.

Like all the Chateau Ste. Michelle Wineries and vineyards, everything has been thoroughly researched and solidly built. No stone has been left unturned in the quest for the ultimate in wine quality. The stainless steel fermentation tanks have been cleverly designed in multiples with plenty of small tanks to ensure all wines can be kept separate at the making stage. This is particularly important because each batch of grapes is unique and one never knows when one will make a totally outstanding wine.

Therefore, being separate, these special wines can then be kept as such and eventually released as reserve wines

In charge of winemaking is Doug Gore, who came to the Ste. Michelle group, in 1982, as an assistant winemaker. Doug had previously graduated from the Food Science degree course at the California Polytechnic State University. He then worked under renowned winemaker, Myron Nightingale, at the Beringer Winery, receiving the best possible practical experience. In 1984, Doug was promoted to a position in charge of all the Chateau Ste. Michelle red wines at the Grandview Winery, before taking over in 1986 at Columbia Crest. Doug spends a great

Columbia Crest Winery

deal of time supervising in the vineyard, believing in the philosophy that the quality of the grapes is the limiting determinant of the ultimate wine quality.

Columbia Crest wines are superbly presented and well priced. It is no wonder that they have become the second biggest selling brand (to Ste. Michelle) almost overnight.

The varietals produced are Gewurztraminer, Johannisberg Riesling, Semillon, Chenin Blanc, Sauvignon Blanc, Chardonnay plus two blended wines, the "Vineyard Reserve White" a Johannisberg Riesling with a touch of spicy Gewurztraminer plus a trace of grapey Muscat Camelli and a "Vineyard

Reserve Blush", made from Grenache.

The long cool fermentations often up to six weeks utilised by Doug Gore retain an enormous amount of mouth-filling flavour in all the wines.

Columbia Crest is the culmination of a great deal of learning by the Stimson Lane/Chateau Ste. Michelle group. They have given it their best shot and the wine consumer is the winner.

COLUMBIA CREST
Address: PO Box 231, Paterson, WA., 99345-0231
Phone: 509/875 2061
Year of Establishment: 1982
Owner: Stimson Lane Wine & Spirits
Winemaker: Doug Gore
Principal Varieties Grown: Chardonnay, Semillon, Sauvignon Blanc, Gewurztraminer, Chenin Blanc, White Riesling, Merlot, Cabernet Sauvignon
Acres Under Vine: 2,000
Average Annual Crush: 6,000 tons

Principal Wines &
Brands
Chardonnay
Semillon
Sauvignon Blanc
Trade Tours – Available
Retail Room Sales – Available
Hours open to Public – 7 days a week from 10am to 5pm

The Hogue Cellars

Mike Hogue is a true wine enthusiast. His modest cellars off the Main Road near Prosser, in the Yakima Valley are a little misleading, because Hogue has quickly become quite a large wine producer. 1988 will see some 80,000 cases produced by the winery, which are now marketed in 38 states plus export sales , particularly to Japan. This is a far cry from the modest 2,000 cases Hogue produced in 1983, most of which were sold from a card table in the winery.

The Hogue family have been growers of fruit, vegetables, hops and spearmint since 1949, when Mike's father set up a 1,300 acre farm. Concord grapes were then grown for grape jelly etc. The business in all the other areas continues, but premium vinifera wines have become an extremely important part of the operation. Hogue now have 250 acres planted to varieties such as Chardonnay, Semillon, Sauvignon Blanc, Johannisberg Riesling, Cabernet Sauvignon and Merlot.

The Hogue Cellars has been rated in the top 10 American wines for 1987 by the "Wine Country Magazine", rating well above many of the respected names of the industry.

The winemaker is Rob Griffin. Although still youthful, he has had ten years' experience in Washington winemaking, firstly with Preston Vineyards in 1977 and, since, 1984 with Hogue.

Many of the Hogue family's other produce such as their pickled fresh asparagus, hot and spicy beans, jars of fruit is available in the tasting and sales area of the winery.

Mike dreamed several years ago of making and selling around 100,000 cases of America's best wines. His goal is very close to being within his grasp.

Franz Wilhelm Langguth Winery

I n one of North America's most isolated locations lies Washington State's second largest winemaking operation. Langguth are one of West Germany's biggest winemakers with their cellars located in the pretty mid-Mosel town of Trarben-Trarbach. In 1981, Langguth formed a partnership with some Seattle investors and commenced planting a 230 acre vineyard.

The Sagebush Country, some 20 miles east of the Columbia River, near Nattawa looks most inhospitable. This is deceiving, however, as the soil and climate are perfect for producing top quality table wines; the only ingredient lacking is water. Once the sandy, loam soil was planted and equipped with a drip irrigation system, a miracle happened and today the starkly contrasting green of 265 acres of vigorous and healthy vines captures one's eye from miles away. The winery was built a year later in front of the vineyards that stretch up the Wahluki slope. The large solid building looks like a fortress in the desert, protecting its precious produce.

Langguth hired Swiss-born and German-speaking winemaker, Max Zellweger, who had worked at Chateau Benoit Winery in Oregon. The first wines were produced in 1982 from purchased grapes and the vineyard came into production the following year. Langguth concentrates on the Germanic Johannisberg Riesling and Gewurztraminer varieties, often making them low in alcohol after the German style. They also produce a Chardonnay and a Cabernet Sauvignon. A second label , Saddle Mountain, is utilised on some of their wines.

Visitors who find their way to this isolated, but striking, part of Washington State receive a warm welcome at the winery

Other Wine producing Regions

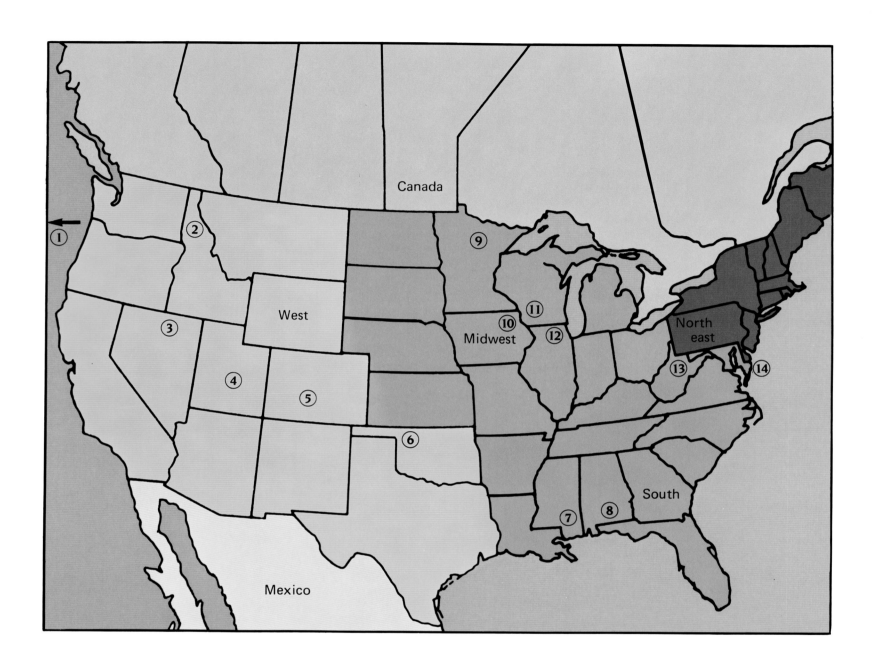

① **Hawaii**	⑧ **Alabama**
② **Idaho**	⑨ **Minnesota**
③ **Nevada**	⑩ **Iowa**
④ **Utah**	⑪ **Wisconsin**
⑤ **Colorado**	⑫ **Illinois**
⑥ **Oklahoma**	⑬ **West Virginia**
⑦ **Mississippi**	⑭ **Delaware/Maryland**

Wineries flourish in 42 of the 50 States of the Union and grapes are grown in every state. Kansas and Nebraska are likely to have wineries operating at any time.

In Canada, grapes are grown in British Columbia, Ontario and Nova Scotia, although wineries operate in most provinces obtaining their grape or juice supply from other Canadian provinces, or from the U.S.A. and sometimes, as is the case with many Quebec wineries, from Europe. Mexico, of course, has a very well established wine industry — the first on the continent and going back 450 years to the time of the Conquistadores.

Although the history of the vine goes back to the very discovery of America by Leif Erikson, the North American people have only embraced wine as the temperate, mealtime beverage of moderation in the last few decades. Some stability and sense of purpose has at last settled on the noble industry of the vine. One can only hope this sanity and positive development can carry on into the future.

Ste Chapelle Winery

Like most other states, Idaho had an active wine industry prior to Prohibition. However, the state monopoly liquor system discouraged wine production and it was not until the laws changed in 1969, allowing wine to be sold in grocery stores, that the incentive to make wine returned to the state.

The first successful winery established was Ste. Chapelle in 1976, when local fruit growers and prominent family, the Symms, with Bill Brioch built a winery to process the Chardonnay, Pinot Noir and Riesling grapes planted on their 1,300 acre ranch in 1971. The Symms took over the operation fully in 1978 and the following year built the striking octagonal winery, on a knoll in the vineyard.

The vineyards are planted at Sunnyslope near Caldwell on the Snake River, which helps moderate the climate, which can be quite harsh in winter. Some 600 acres of

vines are now planted in the region. Ste. Chapelle's annual production of premium wine now amounts to 120,000 cases. 85/of the grapes are from Idaho, although a little of such varieties as Cabernet Sauvignon, Merlot and Chenin Blanc are brought in from Washington State, as the Idaho climate is generally a little cold to grow them successfully.

Mini Mook is their bright young winemaker who has recently come from California, where she worked at the innovative J. Lohr Winery in San Jose. She is assisted by Kevin Mott. The winery was extended in 1986 and now also houses 400 French oak barriques. The Ste. Chapelle Johannisberg Riesling is particularly impressive as is their Late Harvest/Botrytis Blanc, Cabernet Sauvignon, two Blush wines and a Rose. Currently a Methode Champenoise is ageing on tirage — and will be due for release in late 1989. Ste. Chapelle also hold many events in the park complex in front of the winery and in the second floor entertaining area with its 360 degree views of the valley. The "Jazz at the Winery" event each July attracts top musicians and large crowds.

Ste. Chapelle has a real sense of purpose and a promising future in front of it.

Tedeschi Vineyard and Winery

Probably the most unlikely and certainly one of the most beautiful winery locations is that of Tedeschi, high on the slopes of the inactive volcano, Mt. Haelakala, on the Hawaiian island of Maui. The 20 acre vineyard was planted in 1974 by third generation Italian-American winemaker, Emil Tedeschi, who had been making wine in the Napa Valley. Emil and his wife were on holiday the previous year and met Pardee Erdman, owner of the 20,000 acre Ulupalakua Ranch, covering the western slopes of the island, which is mainly concerned with beef cattle raising. Although pineapples, peaches, sugar cane and various vegetables are also grown. Pardee was looking for a crop that would not require too much water. Tedeschi suggested grapes. Hawaii, in fact, has a history of winegrowing going back to 1814, when King Kamehameka the Great, made a grant of land near Honolulu to Spanish horticulturist, Francisco de Paula Marin, for growing vines. Portuguese settlers on various of the islands made wine until the Second World War. Tedeschi, however, is now the only operating winery.

Erdman and Tedeschi formed a partnership and employed Dimitri Tchelistcheff, son of the great Andre, to advise on the vineyard location and the planting of suitable varieties. In all, 140 varieties were tested. The most suitable was found to be the Carnelian grape, developed by Dr. Harold Olmo at U.C. Davis.

Tedeschi planted 20 acres and, whilst waiting for the vines to mature, started making a wine, Maui Blanc, from pineapples, which has proved most successful.

On our visit we happened to arrive on the first day of the 1988 crush, June 22. The mood was high and festive, due to the news that they had just won a gold medal with their Blanc de Noirs Brut Hawaiian Champagne, in Indiana.

Ben Mendez, the assistant winemaker, and his team were busy at work in the winery, which is housed in a group of buildings that formed the vacation home of the former Kings and Queens of Hawaii. The tasting room is in the old stone, former jailhouse and is surrounded by superb gardens, which command a majestic view of the coastline and ocean.

The mountain location over 2,000ft. above sea level is relatively temperate and the wines I found most acceptable. From the carnelian, Tedeschi make a Nouveau Red, a Blush and the Champagne; in addition they have their pineapple based Maui Blanc.

Tedeschi was certainly one of our more

enjoyable stops. I am sure if you are lucky enough to be on this island paradise, you would enjoy a visit. It is located just over 30 miles from the Kahului Airport.

Lynfred Winery

Situated in Roselle, a suburb of Chicago, in a grand old Victorian home, is the Lynfred Winery of Fred and Lynn Koehler, former restaurateurs. The winemaking takes place in the basement and the upstairs area, which has been carefully restored, served as a tasting and sales area. The solidly constructed building has 18 inch thick brick walls and provides a very even temperature for the winemaking and maturation.

The Koehlers utilise grapes from California, Washington and Michigan- the small vineyard plot that adjoins the winery's car park is only for show. The reputation of the Lynfred wines has grown steadily since its founding in 1977. A gift shop is also incorporated in their delightful premises.

LYNFRED WINERY
Address: 15 S. Roselle Road. Roselle. Illinois. 60172
Phone: 312/529-WINE
Year of Establishment: 1979
Owner: Fred E. Kochler
Winemaker: Fred E. Kochler
Average Annual Crush: 100 tons

Principal Wines & Brands	Cellar Potential (Years)
Chardonnay	6-8
Fume Blanc	4-6
Cabernet Sauvignon	10-15
Merlot	8-10
Chancellor	8-10
Villard Blanc	3-4
Select Harvest Riesling	6-8
Late Harvest Zinfandel	10-15

Trade Tours – Available.
Retail Room Sales – Available.
Hours open to Public: 11am to 7pm 7 day a week
Retail Distribution: Illionis

Wollersheim Winery

Bob Wollersheim was looking for a suitable place in Wisconsin to grow grapes and make wine. His search uncovered one of the most significant parts of America's wine history. The building and remnants of a vineyard he found had been built and owned by Agoston Harazathy, who went on to become known as the father of wine in California. Harazathy had started a wine colony near the town he founded "Harazathy" Wisconsin (now known as Sauk City).Unfortunately his vines were killed by the harsh winters and in 1848 he moved on to California. The vineyard was then bought by German immigrant, Peter Kehl, who built a substantial winery on the property from limestone and pine.

Bob Wollersheim his wife Jo Ann and children, Steve, Julie and Eve, have restored the winery cellars and planted vineyards of French hybrids as well as Riesling and Pinor Noir. All vines are trained near to the ground. as they are buried each fall until spring to protect them from the killing winter cold.

The Wollersheims' property is now on the national register of historical places. They also run a deli and a gift shop that also sells home winemaking equipment. Many thousands of people each month visit the winery, which is located on highway 188 across the river from Prairie-du-Sac.

WOLLERSHEIM WINERY
Address: Highway 188, 1 Prairie du Sac, Wisconsin, 53578
Phone: 608/643 6515
Year of Establishment: 1857
Owner: Robert & Joann Wollersheim
Winemaker: Philippe Coquard
Principal Varieties Grown: Chardonnay, Riesling, Seyval Blanc, Pinot Noir, Foch, Millot
Acres Under Vine: 23
Average Annual Crush: 87 tons, 6,500 cases

Principal Wines & Brands	Cellar Potential (Years)
Domaine Reserve	15
Sugarloaf Hill White	5
Domaine Du Sac	5

Trade Tours – Available.
Retail Room Sales – Available.
Hours open to Public: Year round 7 days a week from 10am to 5pm
Retail Distribution: Wisconsin and 3 other states

Index of Wineries

Index of Wineries

Index

Index - Holiday Inns
Located in or near the Wine Regions featured in his book.

Note from the Photographer

In the many years of my photographic career, I have not had as deep an involvement as with photographing the world of wine. At first, it was the "Pictorial Atlas of Australian Wine" and now the North American Atlas. The more involved I became, the more the horizons widened for me.

Wine as a living substance of light and happiness has brought me to many different places on this continent. The rich variety of shapes and colours in the landscape, the many happy hours with winemakers and growers, the days, weeks and months of travel became a photographic experience and a personal joy for me.

Wine does not have geographic and ethnic borders. From the warmest parts of California to the freezing temperatures of Canada, wine makes its own way as a beautiful gift of mother-nature, carefully guided by man and his palate.

As with man, wine can adapt and flourish in the most remote and rugged conditions and create its own character. Colours of the sky, clouds and earth can be found in this liquid form of life. In my photographs, I have tried to capture this ongoing miracle, but a mere lifetime is not nearly enough.

Trying to combine artistic quality and commercial value in photography is always a difficult task, but thanks to my friend and partner, Thomas Hardy, I believe we have achieved this.

Many of the photographs in this book have a special meaning for me, whether it is due to the location or because of the effort it took to capture that special moment in time. On these, I have added my signature. Here it is, American wine as I see it, now it is yours to share and enjoy.

My thanks to the Professional Photography Division of the Eastman Kodak Company, for their help and technical support during this project.

Sponsors

The massive undertaking of producing this Pictorial Atlas, would not have been possible without the assistance of some of North America's Leading Corporations. Whilst I am sure their association with the project as sponsors will be most beneficial to them, their support was absolutely critical to the creation of this volume and we thank them and their staff concerned most sincerely.

Kodak

Eastman Kodak is undoubtably the world's most respected photographic company. Their Professional Photographic Division under the guidance of Vice President, Ray De Moulin have supported the project right from the outset in March 1987. Their faith in us and our ability to carry out our undertaking has been a great source of inspiration for us when times got tough and they certainly did.

Both Milan and I would like to thank Geoff Tucker particularly, for his help and belief in our venture.

We trust the beauty captured and created by Milan with his camera on Kodak film is a lasting tribute to this worthy company's support.

Holiday Inns

When Holiday Inns set out as the world's first roadside motel chain in the early 1950's, I am sure they did not envisage becoming the world's largest hotel chain with around 1,700 properties and over 360,000 rooms. The quality and value for money they offer is second to none as Milan and I can certainly say with confidence, having stayed at literally hundreds of their properties in our 60,000 miles of driving tours, traversing the North American continent.

The Holiday Inn hospitality promise, embraced by all their staff, embodies a philosophy in which wine is an integral part.

Late in the evening after a long day's driving from winery to winery, nothing was so welcome as the sight of the bright green Holiday Inn sign and always knowing its promise of hospitality would be delivered.

To Ray Lewis, whose spontaneous support for our project to his loyal staff, Beverly Robertson, Dorothy Hayes and Margaret Erby, who have made it all happen – sincere thanks.

CONTINENTAL AIRLINES

Continental Airlines

It is very hard to put together a book such as this if you cannot visit every wine region.

Continental Airlines have ensured we have had the ability to not only travel to all corners of the North American continent, but also to our homeland of Australia and to Europe. Continental offer excellent standards and friendly service, that has made these long journeys most pleasurable. To Claude Smith, their director of Pacific Marketing and Rodney Robinson, their Victorian Manager in Australia, for their faith in this project, our heartfelt thanks.